A Glossary
for
English Transformational Grammar

A Glossary
for
English Transformational
Grammar

ROBERT A. PALMATIER
Western Michigan University

APPLETON-CENTURY-CROFTS
Educational Division
MEREDITH CORPORATION
New York

R
425
P171

Copyright © 1972 by

MEREDITH CORPORATION

72 73 74 75 76/10 9 8 7 6 5 4 3 2 1

Library of Congress Catalog Card Number: 79–187737

PRINTED IN THE UNITED STATES OF AMERICA
390–69109–7

To
MARION
DAVID
and
DENISE

PREFACE

Transformational grammar has made many important contributions to English linguistics, not the least of which is a host of new technical terms and new definitions for older terms. Unfortunately, however, the books in which these terms have appeared have not usually contained glossaries; Langendoen's *The Study of Syntax*, 1969, is an exception. Many of the books have even lacked indexes, or at least adequate indexes; Jacobs and Rosenbaum's *English Transformational Grammar*, 1968, is a notable exception. Furthermore, the independent glossaries—dictionaries, lexicons, or handbooks—of linguistic terminology have not kept pace with developments in transformational grammar, and none has concentrated on that particular theory.

The present *Glossary* is an attempt to gather together in one reference work the terminology that has been employed by English transformational grammarians from the beginning of their publication in 1956 until the end of the 1960's. This fourteen-year period has seen considerable change in transformational theory. The *Glossary* recognizes that fact. It separates those terms that apply to first-generation transformational grammar, which reflect the model in Chomsky's *Syntactic Structures* (1957), from those that apply to second-generation transformational grammar, which reflect the model in Chomsky's *Aspects of the Theory of Syntax* (1965). There is also a third category, called here semantic-based transformational grammar. This category refers to the neotransformational investigations of case grammar and generative semantics.

The 72 works that have been surveyed for this *Glossary* include only those sources in English which relate to transformational grammar in general or to English transformational grammar in particular, and which are readily available in book form. That is, the corpus from which the *Glossary* is derived consists only of individual books, monographs, and anthologies of articles on transformational grammar that were written in English and were published or anthologized by the end of 1969. The coverage ranges from Chomsky's "Three Models for the Description of Language" (1956) to King's *Historical Linguistics and Generative Grammar* (late 1969). The places of first publication include both America and Europe.

Within the field of transformational grammar, the individual books and monographs which help form the corpus relate to 1) grammatical theory

(Chomsky's *Syntactic Structures, Aspects of the Theory of Syntax,* and *Topics in the Theory of Generative Grammar;* Katz and Postal's *An Integrated Theory of Linguistic Descriptions;* and Postal's *Constituent Structure*); 2) the psychology and philosophy of language (Chomsky's *Cartesian Linguistics* and *Language and Mind,* and Katz's *Philosophy of Language*); 3) phonological theory (Postal's *Aspects of Phonological Theory,* Harms' *Introduction to Phonological Theory,* and Chomsky and Halle's *The Sound Pattern of English*); 4) complex sentence formation (Lees' *The Grammar of English Nominalizations* and Rosenbaum's *The Grammar of English Predicate Complement Constructions*); 5) historical linguistics (King's *Historical Linguistics and Generative Grammar*); 6) the writing of grammars (Koutsoudas' *Writing Transformational Grammars*); 7) the teaching of grammar (Thomas' *Transformational Grammar and the Teacher of English* and Jacobs' *On Transformational Grammar*); 8) the study of grammar on the college level (Bach's *Introduction to Transformational Grammars,* Jacobs and Rosenbaum's *English Transformational Grammar,* and Langendoen's *The Study of Syntax*); and 9) the study of general linguistics (Lyons' *Introduction to Theoretical Linguistics* and Langacker's *Language and Its Structure*).

The selection of the four anthologies from among the numerous collections of articles on the market was based on their appeal to a professional audience. Of the four, Allen's *Readings in Applied English Linguistics* (2nd ed., 1964) takes up first-generation transformational grammar; Fodor and Katz' *The Structure of Language* (1964) covers the transition from first-generation to second-generation transformational grammar; Reibel and Schane's *Modern Studies in English* (1969) represents primarily second-generation transformational grammar but also introduces semantic-based transformational grammar; and Bach and Harms' *Universals in Linguistic Theory* (1968) represents primarily semantic-based transformational grammar. All four of the articles from Bach and Harms have been surveyed, 23 of those from Reibel and Schane, 12 of those from Fodor and Katz, and three from Allen. It should also be pointed out that the earliest publication in the corpus, Chomsky's "Three Models for the Description of Language" (1956), appears in yet another anthology, Smith's *Communication and Culture,* but is the only article consulted from that source. The 72 sources include introductory remarks by the editors of the collections, Lees' prefaces to later editions of his *The Grammar of English Nominalizations,* Rosenbaum's preface to *The Grammar of English Predicate Complement Constructions,* and Postal's epilogue to Jacobs and Rosenbaum's *English Transformational Grammar.*

The selection of terms from these 72 sources was based solely on their technical nature in relation to the theory of transformational grammar, or to the application of that theory to English grammar. Selection was not based on the frequency of occurrence of a term in the same source or in different sources. It was not based on the simple occurrence of a technical term within the sources, since a number of the works discuss the terminology of earlier or competing theories. It was not based on specific applications of transformational grammar to languages other than English. It was not based on commonly used terms in transformational grammar which occur outside the corpus—such terms as 'gapping,' 'stretching,' and 'raising.' And, finally, selection was not based on terminology that appears to be facetious (such as 'word salad'), nontechnical (such as 'sound'), or remote (such as 'Markov process').

The consequence of this selectional process is that technical terms from traditional grammar and structural linguistics, the two major predecessors of transformational grammar, are not included in the *Glossary* unless their use is maintained in transformational theory. And in the cases of such continued use, no indication of prior origin is given in the *Glossary,* which is comparative only within the development of transformational grammar. The only concession to crosstheoretical comparison is the inclusion of the terms 'traditional grammar' and 'structural linguistics.' Such vital topics in structural linguistics as invariance condition, biuniqueness, and allophonic alternation are discussed in some of the sources in the corpus; however, because they are not within the framework of transformational grammar, they are not entered in the *Glossary.* Terms from traditional grammar have fared somewhat better than those in structural linguistics, since transformationalists generally regard their theory as a direct outgrowth of traditional notions.

The present *Glossary* was designed with the intention of avoiding numerous faults in earlier works of this general type. For example, the definitions are clearly labeled in regard to their bias: toward first-generation transformational grammar (*G–1*), toward second-generation transformational grammar (*G–2*), toward semantic-based transformational grammar (*G–2S*), or toward more than one of these models (e.g., *G–1–2*). In this regard, the reader should be warned that the date of the original publication of a work is not a reliable guide to its *G* classification, since some rather recent materials are either professedly *G–1* (e.g., Koutsoudas, 1966) or else describe contrasts between *G–1* and *G–2* (e.g., Chomsky, 1966a) or between *G–2* and *G–2S* (e.g., McCawley, 1968). On the other hand, some relatively early works in *G–1* anticipate second-generation theory (e.g., Halle, 1959); and some of the authors who identify their work as *G–2* comment on the appearance of semantic-based transformational grammar (e.g., Chomsky, 1965). The reader is advised to regard the generational classifications as relative, not absolute, indicators of underlying orientation.

To avoid the criticism of lack of documentation, the *Glossary* provides each definition of each term with a complete source in the Bibliography: author, date of earliest publication, and page numbers in the source used for this survey. To avoid the patchwork of styles that results from a collection of quotations, the definitions have been paraphrased or summarized in a single consistent style. To clarify the definitions, illustrative English examples have been supplied wherever possible. The examples usually involve the hypothetical characters Tom, Huck, Jim, Becky, and Aunt Polly. To avoid unnecessary repetition and duplication, and to help the reader achieve a full understanding of specific terms, expansive cross-references have been furnished (e.g., "See also DELETION"; "Compare ERASURE"). A complete system of cross-indexing enables the reader to locate related terms (e.g., **"Deletion, node.** See NODE DELETION"). The symbols that are used in the entries are explained in the List of Symbols following this Preface.

The structure of a maximal entry in the *Glossary* follows this plan: First is the *G* notation. Terms are divided into three generational categories (*G–1, G–2, G–2S*). Each generational category is subdivided into as many subcategories (*G–1a, G–1b, G–1c,* and so on) as are necessary to reflect the various senses or part-of-speech classes of the term within that orientation;

these are indicated by the form of the definition rather than by a label. Any particular *G* category opens with one or more representative definitions, in the typical fragment form. Definitions are usually followed by one or more illustrative examples involving Tom, Huck, Jim, and the other characters. After the illustrative examples come one or more encyclopedic statements, which amplify and qualify the definitions. Then follow one or more documentations which cite author, date of first publication, and page numbers in the source used. A documentation applies to everything that precedes it in an entry, up to a preceding documentation or to the *G* label itself. The only exception would be a parenthesized citation inside a definition (which covers only that citation). Most entries conclude with one or more cross-references.

In most cases, the definitions were arrived at inductively from one or more contexts in the corpus. They were usually based on implicit evidence such as usages and illustrations, instead of explicit evidence such as synonyms and glosses. As a result, some definitions may be narrower or broader than the author intended, although the documentation permits the reader to judge for himself. When a definition actually does appear in the corpus, it is paraphrased in the *Glossary;* and when two or more similar definitions occur, they are often synthesized as one. In this connection, the reader should be reminded that the *Glossary* is a collection of terms rather than a collection of concepts. A work of the latter type would focus on the 'notions' associated with English transformational grammar, such as the notion of **Simple transformation**. The names by which this notion has been called—**Singulary transformation, Elementary transformation, Simplex transformation, Unary transformation, Single-base transformation,** etc.—would be of secondary importance to the concept itself. The *Glossary,* however, focuses on the names which have been given to the various concepts in the history of English transformational grammar. Consequently, the catalog is long and unavoidably overlapping. It is hoped that the proliferation of entries, cross-references, and cross-indexes will be tolerated in the light of this function.

I wish to acknowledge—without incrimination—the contributions of several persons to the production of this *Glossary.* Professors Daniel P. Hendriksen and D. P. S. Dwarikesh of the Department of Linguistics at Western Michigan University each read half of the manuscript and made numerous corrections and suggestions, most of which I have accepted. Professor Jean Malmstrom and her colleagues on the English Language staff of the Department of English at Western Michigan University reviewed and tested an earlier, much shorter, version of this work and provided me with valuable feedback. Most of all I wish to acknowledge the silent contribution of the linguists who authored the 72 works in the corpus. Without their development and refinement of the theory of transformational grammar, this *Glossary* would have been neither necessary nor possible.

R. A. P.

LIST OF SYMBOLS

ALPHABETIC SYMBOLS

(NONPHONETIC)

A	Appositive relative clause; agentive case (*G–2S*); a hypothetical category.
α	Alpha-variable.
AD	Acquisition device.
ADJ	Adjective; adjective phrase; adjectival. (Also: Adj.)
ADJP	Adjective phrase.
ADV	Adverb; adverb phrase; adverbial. (Also: Adv.)
ADVP	Adverbial phrase.
AUX	Auxiliary system; auxiliary verb; auxiliary morpheme. (Also: Aux.)
B	Benefactive case (*G–2S*); a hypothetical category.
β	Beta-variable.
C	Concord (*G–1*); consonant; complement; category feature; comitative case (*G–2S*); a hypothetical category.
c	Copulative verb; complement verb (when subscripted to V: V_c).
Comp	Complement verb (when subscripted to V: V_{Comp}); complement. (Also: COMP.)
CS	Complex symbol.
D	Dative case (*G–2S*); a hypothetical category.
d	Determiner (*G–2S*).
DET	Determiner; determiner system. (Also: Det.)
E	A hypothetical category.
ed	Past tense morpheme. (Also: -ed.)
Emph	Emphasis marker (*G–1*).
en	Past participle morpheme; perfective aspect morpheme. (Also: -en.)
Er	Agentive affix (*G–1*).
er	Comparative morpheme. (Also: -er.)

F	Instruction formula (*G–1*); a generalized feature (*G–2*); factitive case (*G–2S*).
G	Grammar; genitive; a generation of transformational grammar (e.g., *G–1, G–2*).
G–1	First-generation transformational grammar.
G–2	Second-generation transformational grammar.
G–2S	Semantic-based transformational grammar.
GEN	Genitive (*G–1*).
I	Imperative marker; instrumental case (*G–2S*).
i	Intransitive (when subscripted to V: V_i).
IMP	Imperative marker. (Also: Imp.)
in	Intransitive (when subscripted to V: V_{in}).
ing	Present participle morpheme; progressive aspect morpheme; gerundive morpheme; gerund morpheme; complementizing morpheme. (Also: -ing.)
K	Kasus.
L	A given language; locative case (*G–2S*).
LAD	Language acquisition device.
M	Modal; morphophonemic rule; marked phonological feature (*G–2*); modality (*G–2S*).
MAN	Manner adverbial.
MV	Main verb.
N	Noun.
n	Indefinite number (when following Rule: Rule *n*).
N°	Number (*G–1*).
NEG	Negative marker. (Also: Neg.)
Nml	Nominalizing morpheme (*G–1*).
Nom	Nominal.
NP	Noun phrase.
O	Objective case (*G–2S*).
P	Preposition; predicate; proposition (*G–2S*).
Pas	Simple past tense.
PDP	Predicate phrase.
pl	Plural (when subscripted to NP: NP_{pl}).
POSS	Possessive morpheme.
PRED	Predicate. (Also: Pred.)
PredP	Predicate phrase.
Prep	Preposition.
PrepP	Prepositional phrase.
Pres	Present tense.
Prev	Preverb.
PRO	Pro-form; pronoun; pronominal feature. (Also: Pro.)

Prop	Proposition (*G–2S*).
Prt	Particle.
Q	Question marker; yes-no question marker.
R	Restrictive relative clause marker.
Rel	Relative clause marker.
S	Sentence; agreement marker (*G–1*).
s	Agreement morpheme; plural morpheme. (Also: -s.)
's	Possessive morpheme. (Also: -'s.)
S′	Embedded sentence.
Σ	Initial symbol.
sing	Singular (when subscripted to NP: NP_{sing}).
sg	Singular (when subscripted to NP: NP_{sg}).
SP	Subordinate adverbial phrase.
T	Article, determiner (*G–1*); tense morpheme; transformation-(al).
t	Transitive (when subscripted to V: V_t).
Tn	Tense morpheme.
U	Unmarked phonological feature (*G–2*).
V	Verb; vowel.
VP	Verb phrase.
W	A generalized content.
WH	Information question marker; relative marker. (Also: Wh, wh.)
X,Y,Z	A generalized context (e.g., X—Y).

NONALPHABETIC SYMBOLS

[ ]	Square brackets. A phonetic transcription; a phonetic representation; a feature; a feature specification; a set of feature specifications; an abbreviator in a phonological rule; a grammatical relation (e.g., [NP, S] 'subject-of').
{ }	Braces. An abbreviator in a grammatical rule; a morpheme; a morphemic transcription (*G–1*).
( )	Parentheses. An optional element in a rule; an abbreviator in a phonological rule; a semantic marker.
< >	Angle brackets. Mutual inclusion in a phonological rule; a selection restriction.
→	Single-shafted arrow. The structural change symbol in a transformational rule (*G–1*); a concatenator in a grammatical rule (a rewriting rule, a morphophonemic rule, a phonological rule).

$\Rightarrow$	Double-shafted arrow. The structural-change symbol in a transformational rule (*G–2*).
/ /	Slashes. A phonological transcription; a phonemic transcription (*G–1*); a systematic phonemic transcription (*G–2*).
/	Slash. An abbreviator in a context-sensitive rewriting rule (e.g., V → CS/__NP: "rewrite Verb as a Complex Symbol in the position immediately preceding a Noun Phrase"); an abbreviator of optional selections in a rewriting rule (e.g., V → V_t/V_i/V_c: "rewrite Verb as transitive, intransitive, or complement").
+	Plus. A concatenator of elements in a string; a syllable boundary; a morpheme boundary; a formative boundary; a word boundary; a positive specification of a syntactic, semantic, or phonological feature (a feature coefficient).
—	Dash. A concatenator of elements in a string. Minus. A negative specification of a syntactic, semantic, or phonological feature (a feature coefficient).
——	Place-marker. A position holder in a context-sensitive rewriting rule (e.g., V → CS/____NP: "rewrite Verb as a Complex Symbol in the position immediately preceding a Noun Phrase").
Ø	Zero. Null string; singular morpheme (*G–1*).
*	Asterisk. Ungrammatical (preceding a linguistic form); ungrammatical, unacceptable (preceding a sentence).
△	Dummy symbol. A dummy element in an underlying phrase-marker (*G–2*).
## ##	Boundary symbol. A word; a phrase; a sentence. (Also: # #.)
=	Prefix boundary. A prefix which cannot receive primary stress.
1,2,3	Indices. Referential indices (e.g., $NP_1 + V + NP_2$); structure indices (e.g., X + Y + Z ⇒ 1,3,2).
	1 2 3
I,II,III	Persons. First person (I); second person (II); third person (III).
/	Primary stress.
∧	Secondary stress.
\	Tertiary stress.

A

Abbreviator. *G–1–2.* The symbol in a grammatical statement which permits the collapsing of two or more rules into one. Abbreviators indicate: optionality of selection of a category—parentheses; free selection of a unit within a category—braces; restricted selection of units within a category—square brackets; or a combination of these instructions, as in:

A → B (C)	rewrite A as B alone or as B plus C
A → $\left\{ \begin{array}{c} B \\ C \end{array} \right\}$	rewrite A as either B or C
A → B $\left(\left\{ \begin{array}{c} C \\ D \end{array} \right\} \right)$	rewrite A as B alone or as B plus either C or D
A → $\left[\begin{array}{c} B \\ C \end{array} \right] \left[\begin{array}{c} D \\ E \end{array} \right]$	rewrite A as either B plus D or as C plus E

(Koutsoudas, 1966, 9–13). Also called **Abbreviatory notation.** (Chomsky and Halle, 1968, 63.) See also NOTATIONAL CONVENTION.

Abbreviatory notation. See ABBREVIATOR.

Abstract. *G–2.* The semantic distinctive feature which is specified in the dictionary entries of nouns, and in the selection restrictions of other categories, to indicate that the lexical item can or cannot refer to something that is not physically oriented in time and space, i.e., is not concrete. (Postal, 1968b, 273.) True abstract nouns have the specification [+abstract] [−count], which distinguishes them from mass nouns—specified [−abstract] [−count]—and prevents them, and also mass nouns, from occurring in such sentences as "Where is . . . ?" Another type of noun is represented by *idea*, which is [+abstract] but also [+count]: *ideas*. (Chomsky, 1965, 230.) Compare CONCRETE.

Abstract inchoative predicate. See INCHOATIVE.

Abstractive nominal. *G–1.* An abstract noun, or nominal, which is derived from an adjective by nominalization, as in: *flatness* (from *flat*), *breadth* (from *broad*), *intensity* (from *intense*). (Lees, 1960a, 85.) See also NOMINALIZATION.

Abstract predicate inversion. *G–1.* An inversion of the type "To steer the raft was hard for Huck" ⇒ "The raft was hard for Huck to steer." (Lees, 1960a, 94–95.)

Abstract syntax. *G–2.* Deep-level syntax; the syntax of underlying structures; generative-transformational syntax. (Rosenbaum, 1967b, ix.) See also SYNTAX, GENERATIVE GRAMMAR.

Acceptability. *G–2.* The concept that characterizes utterances which are

1

acceptable to the native speaker as natural, easy to understand, and likely to be produced, as opposed to utterances that are clumsy, bizarre, and outlandish. Acceptability, like grammaticality, is a matter of degree, but the two concepts are not identical. Acceptability refers to performance, whereas grammaticality refers to competence. A sentence can be both grammatical and acceptable at the same time, as in: "Huck built himself a raft"; or grammatical but unacceptable, as in: "Huck built Huck a raft"; or semigrammatical but acceptable, as in: "The raft built Huck." Sentences that deviate from lower-level syntactic-semantic features, such as [human], are more acceptable than those which deviate from higher-level features, such as [count]. (Chomsky, 1965, 10–11, 150.) Compare GRAMMATICAL-NESS, ADMISSIBILITY.

Accessible. *G–2.* Comprehensible to a native speaker. Deep structures are accessible, to some degree, from surface structures. (Langendoen, 1969, 140.) Compare RECOVERABLE.

Accidental gap. *G–1.* A phonologically admissible nonsense syllable; the nonoccurrence in the lexicon of a syllable that is phonologically admissible under the redundancy rules; one of the three categories of possible lexical items established by the phonological redundancy rules: accidental gap— not occurring, but possible, such as *bling.* (Chomsky, 1964, 64.) See also ADMISSIBILITY.

Account for. *G–1–2.* To provide a theoretical explanation for; to explain how the theory specifies or predicts. For example, a transformational generative grammar 'accounts for' the fact that certain sequences of words are sentences of the language and others are not. (Bach, 1964, 5–8; Rosenbaum, 1967a, 84, 91.) See also PREDICT.

Accusative transformation. *G–2.* The transformation which converts the syntactic feature specification of a noun in the deep structure from [−accusative] to [+accusative] so that the noun will not appear as a grammatical subject in the surface structure, as when: "Becky expected *he* to be brave" ⇒ "Becky expected *him* to be brave." (Jacobs, 1968, 33.) Also called **Case transformation.** (Jacobs and Rosenbaum, 1968, 220–222.)

Acquisition, language. See LANGUAGE ACQUISITION.

Acquisition model. *G–2.* A theory of the strategy which the child uses to construct a correct grammar of his language—to learn his language—on the basis of a restricted sample of primary linguistic data. (Chomsky, 1965, 25, 30.) See also LANGUAGE-ACQUISITION DEVICE.

Acquisition, order of. See ORDER OF ACQUISITION.

Actant. *G–2S.* The case element which dominates a noun phrase within a proposition, as 'locative' dominates the noun phrase *on the raft.* (Fillmore, 1966, 367.) Also called **Case category.** (Fillmore, 1968, 24). See also CASE GRAMMAR.

Action adjective. See ACTION VERBAL.

Action nominal. *G–1.* A noun phrase which results from the nominaliza-tion of a sentence containing an action verb, as in: "Huck rescued Tom immediately" ⇒ "Huck's immediate rescuing of Tom"; "Huck's rescuing of Tom immediately"; "Huck's rescue of Tom." The action nominal re-quires a preposition before a following object, and it permits the adjectivali-zation of a following adverb; but it does not accept an auxiliary verb: *"Huck's having rescued of Tom." (Lees, 1960a, 66–69.) Compare GERUNDIVE NOMINAL, FACTIVE NOMINAL.

Action verb. See ACTION VERBAL.

2

Action verbal. *G–2.* An action verb or an action adjective which can appear in an imperative sentence (action verb: "*Hold* that rope!"; action adjective: "Be *patient!*") or in a sentence with progressive aspect (action verb: "Tom is *holding* the rope"; action adjective: "Huck is being *patient*"). (Jacobs and Rosenbaum, 1968, 63–64.) See also VERBAL.

Active sentence. *G–2.* A nonpassive sentence—that is, a sentence that has not undergone the passive transformation (e.g., "Huck freed Jim"—active —as opposed to "Jim was freed by Huck"—passive). (Rosenbaum, 1967a, 60.) Compare PASSIVE SENTENCE.

Activity verb. *G–1.* A verb from which an action nominal or an agentive nominal can be derived; a verb for which the pro-verb *do* can be substituted, such as *type:* "What does Becky *do*?"; "Becky *types* letters" ⇒ "Becky's *typing* of letters" (action nominal); "Becky is a *typer/typist* of letters" (agentive nominal). (Lees, 1960a, 51, 69.) See also ACTION VERBAL.

Acute. See GRAVE.

Addition. See ADJUNCTION.

Addition, rule. See RULE ADDITION.

Adequacy. *G–1–2.* The correctness of a grammar or a theory of grammar, judged at various levels. A grammar meets the level of observational adequacy if it correctly describes the primary data of a corpus—that is, if it is essentially a structural grammar. It meets the level of descriptive adequacy if it also 1) correctly accounts for the speaker's intuitions, as in an essentially traditional or weakly adequate grammar (Lyons, 1968, 246–247), and 2) assigns a structural description to each sentence as well, as in an essentially generative or strongly adequate grammar (Lyons, 1968, 246–247). A linguistic theory meets the level of explanatory adequacy if it correctly selects the descriptively adequate grammar from among any number of observationally adequate grammars; it would thus be essentially a transformational theory. (King, 1969, 13.) See also DESCRIPTIVE ADEQUACY, EXPLANATORY ADEQUACY, OBSERVATIONAL ADEQUACY, EXTERNAL CONDITION OF ADEQUACY, JUSTIFICATION OF A GRAMMAR.

Adequacy, descriptive. See DESCRIPTIVE ADEQUACY.

Adequacy, empirical. See EMPIRICAL ADEQUACY.

Adequacy, explanatory. See EXPLANATORY ADEQUACY.

Adequacy, external condition of. See EXTERNAL CONDITION OF ADEQUACY.

Adequacy, internal condition of. See JUSTIFICATION OF A GRAMMAR.

Adequacy, observational. See OBSERVATIONAL ADEQUACY.

Adequate, strongly. See ADEQUACY.

Adequate, weakly. See ADEQUACY.

Ad hoc rule. *G–2.* A rule or feature invented by the analyst to account for problems arising from his theoretical assumptions rather than for the purpose of stating a linguistic generalization; thus, an unmotivated rule. (Postal, 1968a, 202–203.) Compare MOTIVATED SYSTEM.

Adjectival. *G–1–2.* Having the characteristics of an adjective. (Chomsky, 1962, 237.) *G–1.* A complex adjective phrase consisting of an adjective plus a prepositional modifier, as in: "happy to comply"; "tired of waiting." (Lees, 1960a, 82–83.) See also ADJECTIVAL COMPLEMENT. *G–2.* A derived adjective, such as: "a *driving* rain"; "a *scary* movie"; "an *impressive* performance." (Chomsky, 1965, 223.) See also ADJECTIVE, ADJECTIVALIZATION.

Adjectival complement. *G–1.* The embedded, and often reduced, modifier of an adjective: "Tom got red *in the face*"; "Tom was shorter *than Huck*." (Lees, 1960a, 84; Smith, 1964, 252.) See also ADJECTIVAL COMPLEMENT CONSTRUCTION.

Adjectival complement construction. *G–2.* A predicate complement construction consisting of *be*+adjective+complement, which is derivationally related to the synonymous verbal complement construction, as in: "Huck was scared to free Jim" (adjectival complement construction); "It scared Huck to free Jim" (verbal complement construction). (Rosenbaum, 1967a, 100.) See also ADJECTIVALIZATION.

Adjectivalization. *G–1a.* The transformation which produces postpositioned phrasal modifiers of adjectives: "sure *to please*"; "afraid *of offending*"; worried *about going*." (Lees, 1960a, 81-82.) *G–1b.* The process which derives single-word adjectivals, also called derived adjectives, from any of the syntactic categories by means of a relative clause—with the addition of an adjectivalization morpheme (Thomas, 1965, 56)—and embeds them before a head noun, as in: "The meeting, *which was a success* . . ." ⇒ "The meeting, *a success* . . ." ⇒ "The meeting, *success-ful* . . ." ("The *successful* meeting . . ."). (Chomsky, 1962, 231.) *G–2.* The process which generates adjectivals, as when: "Huck gave a (the performance *impressed* them) performance" ⇒ "Huck gave an *impress-ing* performance" ⇒ "Huck gave an *impressive* performance." (Chomsky, 1965, 227.)

Adjectivalization morpheme. *G–1.* A morpheme suffix which is used in the adjectivalization transformation to produce derived adjectives, such as *foolish*, from *fool* plus the adjectivalization morpheme *-ish*. (Thomas, 1965, 56.) Also called **Attributivizing suffix.** See also ADJECTIVALIZATION.

Adjective. *G–1–2.* The single-word rewriting of the category ADJ-P or ADJ in the derivation of a kernel sentence; the category symbol ADJ, which is dominated by MV and co-generated with a copula in the phrase structure: $MV \rightarrow V_{copula} + ADJ$. (Chomsky, 1957, 73); a predicate adjective. (Rosenbaum, 1967a, 100, 108.) *G–2a.* The [−verb] subset of the category [+verbal] in the deep structure which will appear with a copula in the surface structure of the sentence. Adjectives are categorized along with verbs as verbals because of the synonymy of such pairs as "That *pleased* Becky" and "That was *pleasing* to Becky." (Jacobs, 1968, 21–22.) *G–2b.* The ADJ or ADJ-P subset of the category 'noun phrase' in the deep structure of a sentence, dominated by NP, just as N is. Adjectives are categorized along with nouns as nominals because they are affected alike by several transformational processes, viz.: question formation ("What is Tom?"; "Tom is *lazy/boss*"); relativization ("That he was *lazy/boss*, which he was, was not surprising"); equation ("Tom is *lazy/boss*"); pseudocleft construction ("What Tom is is *lazy/boss*"); and pro-formation ("Tom is *lazy/boss*, and he acts it"). (Ross, 1969, 357.) Compare ADJECTIVAL, NOMINAL. See also VERBAL.

Adjective, gerundive. See GERUNDIVE ADJECTIVE.

Adjective, intransitive. See INTRANSITIVE ADJECTIVE.

Adjective inversion. *G–2.* The obligatory permutation rule which shifts a single-word adjectival, the residue of a reduced relative clause, from its ungrammatical position following a noun head to its proper position preceding the noun, as in: *"The linen, *dirty* . . ." ⇒ "The *dirty* linen. . . ." (Langacker, 1968, 134.) The transformation is blocked if the adjective has a complement, if the head noun is not in the main sentence, or if the head noun is indefinite, as in: "Something *old,* something *new,* something *borrowed,* something *blue."* Also called **Order-change transformation.** (Smith, 1964, 253.) See also ADJECTIVE TRANSFORMATION.

Adjective, nonstative. See NONSTATIVE VERBAL.

Adjective, predicate. See PREDICATE ADJECTIVE.

Adjective, prenominal. See PRENOMINAL ADJECTIVE.

Adjective, pure See PURE ADJECTIVE.

Adjective, stative. See STATIVE VERBAL.

Adjective transformation. *G–1.* The nominalizing transformation which converts a string of the form article+noun+be+adjective (e.g., *"The raft* is *small"*) into a noun phrase of the form article+adjective+noun (e.g., *"the small raft").* (Chomsky, 1957, 72, 114.) Also called **Adjective inversion.**

Adjective, transitive. See TRANSITIVE ADJECTIVE.

Adjunction. *G–1.* The transformational operation, also called **Addition,** which 'adjoins' one or more branches to a phrase structure, as when: A+B ⇒ A+B+C. (Koutsoudas, 1966, 28–31.)

Adjunction, preposition. See CONJUNCTION.

Adjunction transformation, negative. See NEGATIVE ADJUNCTION TRANSFORMATION.

Adjustment, number. See NUMBER ADJUSTMENT.

Admissibility. *G–1.* The phonological possibility, or permissibility, for a lexical item to occur in the lexicon of a particular language. Three degrees of admissibility are recognized: 1) admissible—occurring and possible, like *bring;* 2) inadmissible—not occurring and not possible, like *bning;* and 3) accidental gap—not occurring but possible, like *bling.* (Chomsky, 1964, 64.) *G–2.* The distance in number of phonological features of a potential lexical item from complete permissibility for the lexicon of a particular language, being analogous to the many degrees of grammaticality. For example, *bling* is more distant from admissibility than *bring,* but less distant than *bning.* The elimination of most of the phonological redundancy rules permits the replacement of the earlier three-way distinction with this sliding scale of admissibility. (Chomsky and Halle, 1968, 417.) Compare ACCEPTABILITY, GRAMMATICALNESS. See also ADMISSIBLE, ACCIDENTAL GAP.

Admissibility, phonological. See PHONOLOGICAL ADMISSIBILITY.

Admissible. *G–1.* Phonologically possible, or permissible, as a lexical item in a particular language; one of the three degrees of admissibility, in which the item both is possible and does occur, like *bring.* (Chomsky, 1964, 64.) See also ADMISSIBILITY. Compare ACCEPTABLE.

Advancement, noun phrase. See NOUN PHRASE ADVANCEMENT.

Adverb. *G–1.* The optional syntactic category ADV, which is dominated by main verb or verb phrase or sentence in the phrase structure of a kernel sentence and which can, or in some cases must, be relocated from its final position within the phrase in which it occurs, as when: "goes *always"* ⇒ *"always* goes"; a single-word replacement for the category ADV in a kernel sentence structure. Adverbs are generally classified semantically according to time, place, or manner; they are classified syntactically according to domination (by MV, VP, or S). (Thomas, 1965, 35–37, 162–171.) *G–2.* The surface structure representation of a deep structure formation consisting of a preposition plus a complement, as in: *at that place* ⇒ *there; at that time* ⇒ *then; in that way* ⇒ *thus; at a local place*

5

⇒ *locally; in quick time* ⇒ *quickly; with ease* ⇒ *easily.* 'Adverb' is not a deep structure syntactic category in *G–2.* (Chomsky, 1966c, 46.) Also called **Adverbial.**

Adverbial. *G–1–2.* Having the characteristics of an adverb. (Lyons, 1968, 327.) *G–2a.* The phrasal residue in the surface structure of a reduced adverbial clause in the deep structure, as in: "Tom approached it (Tom had caution)" ⇒ "Tom approached it *with caution";* "Tom went to school (Tom was in Missouri)" ⇒ "Tom went to school *in Missouri."* (Chomsky, 1965, 219.) *G–2b.* The surface structure representation of an underlying ADV-P construction that refers to time, place, or manner. The term 'adverbial' replaces the earlier term **Adverb.** (Rosenbaum, 1967a, 21, 67; Jacobs and Rosenbaum, 1968, 208.) See also ADVERB. Compare SENTENCE ADVERBIAL.

Adverbial, manner. See MANNER ADVERBIAL.

Adverbial phrase, subordinate. See SUBORDINATE ADVERBIAL PHRASE.

Adverbial, place. See PLACE ADVERBIAL.

Adverbial sentence. *G–2.* A sentence which is embedded as a subordinate phrase (SP) under the immediate domination of S in a main sentence: S → NP+PDP+SP, as in: "Huck built the raft *in order to run away."* (Rosenbaum, 1967a, 16, 17.) See also SUBORDINATE ADVERBIAL PHRASE, SUBORDINATE CLAUSE.

Adverbial, sentence. See SENTENCE ADVERBIAL.

Adverbial, time. See TIME ADVERBIAL.

Adverb, negative preverbal. See NEGATIVE PREVERBAL ADVERB.

Adverb preposing transformation. *G–2.* The optional permutation rule which moves an adverbial time clause to the front of the sentence, as when: "Tom was painting *when Aunt Polly called"* ⇒ *"When Aunt Polly called,* Tom was painting." (Ross, 1967, 189; Jacobs and Rosenbaum, 1968, 210.) Also called **Preposing transformation.** See also TIME-PLACE TEST.

Affirmation transformation. *G–1.* The transformation which accounts for the emphasis of an occurrence of an auxiliary verb in a terminal string, as in: "Huck *can* read!"; "Tom *is* lazy!"; "Tom *does* work!"; "Huck *has* finished!" (Chomsky, 1957, 65.) Also called **Emphasis transformation.** See also EMPHATIC AFFIRMATIVE.

Affirmative, emphatic. See EMPHATIC AFFIRMATIVE.

Affix. *G–1.* A bound morpheme other than a base—thus, a derivational or inflectional morpheme. (Lees, 1960a, 25.) Of the inflectional suffixes, only noun number and auxiliary *-en* and *-ing* are categories of the syntax, introduced by the phrase structure rules. The other inflectional suffixes—verbal concord, noun possessive, comparative/superlative degree, and even some of the aspect forms—are introduced via transformations. Derivational affixes are categories of the lexicon. (Chomsky, 1957, 72–74, 111–113.) See also INFLECTION, DERIVATIONAL SUFFIX. *G–2.* A deep structure feature, [+affix], of the major category to which an inflectional morph will be attached in the surface structure. (Jacobs and Rosenbaum, 1968, 83–84, 110–117.) Most derivational suffixes are surface structure consequences of deep structure embeddings, as in: "Huck is a (Huck swims)" ⇒ "Huck is a *swimmer."* Jacobs and Rosenbaum, 1968, 227–229.) See also AFFIX SEGMENT.

Affix, agentive. See AGENTIVE AFFIX.

Affix, finite verbal. See FINITE VERB.

Affix, Ing-. See ING-AFFIX.

Affix morpheme, nominal. See NOMINAL AFFIX MORPHEME.

Affix, negative. See NEGATIVE AFFIX.

Affix, neutral. See NEUTRAL AFFIX.

Affix, participle. See PARTICIPLE AFFIX.

Affix segment. *G–2.* A constituent of the deep structure which is introduced into a position following a plural noun or a finite or aspect verb in order to carry the feature [+affix] and other relevant features of the head. (Jacobs and Rosenbaum, 1968, 83–89, 110–117.) See also NOUN SUFFIX TRANSFORMATION.

Affix, tense. See TENSE AFFIX.

Affix transformation. See AUXILIARY TRANSFORMATION.

Affricate. *G–1–2.* The natural class of sounds that are positively specified for the phonological distinctive features [consonantal], [delayed release], [strident], and [compact], but that are negatively specified for [vocalic], [continuant], [nasal], and [sonorant]: English /č/ (voiceless, as in *church*) and /ǰ/ (voiced, as in *judge*); a sound that is a member of that class. (Harms, 1968, 33–35; Chomsky and Halle, 1968, 176–177.)

Agent. *G–1.* The performer of an action described by an activity verb in an underlying sentence. (Lees, 1960a, 69, 71.) *G–2S.* The instigator of the action described by the verb in the semantic deep structure of a sentence. (Fillmore, 1968, 28.) See also AGENTIVE.

Agentive. *G–1.* Naming the agent of the action. (Lees, 1960a, 69, 71.) *G–2S.* The case of the instigator—usually animate—of the action described by the verb. (Fillmore, 1966, 363; Fillmore, 1968, 24.) See also CASE GRAMMAR.

Agentive affix. *G–1.* The morpheme *-er,* by which agentive nominals are derived from activity verbs, as in: "Becky types letters" ⇒ "Becky is a type-*er* of letters." (Lees, 1960a, 71.)

Agentive formation. *G–2.* The process by which the verb—usually transitive—of a relative clause is transformed into a nominal of agent by means of an agentive suffix, with the underlying object of the verb either preceding the agent nominal in the possessive case (e.g., "The one who built the raft . . ." ⇒ "The raft's builder . . .") or following it in a prepositional phrase (e.g., "The builder of the raft . . ."). (Ross, 1967, 199.) See also AGENTIVE NOMINAL.

Agentive nominal. *G–1.* A nominal construction which is derived from an activity verb by means of the agentive affix *-er,* as in: "Becky types letters" ⇒ "Becky is a *type-er* of letters." In some cases the resulting agentive nominal is then replaced by a 'professional' noun, as in: "Becky is a *typist*." (Lees, 1960a, 69–71.)

Agentive phrase. *G–2.* The *by*-prepositional phrase in a passive construction, MAN → Prep$_{by}$+NP, as in: "Jim was rescued *by Tom*." The NP of the agentive phrase is the logical subject, or the agent, of the derived sentence. (Rosenbaum, 1967a, 50.) See also PASSIVE TRANSFORMATION.

Agentive preposition. *G–2.* The preposition *by* in the agentive phrase of a passive sentence, MAN → Prep$_{by}$+NP, as in: "Jim was rescued *by* Tom." When the NP object of the preposition is a complement sentence, *by* is sometimes deleted, as when: "To have Tom aboard pleased Huck"

⇒ *"Huck was pleased *by* to have Tom aboard" ⇒ "Huck was pleased to have Tom aboard." (Rosenbaum, 1967a, 21, 84.) See also PASSIVE TRANS-FORMATION.

Agree. See AGREEMENT.

Agreement. *G–1.* The co-occurrence relation 1) involving number concord a) between a subject and present-tense verb (e.g., "The raft floats" and "The rafts float"—in which the verb is said to 'agree' with the subject), b) between demonstrative and head noun (e.g., "this raft" and "these rafts"—in which the demonstrative is said to 'agree' with the noun), and c) between a few noun adjuncts and head nouns (e.g., "woman driver" and "women drivers"—in which the adjunct 'agrees' with the head); and 2) involving person concord in the present singular (e.g., "I/you want" and "He wants." The verb *be* exhibits number agreement in the past tense as well (e.g., "He *was*"; "They *were*") and requires agreement of all three persons in the present singular (e.g., "I *am*"; "You *are*"; "He *is*"). (Koutsoudas, 1966, 97, 256.) Also called **Concord.** The tense element is also called the **Agreement morpheme.** (Thomas, 1965, 58.)

Agreement morpheme. See AGREEMENT.

Agreement transformation. *G–2.* The set of rules which bring about subject-verb agreement by introducing person and number features into the auxiliary to make it agree with the noun phrase subject. The agreement transformation, or subject-verb agreement rule (Langacker, 1968, 127), copies the number and person features of the subject onto the AUX by the auxiliary agreement transformation. It copies these features, plus tense, onto a verb, deleting the AUX by the verb agreement transformation. It then adds a third-singular-present or past tense suffix to the verb by the verb suffix transformation. (Jacobs and Rosenbaum, 1968, 135.) See also AGREEMENT.

Alphabet, universal phonetic. See UNIVERSAL PHONETIC ALPHABET.

Alpha-environment convention. *G–2.* A special convention for handling exceptions to a general phonological rule by combining both the general rule and the succeeding exception rule into a single rule, utilizing the variable alpha (α):

$$[\text{segment}] \rightarrow [\alpha \text{ feature}]/ < \alpha \text{ environment} >$$

"Rewrite a segment as 'plus' a certain feature if the segment occurs in (is 'plus') a certain environment; rewrite a segment as 'minus' a certain feature if the segment does not occur in (is 'minus') a certain environment." (Harms, 1968, 71.) See also ALPHA-SWITCHING RULE, ALPHA-TYPE VARIABLE.

Alpha-switching rule. *G–2.* A phonological exchange rule which reverses —flip flops or shifts—the plus/minus (alpha: α) value of a feature of a segment at the left of an arrow with the value of a feature of a segment at the right of the arrow:

$$[\alpha \text{ feature}_1] \rightarrow [-\alpha \text{ feature}_1]/ < +\text{feature}_2 >$$

"If the segment to the left of the arrow is 'plus' feature # 1, rewrite it as 'minus' feature # 1 in the environment 'plus feature # 2'; if the segment to the left of the arrow is 'minus' feature # 1, rewrite it as 'plus' feature # 1 in the environment 'plus feature # 2'." (Harms, 1968, 61–62.) See also ALPHA-ENVIRONMENT CONVENTION, ALPHA-TYPE VARIABLE, NON-ITERATIVE RULE CONVENTION.

Alpha-type variable. *G–2.* A Greek-letter symbol (α, alpha; β, beta; etc.)

in a phonological rule which indicates agreement in the plus/minus value of one feature with that of another feature in the same rule, and can be negated to indicate lack of agreement. The alpha-type variable can be used to describe the assimilation of nasal consonants to following voiceless stops in English:

$$[+\text{nasal}] \rightarrow \begin{bmatrix} \alpha\,\text{high} \\ \beta\,\text{grave} \end{bmatrix} \Big/ \underline{\hspace{1em}} \begin{bmatrix} \alpha\,\text{high} \\ \beta\,\text{grave} \end{bmatrix}$$

That is, a nasal consonant acquires the value of the features [high] and [grave] of a following voiceless stop: [m](−high, +grave) before *p* (−high, +grave); [n](−high, −grave) before *t* (−high, −grave); [ŋ] (+high, +grave) before *k* (+high, +grave). (Harms, 1968, 59–62.) Also called **Alpha variable, Greek-letter variable.** Compare X-TYPE VARIABLE. See also ALPHA-ENVIRONMENT CONVENTION, ALPHA-SWITCHING RULE, ASSIMILATION.

Alpha variable.   See ALPHA-TYPE VARIABLE.

Alternating stress rule.   See STRESS PLACEMENT RULE.

Alternation, phonological.   See PHONOLOGICAL ALTERNATION.

Amalgam.   See AMALGAMATION.

Amalgamation.   *G–2.* The semantic composition, or projection, of the reading of one branch of a phrase marker with the reading of another branch of that same phrase marker, provided that each of the readings is compatible with the selection restrictions of the other, as in:

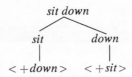

The product of amalgamation is an **Amalgam.** (Katz and Postal, 1964, 21.) See also PROJECTION RULE, READING, SEMANTIC INTERPRETATION.

Ambiguity.   *G–1–2.* The condition under which the surface structure of a sentence can be derived from different underlying syntactic structures—viz., structural or syntactic ambiguity—or under which a sentence has more than one underlying meaning for any of its lexical items—viz., semantic, referential, morphological, or lexical ambiguity—or both. For example, the sentence "Flying planes can be dangerous" is syntactically, or transformationally, ambiguous in at least three ways, as suggested by the following paraphrases: 1. Planes that fly can be dangerous. 2. Causing planes to fly can be dangerous. 3. Flying in planes can be dangerous. Each of these interpretations is, in turn, semantically ambiguous in at least three ways: 2a. Causing airplanes to fly can be dangerous. 2b. Causing carpenters' planes to fly can be dangerous. 2c. Causing brickmakers' planes to fly can be dangerous. (Katz, 1966, 149, 158–159; Lees, 1964b, xxxix.) Syntactic ambiguity is also called **Constructional homonymity.** (Chomsky, 1956, 147; Chomsky, 1957, 28, 86–87.) *G–2S.* The representation of more than one conceptual structure. (Langacker, 1968, 115.) See also TRANSFORMATIONAL AMBIGUITY.

Ambiguity, grammatical.   See AMBIGUITY.

Ambiguity, phonological.   See CONSTRUCTIONAL HOMONYMITY.

Ambiguity, structural. See STRUCTURAL AMBIGUITY.

Ambiguity, syntactic. See AMBIGUITY.

Ambiguity, transformational. See TRANSFORMATIONAL AMBIGUITY.

Ambiguous. See AMBIGUITY.

Analysis. *G–1.* The assignment of an abstract structure to a sentence, as opposed to the segmentation, classification, and labeling of the physical signals, as done in structural linguistics. (Lees, 1960a, xxv-xxvi.) *G–2.* A structural description postulated by a grammarian. Often, more than one analysis can be postulated for the same surface structure, such as: "Huck decided to go," from "Huck decided [to go]" or from "Huck decided [on [to go]]." (Rosenbaum, 1967a, 81.) See also STRUCTURAL DESCRIPTION, STRUCTURAL ANALYSIS, PARSING.

Analysis by synthesis. *G–1.* The model of automatic speech recognition which analyzes the structure of an utterance by generating, or synthesizing, all of the possible representations of sentences, comparing them with the utterance at hand, and selecting the best match. (Halle and Stevens, 1964, 604.) *G–2.* The decision procedure for reducing the number of operations required to assign a structural description to a sentence. (Katz and Postal, 1964, 167.)

Analysis, criteria of. See CRITERIA OF ANALYSIS.

Analysis, feature. See FEATURE ANALYSIS.

Analysis, immediate constituent. See IMMEDIATE CONSTITUENT ANALYSIS.

Analysis, linguistic. See LINGUISTIC ANALYSIS.

Analysis-marker. *G–1.* A bracketing of a string to specify the parts to be permuted or deleted by transformational rule. (Lees, 1960a, 31.)

Analysis, proper. See PROPER ANALYSIS.

Analysis, structural. See STRUCTURAL ANALYSIS.

Analytic grammar. *G–1.* A grammar which is oriented from the viewpoint of the hearer or linguist, as opposed to a synthetic grammar, which takes the point of view of the speaker. (Chomsky, 1962, 240.) Compare SYNTHETIC GRAMMAR.

Analyzability. *G–2.* The notion of derivational relationship which exists within the rewriting rules of the base, permitting the formalization of a derivation as a branching tree or labeled bracketing and allowing the carrying over of features from a complex symbol to its descendants. Based on Boolean conditions, such as the is-a relation, analyzability is the foundation on which the theory of transformational grammar has been developed. (Chomsky, 1965, 56, 98, 121–122, 143–144, 147, 217, 225–226.) See also ANALYZABLE (AS), IS-A RELATION, BOOLEAN CONDITION.

Analyzable (as). *G–1–2.* Having the proper analysis of; having the constituent structure of; bearing an is-a relation to. For example, in the phrase structure A → B+C, the expansion is 'analyzable as' B+C with respect to A; that is, the string B+C is 'analyzable as' A; that is, B+C *is an* A. (Chomsky, 1961a, 131; Chomsky, 1965, 98, 143, 147.) See also ANALYZABILITY, PROPER ANALYSIS, IS-A RELATION.

Analyze. See PARSE.

Anaphoric process. *G–2.* The obligatory pronominalization transformation which reduces, shortens, or simplifies a sentence by deleting from it a noun phrase that is identical to another noun phrase, one dominated by a different S, in the same sentence and replacing the deleted noun phrase with a definite pronoun of the proper number and gender, i.e., by an anaphoric pronoun, or pro-replacement, as when: "Huck said that Huck could swim" ⇒ "Huck said that *he* could swim" (an example of forward pronominalization). Under some circumstances, such as left branching, the anaphoric process can apply to either of the identical noun phrases in different clauses of the same sentence. When the first of the two noun phrases is replaced, the process is referred to as *backward(s) pronominalization,* as when: "After *Tom* had finished painting, Tom disappeared" ⇒ "After *he* had finished painting, Tom disappeared." (Ross, 1967, 187–188.) See also FORWARD PRONOMINALIZATION, BACKWARDS PRONOMINALIZATION, PRONOMINALIZATION.

Anaphoric pronoun. See ANAPHORIC PROCESS.

Anomalous. See ANOMALY.

Anomaly. *G–2.* Lack of intelligibility of a sentence that has not been provided a derived reading in the semantic component because the selection restrictions have blocked amalgamation of its lexical readings, as in: *"The snow sounds red"; *"The varnish was silent." Such a sentence is referred to as **Semantically anomalous,** or simply **Anomalous.** (Katz, 1966, 160.) Violation of a selectional restriction in the deep structure does not necessarily render a sentence anomalous: "It is ridiculous to speak of snow sounding red"; "It is nonsensical to speak of varnish being silent." (McCawley, 1968, 128.) See also ACCEPTABILITY.

Antecedent. See PIVOTAL NOUN.

Anterior. *G–2.* The phonological distinctive feature which applies to sounds whose articulation involves an obstruction in the front of the mouth, forward of the palato-alveolar region of [š]. 'Anterior' sounds include labials, dentals, and alveolars. Anterior is identical with the earlier term **Diffuse,** as applied to consonants. Its minus value is termed **Non-anterior.** (Chomsky and Halle, 1968, 304.) See also DIFFUSE.

Antonymy, sex-. See SEX-ANTONYMY.

A-over-A principle. *G–2.* A restriction on extracting a noun phrase from within another noun phrase for extraposition, relativization, interrogation, cleft transformation, etc., as seen in: "Huck saw Becky's picture of *Tom*"; *"Who did Huck see Becky's picture of?" (Chomsky, 1968, 43, 46.)

Apparatus, derivational. See DERIVATIONAL APPARATUS.

Apparatus, transformational. See TRANSFORMATIONAL MACHINERY.

Apparent counterexample. See COUNTEREXAMPLE.

Application, vacuous. See VACUOUS APPLICATION.

Appositive. *G–1a.* The reduced form of a nonrestrictive relative clause, seen in: "Huck, who was a dropout, went fishing" ⇒ "Huck, *a dropout,* went fishing." (Lees, 1960a, 92.) *G–1b.* Nonrestrictive. (Thomas, 1965, 156.) *G–2.* The marker A, which appears to the right of a noun in a noun phrase with a specified determiner (*a, the*) or a proper name to indicate that a nonrestrictive relative clause will be adjoined to the matrix sentence at that position, as in: NP → N_{Prop}+A ("Huck, who was a dropout, . . ."). (Smith, 1964, 248–251.) See also NONRESTRICTIVE RELATIVE CLAUSE, RELATIVE CLAUSE, RELATIVE TRANSFORMATION.

Appositive clause. See NONRESTRICTIVE RELATIVE CLAUSE.

Appositive relative clause. See NONRESTRICTIVE RELATIVE CLAUSE.

Arbitrary relationship. *G–2.* The conventional, rather than logical, relationship between sound and meaning in a sentence, resulting from the fact that the phonological and semantic components of a grammar operate independently of each other on different aspects of the product of the syntactic component: the semantic component on the deep syntactic structure before transformations, and the phonological component on the surface structure after transformations. (Katz and Postal, 1964, 161.)

Archiphoneme. *G–1.* A phonological representation consisting of features common to two segments, or phonemes. An example is the archiphoneme /N/, which consists of the features common to /m/, /n/, and /ŋ/ in the position immediately before a voiceless stop, where there is no contrast among nasals in English: e.g., /Np/, /Nt/, and /Nk/ in *hump, hunt,* and *hunk,* respectively. (Bach, 1964, 135.) A generalized archiphoneme represents features common to a much broader set, as in: C (for consonant), V (for vowel). (Chomsky, 1964, 89.) *G–2.* A systematic archiphoneme, which reflects the lack of contrast of the features of systematic phonemes in a particular position. (Postal, 1968a, 180, 211.) In Chomsky and Halle, the term **Archi-segment** is used in place of the earlier **Archiphoneme, Generalized phoneme, Systematic phoneme,** and **Systematic archiphoneme** to define any incompletely specified segment in the phonological matrices of a lexicon. (Chomsky and Halle, 1968, 166.) Compare MORPHOPHONEME.

Archiphoneme, generalized. See ARCHIPHONEME.

Archiphoneme, systematic. See ARCHIPHONEME.

Archi-segment. See ARCHIPHONEME.

Argument. *G–1.* The string of symbols comprising the structural analysis of a rule. (Lees, 1960a, 53.) *G–2S.* The noun phrase (NP) of a predicate. A one-place predicate (intransitive) contains one argument (one NP); a two-place predicate (transitive) contains two arguments (two NP's); a three-place predicate contains three arguments (three NP's). (Langendoen, 1969, 97.) See also PREDICATE.

Article. *G–1.* The T node of a noun phrase expansion: NP → T+N. (Chomsky, 1957, 72.) Articles are a subclass of determinatives (Lees, 1960a, 114) or determiners. Articles themselves are subclassified as indefinite (*a/an*) or definite (*the*). A zero article (Ø) appears with nouns which lack overt articles in the surface form. (Thomas, 1965, 79–81.) *G–2.* Articles are not specified for underlying personal pronouns and proper nouns, to which the property of definite/indefinite does not apply. (Postal, 1966, 204, 206–207.) Articles are surface structure manifestations of the underlying specifications of the syntactic/semantic distinctive features of noun phrases (such as: definite, count, concrete) and are largely predictable from these specifications. (McCawley, 1968, 137.) See also DETERMINER.

Article attachment. *G–2.* The rule which attaches the article node to a noun node marked [+Pro] in the reflexivization process. (Postal, 1966, 212.) See also REFLEXIVIZATION. Compare ARTICLE TRANSFORMATION.

Article transformation. *G–2.* The rule which adds to the noun phrase in the surface structure a branch labeled [+article], which contains all of the features of the noun except [+noun]. (Jacobs and Rosenbaum, 1968, 86.) Compare ARTICLE ATTACHMENT.

Articulator feature, oral-. See ORAL-ARTICULATOR FEATURE.

Aspect. *G–2.* The syntactic/semantic distinctive features [perfect] and [progressive], the selection of which for the verb leads to the surface structure forms *have V-en* ("have gone": perfect aspect), *be V-ing* ("are going":

progressive aspect), and *have been V-ing* ("have been going": perfect progressive aspect). (Jacobs and Rosenbaum, 1968, 108.) See also PROGRESSIVE ASPECT.

Aspect, perfect. See ASPECT.

Aspect, progressive. See PROGRESSIVE ASPECT.

Aspiration. *G–2.* A puff of air from the lungs, but without glottal constriction, which obligatorily accompanies the release of English voiceless stops in prevocalic position—not preceded by [s]—and which optionally accompanies their release in word-final position. Aspiration is a phonetic rather than a phonological feature of English. (Chomsky and Halle, 1968, 326.) See also PHONETIC FEATURE.

Assertion. *G–1.* A declarative sentence, or statement, as opposed to an interrogative sentence, or question. (Lees, 1960a, 2.)

Assimilation. *G–2.* The phonological agreement of two adjacent segments in the value of one or more of their features. For example, in *hump* [−mp], *hunt* [−nt], and *hunk* [−ŋk], the nasal is made to agree with the following voiceless stop in respect to place of articulation: labial, alveolar, and velar, respectively. The predictability of this particular assimilation permits the underlying phonological representation of nasals which immediately precede voiceless stops to be in the form of an archiphoneme, or archi-segment: /−Np/, /−Nt/, /−Nk/. (Chomsky and Halle, 1968, 222, 350–352, 419.) Assimilation seems to be motivated by ease of articulation. (King, 1969, 79.) See also ARCHIPHONEME, ALPHA-TYPE VARIABLE.

Atomic element. *G–2.* One of the primitive concepts of a universal vocabulary, such as: the set of phonetic features, like 'nasal'; the set of semantic markers, like 'male'; and the set of grammatical relations, like 'subject-of'. (Postal, 1964c, 32–33.) See also VOCABULARY, PRIME.

Attach. *G–2.* To assign a constituent to the domination of a node other than, and usually higher than, the one by which it was previously dominated. This is an automatic consequence of certain transformations. (Rosenbaum, 1967a, 41.) See also ATTACHMENT TRANSFORMATION.

Attachment, article. See ARTICLE ATTACHMENT.

Attachment transformation. *G–2.* The rule which incorporates a single term dominated by S—such as *Wh*—into one of the phrases within the same sentence, as in: *Wh*+NP+VP ⇒ *Wh*−N+VP. The attachment transformation refines the base-form meaning without changing the meaning of the sentence. (Kuroda, 1969, 332). Compare ATTACH.

Attachment, Wh-. See WH-ATTACHMENT.

Attraction, auxiliary. See AUXILIARY ATTRACTION.

Attribution. *G–1–2.* The process of creating a new semantic unit from a prenominal modifier, or attributive, and a head, the meaning of which is more specific than that of the head alone (e.g., *green ideas*). Prenominal modifiers typically derive from predicate adjectives by relativization (e.g., "*ideas* which are *green*"), but some adjectivals cannot be said to originate in this way (e.g., *heavy* drinker; *former* wife). (Katz and Postal, 1964, 22.) See also ATTRIBUTIVE.

Attributive. *G–1a.* A word which symbolizes a particular attribute of a noun; a modifier of a noun; a prenominal modifier. An attributive within a noun phrase derives from the predicate of a sentence of the type Nom+*be*+Pred, but not if the predicate is an adverb of time: "The raft was *leaky"* ⇒ "The *leaky raft. . . .*" (Thomas, 1965, 173.) See also ATTRIBUTION. *G—1b.* Symbolizing an attribute; functioning as a modifier of a nominal; transformationally related to the predicate of a copulative sentence. (Thomas, 1965, 173–174.)

Attributivizing suffix. *G–1.* A derivational suffix for converting words of other parts of speech into adjectives, as in: *linguist+—ic* ⇒ *linguistic.* (Lees, 1960a, 128.) Also called **Adjectivalization morpheme.** See also ADJECTIVALIZATION.

Automatic consequence. *G–2.* The condition which follows automatically from the application or nonapplication of one or more syntactic rules. For example, the obligatory deletion of IT before a 'that'-complement follows as an 'automatic consequence' of the prevention of application of the extraposition transformation because of the previous application of the passive transformation, as in: "Tom was surprised (by)(IT) that the raft sank." (Rosenbaum, 1967a, 45, 49, 64, 78.)

Auxiliary. *G–1.* The system within the verb phrase which specifies the obligatory concord and optional mood/aspect of English verbs: VP → AUX+MV; AUX → concord (modal) (*have+—en*) (*be+—ing*). The affixes and bases, or 'auxiliaries,' are rearranged correctly by the obligatory auxiliary transformation. (Chomsky, 1957, 38–39.) *G–2.* The system within the base component which specifies the obligatory tense and optional mood and aspect of English verbs: S → NP+AUX+VP; AUX → tense (modal) (perfect aspect) (progressive aspect). (Chomsky, 1965, 43.) Auxiliaries—modals and copulas—may be, but are probably not, only surface structure manifestations of deep structure features of the predicate. (Jacobs and Rosenbaum, 1968, 41.) See also AUXILIARY TRANSFORMATION.

Auxiliary attraction. *G–2.* The step in the Wh-question transformation which moves the first verbal of the auxiliary to the second position in the sentence, following the Wh-word, as when: "Wh-something Huck *can* do" ⇒ "Wh-something *can* Huck do" ("What can Huck do?"). (Chomsky, 1968, 41.) See also QUESTION.

Auxiliary incorporation transformation. *G–2.* The rule which transfers the features of the first segment of the verb phrase (e.g., of *have* or *be*) from the VP node to the auxiliary node, provided that the auxiliary does not contain a modal. (Jacobs and Rosenbaum, 1968, 124–125.)

Auxiliary transformation. *G–1–2.* The obligatory permutation rule which inverts the order of an affix (A) in the auxiliary and a following base (B): A+B ⇒ B+A. The auxiliary transformation applies to a sentence in the following way:

(Tom)	-ed	shall	have	-en	be	-ing	paint	⇒
	1	2	3	4	5	6	7	

(Tom)	shall-ed	have	be-en	paint-ing
	2 1	3	5 4	7 6

("Tom should have been painting.")

(Chomsky, 1957, 62.) Also called **Flip-flop transformation** (Thomas, 1965, 60) and **Affix transformation** (Jacobs and Rosenbaum, 1968, 110). *G–2.* The transformation in the second cycle of noun phrase complementation, involving the POSS-ing complementizer, which inverts POSS with the first NP—and *-ing* with the first verb—of the complement sentence, as in:

POSS-ing Huck steers *the raft* ⇒
1   2   3   4   5

Huck-POSS steer-ing *the raft*
3   1   4   2   5

("Huck's steering the raft.")

(Rosenbaum, 1967a, 46.)

Auxiliary, verbal. See VERBAL AUXILIARY.

B

Back. *G–2*. The phonological distinctive feature that is positively specified for sounds that are articulated by drawing back the body of the tongue from its neutral position: velars ([k], [g], [ŋ]), back vowels ([u], [ʊ], [o], [ɔ], [a]), and the semivowel glide [w]. The negative specification is termed **Nonback.** 'Back' replaces earlier **Grave,** for vowels, and **Pharyngealization,** for consonants. (Chomsky and Halle, 1968, 306.) Compare GRAVE.

Backwards pronominalization. *G–2*. The optional replacement of the first NP, in a subordinate clause, of two identical NP's in the same sentence by an appropriate pronoun, as in: "While *Huck* was sleeping, Huck dreamed" ⇒ "While *he* was sleeping, Huck dreamed." Backwards pronominalization is ordered before forward pronominalization, since, if the former does not apply, the latter must. (Langendoen, 1969, 79–80.) Also called **Backward pronominalization.** (Ross, 1967, 197). Compare FORWARD PRONOMINALIZATION.

Base. *G–2a*. The base component or syntactic base. (Chomsky, 1964, 64; Chomsky, 1966a, 70.) *G–2b*. The labeled bracketing which is the product of the phrase structure rewriting rules; the product of the first cycle of a derivation, in which there are no operations, no transformations: the basis. (Rosenbaum, 1967a, 37.) *G–2S*. The base component or semantic base. (Bach, 1968, 121–122.) See also BASE COMPONENT, BASIS, SEMANTIC-BASED TRANSFORMATIONAL GRAMMAR.

Base component. *G–2*. The subcomponent of the syntactic component which consists of a system of base rules for generating a finite set of basic strings, each with its correct structural description—or labeled bracketing, or labeled tree-diagram, or base phrase-marker: S → NP + PredP; PredP → AUX + VP; etc. The base component performs essentially the same functions as the earlier phrase structure rules, or constituent structure rules—that is, to generate sentence types; but, in addition, it permits embedding and conjunction. (King, 1969, 16.) The base component consists of a categorial component, which is a linear sequence of rewriting rules, and a lexicon, which is an unordered set of lexical entries. (Chomsky, 1966a, 70.) Also called **Base, Syntactic base.** (Chomsky, 1964, 64.) *G–2S*. The semantic base of a linguistic theory. (Bach, 1968, 121–122.) The base component generates deep structures without regard to violation of selectional restrictions. (McCawley, 1968, 135.) See also BASE, BASIS, SEMANTIC-BASED TRANSFORMATIONAL GRAMMAR.

Base phrase-marker. *G–2*. A structural description that is associated with a basic string; an elementary unit out of which deep structures are constituted. (Chomsky, 1965, 17.) The base phrase-marker can be represented as a labeled bracketing or a labeled tree-diagram. (Chomsky, 1966a, 51.) See also BASE COMPONENT, CATEGORIAL COMPONENT, PHRASE-MARKER.

Base rule. See BASE COMPONENT.

Base string. See C-TERMINAL STRING.

Base, syntactic. See BASE.

Basic string. *G–2*. One of the finite set of preterminal strings that are generated by the rewriting, or base, rules of the base component of the syntax. Each basic string has an associated structural description, or base phrase-marker. (Chomsky, 1965, 17.) Also called **Base string**; earlier called **C-terminal string.** (Chomsky, 1966a, 51.) See also BASE COMPONENT, BASE PHRASE-MARKER, C-TERMINAL STRING.

Basis. *G–2*. The output of the base component, to which is automatically assigned a derived phrase-marker by the transformational rules which map it into a surface structure (Chomsky, 1965, 17, 64–65, 102, 220); the sequence of base phrase-markers which make up the underlying deep structure of a sentence: the base form, or basic form, or basic representation of the sentence (Kuroda, 1969, 336). Also called **Base.** See also BASE COMPONENT.

Basis for syntax, semantic. See SEMANTIC BASIS FOR SYNTAX.

Be. See COPULA.

Benefactive. *G–2S*. The case of the animate being which benefits by an action described by the verb. Benefactive is associated with the preposition *for* in English, as in: "Tom did it *for Huck.*" (Fillmore, 1968, 26, 32.) See also CASE.

Biconditional constraint. *G–2*. An if-and-only-if constraint expressed by a lexical redundancy rule, such that the first segment of a formative meets a certain phonetic condition if—and only if—a following segment meets a corresponding condition. (Chomsky and Halle, 1968, 387.) Compare CONDITIONAL CONSTRAINT.

Binary division. *G–1*. The partition of a construction into two disjoint constituents, which is the basis for immediate constituent analysis. Binary divisions are characteristic of constituent-structure phrase-markers but are rarely found in phrase-markers describing actual sentences. (Chomsky, 1961a, 244.) *G–2*. Binary division is no longer expected in the underlying syntactic structure but is required of the underlying interpretive features. Semantic distinctive features are single features with binary specifications, as for [masculine]: [+masculine] (e.g., *boy*); [−masculine] (e.g., *girl*)— the basis for antonyms. Phonological distinctive features are regarded as binary at the phonological level but not necessarily at the phonetic level. (Chomsky, 1965, 232; Langendoen, 1969, 36.) See also BINARY FEATURE HIERARCHY.

Binary feature hierarchy. *G–2*. A system of classification, rather than expansion, in which each specified feature can be subdivided, by redundancy rule, into the plus and minus values of a lower feature, as in: [+A] → [±B], [+B] → [±C], [−B] → [±D], etc. (Rosenbaum, 1967a, 26.) See also BINARY DIVISION.

Binary transformation. See GENERALIZED TRANSFORMATION.

Blank-filling rule. *G–2*. The type of phonological redundancy rule, or morpheme structure rule, which specifies nondistinctive features for unmarked segments, regardless of their environment, such as the specification [−nasal] for all English vowels. (Harms, 1968, 85.) See also PHONOLOGICAL REDUNDANCY RULE, MORPHEME STRUCTURE RULE, SEQUENTIAL CONSTRAINT RULE.

Bleeding order. *G–2.* An ordering of two rules such that the output of rule A, the 'bleeding' rule, is not applicable to rule B, to which rule A has a 'bleeding' relationship. Bleeding order is minimized, diachronically. (Kiparsky, 1968, 196–197; King, 1969, 175.) Compare FEEDING ORDER.

Bleeding relationship. See BLEEDING ORDER.

Bleeding rule. See BLEEDING ORDER.

Block. *G–2a.* To prevent the generation of an ungrammatical sentence by means of certain lexical or grammatical restrictions on transformations; to prevent the application of a transformation which would result in the generation of an ungrammatical sentence. For example, the extraposition transformation 'blocks,' or 'is blocked,' if the sentence contains a POSS-ing complementizer (Rosenbaum, 1967a, 22, 51, 67, 76, 85, 90, 105), and the relative transformation 'blocks' if applied to a sentence without identical noun phrases in the matrix and constituent (Chomsky, 1966a, 67). *G–2b.* The prevention of application of a transformation; the nonapplication of a transformation. A **Mutual block** obtains if, when one transformation is applied, another transformation is prevented from applying, as with negation and apposition; thus: "Becky broke her glasses, which shattered into little pieces"; *"Becky didn't break her glasses, which shattered into little pieces." (Smith, 1964, 258.)

Blocking. *G–2.* The condition under which an expected grammatical process, either a transformation or an interpretation, is prevented from operating, or is blocked, because its input is improperly formulated. (Chomsky, 1966a, 67.) See also BLOCK.

Block, mutual. See BLOCK.

Boolean condition. *G–2.* One of the 'logical' conditions which govern the formulation of a structural analysis and determine the analyzability of a derivation. A Boolean condition, such as the is-a relation, is considered a 'general' condition in the theory and, as such, is not stated in a particular grammar. (Chomsky, 1965, 56, 121–122, 143–144, 147, 217, 225–226.) So called after George Boole, the developer of an algebra for the symbolic analysis of logic—symbolic logic. See also ANALYZABILITY.

Boundary. *G–2.* A grammatical juncture which marks the beginning and end of a unit in a terminal syntactic string. The formative boundary is the concatenator +, except that a prefix is typically followed by =; the word boundary is #; and the phrase boundary is ##. Boundaries are negatively specified for the feature [segment] in the terminal string, but, like segments, their features are given in the universal theory, although their only possible manifestation is pause. The formative boundaries are either inserted between all elements in the string by a low-level transformation (Harms, 1968, 114) or provided by the lexicon. All other boundaries are automatically introduced by universal or language-particular boundary insertion rules according to the labeled bracketing of the derived phrasemarker. Boundaries fall into the natural hierarchy ##, #, =, and +, so that phonological rules will apply, cyclically, only within the domain of a particular boundary. (Chomsky and Halle, 1968, 364–366, 371.)

Boundary insertion rule. See BOUNDARY.

Boundary, sentence. See SENTENCE BOUNDARY.

Bound morpheme. *G–2.* A morpheme that cannot occur independently as a word—that is, it cannot appear between word boundaries—and, in many cases, lacks independent meaning of its own. It is an 'empty' morpheme. With the exception of the bound bases *-spire, -ceive,* etc., and the bound pre-bases *cran-, huckle-,* etc., 'bound morpheme' is synonymous with **Affix.** A morpheme which is not 'bound' is a **Free morpheme,** or a **Free base.** (Langacker, 1968, **73.**) See also AFFIX. Compare FREE MORPHEME.

Bracketing. See LABELED BRACKETING.

Bracketing, labeled. See LABELED BRACKETING.

Branch. *G–2a.* The path between a dominating and an immediately dominated node in a tree diagram. (Rosenbaum, 1967a, 6.) *G-2b.* To expand into, or be replaced by, two or more constituents. For example, in

the S node 'branches' into NP, VP. But in

the S node does not 'branch.' (Ross, 1966, 289.) See also BRANCHING DIAGRAM.

Branching. See BRANCHING DIAGRAM.

Branching diagram. *G–1–2.* A graphic display, in the form of an upside-down, rootless tree, of a phrase-structure derivation. The trunk of the inverted tree represents the initial string S, the branches indicate relations, and the crotches, or nodes, stand for categories. A branching diagram is mechanically associated with a set of phrase-structure rewrite rules, or branching rules (Chomsky, 1965, 12, 79, 136), by drawing connecting lines from each upper category to the lower categories which constitute it:

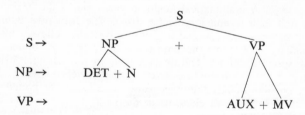

The upper node is said to dominate the lower nodes depending from it and depending from them, and these lower nodes are said to be dominated by the upper node and co-dominated with each other. (Postal, 1964b, 143.) Branching in the underlying tree is binary; in the output tree it is multinary. (Lees, 1964b, xxxvii.) Other terms for a branching diagram, or the structure which it reflects, are: **Tree diagram, Tree, Branching tree, Tree of deriva-**

tion, Labeled tree diagram, Labeled branching diagram, Labeled bracketing, Constituent-structure marker, Phrase-structure marker, and Phrase-marker (Phrase marker, P-marker). See also TREE.

Branching rule. See BRANCHING DIAGRAM.

C

Capacity, strong generative. See STRONG GENERATIVE CAPACITY.

Capacity, weak generative. See WEAK GENERATIVE CAPACITY.

Cartesian linguistics. *G–2*. The rationalist theory of language which stresses the search for universal principles and rational explanations of linguistic fact. Cartesian linguistics assumes that the surface organization of a sentence gives an incomplete and distorted representation of the grammatical relations that partially determine its semantic content. A rational grammar goes beyond a description of the surface form of a sentence by deriving it from its underlying deep structure. Cartesian linguistics, or philosophical grammar, was developed in Europe during the period 1650–1850 by Descartes, the Port Royal grammarians, and von Humboldt, but it is currently associated with the Transformational theory of Noam Chomsky. (Chomsky, 1966c, 59, 100.)

Case. *G–2S*. One of the underlying syntactic-semantic relationships in language which make up a universal set of innate concepts that explain judgments about such notions as "Who did what to whom?" Case relationships are manifested in the noun phrases of particular languages as affixes, particles, and word orders, and they include at least the following categories: agentive, benefactive, comitative, dative, factitive, instrumental, locative, and objective, or neutral. A particular case can occur only once in a simple sentence, unless there is noun phrase conjunction; but different noun phrases can have different cases, and complex sentences, which involve recursion under the case category 'objective,' can feature more than one occurrence of a given case. In the deep structure of a sentence, every noun phrase is co-dominated with the element K, for 'kasus,' and dominated by one of the category labels. For English, which typically employs prepositions rather than affixes to express case relationships, the underlying kasus associates: agentive with the preposition *by;* benefactive with *for;* comitative with *with;* dative with *to;* factitive and objective with Ø; instrumental with *by*—or *with,* when accompanied by agentive; and locative with a variety of lexical selections. Transformational rules account for the surface subject and objects, establish their order, and delete or replace the prepositions. (Fillmore, 1968, 19, 21, 25–26, 32–33, 41.) See also CASE GRAMMAR, ACTANT.

Case category. See CASE GRAMMAR.

Case frame. *G–2S*. The underlying array of cases in a sentence which determine the environment into which a given verb may be inserted. For example, the verb *read* may be inserted into the case frame [__objective] because its lexical entry contains frame features which permit this selection. (Fillmore, 1968, 27.) See also CASE.

Case grammar. *G–2S.* A modification of the theory of transformational grammar which reintroduces the conceptual framework of case relationships from traditional grammar but maintains a distinction between deep and surface structure from generative grammar, with the word 'deep' signifying 'semantic deep.' The deep structure of a sentence consists of a modality, which contains tense, mood, aspect, negation, etc., and a proposition, which contains a verbal plus one or more different case categories, or actants. These categories, which comprise a set of universal, innate concepts, include at least the following cases: agentive, benefactive, comitative, dative, factitive, instrumental, locative, and objective. The case category is automatically realized as a kasus—a preposition or case affix—plus a noun phrase or embedded S, as in:

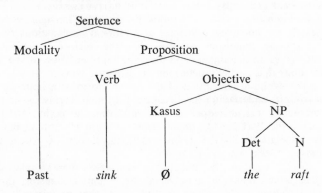

The selection of the surface subject of the sentence is based on the case constituency of the proposition. If there is only one case, it becomes subject:

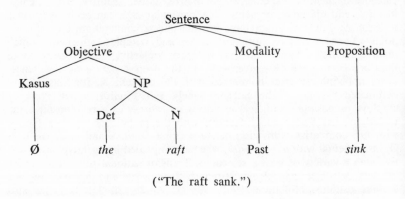

("The raft sank.")

(Fillmore, 1968, 21.) See also CASE, MODALITY, PROPOSITION, ACTANT, AGENTIVE, INSTRUMENTAL, DATIVE, FACTITIVE, LOCATIVE, COMITATIVE, OBJECTIVE, BENEFACTIVE.

Case marking transformation. *G–2.* The transformation which attaches the proper case affix to personal pronouns. (King, 1969, 143.)

Case, paradigm. See PARADIGM CASE.

Case transformation. See ACCUSATIVE TRANSFORMATION.

Categorial component. *G–2.* That part of the syntactic base, other than the lexicon and subcategorization rules, which consists of a system of context-free rewriting, or branching, rules for defining grammatical relations and establishing the order of elements in deep structures. The categorial component is essentially equivalent to the simple phrase structure grammar of *G–1*, but differs from it in that its terminal vocabulary consists only of grammatical morphemes and of $\triangle$, into which lexical items are mapped by insertion transformation, and that its rules permit embedding and conjunction. (Chomsky, 1965, 120–124; Chomsky, 1966a, 70.) Compare PHRASE STRUCTURE GRAMMAR. See also BASE COMPONENT.

Categorial segment, natural. See NATURAL CATEGORIAL SEGMENT.

Categorial sequence, natural. See NATURAL CATEGORIAL SEQUENCE.

Category. *G–1.* A primitive unit of the vocabulary of the phrase structure grammar; a labeled node of a branching diagram, or a labeled bracket of a bracketed string, such as: S, NP, VP, etc. The original categories of *G-1*, also called **Grammatical categories,** are: #Sentence# (sentence), NP (noun phrase), VP (verb phrase), T (article), N (noun), AUX (auxiliary), and V (verb). (Chomsky, 1956, 146–147; Chomsky, 1957, 27, 39.) Additional categories are PP (prepositional phrase), P (preposition), ADJ (adjective) (Postal, 1964a, 56); Nucleus, DET (determiner), MV (main verb), ADV (adverb), Q (question) (Katz and Postal, 1964, 104); and Predicate (Katz, 1966, 125). *G-2.* In *G-2*, the initial string is sometimes distinguished from the embedded string (i.e., #S#, as opposed to S′ or S), the dummy symbol $\triangle$ is used for the first time, and predicate-phrase is co-generated with NP (Chomsky, 1965, 129); MV is dropped, VB (verbal) covers both verbs and adjectives, and ADV is eliminated (Jacobs, 1968, 46; Jacobs and Rosenbaum, 1968, 48). *G-2S.* Fillmore rewrites S as M (modality) and P (proposition) and recognizes a number of case categories under P, each of which is rewritten as K (kasus) plus NP. (Fillmore, 1968, 83.) Langendoen rewrites S as P (predicate) plus one, two, or three NP arguments. (Langendoen, 1969, 137.) See also CATEGORY FEATURE, INITIAL CATEGORY, LEXICAL CATEGORY, CATEGORY INCLUSION RELATION.

Category feature. *G–2.* A contextual feature of the sort [±C], where C is a lexical category. A lexical item which is positively specified for the category feature [C] can replace a dummy element, $\triangle$, only when $\triangle$ is dominated by the category symbol C. (Chomsky, 1966a, 72.) See also CONTEXTUAL FEATURE.

Category, grammatical. See CATEGORY.

Category inclusion relation. *G–2.* The relation which holds between two semantic markers when one marker, such as (human), represents a conceptual category that is a subcategory of the category represented by the other, such as (animate). Category inclusion rules in the semantic component satisfy conditions of simplicity by establishing these relations in the readings of the lowest nodes of underlying phrase-markers. (Katz and Postal, 1964, 16–17.) See also SEMANTIC MARKER.

Category, initial. See INITIAL CATEGORY.

Category, lexical. See LEXICAL CATEGORY.

Category symbol. See CATEGORY.

Causative. See CAUSATIVE TRANSFORMATION.

Causative transformation. *G–2.* The set of rules which convert underlying sentences of the type "Huck caused #S#" into surface structures in which the main verb is replaced by an element from the embedding, as when: "Huck caused (the water spilled)" ⇒ "Huck spilled the water"; "It made (Tom was sad)" ⇒ "It saddened Tom." Adjectives and verbs are classified in the lexicon according to whether or not they undergo the causative transformation. (Chomsky, 1965, 189.) See also CAUSATIVE VERB, ERGATIVE.

Causative verb. *G–1.* A verb which can participate in a transformation of the type: "Paper *burns*"+"Tom caused the paper to *burn*" ⇒ "Tom *burned* the paper"; "Water *boils*"+"Huck caused the water to *boil*" ⇒ "Huck *boiled* the water." (Lees, 1960a, 34.) See also CAUSATIVE TRANSFORMATION.

Cell. *G–2.* One of the boxes or squares of a feature matrix, in which a segment is specified for a particular feature. (Postal, 1968a, 163.) See also MATRIX.

Change, linguistic. See LINGUISTIC CHANGE.

Change, phonological. See PHONOLOGICAL CHANGE.

Change, primary. See RULE ADDITION.

Change, sound. See SOUND CHANGE.

Change, structural. See STRUCTURAL CHANGE.

Change, syntactic. See SYNTACTIC CHANGE.

Class, equivalence. See EQUIVALENCE CLASS.

Classificatory feature. *G–2.* A universal phonological feature which combines with other such features to represent morphemes as a classificatory matrix, which is a sequence of columns containing plus or minus specifications for distinctive features and zero specifications for nondistinctive features. The resulting classificatory matrix can be converted into a tree diagram to test its binarity. The list of classificatory features has been revised frequently since it was first conceived by Jakobson in 1928, but such inventories usually include syllabicity features, oral features, qualifying features, manner features, nonaural features, and prosodic features. (Harms, 1968, 14–23.) See also DISTINCTIVE FEATURE, PHONOLOGICAL DISTINCTIVE FEATURE, JAKOBSONIAN DISTINCTIVE FEATURE, PHONETIC FEATURE.

Classificatory matrix. See CLASSIFICATORY FEATURE.

Class, natural. See NATURAL CLASS.

Class, productive. See PRODUCTIVE CLASS.

Clause. See MAIN CLAUSE.

Clause, appositive. See NONRESTRICTIVE RELATIVE CLAUSE.

Clause, appositive relative. See NONRESTRICTIVE RELATIVE CLAUSE.

Clause complementizer. *G–2.* The formative *that*, which introduces the clausal complement of a noun, as in: "the report *that* Twain had died." Also called **Clause-introducer.** The clause complementizer can be distinguished from the relative pronoun *that*, which plays a grammatical role in the relative clause, such as the underlying object in "the report *that* Twain received." (Jacobs, 1968, 51.) See also COMPLEMENTIZER, 'THAT' COMPLEMENTIZER.

Clause, infinitival. See INFINITIVE.

Clause, main. See MAIN CLAUSE.

Clause, nonrestrictive. See NONRESTRICTIVE CLAUSE.

Clause, nonrestrictive relative. See NONRESTRICTIVE RELATIVE CLAUSE.

Clause, relative. See RELATIVE CLAUSE.

Clause, subordinate. See SUBORDINATE CLAUSE.

Clause, 'that'-. See 'THAT'-CLAUSE.

Clause transportation rule. *G–2.* The rule which permutes a subject 'that'-clause with the following part of the matrix sentence, as when: *"That Tom was alive* surprised Huck" ⇒ "It surprised Huck *that Tom was alive."* (Langacker, 1969, 183.) Also called **Extraposition.**

Cleft-complement. *G–1a.* The element 'cleft-comp,' in an underlying string, which marks the place for the embedding of a cleft-sentence. (Lees, 1964a, 145–146.) *G–1b.* The cleft-sentence which is embedded in an underlying string in place of the element 'cleft-comp.' (Lees, 1964a, 146.) See also CLEFT SENTENCE.

Cleft-sentence. *G–1.* A sentence of the type "It is the children who suffer," which derives from a complement-sentence—"It is cleft-complement the children suffer"—by means of a Wh-transformation: "It is the children *wh*-the children suffer" ⇒ "It is the children who suffer" (Lees, 1964a, 145; Lees, 1964b, xlii); a sentence in which a constituent of the subordinate clause is also a constituent of the main clause (Koutsoudas, 1966, 288). Also: **Cleft sentence.** *G–2.* A sentence of the type "What hit the window was a snowball," in which *what* is an independent relative pronoun without an antecedent (Kuroda, 1968, 264); a sentence of the type "What Tom painted was a fence" or "What Tom was was lazy," which derives by way of a cleft sentence transformation (Jacobs and Rosenbaum, 1968, 39–40).

Cleft sentence test. *G–2.* The process for determining the NP status of a word or group of words by the use of the cleft sentence transformation: *what* is placed first in the string; *be* is placed last; and the words to be tested are transposed to the very end. If the resulting sentence is grammatical, the transposed words are likely to be a noun phrase, though some adjective phrases can also be shifted. (Jacobs and Rosenbaum, 1968, 39–40.) See also CLEFT SENTENCE TRANSFORMATION.

Cleft sentence transformation. *G–2.* The transformation which places *what* at the front of a string and an appropriate form of *be* at the end, then shifts an NP, or ADJ-P, to the final position, as when: "Huck steered *the raft"* ⇒ **"What* Huck steered *the raft was"* ⇒ *"What* Huck steered *was the raft."* If the shifted NP is [+human], the sentence will be ungrammatical: *"What steered the raft was Huck." The cleft sentence transformation provides a partial test—the cleft sentence test—for noun phrases. (Jacobs and Rosenbaum, 1968, 39–40.) Also called **Pseudo-cleft process, Pseudo-cleft transformation** (Rosenbaum, 1967c, 318–319), **Pseudocleft sentence transformation** (Rosenbaum, 1967a, 13, 75), and **Cleft transformation** (Jacobs, 1968, 30). See also PSEUDO-CLEFT TRANSFORMATION.

Cleft transformation. See CLEFT SENTENCE TRANSFORMATION.

Closer. *G–2.* Less distant from another node in a tree than some third node is, as measured by the number of branches in the paths connecting the nodes. (Rosenbaum, 1967a, 50.) See also DISTANCE.

Cluster, feature. See FEATURE CLUSTER.

Cluster, strong. See STRONG CLUSTER.

Cluster, weak. See WEAK CLUSTER.

Coefficient, feature. See FEATURE COEFFICIENT.

Co-generated. *G–2*. Immediately dominated by the same phrase structure node. For example, determiner and noun are cogenerated by noun phrase in the expansion NP → DET+N. (Gruber, 1967, 423.)

Cognate. *G–2*. Synonymous in truth value, because of the same underlying structure, but different in derived structure. (Rosenbaum, 1967a, 100.) See also COGNATE SENTENCES.

Cognate sentences. *G–2*. Sentences which are synonymous in truth value, because of the same underlying structure, but different in derived structure, as in: "Huck was scared to go"; "It scared Huck to go"; "To go scared Huck"; 'paradigmatic' sentences. (Rosenbaum, 1967a, 72.) See also SYNONYMY.

Cognitive model. *G–2*. A theory of language which accounts for mentalistic phenomena such as the child's unconscious acquisition of a language. (King, 1969, 13.) See also ACQUISITION MODEL, LANGUAGE ACQUISITION, LANGUAGE ACQUISITION DEVICE.

Collapse. *G–2*. To combine or merge two or more rules, such as to collapse the separate deletion rules for the various complementizers into a single, more general, deletion rule. (Rosenbaum, 1967a, 42.) See also COLLAPSING TRANSFORMATION.

Collapsing transformation. *G–2*. A transformation which collapses same constituents into one constituent, as in a 'respectively' string of the type: "The boys and the boys are tall and short respectively" ⇒ "The boys are tall and short." (McCawley, 1968, 144.)

Comitative. *G–2S*. The case category C of a noun phrase which bears a conjunctive relationship to another noun phrase in the sentence, as in: "Tom ran away *with Huck*"; "Tom *and Huck* ran away." The preposition associated with the comitative case is *with*. (Fillmore, 1966, 366, 371–373; Fillmore, 1968, 81–83.) See also CASE.

Comma intonation. *G–1*. Nonterminal intonation and pause which reflect the boundaries of a series of constituents and which are reflected, in turn, by commas in orthography, as in: "Tom, Huck, and Jim were on the raft." (Katz and Postal, 1964, 107.) Also called **Parenthetic-type intonation.** (Lees, 1960a, 86.)

Command. *G–2*. The primacy relation, or command relation, that holds between two constituents in a phrase-marker. A node 'commands' another node if neither dominates the other and if the S-node most immediately dominating the former also dominates the latter. A noun phrase which commands, and also precedes, another identical noun phrase cannot be pronominalized by that noun phrase: *"*He* is much smarter than Tom seems." (Langacker, 1969, 167–169.)

Command relation. See COMMAND.

Comment, topic and. See TOPIC AND COMMENT.

Common noun. *G–2*. A noun which has the syntactic feature [determiner ——] in its dictionary entry, such as: "the *raft*"; "a *worm*." Proper nouns have the feature [——]—that is, no determiner. (Chomsky, 1965, 100.) Compare PROPER NOUN. *G–2S*. All common nouns derive from the rule NP → DET+*one*+S, where S is a relative clause of the type NP+*be*+NP, as in: "Huck knew *someone who was a pilot*"; "Huck knew *a pilot*." (Bach, 1968, 91–93, 121.)

Common underlying structure. *G–2*. The single deep structure which underlies two or more sentences and establishes both their syntactic relatedness and their truth value synonymy. (Rosenbaum, 1967a, 34–35; Rosenbaum, 1967b, ix.) See also SYNONYMY.

Compact. *G–1.* The phonological distinctive feature which is positively specified for vowels articulated in the forward part of the oral cavity, and which is negatively specified, as noncompact or diffuse, for vowels that are not so articulated. (Halle, 1962, 327.) Compare DIFFUSE.

Comparative. See COMPARATIVE TRANSFORMATION.

Comparative introduction. See COMPARATIVE TRANSFORMATION.

Comparative transformation. *G–1.* The set of rules which embed elements of a constituent sentence as an adverbial modifier of an adjective or adverb in a main sentence. Morphophonemic rules provide comparative adjectives with their proper phonemic shape and convert *more*+adjective into adjective+*-er*. The comparative construction is 'affective' in the sense that it may contain *ever* or *any*, and it may also accommodate the special negative pre-modifier *no*, as in: "Becky is *no* smart*er than anyone else.*" (Lees, 1961, 307–308, 314.) *G–2.* An erasure operation in which an adjective of the matrix sentence deletes an associated adjective in the embedding, after inversion of *than*+S with the matrix adjective, as when: "Huck is more than (Tom is *handsome*) *handsome*" ⇒ "Huck is more *handsome* than Tom (is)" (Chomsky, 1965, 178–179); a set of rules, called **Comparative introduction,** which operate on an underlying sentence of the type "Tom is handsome to an extent to which Huck is not handsome" by adding *-er* or *more* to the adjective of the main sentence, replacing *which* with *than,* and deleting *to an extent to, not,* and the embedded adjective, as in: "Tom is more handsome than Huck (is)." (Ross, 1966, 294, 296.)

Competence. *G–2.* The native speaker-hearer's unconscious, tacit, intrinsic, implicit, intuitive, and finite knowledge of his language; the information available to a fluent speaker concerning his language which allows him to understand and produce sentences which he has never heard or uttered before and to discriminate between ambiguous and unambiguous sentences, synonymous and nonsynonymous sentences, acceptable and unacceptable sentences, grammatical and ungrammatical sentences, etc.; the abstract and finite system of rules underlying a speaker's linguistic behavior which permit him to analyze and synthesize correctly the sound-meaning correspondence of an indefinite number of sentences; the potential performance of an idealized speaker-hearer who is not affected by such unpredictable behavior as hesitations, false starts, lapses of memory, sloppy enunciation, etc.; the internalized grammar which provides the basis for a theory of language and a model of linguistic description—a competence-model grammar (or generative grammar) which attempts to account for linguistic competence. (Chomsky, 1965, 4, 18, 24, 140; Chomsky, 1966a, 9–11, 29, 91; Chomsky, 1968, 4, 23, 52, 62–63.) Compare PERFORMANCE.

Competence, linguistic. See COMPETENCE.

Competence-model grammar. See COMPETENCE.

Complement. *G–1.* The product of a complementation transformation, or complement-embedding, which inserts transforms into the Comp position after certain nouns, adjectives, adverbs, and complement verbs: N_c+Comp (e.g., "the man *to see*"); ADJ_c+Comp (e.g., "nice *to know*"); ADV_c+Comp (e.g., "hard *to miss*"); V_c+Comp (e.g., "find *him able*"). (Lees,

1964a, 144.) *G–2.* The functional notion surrounding right-hand embeddings inside phrases. 'Complement' has been eliminated as a category symbol in *G–2* and replaced by S: N+S (e.g., "the man—*you see the man"*). (Chomsky, 1965, 224.) See also PREDICATE COMPLEMENT, COMPLEMENT-SENTENCE. *Related terms:* **Complementation** is the general term for the process of embedding sentences as complements in other sentences. (Rosenbaum, 1967a, 1, 8.) A **Complement-sentence** is a sentence which is embedded in the complement position of a main sentence. (Lees, 1964a, 145.) A **Complement system** is a set of rules for explaining a particular type of complementation, such as predicate complementation. (Rosenbaum, 1967a, 1, 8.) A **Complementizer,** or **Complementizing morpheme,** is a morpheme or set of paired morphemes associated with the predicate complement system. (Rosenbaum, 1967a, 24–25.) A **Complementizing feature** is a lexical feature which marks verbs for co-occurrence with a particular complementizer. (Rosenbaum, 1967a, 27–28.) **Complementizer selection** is the selection of a complementizing morpheme on the basis of the complementizing feature. (Rosenbaum, 1967a, 33–34.) **Complementizer introduction,** or **Complementizer placement,** is the insertion of a complementizing morpheme into a derivation. (Rosenbaum, 1967a, 5, 25, 75.)

Complement, adjectival. See ADJECTIVAL COMPLEMENT.

Complementary distribution. *G–2.* Noncontrastive distribution of mutually exclusive items in a set, such as the distribution of complementizers with certain prepositions. (Rosenbaum, 1967a, 81.) The principle of complementary distribution is an analytic one, without theoretical significance. (Chomsky, 1964, 104.) Compare FREE VARIATION.

Complementation. See COMPLEMENT SYSTEM.

Complementation, intransitive oblique noun phrase. See INTRANSITIVE OBLIQUE NOUN PHRASE COMPLEMENTATION.

Complementation, intransitive verb phrase. See INTRANSITIVE VERB PHRASE COMPLEMENTATION.

Complementation, noun phrase. See NOUN PHRASE COMPLEMENTATION.

Complementation, object. See OBJECT COMPLEMENTATION.

Complementation, object noun phrase. See OBJECT COMPLEMENTATION.

Complementation, oblique noun phrase. See OBLIQUE NOUN PHRASE COMPLEMENTATION.

Complementation, oblique verb phrase. See OBLIQUE VERB PHRASE COMPLEMENTATION.

Complementation, predicate. See PREDICATE COMPLEMENTATION.

Complementation, prepositional. See PREPOSITIONAL NOUN PHRASE COMPLEMENTATION.

Complementation, prepositional noun phrase. See PREPOSITIONAL NOUN PHRASE COMPLEMENTATION.

Complementation, sentential. See SENTENTIAL COMPLEMENTATION.

Complementation, subject. See SUBJECT COMPLEMENTATION.

Complementation, subject noun phrase. See SUBJECT COMPLEMENTATION.

Complementation transformation. See COMPLEMENT.

Complementation, transitive oblique. See TRANSITIVE OBLIQUE COMPLEMENTATION.

Complementation, transitive oblique noun phrase. See TRANSITIVE OBLIQUE COMPLEMENTATION.

Complementation, transitive verb phrase. See TRANSITIVE VERB PHRASE COMPLEMENTATION.

Complementation, verb phrase. See VERB PHRASE COMPLEMENTATION.

Complement, cleft-. See CLEFT-COMPLEMENT.

Complementizer. *G–2.* The morpheme *that* or one of the sets of paired morphemes *for . . . to* or *'s . . . ing* which is inserted by complementizer placement transformation into a position before a complement sentence, or S complement, in the deep structure of a sentence containing a complement verb, as in: V+*that*+S (e.g., "said *that* he sang"); V+*for . . . to*+S (e.g., "asked *for* him *to* sing"); V+*'s . . . ing*+S (e.g., "opposed his sing*ing*"). The first part of the complementizer is optionally, sometimes obligatorily, deleted by the complementizer deletion transformation, as in: "said (*that*) he sang"; "asked (*for*) him to sing"; "opposed him (*'s*) singing." (Jacobs, 1968, 49, 51.) Complementizers, including *Wh* and *if,* are transformationally derived markers unique to predicate complementation. (Rosenbaum, 1967a, 24–25, 32; Rosenbaum, 1967b, ix.) See also COMPLEMENTIZING MORPHEME, CLAUSE COMPLEMENTIZER, 'THAT' COMPLEMENTIZER, FOR-TO COMPLEMENTIZER, POSS-ING COMPLEMENTIZER.

Complementizer, clause. See CLAUSE COMPLEMENTIZER.

Complementizer deletion transformation. See COMPLEMENTIZER.

Complementizer deletion transformation, obligatory. See OBLIGATORY COMPLEMENTIZER DELETION TRANSFORMATION.

Complementizer deletion transformation, optional. See OPTIONAL COMPLEMENTIZER DELETION TRANSFORMATION.

Complementizer feature. See COMPLEMENTIZING FEATURE.

Complementizer, for-to. See FOR-TO COMPLEMENTIZER.

Complementizer, gerundive. See GERUNDIVE COMPLEMENTIZER.

Complementizer, infinitive. See INFINITIVE COMPLEMENTIZER.

Complementizer insertion. See COMPLEMENTIZER INTRODUCTION.

Complementizer introduction. *G–2.* The insertion of a complementizing morpheme into a derivation. Also called **Complementizer insertion**—by **Complementizer placement transformation.** (Rosenbaum, 1967a, 5, 25, 75.) See also COMPLEMENTIZER.

Complementizer placement transformation. *G–2.* The rule which introduces a complementizing morpheme into an embedded sentence in the second cycle of predicate complementation. (Rosenbaum, 1967a, 5.) See also COMPLEMENTIZER.

Complementizer, POSS-ing. See POSS-ING COMPLEMENTIZER.

Complementizer selection. *G–2.* The selection of a complementizing morpheme, or pair of morphemes, for a noun phrase complement construction on the basis of the markers on the verb of the main sentence. (Rosenbaum, 1967a, 33–34.) See also COMPLEMENTIZER.

Complementizer, 'that.' See 'THAT' COMPLEMENTIZER.

Complementizing feature. *G–2.* One of the binary features in the lexicon which mark verbs for the complementizers which can appear in their noun phrase and verb phrase complements. Also called **Complementizer feature.** (Rosenbaum, 1967a, 27–28.) See also COMPLEMENTIZER.

Complementizing morpheme. *G–2.* One of the unique set of morphemes which, singly or paired, mark predicate complement constructions and distinguish them from other types of complements. The complementizing morphemes, also called **Complementizers,** are *that, for, to, POSS, ing,*

Wh, if, etc. The complementizers, also called **Complementizing morphemes,** are *that, for-to, POSS-ing, Wh, if,* etc. (Rosenbaum, 1967a, 24, 32.) See also COMPLEMENTIZER.

Complement, noun phrase. See NOUN PHRASE COMPLEMENT.

Complement, object. See OBJECT COMPLEMENT.

Complement, oblique noun phrase. See OBLIQUE NOUN PHRASE COMPLEMENT.

Complement, predicate. See PREDICATE COMPLEMENT.

Complement-sentence. *G–1.* A sentence which is embedded in the complement position of a main sentence. (Lees, 1964a, 145.) *G–2.* The entire predicate complement construction, including the complementizer and other morphemes, which is dominated by S in the underlying structure of a main sentence, such as the complement sentence "that Huck returned" in the main sentence "It *that Huck returned* pleased Tom." Rosenbaum, 1967a, 75.) See also COMPLEMENT, PREDICATE COMPLEMENT.

Complement, sentence. See SENTENCE COMPLEMENT.

Complement sentence marker. *G–2.* A complementizing morpheme, or complementizer. (Rosenbaum, 1967a, 118.) See also COMPLEMENTIZER.

Complement, sentential. See SENTENTIAL COMPLEMENT.

Complement, subject. See SUBJECT COMPLEMENT.

Complement system. *G–2.* One of the sets of rules for explaining complementation or sentence embedding. The sets are: the noun phrase complement system; the verb phrase complement system; the predicate complement system, which encompasses the first two; and the sentential complement system, which includes the predicate complement system and all other such systems. (Rosenbaum, 1967a, 1, 8.) See also NOUN PHRASE COMPLEMENTATION, VERB PHRASE COMPLEMENTATION, PREDICATE COMPLEMENTATION, SENTENTIAL COMPLEMENTATION.

Complement system, predicate. See PREDICATE COMPLEMENT SYSTEM.

Complement, transitive oblique. See TRANSITIVE OBLIQUE COMPLEMENTATION.

Complement verb. See COMPLEMENT.

Complement, verb phrase. See VERB PHRASE COMPLEMENT.

Complex nominal compound. *G–1.* A nominal compound whose first member is itself a nominal compound, such as *basketball game,* in which *basketball* is also a compound. The entire complex functions like a simple noun. (Lees, 1960a, 164.) See also NOMINAL COMPOUND.

Complex sentence. *G–1.* A matrix sentence in which one or more simplex sentences are embedded. (Lees, 1964b, xxxix.) *G–2.* A sentence that is generated by a set of rules of which one or more contain S on the right-hand side (Lyons, 1968, 225); a sentence which contains a complement (Rosenbaum, 1967b, ix). *G–2S.* A sentence that consists of a conceptual structure which contains other conceptual structures that can underlie sentences. (Langacker, 1968, 105.) See also COMPLEMENT, MATRIX SENTENCE.

Complex sentence formation. *G–2.* The generation of sentences which contain embedded sentences, or complements. (Rosenbaum, 1967b, ix.) See also COMPLEX SENTENCE.

Complex symbol. *G–2.* A set of positively or negatively specified syntactic-semantic features, inherent and contextual, which, along with a phonological matrix, make up the dictionary entry of a lexical item, such as:

N → [phonological matrix, complex symbol] (Chomsky, 1965, 122); a paired category symbol and set of indices. (Chomsky, 1966a, 42.)

Complex transformation. See GENERALIZED TRANSFORMATION.

Component. *G–1*. A distinct set of rules of the grammar: the syntax, which enumerates an infinite set of strings plus their structural descriptions, or the phonology, which maps the strings into their phonetic representations. (Lees, 1960b, 150.) *G–2*. A distinct set of rules within a grammar, such as the components of a generative grammar: the syntactic component (consisting of a base component and a transformational component); the semantic component; and the phonological component. (Chomsky, 1965, 16.) See also BASE COMPONENT, PHONOLOGICAL COMPONENT, SEMANTIC COMPONENT, SYNTACTIC COMPONENT.

Component, base. See BASE COMPONENT.

Component, categorial. See CATEGORIAL COMPONENT.

Component, lexical. See LEXICAL COMPONENT.

Component, morpheme structure. See MORPHEME STRUCTURE COMPONENT.

Component, phonological. See PHONOLOGICAL COMPONENT.

Component, semantic. See SEMANTIC COMPONENT.

Component, syntactic. See SYNTACTIC COMPONENT.

Composition. *G–2*. The normal, natural, and logical amalgamation of the semantic readings of individual morphemes in a word $(1+2=3)$, without the need for special rules of derivation. The postulation of composition in the lexicon reduces the number of dictionary entries, since a prefix such as *dis-* and a base such as *band* need be entered only separately and not as an idiom, *disband*. 'Compositionality' of bases and affixes must be indicated in the lexical entry for the base. For example, *dis-* and *band* are 'compositional' because *band* is semantically marked for reversibility. (Katz and Fodor, 1963, 501.) See also AMALGAMATION.

Compositional. See COMPOSITION.

Compositionality. See COMPOSITION.

Compound. *G–1*. A complex nominal that is generated by one of a set of compounding transformations and has the stress superfix $/ + \backslash$ (or $\wedge + /$ for N+N combinations); a compound-noun; a nominal compound. English nominal compounds derive from several different sentence types and all sorts of grammatical relations, such as: subject-predicate (*earthquake*); verb-object (*flashlight*); subject-object (*fingerprint*); etc. (Lees, 1960a, 115, 118–120, 180–181.) *G–2*. A double-base construction containing two or more items of the same grammatical weight. A compound 'word,' or compound, is a lexical unit which consists of two or more base (full, root) morphemes, and therefore resembles a phrase but functions as a single word, such as *flower pot*, a compound noun. A compound 'phrase' is a phrase which contains two or more coordinated elements in conjunction (*bread and butter*) or disjunction (*life or death*). A compound 'sentence' is a sentence which contains two or more coordinated sentences in conjunction (*"Open your books and repeat after me"*) or disjunction (*"Stop or I'll shoot!"*). (Koutsoudas, 1966, 150; Lyons, 1968, 234.) Stress is assigned to compound words by the compound rule, part of the main stress rule. (Chomsky and Halle, 1968, 92–93.) See also NOMINAL COMPOUND, CONJUNCTIVE COMPOUND, DISJUNCTIVE COMPOUND, COMPLEX NOMINAL COMPOUND, ENDOCENTRIC COMPOUND, SENTENTIAL COMPOUND, EXOCENTRIC COMPOUND.

Compound, complex nominal. See COMPLEX NOMINAL COMPOUND.

Compound, conjunctive. See CONJUNCTIVE COMPOUND.

Compound, disjunctive. See DISJUNCTIVE COMPOUND.

Compound, endocentric. See ENDOCENTRIC COMPOUND.

Compound, exocentric. See EXOCENTRIC COMPOUND.

Compounding-stress-pattern. *G–1.* The stress superfix $/+\backslash$, which characterizes nominal compounds. (Lees, 1960a, 154.) See also COMPOUND.

Compounding transformation. See COMPOUND.

Compound, nominal. See NOMINAL COMPOUND.

Compound rule. *G–2.* The phonological rule—part of the main stress rule—which assigns primary stress to a primary-stressed vowel which is followed by another primary-stressed vowel in a noun phrase, as in *bláck bóard* ⇒ *bláckboard,* as opposed to *black bóard,* to which stress is assigned by the nuclear stress rule. (Chomsky and Halle, 1968, 17.) Compare NUCLEAR STRESS RULE. See also MAIN STRESS RULE.

Compound, sentential. See SENTENTIAL COMPOUND.

Comprehension set. *G–2.* A set of sentences whose meanings are transferred to a semi-sentence by transfer rules and whose structures can be recovered mechanically from the semi-derivation of that semi-sentence. (Katz, 1964b, 411–412.) See also SEMI-DERIVATION, SEMI-SENTENCE.

Concatenation. *G–1–2.* The operation which chains together various vocabulary symbols called **Primes** by means of various linking symbols called **Concatenators,** such as $+$ and $\#$, to form a linear sequence of linguistic elements, called a **String.** (Chomsky, 1965, 222; Koutsoudas, 1966, 8.) The symbol $+$ is sometimes referred to as the **Concatenator sign.** (Lees, 1960a, 50.) See also VOCABULARY, PRIME.

Concatenator. See CONCATENATION.

Conceptual structure. *G–2S.* The abstract underlying structure of a sentence; the structure of the meaning of a sentence—the conceptual situation; the organization of concepts in a sentence (e.g., 'boy' 'meet' 'girl'); the input to the lexical and syntactic systems, which modify the abstract structure of a sentence until it becomes a surface structure. (Langacker, 1968, 89–92, 114.) See also SEMANTIC DEEP STRUCTURE.

Concord. *G–1.* The obligatory tense morpheme C in the auxiliary system: AUX → C. . . . (Chomsky, 1957, 39.) *G–1–2.* The condition under which two or more grammatical constructions are mutually dependent— they agree—in regard to person or number. The concord, or agreement, may be between items in an exocentric construction (e.g., "I grow"—"It grows"; "Hair grows"—"Hairs grow") or between those in an endocentric construction (e.g., "this book"—"these books"; "that book"—"those books"). (Lyons, 1968, 241–242.) See also AUXILIARY, AGREEMENT.

Concrete. *G–1.* Able to function as the subject or object of a sense verb— one of the characteristics of a count or mass noun that distinguishes it from a nominalization, as in: "(The) *water* tastes good" (concrete); **"Watering* tastes good" (abstract). (Lees, 1960a, 14.) *G–2.* The negative specification of the semantic distinctive feature [abstract], indicating that the lexical item refers to something that is physically oriented in time and space. (Postal, 1968b, 273.) Compare ABSTRACT.

Conditional constraint. *G–2.* An if-then constraint expressed by a lexical redundancy rule such that, if the first segment of a formative meets a certain phonetic condition, a following segment must meet a corresponding condition. (Chomsky and Halle, 1968, 387.) Compare BICONDITIONAL CONSTRAINT.

Condition, Boolean. See BOOLEAN CONDITION.

Condition, general. See GENERAL CONDITION.

Condition, global. See GLOBAL CONSTRAINT.

Condition, naturalness. See NATURALNESS CONDITION.

Condition, necessary. See NECESSARY CONDITION.

Condition of adequacy, external. See EXTERNAL CONDITION OF ADEQUACY.

Condition of adequacy, internal. See JUSTIFICATION OF A GRAMMAR.

Condition of generality. *G–1.* A requirement that the grammar of a language be constructed according to a theory of linguistic structure in which the primary terms are defined independently of any given language. (Chomsky, 1957, 50.) See also GENERALITY.

Condition, structural. See STRUCTURAL CONDITION.

Configuration. *G–2.* The profile of the structure of a sentence, as in a branching diagram or labeled bracketing. (Rosenbaum, 1967a, 87.) See also BRANCHING DIAGRAM, LABELED BRACKETING.

Configuration, phrase structure. See PHRASE STRUCTURE CONFIGURATION.

Conjoining, either-. See EITHER-CONJOINING.

Conjunct. *G–1–2.* A constituent that is conjoined to another constituent by a conjunction, as in: *"Huck* and *Tom"; "ate* and *drank"; "Huck ate* and *Tom drank"*; etc. (Jacobs and Rosenbaum, 1968, 257.) See also CONJUNCTION.

Conjunction. *G–1.* The transformational process which joins two sentences into a compound construction with *and,* which is also called a conjunction, and obligatorily deletes the overlapping material to form a coordinate construction, as when: "Huck fished" + "Tom fished" ⇒ "Huck fished and Tom fished" (a compound construction); *"Huck and Tom* fished" (a coordinate construction). Constituents cannot be conjoined unless they are dominated by the same node—that is, the underlying phrase-markers must have the same general structure. (Koutsoudas, 1966, 249–250.) The morpheme *and* is introduced transformationally and has no phrase structure origin. The phrase structure which results from a conjunction transformation is also called a **Conjunction,** or a **Coordination.** (Postal, 1964a, 92.) *G–2.* The transformation which generates conjoined elements with multiple branching, rather than left-branching or right-branching or nesting, from underlying conjoined sentences, obligatorily reducing these sentences by conjunction reduction transformation, as in: "Huck fished and Tom fished and Jim fished" (a compound sentence) and *"Huck and Tom and Jim* fished" (a coordinate construction) (Chomsky, 1965, 196–197); a multiple-branching structure of different conjoined sentences (a sentential compound) or of different conjoined noun phrases (a phrasal conjunction). The sentential compound (or compound sentence) is sometimes reduced to a sentence with a 'separate-entity plural NP.' The phrasal conjunction (or compound noun phrase) does not derive from the conjoining of sentences but is generated as a 'unit plural NP' in the base component (e.g., *"Tom and Becky* embraced"). (Lakoff, 1966, 115.) *Sentence conjunction vs. phrasal conjunction:* The conjunction *and* appears in the base rules for phrasal conjunction but is introduced by transformation for sentence conjunction. Paraphrasability by a full sentence or the word *both* indicates underlying conjoined sentences (e.g., *"Both* Tom and

31

Huck attended the play"); paraphrasability by the word *with* (the 'with'-transformation) indicates underlying conjoined phrases (e.g., "Tom attended the play *with Huck*"—where *with* replaces *and* by preposition adjunction, and *with Huck* moves to the end of the sentence by conjunct movement). (Lakoff and Peters, 1966, 113–119, 121–131.) In sentence conjunction, the order of the conjuncts is related to their temporal sequence or their importance; in phrasal conjunction, the dominance relation is neutralized. (Langacker, 1969, 171–172.) Reciprocal conjunction (e.g., "Tom and Huck respected each other") is a type of phrasal conjunction; reflexive conjunction (e.g., "Tom and Huck liked themselves") is a type of sentence conjunction. (Gleitman, 1965, 100–101.) See also COMPOUND. Compare DISJUNCTIVE COMPOUND.

Conjunction, disjunctive. See CONJUNCTION.

Conjunction, phrasal. See CONJUNCTION.

Conjunction, reciprocal. See RECIPROCAL CONJUNCTION.

Conjunction reduction transformation. *G–2.* The rule, or rule schema, which deletes all but one of the identical parts of shared constituents in a compound sentence, as when: "Tom *left the raft* and Huck *left the raft* and Jim *left the raft*" ⇒ "Tom, Huck, and Jim *left the raft.*" (Langendoen, 1969, 32, 88–89.) No conjunction rule is needed to derive "Tom and Becky embraced," because the deep structure is a simple sentence with a conjoined subject. (McCawley, 1968, 151.) Also called **Identical conjunct reduction.** (Jacobs and Rosenbaum, 1968, 257.)

Conjunction, reflexive. See CONJUNCTION.

Conjunction, sentence. See CONJUNCTION.

Conjunction transformation. See CONJUNCTION.

Conjunctive compound. *G–2.* A coordination of two sentences with *and,* as opposed to a disjunctive compound, which is coordinated with *or:* S → S *and* S; "Huck fished and Tom slept." (Jacobs and Rosenbaum, 1968, 253.) Compare DISJUNCTIVE COMPOUND.

Conjunctive ordering. *G–2.* The ordering of rules in a cycle which allows a following rule to apply after a preceding rule has already applied. (Chomsky and Halle, 1968, 60.) Compare DISJUNCTIVE ORDERING.

Conjunct movement. See CONJUNCTION.

Conjunct reduction, identical. See IDENTICAL CONJUNCT REDUCTION.

Connected noun phrase. *G–2.* One of two noun phrases in a complex sentence which are related by identity, and either of which can be deleted; that is, the erasing noun phrase in the main sentence or the erased noun phrase in the complement sentence, as in: "It was kind of Tom (for Tom) to free Jim"; "It was kind (of Tom) for Tom to free Jim." (Rosenbaum, 1967a, 106). See also IDENTITY.

Connection erasure. *G–2.* The deletion of one of the identical noun phrases in a complex sentence—either the erasing noun phrase in the main sentence, or the erased noun phrase in the complement sentence. It is a type of identity erasure, but with an option involved. (Rosenbaum, 1967a, 106.) See also IDENTITY ERASURE TRANSFORMATION, IDENTICAL NOUN PHRASE DELETION.

Consequence, automatic. See AUTOMATIC CONSEQUENCE.

Consonant. *G–1.* A phonological segment which is specified [+consonantal] and [−vocalic]: [p], [t], [k], [b], [d], [g], [f], [θ], [s], [š], [v], [ð], [z], [ž], [č], [ǰ], [m], [n], etc. Liquids, [l], [r], are specified [+consonantal] [+vocalic].

Glides, [w], [y], [h], are specified [−consonantal] [−vocalic]. The velar nasal, [ŋ], is analyzed phonemically as /ng/. (Halle, 1959, 326–327.) *G–2*. A phonological segment that is specified [+consonantal], [+obstruent], and [−vocalic]—the 'true' consonants: [p], [t], [k], [b], [d], [g], [f], [θ], [s], [š], [v], [ð], [z], [ž], [č], [ǰ], [m], [n], [ŋ]. Liquids are [+consonantal], [−obstruent], and [+vocalic]: [l], [r], etc. Glides are [−consonantal], [+obstruent], and [−vocalic]: [w], [y], [h], [ʔ]. (Chomsky and Halle, 1968, 224.) Compare VOWEL.

Consonantal. *G–1.* The phonetic distinctive feature which is positively specified for sounds that are produced with contact of an upper and lower articulator in the oral cavity, and which are negatively specified, or nonconsonantal, for oral sounds with less narrowing. (Halle, 1959, 326.) *G–2.* The phonological distinctive feature which is positively specified for sounds that are produced with radical obstruction in the vocal tract, as with true consonants and liquids, and that are negatively specified, nonconsonantal, for oral sounds without such obstruction, as with vowels and glides. (Chomsky and Halle, 1968, 302.) Compare VOCALIC.

Consonant, nasal. See NASAL.

Consonant, true. See TRUE CONSONANT.

Constituency. *G–2.* The make-up of a string, more in regard to its constituents than to its structure. (Rosenbaum, 1967a, 39.) See also STRING, CONSTITUENT.

Constituency, internal. See INTERNAL CONSTITUENCY.

Constituent. *G–1–2.* A boundaried, or bracketed, element in a string: a morpheme, a word, a phrase, or an embedded sentence. (Rosenbaum, 1967a, 35, 82.) See also STRING.

Constituent, discontinuous. See DISCONTINUOUS CONSTITUENT.

Constituent-membership rule. *G–2S.* A phrase structure rule or constituent-structure rule, such as: S → Pred+NP. (Langendoen, 1969, 20, 23.) See also PHRASE STRUCTURE RULE.

Constituent negation. *G–2.* The negation of a constituent of a sentence rather than of the sentence as a whole—which may have its own sentence negation. Constituent negation may take the same form as the sentence negator *not* (e.g., "*not* far away"), or it may surface as an affix (e.g., "*un*certain"; "*in*consistent"). (Klima, 1964a, 308–309.) Compare SENTENCE NEGATION.

Constituent phrase-marker. See CONSTITUENT SENTENCE.

Constituent sentence. *G–1.* The second source-sentence in a generalized transformation, the first source-sentence being the matrix sentence (Lees, 1961, 309); the sentence that is represented by a constituent P-marker, which is the structure that is embedded in a matrix P-marker (Katz and Postal, 1964, 48). Both underlying and derived phrase-markers can serve as constituent phrase-markers. (Koutsoudas, 1966, 315.) Also called **Insert sentence, Insert, Embedded sentence.** See also EMBEDDING.

Constituent-structure grammar. *G–1–2.* The subcomponent of the syntactic component which consists of an ordered set of context-free rewriting rules which generate C-terminal strings of formatives (Chomsky, 1964, 54); a phrase structure grammar (Chomsky, 1965, 67); a grammar made up only of constituent-structure or expansion rules. A language generated by such a grammar is a **Constituent-structure language.** (Langendoen, 1969, 23.) See also PHRASE STRUCTURE GRAMMAR.

Constituent-structure rule. See PHRASE STRUCTURE RULE.

Constituent-structure tree. See TREE.

Constituent, ultimate. See ULTIMATE CONSTITUENT.

Constraint. *G–2.* Any lexical, syntactic, semantic, or phonological restriction on the privilege of occurrence of a morpheme, word, or phrase in a sentence. (Rosenbaum, 1967a, 107.) See also SELECTION RESTRICTION.

Constraint, global. See GLOBAL CONSTRAINT.

Constraint, positional. See POSITIONAL CONSTRAINT.

Constriction. *G–1.* The least extreme degree of narrowing in the oral tract, characterizing the articulation of high, or diffuse, vowels: [i], [u]. Halle, 1959, 326.) See also NARROWING.

Construct. See CONSTRUCTION.

Construction. *G–1–2.* A syntactic structure, one constituent of which is said to be 'in construction with' another if the former, on one branch, is dominated by a node which immediateley dominates the latter on another branch. For example in the phrase-marker

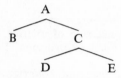

B is 'in construction with' C, and vice versa; D is 'in construction with' E, and vice versa; and D or E is 'in construction with' B, but not vice versa, and not with C. (Klima, 1964a, 297–298.) Also called **Construct.** (Rosenbaum, 1967a, 21.)

Construction, adjectival complement. See ADJECTIVAL COMPLEMENT CONSTRUCTION.

Constructional homonymity. *G–1a.* The condition which holds when a sentence can be associated with two or more nonequivalent derivations (Chomsky, 1956, 147, 151; Chomsky, 1957, 28)—that is, when two or more different phrase-markers can represent the same string (Bach, 1964, 40). Also called **Structural ambiguity, Grammatical ambiguity, Syntactic ambiguity, Transformational ambiguity.** *G–1b.* The condition which holds when a phoneme sequence can be analyzed in more than one way on a particular level, as in: /ə neym/ as *a name* or *an aim*; the ambiguous representation of a sequence of phonemes. (Chomsky, 1957, 86.) Equivalent to **Phonological ambiguity** in *G–2.* (Katz, 1966, 158–159.) Also called **Dual representation.** (Chomsky, 1957, 107.) See also AMBIGUITY, TRANSFORMATIONAL AMBIGUITY.

Construction, coordinate. See CONJUNCTION.

Construction, multiple-branching. See MULTIPLE-BRANCHING CONSTRUCTION.

Construction, pseudocleft. See CLEFT-SENTENCE.

Construction, right-branching. See RIGHT-BRANCHING CONSTRUCTION.

Contact. *G–1.* The closure of an upper and a lower articulator in the production of a stop consonant, as in [p], [t], [k]. Contact is the most extreme degree of narrowing. (Halle, 1959, 326.) See also NARROWING.

Contentive. *G–2S.* The category in the base which represents the three categories noun, verb, and adjective. (Bach, 1968, 115.) Compare PROPOSITION.

Context. *G–1*. The environment in which a linguistic element occurs. Context may condition the rule which specifies the element, in which case it is a context-sensitive or context-restricted rule; or it may be irrelevant to the specifications and be a context-free rule. (Koutsoudas, 1966, 117.) See also CONTEXT-FREE RULE, CONTEXT-SENSITIVE RULE, DISTRIBUTION.

Context-free rule. *G–1–2*. A rewrite rule with indifferent context—that is, a rule of the type $A \to B$ rather than $A \to B/X\text{——}Y$ or $XAY \to XBY$. A grammar based on context-free rules alone—not also on transformations —is a context-free grammar, or a structural grammar. (Chomsky, 1964, 53.) A language cannot be described by context-free rules alone. (Postal, 1964b, 146.) Compare CONTEXT-SENSITIVE RULE. See also PHRASE STRUCTURE RULE.

Context-sensitive rule. *G–1*. A rule of the type $XAY \to XBY$ or $A \to B/X\text{——}Y$, in which the context, $X\text{——}Y$, conditions the occurrence of the constituent to be rewritten; a context-restricted or context-dependent rule (Bach, 1964, 16, 36); a transformational rule (Lyons, 1968, 262). English cannot be described by a context-sensitive phrase structure grammar. (Bach, 1964, 173.) Context-sensitive rules are unavoidable in grammatical descriptions, regardless of the theoretical model. (Chomsky, 1961a, 122.) *G–2*. A phrase structure rule which permits the rewriting of an element along with its defining context—permitting more than one symbol on the left-hand side of the arrow. A generative-transformational grammar pairs a set of context-*free* rewriting rules with a set of transformations, thus rendering context-sensitive rewriting rules unnecessary in most analyses. Also called **Context-sensitive rewriting rule.** (Rosenbaum, 1967a, 25.) See also PHRASE STRUCTURE RULE. Compare CONTEXT-FREE RULE.

Context-sensitive subcategorization rule. *G–2*. A rule which subcategorizes a lexical category other than noun according to the context in which it can appear. Such rules are of two subtypes. One subtype is composed of strict subcategorization rules, in which the context consists of a frame of category symbols, as in: $[+V_t \to CS/\text{——}NP]$; that is, rewrite transitive verb as a complex symbol in the environment preceding a noun phrase. The other subtype is composed of selectional rules, in which the context consists of a frame of both category symbols and syntactic features, as in: $[+V_t \to CS/\text{——}DET\ [+animate]]$; that is, rewrite transitive verb as a complex symbol in the environment preceding a noun phrase consisting of a determiner and an animate noun. (Chomsky, 1965, 113.) See also STRICT SUBCATEGORIZATION RULE, SELECTIONAL RULE.

Contextual feature. *G–2*. A feature which specifies a context—that is, a syntactic context, specified by a strict subcategorization feature, or a lexical context, specified by a selectional feature (Chomsky, 1966a, 72); a syntactic feature which is positively or negatively specified for a lexical category or for the lexical item that belongs to that category. For example, transitive verbs are positively specified for the contextual feature [——NP], and a lexical item that belongs to the transitive verb category is specified [+V, +——NP]. The context can be stated in the form of category symbols alone—a strict subcategorization rule—or as category symbols plus syntactic features—a selectional rule. (Chomsky, 1965, 93–94.) See also CONTEXT-SENSITIVE SUBCATEGORIZATION RULE, STRICT SUBCATEGORIZATION FEATURE, STRICT SUBCATEGORIZATION RULE, SELECTIONAL FEATURE, SELECTIONAL RESTRICTION, SELECTIONAL RULE. Compare INHERENT FEATURE.

Continuant. *G–1.* The phonological distinctive feature which describes sounds that are articulated without closure—without contact—in the vocal tract, as opposed to interrupted sounds, which are produced with closure; a sound which is articulated without such closure. (Halle, 1959, 327.) *G–2.* The phonological distinctive feature which is positively specified for sounds which are articulated without oral blockage of the air flow, as opposed to noncontinuants, or true stops and affricates, which have oral blockage; a sound which is articulated without such blockage. (Chomsky and Halle, 1968, 317–318.) Compare STOP.

Contour, prosodic. See INTONATION.

Contraction. *G–1.* Introduction of the morpheme Cntr after the modal or *have* or *be* in the auxiliary of a negative sentence: $X+not-Cntr+Y \Rightarrow X+n't+Y$; the contracted form of the negative morpheme. (Lees, 1960a, 41.) *G–2.* A phonological transformation, the contraction rule, which converts a sentence with the full form of the negator *not* into a sentence with the contracted form of *not* ([nt]). (Jacobs, 1968, 20.) See also NEGATION.

Contraction rule. See CONTRACTION.

Contradiction, internal. See INTERNAL CONTRADICTION.

Convention. *G–2.* A universal principle provided by the theory and therefore not needing a specific statement in the grammar of a particular language. Conventions play a role in insuring that each transformation properly constructs its derived phrase-markers (Koutsoudas, 1966, 27) and in eliminating redundant specifications from lexical entries. (Chomsky, 1965, 168.) Also called **Metarule.**

Conventional orthography. *G–2.* The near optimal system used for the lexical representation of English words. It is near optimal because it does not indicate phonetic variation predictable by general rule and therefore known to the native speaker. An optimal orthography—the simplest orthography— would have only one spelling for any given lexical item. (Chomsky and Halle, 1968, 49, 221.) Compare PHONETIC TRANSCRIPTION.

Convention, alpha-environment. See ALPHA-ENVIRONMENT CONVENTION.

Convention, minus-next-rule. See MINUS-NEXT-RULE CONVENTION.

Convention, noniterative rule. See NONITERATIVE RULE CONVENTION.

Convention, notational. See NOTATIONAL CONVENTION.

Convert. *G–2.* To transform, as to convert a string of one form into a string of a different form. (Rosenbaum, 1967a, 64.) See also TRANSFORM.

Co-occur. *G–2.* For two morphemes to mutually include each other in a structure, as with the 'co-occurrence' of the complementizing morpheme *for* with the complementizing morpheme *to,* as a pair, neither occurring without the other in the underlying structure, though *for* can be deleted from the derived structure. (Rosenbaum, 1967a, 24.) See also MUTUAL INCLUSION, SELECTION RESTRICTION.

Co-occurrence. See CO-OCCUR.

Co-occurrence relation. See SELECTION RESTRICTION.

Coordinate construction. See CONJUNCTION.

Coordination. See CONJUNCTION.

Copula. *G–1.* The class of linking or copulative verbs, not including *be: become, seem,* etc. (Thomas, 1965, 33–34.) *G–2a.* The form *be,* which is entered in the lexicon as a true verb, $[+V, -ADJ]$, and can appear in the deep structure predicate of a sentence, where it can take an abstract noun phrase object, just as transitive verbs can, as in: "Huck *is* (it hungers Huck)" ⇒ "Huck *is* hungry." (Ross, 1969, 353, 355.) *G–2b.* The form *be,* which is an empty morpheme that is not entered in the lexicon but must be introduced as [+copula] by the copula transformation into the auxiliary of a sentence with a predicate adjective in order to carry person and number inflections. (Jacobs and Rosenbaum, 1968, 101.) *G–2c.* The form *have* or *be,* which is introduced by transformation into the auxiliary of certain sentences. (King, 1969, 153.)

Copula transformation. See COPULA.

Copula-type sentence. *G–1.* A predicative sentence, containing a predicate noun or predicate adjective. (Lees, 1960a, 7.) See also PREDICATE NOUN, PREDICATE ADJECTIVE.

Copula-type verb. *G–1.* A predicative verb like *be,* which cannot take manner adverbials, as opposed to activity verbs such as *become,* which can take manner adverbials, as in: "Huck *became* tired *quickly.*" (Lees, 1960a, 8.) See also COPULA.

Copy. *G–2.* To duplicate a constituent as a new constituent of the sentence, sometimes accompanied by deletion of the original constituent. (Langendoen, 1969, 24.) *G–2S.* To duplicate a case element of a simple sentence in subject position by means of a copying transformation. (Fillmore, 1968, 41.)

Copying transformation. See COPY.

Coreferential. See REFERENTIAL INDEX.

Coronal. *G–2.* The phonological distinctive feature which is positively specified for sounds that are articulated with the blade of the tongue raised from the neutral position. Coronal sounds (earlier [−grave] for consonants) include the interdentals, [θ], [ð], the alveolars, [t], [d], [s], [z], [č], [j], [n], the palato-alveolars, [š], [ž], and the lateral liquid [l]. (Chomsky and Halle, 1968, 304.) Compare GRAVE.

Correct. *G–1.* Grammatical; well formed. (Koutsoudas, 1966, 1.) *G–2a.* Strongly adequate—said of a structural description of a sentence. One structural description can be more strongly adequate, or more correct, than another. (Lyons, 1968, 247.) *G–2b.* Most highly motivated, most general, most economical, most explanatory. For example, in a 'correct' derivation, the grammar 'correctly' generates, or most satisfactorily explains the derivation of, a string. (Rosenbaum, 1967a, 26, 90.) See also ADEQUACY.

Cost. *G–2.* Expense to the theory, or lack of economy in the analysis, due to the number or complexity of operations required in a particular description. (Rosenbaum, 1967a, 39, 61, 90.) See also EXPENSIVE.

Counterexample. *G–1–2.* A datum which disproves a linguistic hypothesis or theory of language. A 'genuine' counterexample is one which leads to the discarding of a hypothesis. An 'apparent' counterexample is one which can itself be disproved. An 'uninteresting' counterexample is one which leads to the refinement of a theory. (Chomsky, 1957, 100; Katz and Postal, 1964, 120; Chomsky and Halle, 1968, ix.) Also: **Counter-example.** (King, 1969, 65.)

Counterexample, apparent. See COUNTEREXAMPLE.

Counterexample, genuine. See COUNTEREXAMPLE.

Cover symbol. *G–2.* The capitalized Roman-letter symbol X or Y or Z which is used in a grammatical rule to indicate that the variable composition of that context is not relevant to the operation of that transformation, as in: X+affix+verb+Y ⇒ X+verb+affix+Y (the auxiliary transformation). (King, 1969, 144.) See also X-TYPE VARIABLE.

Covert negation. *G–2.* Negation without an overt negative element such as *not, un-, in-,* etc.: a negative predicate like *doubt* or *deny,* or a negative adverb like *hardly* or *scarcely.* (Langendoen, 1969, 127.) Compare OVERT NEGATION.

Criteria of analysis. *G–1.* The constraints that a linguist imposes on a linguistic theory to insure that it will exhibit features of explanatory adequacy. (Lees, 1960a, xxv.) See also EXPLANATORY ADEQUACY.

Critically ordered. *G–2.* Strictly ordered; without exception in the order of application, as with the passive transformation preceding the extraposition transformation. (Rosenbaum, 1967a, 40.) Compare PARTIALLY ORDERED.

Cross-classification. *G–2.* The specification of a syntactic, semantic, or phonological feature in various combinations in the representation of lexical items. (Chomsky, 1966a, 69.) See also CROSS-CLASSIFYING FEATURE.

Cross-classifying feature. *G–2.* A syntactic, semantic, or phonological feature which is specified in various combinations in the representation of lexical items, as: for semantic features, *man* [+human], [+masculine]; *woman* [+human], [−masculine]; *rooster* [−human], [+masculine]; *hen* [−human], [−masculine]; etc. (Chomsky, 1966a, 69; Langendoen, 1969, 37.) See also INHERENT FEATURE, DISTINCTIVE FEATURE, SEMANTIC FEATURE, PHONOLOGICAL DISTINCTIVE FEATURE.

Cross-over principle. *G–2.* The principle of noninvertibility of identical noun phrases, as seen in: "The raft steered itself" ⇒ *"Itself was steered by the raft." (Jacobs and Rosenbaum, 1968, 147.) See also NONIDENTITY.

C-terminal string. *G–1.* A constituent-terminal string, which is the string of morphemes or formatives that is the output of a constituent-structure grammar, or phrase structure grammar (Chomsky, 1964, 54); a base string (Chomsky, 1966a, 51). Also called **Basic string.**

Cycle. *G–2a.* One pass of an ordered set of rules, not all of which need apply in a particular derivation. The grammar has three cycles: one each for phrase structure rules (the first cycle), transformational rules (the second cycle), and morphophonemic rules (the post cycle). (Rosenbaum, 1967a, 38.) *G–2b.* The iterative operation of certain ordered phonological rules, such as stress assignment and vowel reduction, on the labeled bracketing of a surface structure. All of the rules of the cycle apply first to the innermost constituent of the bracketing, whose brackets are then erased; subsequently the entire order of rules applies to the smallest remaining constituent, etc., until even S is erased. (Chomsky, 1968, 37–39.) Cyclic rules apply only to prosodic features and cannot account for segmental features. (Chomsky and Halle, 1968, 350.) See also TRANSFORMATIONAL CYCLE.

Cycle, iterative. See ITERATIVE CYCLE.

Cycle, post. See POST CYCLE.

Cycle, transformational. See TRANSFORMATIONAL CYCLE.

Cyclic principle. *G–2.* The principle of sequential application of ordered rules in a set, and of ordered sets of rules in a system. (Rosenbaum, 1967a, 5.) The validity of the cyclic principle has been questioned. (Rosenbaum, 1967b, ix.) See also CYCLE.

D

Data, primary linguistic. See PRIMARY LINGUISTIC DATA.

Dative. *G–2S.* The case category of the noun phrase, typically identified by *to* in the surface form, which is affected by the action or state of the verb, as in: "Tom obeyed *Aunt Polly*"; "Tom showed *Aunt Polly* obedience"; "Tom was obedient *to Aunt Polly*"; "Tom showed obedience *to Aunt Polly*." (Fillmore, 1968, 29.) See also CASE, INDIRECT OBJECT.

Decision procedure. *G–1.* The unachievable demand on a linguistic theory that it provide a mechanical procedure for deciding whether a proposed grammar of a corpus is the best grammar of the language. (Chomsky, 1957, 51.) Compare EVALUATION PROCEDURE.

Decompose. *G–2.* To break down a complex symbol into its atomic concepts, as to decompose the meaning of a lexical item by means of semantic markers and distinguishers in a dictionary entry. (Katz and Fodor, 1963, 496.) Compare AMALGAMATION.

Deep level. *G–2S.* The level of the semantic representation of a sentence, as opposed to the surface level, or physical representation. The structure of a sentence on the deep level is its deep structure, and, at the surface level, its surface structure. The grammatical relationships which hold at the surface level do not necessarily hold at the deep level. (Langendoen, 1969, 14, 23–24.) Compare DEEP STRUCTURE, SURFACE LEVEL, SURFACE STRUCTURE.

Deep-level structure. See DEEP STRUCTURE.

Deep structure. *G–2a.* The phrase-markers of the underlying strings of a sentence, plus the transformation-marker, which, together, contain all of the information needed for semantic interpretation. (Chomsky, 1964, 55; Chomsky, 1966a, 55.) *G–2b.* The abstract underlying form of a sentence which determines its meaning but is not necessarily represented in the physical utterance (Chomsky, 1966b, 4); a generalized phrase-marker, generated by the base component, which underlies a well-formed surface structure (Chomsky, 1965, 16–18). Sentences that have different meanings have different deep structures. (Chomsky, 1966b, 4.) Transformations filter out generalized phrase-markers that do not qualify as deep structures. (Chomsky, 1965, 135–136.) *G–2c.* The underlying abstract structure of the language. (Chomsky, 1965, 122.) *G–2d.* The systematic phonemic structure that underlies a phonetic surface form. (King, 1969, 126.) *G–2S.* The notion of **Syntactic deep structure** has been abandoned by some linguists in favor of a deeper and more abstract structure that is identical with semantic representation. (Bach and Harms, 1968, viii.) Deep structures are identical in different languages and are much more abstract than was previously thought. For example, 'noun,' 'verb,' and 'adjective' are not differentiated in the deep structure. (Bach, 1968, 121.) The earlier syntactic deep structure was an artificial intermediate level between **Semantic deep structure,** or **Conceptual structure** (Langacker, 1968, 114), and **Phonological surface structure.** A semantically justified universal syntactic theory converts order-free semantic deep structures into ordered surface forms of sentences. (Fillmore, 1968, 88.) Also called **Underlying struc-**

ture (Postal, 1964c, 22), **Deep-level structure** (Langendoen, 1969, 24). Compare SURFACE STRUCTURE.

Deep structure, semantic. See SEMANTIC DEEP STRUCTURE.

Deep structure, syntactic. See DEEP STRUCTURE.

Deep subject. *G–2*. The noun phrase subject of the deep structure of a sentence, which may or may not appear as the surface structure subject. (Jacobs and Rosenbaum, 1968, 77.) Also called **Underlying subject.** Compare DERIVED SUBJECT, SUPERFICIAL SUBJECT.

Define. *G–2*. To provide with an analysis which correctly describes and explains the environment for, and operation of, a transformation, as to 'define' identity erasure. (Rosenbaum, 1967a, 50–51.) See also PREDICT.

Defined on/upon/over. *G–2*. Predicted, or triggered, as an automatic consequence of the appropriate environment's being met in the structural description of a particular string. Said of a transformation. For example, the extraposition transformation is 'defined on' complements containing the 'that' complementizer, among other things, but is not 'defined on' complements containing the POSS-ing complementizer. (Rosenbaum, 1967a, 40, 42, 45, 78, 80.) Also: **Sensitive to.** (Rosenbaum, 1967a, 26, 39, 69, 81.) See also STRUCTURAL DESCRIPTION, NECESSARY CONDITION.

Definite noun phrase. *G–1–2*. A noun phrase which contains either a zero determiner—a unique NP, or proper name, which can be followed only by an appositive relative—or *the/this/that*—a specified NP, which can be followed by a restrictive or an appositive relative. (Smith, 1964, 248–249.)

Definitization. *G–2*. The specifying of a Pro-noun as [+definite] and usually also [−demonstrative]—that is, as a personal pronoun. (Postal, 1966, 209.) See also PERSONAL PRONOUN.

Deformation rule. *G–2*. A singulary transformation which converts an embedding into a derived nominal, as when: "Tom is a (he leads)" ⇒ "Tom is a leader"; "Huck smashed the (the raft has a rudder) rudder" ⇒ "Huck smashed the raft's rudder." (Katz and Postal, 1964, 142, 146.) See also DERIVATION.

Degree of grammaticalness. *G–1*. The formal remoteness, or distance, of an utterance from the set of perfectly well-formed sentences of the language. Grammaticalness is measured along a scale that includes three degrees: fully grammatical, semi-grammatical, and ungrammatical. A fully grammatical sentence is not necessarily fully acceptable on semantic and phonological grounds (e.g., "Colorless green ideas sleep furiously"). Semi-grammatical sentences, or semi-sentences, are characteristic of the English of non-fluent speakers, as in: "You like?" (Chomsky, 1957, 36, 43; Chomsky, 1961b, F&K, 387.) Also called **Degree of grammaticality.** See also SCALE OF GRAMMATICALNESS, GRAMMATICALNESS. Compare ACCEPTABILITY.

Deletability, free. See FREE DELETABILITY.

Deletion. *G–1–2*. The operation which eliminates nodes, up to a certain number, that do not dominate a terminal string in a derivation. (Chomsky, 1961a, 136.) A transformation can delete only those elements that are recoverable—that is, only formatives present in the structural description (e.g., the *you* of an imperative sentence), or dummy elements or proforms (e.g., Something), or a repeated element (e.g., "Huck is taller than

Tom *is tall*"). (Chomsky, 1964, 136; Chomsky, 1965, 144–145.) Compare ERASURE.

Deletion, equi-NP-. See EQUI-NP-DELETION.

Deletion, identical noun phrase. See IDENTICAL NOUN PHRASE DELETION.

Deletion, identical verb phrase. See IDENTICAL VERB PHRASE DELETION.

Deletion, indefinite noun phrase. See IDENTICAL NOUN PHRASE DELETION.

Deletion, node. See NODE DELETION.

Deletion, preposition. See PREPOSITION DELETION.

Deletion rule, noun phrase. See IDENTICAL NOUN PHRASE DELETION.

Deletion rule, preposition. See PREPOSITION DELETION TRANSFORMATION.

Deletion rule, verb. See VERB DELETION RULE.

Deletion transformation, complementizer. See COMPLEMENTIZER.

Deletion transformation, indefinite pronoun. See INDEFINITE PRONOUN DELETION TRANSFORMATION.

Deletion transformation, 'it'. See 'IT' DELETION TRANSFORMATION.

Deletion transformation, noun segment. See NOUN SEGMENT DELETION TRANSFORMATION.

Deletion transformation, obligatory complementizer. See OBLIGATORY COMPLEMENTIZER DELETION TRANSFORMATION.

Deletion transformation, optional complementizer. See OPTIONAL COMPLEMENTIZER DELETION TRANSFORMATION.

Deletion transformation, preposition. See PREPOSITION DELETION TRANSFORMATION.

Deletion transformation, pronoun. See PRONOUN DELETION TRANSFORMATION.

Deletion transformation, question. See QUESTION DELETION TRANSFORMATION.

Deletion transformation, relative 'be'. See RELATIVE 'BE' DELETION TRANSFORMATION.

Deletion transformation, relative pronoun. See RELATIVE PRONOUN DELETION TRANSFORMATION.

Deletion transformation, 'that'. See 'THAT' DELETION TRANSFORMATION.

Deletion transformation, time-place. See TIME-PLACE DELETION TRANSFORMATION.

Deletion transformation, 'to'. See 'TO' DELETION TRANSFORMATION.

Deletion transformation, to-be. See TO-BE DELETION TRANSFORMATION.

Dependent, structure-. See STRUCTURE-DEPENDENT.

Derivation. *G–1–2a.* The transformational process which generates, or derives, complex words from embeddings (Chomsky, 1962, 222); the creation of stems with derivational suffixes by deforming transformations involving relative phrases (Katz and Postal, 1964, 144–148); the lexical and transformational processes which produce complex stems. Some complex stems—such as some verbs consisting of prefix plus bound base—are created by processes internal to the lexicon and do not involve syntactic rules; others have affixes added by transformation. (Chomsky and Halle, 1968, 370.) Much of English morphological derivation is part of syntactic derivation and can be accounted for in the syntax. (Chomsky and Halle, 1968, 8.) *G–1–2b.* A finite sequence of strings of symbols, beginning with the initial symbol #S# and proceeding through successive intermediate strings, each formed by the expansion—rewriting or replacing—of only one symbol at a time in the preceding string until the terminal string of morphemes is reached, none of which can be rewritten. Because a syntactic derivation reveals, through its sequence of strings, the order in which the phrase structure rules were applied to form it (i.e., its derivational history), it can be represented as a labeled tree; but the order is lost in the tree, so the representation is not reversible. (Koutsoudas, 1966, 15, 17.) *G–2*. An analysis of the transformational history of a surface structure. (Rosenbaum, 1967a, 34.)

Derivational apparatus. *G–2*. The set of transformations necessary to explain the derivation of syntactic constructions within a system like the complementation system. (Rosenbaum, 1967a, 93.) See also DERIVATION.

Derivational history. *G–1*. The record of the generation of an underlying phrase-marker of a sentence, based on the successive selection and expansion of phrase structure rules (Koutsoudas, 1966, 28); a **Phrase-structure history** or **Derivation history** (Lees, 1960a, 101). See also DERIVATION.

Derivational path. *G–1*. The lines of a syntactic derivation which connect the initial symbol S to a particular terminal symbol by way of various intermediate nodes. (Bach, 1964, 72.) See also BRANCHING DIAGRAM, DERIVATION, PATH.

Derivational status. *G–2*. The identification of a constituent in a derivation, such as the 'derivational status' of the morpheme *for* as a preposition rather than as a complementizer in the sentence "Huck hoped *for* Tom to return." (Rosenbaum, 1967a, 85.) See also DERIVATION.

Derivational suffix. *G–1–2*. A grammatical morpheme that is suffixed to a base in the generation of complex stems, such as: *-er,* the agentive suffix; *-ee,* the objective suffix (Katz and Postal, 1964, 144–148); *-ness,* the nominalization morpheme (Thomas, 1965, 51); etc. The derivational suffixes *-y, -ate, -ize, -i-on, -ic-al, -i-ty,* and *-i-fy* place primary stress on the next to last syllable of the stems to which they are added—counting *-i-* and *-ic-* as part of the stem. (Chomsky and Halle, 1968, 86–87.) Also called **Derivative suffix, Derivative morpheme.** See also DERIVATION.

Derivation, formal. See FORMAL DERIVATION.

Derivation, semi-. See SEMI-DERIVATION.

Derivative morpheme. *G–1*. A category-change affix such as *-ish,* as in: *fool,* noun; *foolish,* adjective. Also called **Derivative affix.** (Lees, 1960a, 109.) See also DERIVATIONAL SUFFIX.

Derivative morphology. *G–1*. The subset of morphological rules that operate in or near the lexicon—low-level morphology. (Lees, 1960a, 109.) '

Derive. See DERIVATION.

Derived phrase-marker. *G–1*. The phrase-marker resulting from the application of a simple or generalized transformation to one or more underlying phrase-markers. Also: **Derived P-marker.** (Chomsky, 1961a, 131, 134.) *G–2*. The phrase-marker resulting from the application of a singular transformation to a single generalized phrase-marker. The final derived phrase-marker represents the surface structure of a sentence. (Chomsky, 1966a, 66.) See also PHRASE-MARKER, GENERALIZED PHRASE-MARKER.

Derived phrase-marker, final. See FINAL DERIVED PHRASE-MARKER.

Derived sentence. *G–1*. A sentence which has undergone one or more optional transformations, as well as all obligatory transformations that apply—a nonkernel sentence. (Chomsky, 1962, 223.) *G–2*. A sentence that has its origin in the structures underlying other sentences. Sentences are 'derived' from underlying structures rather than from surface structures or actual utterances. (Chomsky, 1968, 54.) Compare SOURCE SENTENCE, KERNEL SENTENCE.

Derived structure. *G–1–2*. The structure onto which a set of transformational rules map an underlying structure. (Rosenbaum, 1967a, 1.) See also DERIVED PHRASE-MARKER.

Derived subject. *G–2*. The subject of a superficial structure, sometimes different from the subject of the underlying structure, as in the case of the grammatical subject of a passive sentence, which is a direct object in the active sentence (e.g., *"Jim* was freed by Tom"). (Rosenbaum, 1967a, 18.) Also called **Superficial subject.** Compare DEEP SUBJECT, UNDERLYING SUBJECT.

Derived word. *G–2*. A complex lexical item which derives by way of lexical or transformational rules. The nominalization transformation is responsible for the words *destruction* and *refusal* (e.g., "Huck's *destruction* of the raft"; "Tom's *refusal* to leave"), which are not entered in the lexicon as such but as the verbs *destroy* and *refuse,* along with a feature specification of their phonetic form in nominalized sentences. Phonological rules determine that Nom-*destroy* will become *destruction* and Nom-*refuse* become *refusal,* according to the inherent features of the items. *Destruction* and *refusal,* in the examples above, are transforms, or, specifically, defective predicates, rather than nouns, though such forms could be nouns (e.g., "Tom's *refusal* was unexpected"; "Its *destruction* interested Huck"). There are no general rules for deriving such items as *horror, horrid, horrify* or *telephone, telegraph, teletype.* They must be entered directly in the lexicon, even though they clearly have internal structure and their meanings are predictable to some degree from the semantic properties of their morphemes. Native intuition is against deriving these idioms syntactically, so there may be some internal computation in the lexicon. (Chomsky, 1965, 184–187.) See also DERIVATION.

Descendant. See GRAMMATICAL FUNCTION.

Description, grammatical. See GRAMMATICAL DESCRIPTION.

Description, linguistic. See LINGUISTIC DESCRIPTION.

Description, structural. See STRUCTURAL DESCRIPTION.

Description, syntactic. See SYNTACTIC DESCRIPTION.

Descriptive adequacy. *G–1–2*. The level of adequacy of a grammar which correctly accounts for the linguistic intuition of an idealized native speaker (Chomsky, 1964, 63) by correctly pairing signals with syntactic descriptions that support semantic interpretations (Chomsky, 1966a, 14). The structural descriptions and the assessments of grammaticality must match the native speaker's intrinsic competence. (Chomsky, 1965, 24.) At the level of descriptive adequacy, a grammar is justified on purely external grounds. (Chomsky, 1965, 26–27.) A descriptively adequate *grammar* is an adequate account of semantic interpretation; a descriptively adequate *theory* is one which provides a descriptively adequate grammar for each language. (Chomsky, 1965, 24, 76.) See also ADEQUACY. Compare EXPLANATORY ADEQUACY, OBSERVATIONAL ADEQUACY.

Descriptive grammar. *G–2*. A descriptively adequate grammar—that is, a grammar which assigns to each sentence of the language an abstract deep structure that determines the sentence's semantic interpretation, and a surface structure that determines its phonetic form. (Chomsky, 1966c, 52.) See also DESCRIPTIVE ADEQUACY.

Descriptive linguistics. *G–1–2.* The scientific analysis of a language at one point in time. (Langacker, 1968, 6.) Compare HISTORICAL LINGUISTICS.

Detail rule. *G–2.* A context-sensitive phonological rule which rewrites the plus and minus values of a phonological feature as multinary values of a phonetic feature—that is: phonological feature → phonetic feature/ X——Y. (Postal, 1968'a, 69.) Compare PHONOLOGICAL REDUNDANCY RULE, BLANK-FILLING RULE.

Determinative. See DETERMINER.

Determinative, pre-nominal. See PRE-NOMINAL DETERMINATIVE.

Determiner. *G–1.* The syntactic category DET, or Det, which must occur in any noun phrase that contains a count noun, and which may occur in an NP containing a mass noun—that is, NP → DET+N_c; the system which expands the 'determiner' category as follows: DET → (predeterminer) (prearticle) article/demonstrative/genitive/∅ (postdeterminer). (Thomas, 1965, 79–86.) DET can also expand to include the relative marker R, which permits a restrictive relative clause, and/or the appositive marker A, which permits a nonrestrictive, or appositive, clause. (Smith, 1964, 247–249.) Also called **Determinative.** (Lees, 1960a, 14). *G–2.* The syntactic feature of definiteness—the earlier **Articles**—and order—the earlier **Postdeterminers**—which are specified for noun phrases in the categorial subcomponent of the base. Predeterminers and prearticles have been eliminated by the positing of an underlying noun identical to the head noun, as in: "each *book* of these *books*," rather than "each of these books"; then, by reduction and deletion transformations, various strings can result, such as: "each book"; "each of these books"; "each of these"; "each"; etc. (Postal, 1966, 206; Langacker, 1969, 182.) See also ARTICLE.

Determiner, generic. See GENERIC DETERMINER.

Deviance. See DEVIATION.

Deviation. *G–1–2.* Departure from well-formedness of sentences (Chomsky, 1961b, 184); the distance of a string from complete grammaticalness. Deviation is measured in degrees on a scale of deviance that is based on a hierarchy imposed by the selectional rules: the higher the violation in the dominance hierarchy, the greater the deviation. That is, the violation of a lexical category is more serious than the violation of a subcategory; the violation of a subcategory is more serious than the violation of a selectional rule; and the violation of a high-level selectional feature is more serious than the violation of a low-level selectional feature, as in: "Honesty may serious Tom"; "Honesty may swivel Tom"; "Honesty may file Tom"; "Honesty may fire Tom." (Chomsky, 1965, 152–153, 227.) See also DEGREE OF GRAMMATICALNESS.

Device, language-acquisition. See LANGUAGE-ACQUISITION DEVICE.

Diacritic feature. *G–2.* A feature in a lexical entry which indicates which exceptional grammatical rules can apply to that particular lexical item. For example, a negative specification of the diacritic feature [Germanic] indicates that a special 'foreign' rule applies, perhaps [+Greek] or [+Romance]. By universal convention, the diacritic features are distributed to all of the segments of a given lexical item. (Chomsky and Halle, 1968, 374.) See also EXCEPTION, EXCEPTION FEATURE.

Diagram. *G–1–2.* A graphic representation of the syntactic structure of a sentence—a branching tree. (Rosenbaum, 1967a, 34.)

Diagram, branching. See BRANCHING DIAGRAM.

Dialect. *G–2.* A regional or social variant of a language, defined abstractly according to the rules of the grammar of that variant in contrast with the rules of the grammars of other variants rather than according to a comparison of phonemic or morphemic inventories, as in structural linguistics. (King, 1969, 38–39.) Minor syntactic differences among dialects are not attributable to the base rules but are a result of differences in the lexicon, in the number of transformational rules, and in the ordering of transformational rules. (Postal, 1966, 222.) See also DIASYSTEM.

Diaphoneme. See DIASYSTEM.

Diasystem. *G–1.* The systematic concept which characterizes dialect differences in cognate items as phonemic correspondences—that is, as different realizations of the same shared phoneme, or diaphoneme. For example, the diaphoneme /ay/ is shared by all English dialects in certain cognates, although it is manifested variously as /æy/, /əy/, /oy/, /ah/, etc. (King, 1969, 31–32.) See also DIALECT.

Dictionary. *G–2.* The component of a semantic theory, other than the set of projection rules, which provides representations of the semantic properties of each of the lexical items—morphemes, words, idioms—of the language; a finite set of rules, or dictionary entries, which pair words with representations of their meanings, or readings, in some normal form of distinctive feature complexes. (Katz and Fodor, 1963, 492–493, 501.) A complete linguistic description contains both a dictionary, in the semantic component, and a lexicon, in the syntactic component. (Katz and Postal, 1964, 161.) See also DICTIONARY ENTRY, SEMANTIC COMPONENT. Compare LEXICON.

Dictionary entry. *G–2a.* That part of a semantic theory which pairs a word with its meaning by supplying all of the grammatical and semantic information necessary for the operation of the projection rules, which are the other part of the theory. The grammatical portion of a dictionary entry represents the part-of-speech classification of the lexical item, while the semantic portion provides each of the meanings that the lexical item normally has when it occurs as a given part of speech. The grammatical information is given in a grammatical or syntactic marker, such as noun, verb, adjective, adverb. The semantic information is given in three types of markers: a semantic marker, such as (animal), (human), (male), etc.; a distinguisher, consisting of a single definition; and a selection restriction, which describes the required context. A dictionary entry can be displayed in the form of a tree diagram. (Katz and Fodor, 1963, 494–501.) *G–2b.* A collection of those properties of a word which are unpredictable by universal or particular rule; that is: syntactic properties such as [+noun], [+animate]; semantic properties such as [+animal], [+physical object]; and phonological properties—a feature matrix. (Postal, 1968a, 155.) Also called **Lexical entry.** (Chomsky, 1965, 160–161.) *G–2S.* There is no good reason for organizing the dictionary on the basis of phonological identity rather than on the basis of semantic identity. Dictionary entries are not necessary at all if 'lexical item' is taken to mean the combination of one syntactic category, one semantic reading, one phonological shape, and one set of exception features. The four-way ambiguous dictionary entry for "bachelor," described in Katz and Kodor, 1963, 494–496, would simply be four different lexical items pronounced the same way. Because transformations which demand identity of lexical items demand identity of specific readings, each terminal node in the deep structure must have only one semantic reading. (McCawley, 1968, 125–127.) See also LEXICAL ENTRY.

Diffuse. *G–1.* The phonetic distinctive feature which is positively specified for sounds that are produced with constriction or contact of articulators in the front part of the vocal tract—that is to say, forward of the palatal region for consonants, and anywhere in the oral cavity for vowels. The negative specification is called **Nondiffuse.** (Halle, 1959, 327.) Compare COMPACT.

Dimensional. *G–2.* A nonbinary semantic feature corresponding to the three independent dimensions of human visual perception, as: [1-dimensional], length; [2-dimensional], area; [3-dimensional], volume—and perhaps [0-dimensional], without length, area, or volume. (Langendoen, 1969, 40.)

Diphthong. *G–2.* A vocalic nucleus which consists phonetically of a vowel plus a glide and which is derived by diphthongization from a phonological single vowel, or monophthong, as in: [īy], from /ē/; [ēy], from /ǣ/; [āy], from /ī/; [ūw], from /ō/; [ōw], from /ɔ̄/; [ǣw], from /ū/. The true phonetic diphthongs—[āy], [āw], and [ɔy]—consist of a low vowel followed by a glide ([y] or [w]). (Chomsky and Halle, 1968, 189, 198.) Compare VOWEL.

Direct object. *G–1.* The grammatical relation which holds between a noun phrase, NP, and the main verb, MV, that immediately dominates that NP and also immediately dominates a transitive verb, V_t, as in:

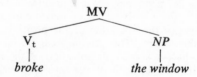

Under passive transformation, the direct object NP becomes the surface grammatical subject of the passive transform, as when: "Huck broke *the window*" ⇒ "*The window* was broken by Huck." (Thomas, 1965, 34.) *G–2.* The grammatical relation which holds between an NP and a VP in the deep structure when the VP directly dominates the NP:

The direct object relation can be symbolized as [NP, VP]: noun phrase directly dominated by verb phrase. (Chomsky, 1965, 69, 71.) Also called **Object.** (Jacobs and Rosenbaum, 1968, 72.) Compare MIDDLE OBJECT.

Disambiguation. *G–2.* The application of context in selecting the intended reading of an ambiguous utterance and in rejecting the readings which violate selection restrictions. Disambiguation is not covered by a general theory of understanding in context. (Postal, 1964c, 35.) See also AMBIGUITY, AMBIGUOUS SENTENCE.

Discontinuous constituent. *G–1.* A constituent that has undergone permutation from its contiguous form in the phrase structure and appears in the surface structure as an interrupted form, as in: "Q Huck *can sing*" ⇒ *"Can* Huck *sing?"* Discontinuities cannot be explained by phrase structure rules alone but must involve transformations. (Postal, 1964a, 20, 67–69, 94, 112.)

Discourse paraphrase. *G–2.* The paraphrase, as a sequence of simple sentences, of a generalized base form. For example, the complex sentence "The raft that Huck built sank" can be given the discourse paraphrase "Huck built the raft"; "The raft sank." (Kuroda, 1969, 340.) See also PARAPHRASE.

Discovery procedure. *G–1.* The mechanical method for constructing the grammar of a language by segmentation and classification of a corpus of utterances. It is the strongest requirement that could be made of the relationship between a linguistic theory and a particular grammar (corpus → theory → grammar). It is questionable whether there can be a successful discovery procedure for grammars. (Chomsky, 1957, 50–52.) See also STRUCTURAL LINGUISTICS.

Disjunction. See DISJUNCTIVE COMPOUND.

Disjunctive compound. *G–2.* A compound sentence which employs the disjunctive conjunction *or* (e.g., "Stop *or* I'll shoot!"), as opposed to a conjunctive compound, which employs the conjunction *and* (e.g., "Close your books *and* repeat after me"). (Jacobs and Rosenbaum, 1968, 253.) Also called **Disjunction.** (Langendoen, 1969, 124.) Compare CONJUNCTION.

Disjunctive conjunction. See DISJUNCTIVE COMPOUND.

Disjunctive ordering. *G–2a.* The ordering of phonological rules in a cycle, such that if one of the rules applies, the other rules cannot apply in that stage of the cycle. (Chomsky and Halle, 1968, 60, 63.) *G–2b.* The convention by which only the earliest—that is, fullest—expansion of a rule applies to a given form. (Harms, 1968, 64, 66.) Compare CONJUNCTIVE ORDERING.

Distance. *G–2a.* The number of branches in the path which connects two nodes in a tree. (Rosenbaum, 1967a, 6, 17.) See also PATH, CLOSER. *G–2b.* The degree of deviation of a lexical item from the lexicon, or of a sentence from the corpus. (Chomsky and Halle, 1968, 417–418.) See also ADMISSIBILITY, DEGREE OF GRAMMATICALNESS.

Distinctive feature. *G–1.* A phonetic property of sounds, defined in acoustic and articulatory terms. (Halle, 1959, 324.) *G–2.* A phonetic or phonological property of sounds, usually defined in articulatory terms (Chomsky, 1965, vii, 22); one of the minimal elements of an alphabetic symbol in a phonetic or phonological transcription; a phonetic feature which contributes to systematic recognition of differences among morphemes (Langacker, 1968, 153); the fundamental unit of generative phonology; a universal set of gross phonetic features in complementary distribution (Harms, 1968, 1, 6); a row in a phonological matrix of phonological features, or a row in a phonetic matrix of phonetic features (Chomsky and Halle, 1968, 169). A bundle of distinctive features is called a **Feature complex.** (Chomsky and Halle, 1968, 64.) The major class distinctive features are [sonorant], [consonantal], and [vocalic]. (Chomsky and Halle, 1968, 303.) See also PHONOLOGICAL DISTINCTIVE FEATURE, PHONETIC FEATURE, MATRIX.

Distinctive feature, Jakobsonian. See JAKOBSONIAN DISTINCTIVE FEATURE.

Distinctive feature, phonological. See PHONOLOGICAL DISTINCTIVE FEATURE.

Distinguisher. *G–2.* A formal element in a dictionary entry which reflects the idiosyncratic meaning of a lexical item within its semantic marker, such as: "one who has never married"—a distinguisher of one of the meanings of *bachelor* or *maid.* (Katz and Postal, 1964, 14.) See also DICTIONARY ENTRY.

Distribution. *G–1.* The infinite class of environments for which a linguistic form is specified by generative rules. The primary task of a linguistic description is the specification by rules of the possible distributions for each of the forms of the language. (Bach, 1964, 152–153.) See also CONTEXT.

Distribution, complementary. See COMPLEMENTARY DISTRIBUTION.

Division, binary. See BINARY DIVISION.

'Do', dummy carrier. See DUMMY CARRIER 'DO'.

Domain. *G–1.* The structural description of a transformational rule, specifying the form that strings must have in order for the rule to apply. (Koutsoudas, 1966, 24.) See also STRUCTURAL DESCRIPTION.

Dominance relation. See COMMAND.

Dominate. See DOMINATION.

Domination. *G–1–2.* The relation between a higher-order constituent (e.g., node A) and a lower-order constituent on the same derivational path (e.g., node B or node C) by which A is said to dominate B and C; B and C are said to be dominated by, or to be co-generated by, or to be descendants of, A; and the string B+C *is an* A:

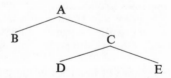

In the diagram, A immediately dominates B and C, and C immediately dominates D and E. A dominates B, C, D, and E; and C dominates D and E. The string B+C—or B+D+E—*is an* A; and the string D+E *is a* C. (Koutsoudas, 1966, 17-18; Rosenbaum, 1967a, 9, 94.) Compare IS-A RELATION.

Domination, immediate. See IMMEDIATE DOMINATION.

'Do'-support. *G–1.* The introduction of the dummy carrier *do* before an unattached tense affix in the auxiliary. Do-support is needed in negative sentences (e.g., "Tom *does*n't like fish"), in questions of all types (e.g., "*Does* Tom like fish?"; "Why *does* Tom like fish?"; "Tom likes fish, *does*n't he?"), in complex comparative sentences (e.g., "Huck likes fish better than Tom *does*"), in cleft sentences (e.g., "What Huck *does* is catch fish"), etc. (Klima, 1964a, 321.) See also DUMMY CARRIER 'DO.'

Double-base transformation. See GENERALIZED TRANSFORMATION.

Double-object verb. *G–1.* A verb with two objects—an indirect object and a direct object—and two passive forms, as in: "Huck *gave* Tom a knife" ⇒ "Tom *was given* a knife by Huck" or "A knife *was given* Tom by Huck." (Lees, 1960a, 10.)

Drift. *G–2.* The independent addition of the same rule in separated members of a family of languages. (Postal, 1968, 257.)

Dual representation. See CONSTRUCTIONAL HOMONYMITY.

Dummy. *G–2.* An unspecified constituent in an underlying structure whose presence is required to explain a set of derivations. (Rosenbaum, 1967a, 64.) See also DUMMY SYMBOL.

Dummy carrier 'do.' *G–1.* The empty, or meaningless, morpheme *do,* which is not entered in the lexicon but is introduced by obligatory transformation when a base is needed to bear an unattached tense morpheme. (Chomsky, 1957, 100.) Also called **Pro-verb.** See also 'DO'-SUPPORT.

Dummy symbol. *G–1.* The terminal symbol in a matrix phrase-marker which is obligatorily replaced, through an embedding transformation, by a constituent phrase-marker which takes on the structure of the node of the dummy symbol. (Koutsoudas, 1966, 308.) *G–2a.* A morpheme which is never a formative, and is therefore a dummy element, but is found only in the last line of a matrix phrase-marker, labeled 'matrix dummy' or 'md', in order to permit relative and complement embedding—the former in the determiner, the latter in the NP. (Katz and Postal, 1964, 48–49.) *G–2b.* The fixed symbol △, which is generated in the categorial component by a rule of the type A → △ ("rewrite lexical category A as a dummy symbol") and positioned in a phrase-marker to mark that category for replacement by a complex symbol; a marker for a lexical category. (Chomsky, 1965, 122.)

E

Early rule. *G–2.* A rule which is not located close to the end of the set of ordered rules comprising a given component of the grammar; a rule of the phonology, like the main stress rule, which radically changes the form it acts on. Changes in the early rules of a grammar are made only by children. (King, 1969, 26, 79.) Compare LATE RULE.

Echo question. *G–1–2.* A special type of Wh-question, with rising intonation from the Wh-word on, which echoes a preceding statement or question and is normally followed by a repetition of that statement or question with falling intonation and greater emphasis on the questioned element, as in: "Huck catches fish" (statement); "Huck catches WHAT?" (echo); "Huck catches FISH" (repeat). (Katz and Postal, 1964, 112; Kuroda, 1969, 345.) See also QUESTION.

Economy. *G–2.* Generality and simplicity of analysis. The simpler and more general the analysis, the more 'economical' it is. (Rosenbaum, 1967a, 94, 103.) See also COST.

E-grammatical. *G–2.* Generated by the grammar of modern standard American English. (Langendoen, 1969, 3.) Compare E-UNGRAMMATICAL.

Either-conjoining. *G–1*. The introduction of a negative sentence into the framework *and . . . either,* as in: "Tom doesn't like fish, *and* Becky doesn't like it *either*." The appended sentence may contain a negative pre-verbal adverb, such as: "Tom doesn't like fish, *and* Becky *scarcely* likes it *either*." (Klima, 1964a, 261.) See also NEGATIVE PRE-VERBAL ADVERB.

Elementary transformation. *G–1*. A transformation which reorders, adds to, or deletes from a string of lexical categories, rather than a string of actually occurring morphemes or words, and whose effect is independent of the particular string to which it applies (Chomsky, 1961a, 132); a transformation which operates on only one phrase structure string, either permuting some of its elements—by permutation, rearrangement, inversion, or juxtaposition—or deleting them—by deletion—or replacing them with substitutes—by substitution—or adding other elements to the string—by adjunction or addition (Koutsoudas, 1966, 27). *G–2*. Any transformation, or any operation performed by a transformation: adjunction, substitution, or deletion. (Chomsky, 1965, 144; Jacobs and Rosenbaum, 1968, 26.) Also called **Singulary transformation** (Chomsky, 1961a, 136), **Single-base transformation** (Lyons, 1968, 265), **Simple transformation** (Chomsky, 1957, 114), **Simplex transformation** (Lees, 1965, xlvi), **Unary transformation** (Gleitman, 1965, 90). See also OPERATION, SINGULARY TRANSFORMATION.

Element, atomic. See ATOMIC ELEMENT.

Element, presentence. See PRESENTENCE ELEMENT.

Elicitation. *G–2*. A technique, usually introspective, for judging the acceptability and grammaticality of linguistic products. (Langendoen, 1969, 3.) See also INTROSPECTION.

Ellipsis. *G–2*. The deletion from the deep structure of one or more constituents that are understood in the context of the surface sentence, as in: "Huck put one end of the board on the raft and (Huck put) the other end (of the board) on the shore." The deleted constituent is said to have been **Elided.** (Langendoen, 1969, 15.) See also DELETION. Compare ELLIPTICAL TRANSFORMATION, ELLIPTIC TRANSFORMATION.

Elliptical transformation. *G–1*. An optional singulary transformation which deletes the agent from a passive transform, as when: "The fish had been cleaned *by Huck*" ⇒ "The fish had been cleaned. . . ." (Chomsky, 1957, 81, 89.) Compare ELLIPTIC TRANSFORMATION, ELLIPSIS.

Elliptic transformation. *G–1*. The optional singulary transformation which deletes everything following the finite verb in a sentence, as when: "Tom will *help free Jim*" ⇒ "Tom will." (Chomsky, 1962, 228.) Compare ELLIPSIS, ELLIPTICAL TRANSFORMATION.

Embedded sentence. *G–2*. An S under the ultimate domination of another S in the base; a recursive S, as in:

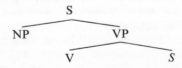

(Rosenbaum, 1967a, 65.) See also EMBEDDING.

Embedded sentences, grammar of. See GRAMMAR OF EMBEDDED SENTENCES.

Embedding. *G–1a.* A phrase-marker which is introduced into a matrix sentence by embedding rules. (Langacker, 1968, 110.) Also called **Constituent phrase-marker, Constituent sentence, Subordinate sentence, Embedded sentence, Underlying phrase-marker, Underlying sentence, Insert sentence, Insert.** Compare EMBEDDED SENTENCE. *G–1b.* The process which transforms a pair of phrase-markers into a single derived phrase-marker by inserting one of them, the constituent phrase-marker, into the other, the matrix phrase-marker. (Katz and Postal, 1964, 48.) Also called **Insertion, Nesting, Self-embedding.** Compare RECURSION. *G–2.* The substitution transformation by which one phrase-marker, the embedded phrase-marker, takes on the structure of the dummy symbol that it replaces in the matrix phrase-marker. (Koutsoudas, 1966, 309–310, 317–318.)

Embedding, multiple. See MULTIPLE EMBEDDING.

Embedding, self-. See SELF-EMBEDDING.

Embedding, sentential. See SENTENTIAL COMPLEMENTATION.

Embedding transformation. See EMBEDDING.

Emphasis transformation. See AFFIRMATION TRANSFORMATION.

Emphatic affirmative. *G–1.* The transformation which converts a string of the form $X+Y+E+Z$ (e.g., "Tom was emphasis-morpheme lost") into a string of the form $X+\acute{Y}+Z$ ("Tom *was* lost!"). The **Emphasis-morpheme**, or **E-morpheme**, is a signal for affirmative stress. (Lees, 1960a, 49.) See also AFFIRMATION TRANSFORMATION.

Empirical adequacy. *G–2.* Accountability of a linguistic description in the light of performative evidence. (Rosenbaum, 1967a, 10.) See also OBSERVATIONAL ADEQUACY.

Empty morpheme. *G–2.* A member of the closed class of morphemes which perform grammatical functions but are relatively empty of meaning, such as prepositions, conjunctions, articles, inflections, etc. (Langacker, 1968, 72–74.) Compare FULL MORPHEME.

Ending, inflectional. See INFLECTION.

Endocentric compound. *G–1.* A nominal compound which can occur in the same context where its head can occur alone, as in: "Tom cut his *(finger)nails*." (Lees, 1960a, 128–130.) Compare EXOCENTRIC COMPOUND.

Entry, dictionary. See DICTIONARY ENTRY.

Entry, lexical. See LEXICAL ENTRY.

Enumerate. *G–1–2.* To predict, or specify, or generate—as for a phrase structure rule to 'enumerate' a set of underlying strings. (Rosenbaum, 1967a, 9.) See also PREDICT, GENERATE.

Environment. *G–1–2.* The constituency of a syntactic structure on which a transformation is defined. If the necessary environment is not satisfied, the transformation will not apply. (Rosenbaum, 1967a, 41.) See also CONTEXT, DISTRIBUTION.

Environment, necessary. See NECESSARY CONDITION.

Epi-rule. *G–2.* A general rule which guides the application of other rules in deriving sentences from underlying constituent structures. (Lees, 1964b, xxxvi.) See also TRAFFIC RULE.

Equidistant. *G–2.* Having the same number of branches in the paths leading from one node in an embedded sentence to two other identical nodes in the main sentence, in which case the relationship of the 'equidistant' nodes to the embedded node is ambiguous. (Rosenbaum, 1967a, 18–19.) See also DISTANCE.

Equi-NP-deletion. *G–2.* The cyclic rule which deletes the subject noun phrase of an embedded complement containing *'s . . . ing* or *for . . . to* if that noun phrase is identical to one in the matrix sentence, as when: *"Huck's* knowing the truth didn't bother *Huck"* ⇒ "Knowing the truth didn't bother *Huck*." (Ross, 1967, 194–195.) See also IDENTICAL NOUN PHRASE DELETION.

Equivalence class. *G–1.* The class of sentences which are related by a meaning-preserving transformation and which have therefore received the same semantic interpretation, since every nonkernel sentence in the set automatically receives the semantic interpretation of the kernel. (Katz and Fodor, 1963, 515.) See also RELATED SENTENCES.

Equivalence, weak generative. See WEAK GENERATIVE EQUIVALENCE.

Equivalent grammars. *G–2.* Grammars that generate the same set of sentences—**Weakly equivalent grammars.** Equivalent grammars that also assign the same structural descriptions to their sentences are **Strongly equivalent grammars.** (Lyons, 1968, 226.) See also WEAK GENERATIVE EQUIVALENCE.

Erase. *G–2.* To delete from a string, as when a noun phrase in a main sentence—the 'erasing' noun phrase—'erases' an identical noun phrase in the complement sentence—the 'erased' noun phrase. For example, "Huck preferred (Huck) to steer." (Rosenbaum, 1967a, 49.) See also ERASURE PRINCIPLE, ERASED NOUN PHRASE, ERASING NOUN PHRASE, DELETION.

Erased noun phrase. *G–2.* The noun phrase, following the complementizer in a complement sentence, which is deleted, through identity erasure transformation, by an identical noun phrase—the 'erasing' noun phrase—in the main sentence. (Rosenbaum, 1967a, 18, 68.) Compare ERASING NOUN PHRASE. See also IDENTITY ERASURE TRANSFORMATION.

Erasing noun phrase. *G–2.* The noun phrase, in the main sentence of a complex sentence, which deletes, through identity erasure transformation, an identical noun phrase—the 'erased' noun phrase—following the complementizer in a complement sentence. (Rosenbaum, 1967a, 18, 49.) Compare ERASED NOUN PHRASE. See also IDENTITY ERASURE TRANSFORMATION.

Erasure. *G–2.* Deletion of a noun phrase, following a complementizer in a complement sentence, by an identical noun phrase in the main sentence. This operation is performed by the identity erasure transformation. (Rosenbaum, 1967a, 50.) See also ERASURE PRINCIPLE, IDENTITY ERASURE TRANSFORMATION.

Erasure, connection. See CONNECTION ERASURE.

Erasure, identity. See IDENTITY ERASURE.

Erasure principle. *G–2a.* The principle which prescribes that the subject of an embedded sentence is deleted, through erasure transformation, by the nearest identical noun phrase outside that embedding, as when: *"The girl* Wh-*the girl* arrived soon left" ⇒ *"The girl who* arrived soon left."* (Chomsky, 1965, 145; Chomsky, 1968, 48.) Compare LEFT-IDENTITY HYPOTHESIS. *G–2b.* The conditions which govern the application of the identity erasure transformation, namely that the sentence contain two identical noun phrases, one—the 'erased' noun phrase—dominated by an embedded S, and the other—the 'erasing' noun phrase—neither dominating nor dominated by the embedded S. (Rosenbaum, 1967a, 6, 8, 18.) See also IDENTITY ERASURE TRANSFORMATION.

Erasure transformation. See ERASURE PRINCIPLE.

Erasure transformation, identity. See IDENTITY ERASURE TRANSFORMATION.

Ergative. *G–2.* Causative, referring to the syntactic relation that holds between a sentence like "The raft moved" and "Huck moved the raft," in which *Huck* is the 'ergative' subject—agent or cause of the action. (Lyons, 1968, 352.) See also CAUSATIVE TRANSFORMATION, AGENTIVE.

E-ungrammatical. *G–2.* Not generated by the grammar of modern standard American English. (Langendoen, 1969, 3.) Compare E-GRAMMATICAL.

Evaluation procedure. *G–1.* The requirement which demands that a linguistic theory provide a practical procedure for evaluating two or more proposed grammars of the same corpus and for selecting the better grammar of the language. This is the weakest and only reasonable requirement of a linguistic theory—weaker than decision procedure and discovery procedure. (Chomsky, 1957, 51.) *G–2.* A simplicity measure—that is, a hypothesis about universal properties of language and the prerequisites for acquisition of language. (Chomsky, 1966a, 22.) Compare DECISION PROCEDURE, DISCOVERY PROCEDURE. See also SIMPLICITY METRIC.

Exception. *G–2a.* A lexical item which is listed in the lexicon as being in conflict with a general rule and requiring a separate statement. For example, *have,* in "A good time was *had* by all," is a marginal 'exception' to the categorization of *have* as a nonpassive verb. (Chomsky, 1965, 218.) *G–2b.* The specification by lexical categorization or lexical redundancy rule—that is, an exception rule or minus rule (King, 1969, 135)—that a formative is excepted from undergoing a general phonological rule of the grammar but demands a special statement. In lexical categorization, the distinctive feature [±rule] is, by convention, specified positively for all lexical items for all rules; exceptional items must then be specified as [−rule n] for a particular rule—thus, if they are not derived like Romance words: [−Romance]. Classes of exceptions can be handled by a redundancy rule, following the general rule, instead of individual lexical marking: A →−Rule n/X——Y. (Chomsky and Halle, 1968, 172–175.) *G–2c.* A counterexample to a syntactic principle. For example, the sentence "Huck promised Tom (for Huck) to build a fire" is an apparent exception to the erasure principle, since the erased noun phrase, (for) *Huck,* is not identical to the erasing noun phrase, *Tom.* (Rosenbaum, 1967a, 68.) See also COUNTEREXAMPLE, MINUS-NEXT-RULE CONVENTION.

Exception feature. *G–2.* A morphological feature in the dictionary which indicates unpredictable properties of morphemes, such as [−Romance] for lexical items that are not derived like Romance words. (Postal, 1968a, 133.) Also called **Morpheme feature, Morphological feature.** See also EXCEPTION, MINUS-NEXT-RULE CONVENTION.

Exception rule. See EXCEPTION.

Exchange rule. See ALPHA-SWITCHING RULE.

Exclusion, mutual. See MUTUAL EXCLUSION.

Exocentric compound. *G–1.* A compound which cannot occur in the same context as its head, such as: "Tom was a *greenhorn*"; *"Tom was a horn." (Lees, 1960a, 128–130.) Compare ENDOCENTRIC COMPOUND.

Expansion. *G–1–2.* The branching, or rewriting, of a constituent into two or more constituents. For example, NP can be expanded into DET,

N, S—an example of noun phrase complementation. (Rosenbaum, 1967a, 3, 33.) See also EXPANSION RULE.

Expansion rule. *G–1.* A grammatical rule which replaces a single symbol, with or without context, to the left of an arrow by one or more non-null symbols to the right of the arrow. Also called **One-many rule, Rewrite rule, Rewriting rule, Phrase structure rule, Constituent structure rule.** (Bach, 1964, 35.) See also PHRASE STRUCTURE RULE, REWRITING RULE, PHRASE-STRUCTURE EXPANSION RULE.

Expansion rule, phrase-structure. See PHRASE-STRUCTURE EXPANSION RULE.

Expense. See COST.

Expensive. *G–2.* Leading to greater complexity; uneconomical to the analysis; costly to the theory. For example, it is more 'expensive' to refer to complementizers separately than to refer to them together. (Rosenbaum, 1967a, 26.) See also COST.

Explain. *G–1–2.* To account for the grammatical properties of a sentence through a syntactic formulation or derivation. (Rosenbaum, 1967a, 60, 74.) See also EXPLANATORY ADEQUACY.

Explanation. *G–1–2.* An accounting for the grammatical properties of a sentence in a syntactic formulation or derivation. (Rosenbaum, 1967a, 75.) See also EXPLANATORY ADEQUACY.

Explanatory adequacy. *G–1–2.* The level of adequacy achieved by a universal linguistic theory which provides an internally justified basis for selecting the descriptively adequate grammar of each language. (Chomsky, 1964, 63; Chomsky, 1965, 25, 27, 36, 38; Chomsky, 1968, 13, 22, 30.) See also ADEQUACY. Compare DESCRIPTIVE ADEQUACY, OBSERVATIONAL ADEQUACY, EMPIRICAL ADEQUACY.

Expletive. *G–2S.* The pro-form *it,* which replaces a 'that'-clause that has been copied in the subject position, as when: "(That a fly is in Tom's soup) is true that a fly is in Tom's soup" ⇒ "*It* is true that a fly is in Tom's soup"; the pro-form *there,* which replaces a locative actant that has been copied in subject position, as when: "(In Tom's soup) is (with) a fly is in Tom's soup" ⇒ "*There* is a fly in Tom's soup." (Fillmore, 1966, 370.) Also called **Impersonal subject.** See also PRONOUN 'IT'.

External condition of adequacy. *G–1.* The condition on grammars that the sentences generated by them must be acceptable to one or more native or fluent speakers. (Chomsky, 1957, 49–50.) See also ACCEPTABILITY, EMPIRICAL ADEQUACY, JUSTIFICATION OF A GRAMMAR.

Extrapose. *G–2.* To move a complement sentence from sentence-initial position to sentence-final position by extraposition transformation. Fo. example, the complement sentence *that Tom returned* can be 'extraposed' from initial position to final position in the sentence "It *that Tom returned* pleased Huck": "It pleased Huck *that Tom returned*." (Rosenbaum, 1967a, 13, 124.) See also EXTRAPOSITION.

Extraposition. *G–2.* The transformational process which moves the complement sentence—a sentence with complementizer—or unreduced relative clause to the end of the main sentence, optionally replacing the complemented subject noun with *it,* as when: "*That he stole the* raft is certain" ⇒ "*It* is certain *that he stole the raft*"; "The man *who stole the raft* escaped" ⇒ "The man escaped *who stole the raft*." (Ross, 1966, 290–291; Rosenbaum, 1967c, 327; Jacobs, 1968, 51; Jacobs and Rosenbaum, 1968, 177; Langendoen, 1969, 25, 54, 65.) Also called **'It'-inversion**

(Lees, 1961, 314) and **Clause transportation** (Langacker, 1969, 183). See also EXTRAPOSITION TRANSFORMATION.

Extraposition transformation. *G–2*. The transformation which transports a complement sentence from initial position, following the pronoun *it,* to final position in a string, as when: "It *that Tom returned* pleased Huck" ⇒ "It pleased Huck *that Tom returned.*" (Rosenbaum, 1967a, 6, 13.) See also EXTRAPOSITION.

F

Factitive. *G–2S*. The case of the result of the action or state expressed in the verb. (Fillmore, 1968, 25.) See also CASE.

Factive. *G–2*. A construction which is an underlying complement of the noun *fact*, as in: "I believe (the fact) *that spring is late*"; "It is a fact *that spring is late*"; "*That spring is late* is a fact"; "The fact is *that spring is late*"; etc. (Katz and Postal, 1964, 122, 142.) See also FACTIVE NOMINAL.

Factive nominal. *G–1*. A 'that'-clause assertion or question-word clause which answers a question, as in: "Tom knew *that he was lost*"; "Tom knew *what kind of trouble he was in.*" (Lees, 1960a, 59.) See also FACTIVE.

Family of transformations. *G–1–2*. An ordered set of operations which accomplish a complete structural change (Lees, 1960a, 57); a transformation—any transformation, even if it contains only a single rule (Katz and Postal, 1964, 153). See also TRANSFORMATION, OPERATION.

Feature. *G–2*. A syntactic, semantic, or phonological property of lexical items, which are positively or negatively specified for that property (Lyons, 1968, 332); a marker on a lexical item which determines its co-occurrence with other lexical items and restricts the transformations that can apply to it (Rosenbaum, 1967a, 81). See also DISTINCTIVE FEATURE, SEMANTIC FEATURE.

Feature analysis. *G–2*. The assignment of inherent distinctive features— syntactic, semantic, and phonological—to morphemes in the lexicon. (Jacobs and Rosenbaum, 1968, 83.)

Feature, category. See CATEGORY FEATURE.

Feature, classificatory. See CLASSIFICATORY FEATURE.

Feature cluster. *G–2*. A set of plus or minus feature specifications which can be realized morphophonemically as a particular morpheme. (Rosenbaum, 1967a, 29.) See also MORPHEME, FORMATIVE.

Feature coefficient. *G–2*. The value assigned to a lexical or phonological feature by the symbols + (plus), − (minus), or α (alpha), as in: [+ nasal], [− nasal], [α nasal] (= plus or minus nasal). (Rosenbaum, 1967a, 29; Chomsky and Halle, 1968, 351.) See also FEATURE.

Feature, complementizing. See COMPLEMENTIZING FEATURE.

Feature, contextual. See CONTEXTUAL FEATURE.

Feature, cross-classifying. See CROSS-CLASSIFYING FEATURE.

Feature, diacritic. See DIACRITIC FEATURE.

Feature, distinctive. See DISTINCTIVE FEATURE.

Feature, exception. See EXCEPTION FEATURE.

Feature, frame. See CASE FRAME.

Feature, general. See GENERAL FEATURE.

Feature, hierarchic semantic. See HIERARCHIC SEMANTIC FEATURE.

Feature hierarchy, binary. See BINARY FEATURE HIERARCHY.

Feature, inherent. See INHERENT FEATURE.

Feature, Jakobsonian distinctive. See JAKOBSONIAN DISTINCTIVE FEATURE.

Feature, major class. See MAJOR CLASS FEATURE.

Feature, manner. See MANNER FEATURE.

Feature, morpheme. See MORPHEME FEATURE.

Feature, morphological. See MORPHOLOGICAL FEATURE.

Feature, nonoral-articulator. See NONORAL-ARTICULATOR FEATURE.

Feature notation. *G–2a*. The interpretation of systematic phonemic segments as phonological feature specifications rather than as autonomous phonemic entities. (Chomsky, 1965, 45.) *G–2b*. The interpretation of certain higher-level syntactic markers in the base structure, such as Wh or manner adverbial, as syntactic feature specifications assigned to S rather than as syntactic categories or formatives, in order to neutralize the arbitrariness of their ordering in respect to other constituents. The feature notation is then correctly positioned and assigned to a lower-level constituent by attachment transformation. (Kuroda, 1969, 349–350.) See also FEATURE SPECIFICATION.

Feature, oral-articulator. See ORAL-ARTICULATOR FEATURE.

Feature, phonemic. See PHONEMIC FEATURE.

Feature, phonetic. See PHONETIC FEATURE.

Feature, phonological distinctive. See PHONOLOGICAL DISTINCTIVE FEATURE.

Feature, pronominal. See PRONOMINAL FEATURE.

Feature, prosodic. See PROSODIC FEATURE.

Feature, qualifying. See QUALIFYING FEATURE.

Feature, release. See RELEASE FEATURE.

Feature, selectional. See SELECTIONAL FEATURE.

Feature, semantic. See SEMANTIC FEATURE.

Feature specification. *G–2*. A specification of the plus or minus value of a syntactic, semantic, or phonological feature. (Rosenbaum, 1967a, 15, 29.) See also FEATURE NOTATION.

Feature, strict subcategorization. See STRICT SUBCATEGORIZATION FEATURE.

Feature, strict subclassificational. See STRICT SUBCATEGORIZATION MARKER.

Feature, syntactic. See SYNTACTIC FEATURE.

Feature system. *G–2*. A set of feature specifications which distinguish a unique set of morphemes, such as the system of complementizing features which distinguish the unique set of complementizing morphemes. (Rosenbaum, 1967a, 27.)

Feeding order. *G–2*. An ordering of two rules such that the output of rule A, the 'feeding' rule, is applicable to rule B, to which rule A has a 'feeding' relationship. Feeding order is maximized, diachronically. (Kiparsky, 1968, 196–197; King, 1969, 175.) Compare BLEEDING ORDER.

Feeding relationship. See FEEDING ORDER.

Feeding rule. See FEEDING ORDER.

Field property. *G–2*. A semantic attribute of morphemes that is outside the lexicon but is characterized in the semantic component of a grammar. Violation of field properties results in sentences that are false (e.g., *"The fly has a goiter"), senseless (e.g., *"The wing has a fly"), or otherwise deviant. (Chomsky, 1965, 160–161.)

Filter. *G–2a.* A transformation—that is, a rule which interprets objects derived by the phrase structure rules, marks them as well-formed or ill-formed, and rejects the ill-formed structures. (Rosenbaum, 1967a, 25.) *G–2b.* For a transformation to reject an ill-formed sentence structure—for it to filter out or block that structure. (Rosenbaum, 1967a, 25.) See also BLOCK.

Filtering. *G–2.* The function performed by transformational rules, as filters, of blocking or filtering out the infinitely many ill-formed base phrase-markers and allowing only well-formed phrase-markers to qualify as deep structures. (Katz, 1966, 148; Postal, 1968a, 205.) Filtering applies only to the embedding process in generalized phrase-markers. (Chomsky, 1965, 138–139; Kuroda, 1969, 339–341.) Transformations that serve a filtering function are called **Filter transformations.** (Closs, 1965, 408.) See also BLOCKING.

Filter transformation. See FILTERING.

Final derived phrase-marker. *G–2.* The last phrase-marker derived by the final transformational rule, viz., the superficial phrase-marker, or surface structure. (Postal, 1964c, 25.) See also SUPERFICIAL PHRASE-MARKER, SUPERFICIAL STRUCTURE, SURFACE STRUCTURE. Compare UNDERLYING PHRASE STRUCTURE, UNDERLYING STRUCTURE, DEEP STRUCTURE.

Finite. *G–1–2.* Limited; terminated, as in a finite string. For example, the number of symbols in the grammar is 'finite,' but the number of strings in the language is 'infinite.' (Bach, 1964, 163.) Compare INFINITE.

Finite verb. *G–1.* The verb with the finite verbal affix—the concord or tense morpheme; the leftmost of the verbal auxiliaries. (Lees, 1960a, 6.) See also CONCORD.

Finite verbal affix. See FINITE VERB.

First-generation transformational grammar. *G–1.* A term used by Jacobs (1968, 62) to describe the generative theory found in or based on Chomsky's *Syntactic Structures* (1957), which furnished the major model of transformational grammar from that date until 1962 for phonology (Halle), 1963 for semantics (Katz and Fodor), and 1964 for syntax (Katz and Postal). These refinements contributed to the major statement of second-generation transformational grammar, Chomsky's *Aspects of the Theory of Syntax* (1965). First-generation transformational grammar (*G–1*) was characterized by 1) the lack of a semantic component, 2) transformations that changed meaning, 3) a basically structural approach to phonology and morphology, 4) no separation of deep and surface structure, 5) independent formation of matrix and constituent sentences, 6) generalized embedding transformations, 7) subcategorization by rewrite rules, 8) precise statements of environmental conditions, 9) inability to handle cross-classification, 10) assignment of recursion to the transformational rules, and 11) an overconcern with formalism. (Jacobs, 1968, 62; Reibel and Schane, 1969, viii–ix.) Compare SECOND-GENERATION TRANSFORMATIONAL GRAMMAR, SEMANTIC-BASED TRANSFORMATIONAL GRAMMAR.

First lexical pass. *G–2.* The introduction of lexical items into deep structures before transformations, as opposed to the 'second lexical pass,' which occurs after the application of all transformations and replaces segments introduced by transformation and, possibly, also certain items from the first lexical pass. (Jacobs and Rosenbaum, 1968, 84.) Compare SECOND LEXICAL PASS.

Flat. *G–1*. The distinctive feature which is positively specified for sounds that are articulated with a secondary narrowing at the periphery of the oral cavity, such as rounded vowels. (Halle, 1959, 326.)

Flip-flop transformation. See AUXILIARY TRANSFORMATION.

Formal. See FORMAL THEORY.

Formal derivation. *G–2*. A sequence of strings of labeled bracketings which describe and explain the generation of a sentence from its underlying structure—its deep structure, or base—through its various derived structures, to its superficial structure, or surface structure. (Rosenbaum, 1967a, 75–76.) See also DERIVATION.

Formalize. *G–2*. To represent a syntactic structure either as a branching diagram, or tree, or as a labeled bracketing, or formulation. For example, the sentence "Huck was lost" can be formalized broadly either as

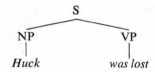

or as [[Huck]₍NP₎ [was lost]₍VP₎]₍S₎. (Rosenbaum, 1967a, 12, 37.) See also FORMULATION.

Formal linguistics. See FORMAL THEORY.

Formal theory. *G–1*. A theory which is technically developed, precisely constructed, rigorously stated, applied strictly to linguistic material, based on form rather than meaning or use, mechanical (Kuroda, 1968, 266), objective, and tightly formulated (i.e., containing no ad hoc adjustments). A formal theory, or formalized theory, is developed in formal linguistics. (Chomsky, 1957, 5, 93–94, 100–101, 103.) See also LINGUISTIC THEORY.

Formal universal. *G–2*. A specification of the kinds of grammatical rules that the linguistic theory permits, along with their ordering and their domains, such as the formal universal that some of the syntactic rules must be transformational. (Katz and Postal, 1964, 160; Chomsky, 1965, 29–30; Chomsky and Halle, 1968, 4.) Compare SUBSTANTIVE UNIVERSAL.

Formant. *G–2*. An underlying element of the deep structure which triggers the application of an associated transformation and may be realized as a morpheme in the surface structure, such as: IMP (Imperative), NEG (Negative). (Klima and Bellugi-Klima, 1966, 450–454.) Also called SCOPE MARKER, PRESENTENCE ELEMENT.

Formation, agentive. See AGENTIVE FORMATION.

Formation, complex sentence. See COMPLEX SENTENCE FORMATION.

Formation rule. See PHRASE STRUCTURE RULE.

Formation, rule of. See PHRASE STRUCTURE RULE.

Formative. *G–2*. A minimal syntactic element functioning in a well-formed string (Chomsky, 1964, 85); a minimal terminal symbol in the surface syntactic string which is originally provided by the lexicon with specifications, which is inputted to the phonological component, and which is modified by readjustment rules—as opposed to a morpheme, which is a terminal element of a deep syntactic structure (Postal, 1968a, 156; Chomsky and Halle, 1968, 7, 164). There are two types of formatives. Grammatical formatives, such as class markers, junctures, and boundaries, are represented by one symbol each. Lexical formatives are represented as a string of symbols, each with a set of inherent and transformational features. (Katz and Postal, 1964, 1; Chomsky, 1965, 65, 181, 233.) See also GRAMMATICAL FORMATIVE, LEXICAL FORMATIVE. Compare MORPHEME.

Formative, grammatical. See GRAMMATICAL FORMATIVE.

Formative, lexical. See LEXICAL FORMATIVE.

Formula, instruction. See INSTRUCTION FORMULA.

Formulation. *G–2.* A formalization of a syntactic structure as a string of labeled bracketings, as in: [[Huck]$_{NP}$ [was lost]$_{VP}$]$_S$. (Rosenbaum, 1967a, 75–76.) See also FORMALIZE.

For-to complementizer. *G–2.* The pair of mutually inclusive complementizing morphemes *for* and *to*, which mark one type of predicate complementation, as in: "Huck hoped *for* Tom *to* return"; "Huck wanted (*for*) Tom *to* return." (Rosenbaum, 1967a, 24, 26.) See also COMPLEMENTIZER.

Forward pronominalization. *G–2.* The obligatory replacement of the second of two identical noun phrases in the same sentence by an appropriate pronoun, as in: "While *Huck* was sleeping, *Huck* dreamed" ⇒ "While Huck was sleeping, *he* dreamed." (Ross, 1967, 188.) Also called **Forwards pronominalization.** (Langendoen, 1969, 80.) Compare BACKWARDS PRONOMINALIZATION.

Frame, case. See CASE FRAME.

Frame feature. See CASE FRAME.

Free deletability. *G–2.* The property associated with the dummy terminal symbol, or PRO, of a major category—noun, verb, etc.—whereby the dummy can be deleted from an underlying string in which it is not a repetition, as in: "Huck was whittling (Something)." (Katz and Postal, 1964, 80–81.) See also DUMMY SYMBOL, RECOVERABILITY.

Free morpheme. *G–1–2.* A morpheme that can stand alone as an independent word, such as *color, green, idea, sleep,* etc. (Langacker, 1968, 73.) Compare BOUND MORPHEME.

Free variation. *G–2a.* The condition which holds among the stylistic variants resulting from the operation of an optional singulary transformation on a single phrase-marker, as in: "Huck smokes?"; "Does Huck smoke?"; "Huck smokes, doesn't he?"; etc. (Katz and Postal, 1964, 113.) *G-2b.* Noncontrast between utterances which are assigned by phonological rules to the same systematic phonological representations. (Postal, 1968a, 14.) Compare COMPLEMENTARY DISTRIBUTION.

Fricative. *G–1.* An occlusive consonant: English [f], [v], [θ], [ð], [s], [z], [š], [ž], [h]. (Halle, 1959, 326.) *G-2.* A 'true' consonant—consonantal, nonvocalic, nonsonorant or obstruent—which is also a continuant. True consonants of English are those listed in *G-1*, minus [h]. (Chomsky and Halle, 1968, 302.) See also TRUE CONSONANT, CONTINUANT.

Full morpheme. *G–2.* A member of the large, open class of content morphemes which have some degree of independent meaning—a noun, verb, adjective, or adverb base. Most full morphemes are 'free.' (Langacker, 1968, 72–73.) Compare EMPTY MORPHEME. See also FREE MORPHEME.

Function, *G–1–2.* The grammatical role of a syntactic category. (Chomsky, 1966a, 56–58.) See also GRAMMATICAL FUNCTION.

Functional information. *G–2.* The relational information, vital to semantic interpretation, which is furnished by the organization of higher- and lower-level nodes in deep structures. For example, the relation [NP,S] furnishes the functional information "noun phrase 'subject' of the sentence." (Jacobs and Rosenbaum, 1968, 71.) See also GRAMMATICAL FUNCTION.

Function, grammatical. See GRAMMATICAL FUNCTION.

G

Gap, accidental. See ACCIDENTAL GAP.

General condition. *G–2.* A universal condition in the grammatical theory, such as the identity condition, which need not be stated in a particular grammar. (Chomsky, 1965, 225.) See also CONDITION OF GENERALITY.

General feature. *G–2.* Either of the two phonological distinctive features [consonantal] or [vocalic], which are the basis for the universal division of systematic phonemes into four general classes: true consonants, [+consonantal] [−vocalic]; vowels, [−consonantal] [+vocalic]; glides, [−consonantal] [−vocalic]; and liquids (resonants), [+consonantal] [+vocalic]. The features [obstruent] and [syllabicity] have also been employed as 'general features,' though they are redundant for the classification of English segments. (Harms, 1968, 22–26.) Also called **Major class feature,** which includes [sonorant]. (Chomsky and Halle, 1968, 299.) See also MAJOR CLASS FEATURE.

Generality. *G–2a.* The degree of application of a phonological rule to larger classes, more natural classes, or more members of a natural class. The more 'general' the rule, the lower the number of features, the broader the application, and the greater its 'generality.' (King, 1969, 58–60.) *G–2b.* The simplicity, economy, universality, and explanatory power of a linguistic rule, though not necessarily a phonological rule. The greater the generality of a rule, the more interesting it is to the theory. (Rosenbaum, 1967a, 10, 104–105.) A rule with the characteristics of generality is called a **Generalization.** (Chomsky, 1965, 42.) See also SIMPLICITY METRIC.

Generality, condition of. See CONDITION OF GENERALITY.

Generalization. *G–2.* Simplification of a set of distinct rules into a single rule which need be stated only once in the grammar, thereby achieving economy, universality, and explanatory power; the single rule which is a result of such simplification. For example, the optional complementizer deletion rule is a generalization which captures two separate cases of deletion, those of POSS and of *for.* (Rosenbaum, 1967a, 46, 107.) Compare SIMPLIFICATION.

Generalize. *G–2.* To state a rule only once in the grammar instead of once for each case to which it applies, thereby gaining simplicity, economy, universality, and explanatory power. (Rosenbaum, 1967a, 21, 46, 98.) See also COLLAPSE.

Generalized archiphoneme. See ARCHIPHONEME.

Generalized phrase-marker. *G–2*. The deep structure output of the base component of a second-generation transformational grammar, and the input to the semantic component and the transformational component, which contains only singulary transformations and which generates derived phrase-markers. The generalized phrase-marker reflects the assumption by the base component of the embedding functions of the earlier generalized transformations. The symbol S is allowed to appear on the right of certain branching rules, and the transformational rules then apply cyclically—preserving their order—to the occurrences of S, provided that certain compatibility conditions exist. The generalized phrase-marker terminates in a **Generalized string,** or **G-string.** (Katz and Postal, 1964, 57, 67, 172; Chomsky, 1965, 135; Chomsky, 1966a, 63.) Compare DERIVED PHRASE-MARKER. See also PHRASE-MARKER.

Generalized transformation. *G–1*. An optional embedding transformation which operates on two underlying strings at once, inserting one of them, the constituent sentence, into a designated position in the other, the matrix sentence. Generalized transformations are unordered in respect to each other and to singulary transformations, and they provide the basic recursive power of a first-generation transformational grammar. The product of a generalized transformation is a **Derived phrase-marker,** or **Generalized transform,** or **Complex sentence.** (Chomsky, 1961a, 134; Katz and Postal, 1964, 12; Chomsky, 1965, 132–133; Chomsky, 1966a, 60–65.) In *G–2*, generalized transformations have been eliminated in favor of the introduction of S into the base by rewriting rules. (Chomsky, 1966a, 65.) Also called **Embedding transformation, Complex transformation, Double-base transformation, Two-string transformation, Binary transformation, Insertion transformation.** Compare SINGULARY TRANSFORMATION, ELEMENTARY TRANSFORMATION.

General linguistics. *G–2*. The branch of linguistics which attempts to develop a theory of natural language—a system of hypotheses about the essential characteristics of any human language. (Chomsky and Halle, 1968, 4.) See also LINGUISTICS.

Generatable. See GENERATE.

Generate. *G–1–2*. To characterize—or predict, or specify, or enumerate, or describe—the infinite set of potential deep structures of a language (Chomsky, 1968, 26); to enumerate underlying structures by phrase structure rules and to specify derived structures by transformational rules; to yield, or produce (Rosenbaum, 1967a, 4, 36–37, 40, 60, 75, 82). 'Generation' of 'generatable' structures (Lees, 1960a, 140) is not production—that is, it is neutral as between speaker and hearer. (Postal, 1964a, 90.) Compare DERIVE. See also PREDICT.

Generate, weakly. See WEAK GENERATIVE EQUIVALENCE.

Generation. *G–1–2*. The specification or enumeration of underlying structures by phrase structure rules, and of derived structures by transformational rules. (Rosenbaum, 1967a, 1, 5). See also DERIVATION.

Generative capacity, strong. See STRONG GENERATIVE CAPACITY.

Generative capacity, weak. See WEAK GENERATIVE CAPACITY.

Generative equivalence, weak. See WEAK GENERATIVE EQUIVALENCE.

Generative grammar. *G–1.* A grammar which specifies precisely and explicitly the well-formedness of utterances; a transformational model of the type described in *Syntactic Structures,* 1957 (Chomsky, 1961b, 177, 182–183); a system of explicit rules that assign to each utterance a structural description which represents the utterance on each of the linguistic levels and determines whether it is properly formed or deviant (Chomsky, 1961b, 174–175); a grammar which generates—describes, defines, characterizes, specifies, enumerates, or predicts—all of and only the well-formed sentences of the language: a sentence-generating grammar (Halle, 1962, 334); a theory which attempts to specify formal linguistic universals (Chomsky, 1964, 57). *G–2.* The system of rules which express the native speaker's internalized knowledge of his language and his tacit competence or intuition that underlies his perceptual and productive performance (Chomsky, 1965, 8–9, 42; Chomsky, 1966c, 75); a hypothesis as to how a speaker-hearer interprets utterances (Chomsky, 1966c, 75); a system of rules which determine deep and surface structures, establish the relation between them, and provide phonetic interpretations of them (Chomsky, 1966b, 10); a formal or explicit grammar (Lyons, 1968, 155–157); a system of rules relating signals to semantic interpretations (Chomsky, 1966a, 12). See also TRANSFORMATIONAL GRAMMAR, TRANSFORMATIONAL GENERATIVE GRAMMAR, GENERATIVE-TRANSFORMATIONAL GRAMMAR.

Generative grammar, transformational. See TRANSFORMATIONAL GENERATIVE GRAMMAR.

Generative phonology. *G–2.* The theory of generative grammar which explains the native speaker's competence, in respect to the sounds of his language, by means of phonological generalizations; the study of the components of a generative grammar which contribute to the phonetic representations of the utterances of a language: the lexicon, the morpheme structure rules, and the phonological rules. The articulatory distinctive feature is the fundamental unit of generative phonology, along with boundary phenomena and syntactic bracketing. (Harms, 1968, 1, 5, 12.) See also SYSTEMATIC PHONEMICS.

Generative-transformational grammar. *G–2a.* A grammar that is both generative—i.e., supplies structural descriptions for its grammatical outputs—and transformational—i.e., relates deep structures to surface structures by means of transformations. (Langendoen, 1969, 24.) *G–2b.* The linguistic theory which postulates a grammatical constituency, rather than the traditional logical constituency, for sentences, provides a formal apparatus to allow recursive specification of well-formed sentences, and has as its primary goal the explanation or justification, rather than simply the description, of sentences. (Rosenbaum, 1967a, 109, 113.) Also called **Transformational generative grammar, Generative grammar, Transformational grammar.** Compare NONGENERATIVE TRANSFORMATIONAL GRAMMAR.

Generic determiner. *G–1.* The nonanaphoric use of the article *the* before a count noun with a singular number affix, as in: *"The* human is a biped." The noun in such a frame is a **Generic noun,** and the sentence which contains such a noun is a **Generic sentence.** (Smith, 1964, 263.) See also DETERMINER, ARTICLE.

Generic noun. See GENERIC DETERMINER.

Generic sentence. See GENERIC DETERMINER.

Genitive. *G–1.* The relation which holds, in most instances, between the subject and object of the middle verb *have,* as in: *"Huck has a pipe"* ⇒ "Huck's pipe. . . ." (Lees, 1960a, 131.) All genitives are transformational in origin. (Lees and Klima, 1963, 152.) *G–2.* The syntactic marker [genitive], which is negatively specified for all nouns in the deep structure but positively specified for some nouns by transformation. (Postal, 1966, 214.) *G–2S.* The case modification which is usually involved in nominalization transformation. (Fillmore, 1968, 51.) See also GENITIVE TRANSFORMATION, POSSESSIVE.

Genitive periphrasis. *G–1.* A phrasal genitive, such as "the owner *of the raft,"* as opposed to an inflectional genitive, such as "the *raft's* owner." (Lees, 1960a, 67, 104.) Compare POSSESSIVE GENITIVE.

Genitive, possessive. See POSSESSIVE GENITIVE.

Genitive transformation. *G–1–2a.* The set of grammatical rules which generate genitive transforms of the type "N *that Tom has"* or "N *of Tom"* or *"Tom's* N." A genitive transform usually originates in an underlying sentence with *have* (e.g., "Tom *has* a knife"). This sentence is embedded as a relative clause after a noun which is identical to the one following *have* (e.g., "The knife *which Tom has* fell apart"). The relative clause is then optionally transformed into an *of*-phrase (e.g., "The knife *of Tom* fell apart") or reduced to a genitive noun (*"Tom's"*) and moved into the head noun phrase to replace the definite article (e.g., *"Tom's* knife fell apart"). (Lees and Klima, 1963, 152; Jacobs and Rosenbaum, 1968, 212, 231–232.) *G–1–2b.* The set of transformational rules which transform an embedded sentence into a genitive of the type "N *which is Tom's"* or "N *of Tom's"* or *"Tom's* N." A genitive originates in an embedded sentence with *have* and a [+genitive] noun phrase, as in: "The knife (*Tom+G has a knife*) fell apart." This embedding is rearranged as a sentence with the original object as a definite subject, *have* is replaced by *be,* and the original subject appears as a genitive phrase, as in: "The knife (*the knife is Tom's*) fell apart." The embedding is then relativized, as in: "The knife (*which is Tom's*) fell apart"; and *which is* is optionally replaced by *of,* as in: "The knife (*of Tom's*) fell apart." For a prenominal genitive, *of* is deleted, and the genitive phrase is moved to the left of the head noun to replace the definite article, as in: *"Tom's* knife fell apart." Genitive nominals of the type *"Huck's wrecking the raft . . ."* and *"Huck's wrecking of the raft . . ."* derive by way of gerundive and factive nominalization rather than by relativization. (Katz and Postal, 1964, 138, 142; Smith, 1964, 258.)

Genuine counterexample. See COUNTEREXAMPLE.

Gerund. *G–1–2.* A nominal, derived transformationally from a verb by means of the verbal suffix *-ing*—the gerund *-ing* (Lees, 1960a, 67)—as when: "Huck *steered* the raft skillfully" ⇒ "Huck's skillful *steering* of the raft." (Lakoff and Peters, 1966, 132.) Compare GERUNDIVE NOMINAL, ACTION NOMINAL.

Gerundive adjective. *G–1.* An adjective derived transformationally from a verb by means of the verbal suffix *-ing,* as when: "The raft *floated* aimlessly" ⇒ "The aimlessly *floating* raft . . ."; thus, also, the source of one type of compound: *wáshing machine, stéering wheel.* (Lees, 1960a, 96, 137.) Compare GERUND, GERUNDIVE NOMINAL.

Gerundive complementizer. *G–2.* The sequence of suffixes *'s . . . ing,* which, when introduced into the noun node of a noun phrase subject, form a gerundive complement, as when: "It (Becky had refused) surprised Tom" ⇒ "(It) Becky's having refused surprised Tom." That is, the subject of the embedding takes the possessive affix, and the first verb of the embedding takes the progressive affix. The *it* is then removed by the 'it' deletion rule. (Jacobs, 1969, 51.) Also called **POSS-ing complementizer.**

Gerundive nominal. *G–1.* A noun phrase which results from the nominalization of a sentence structure as an expression of fact, as when: "Huck rescued Tom immediately" ⇒ "Huck's rescuing Tom immediately"; "Huck's having rescued Tom immediately." The gerundive nominal can accept an auxiliary verb, but it does not permit the adjectivalization of a following adverb or the use of a preposition before a noun phrase object, as in: *"Huck's *immediate* rescuing Tom"; *"Huck's having rescued *of* Tom." (Lees, 1960a, 71–73.) Compare ACTION NOMINAL, INFINITIVE NOMINAL.

Glide. *G–1.* A member of the natural class defined by the distinctive feature specifications [−consonantal], [−vocalic]: /w/, /y/, /h/. (Halle, 1959, 327.) *G–2.* A member of the natural class defined by the distinctive feature specifications [+sonorant], [−consonantal], [−vocalic]: /w/, /y/, /h/, /ʔ/. (Chomsky and Halle, 1968, 68, 303.) Also called **Semi-vowel.** See also DIPHTHONG.

Global. *G–2.* Affecting an entire string throughout the course of its derivation. (Chomsky, 1965, 12.) See also GLOBAL OPERATION, GLOBAL CONSTRAINT.

Global condition. See GLOBAL CONSTRAINT.

Global constraint. *G–2.* One of the contextual restrictions, supplied by a transformational rule, that an entire deep structure must meet in order to survive the filtering process. (Chomsky, 1966a, 67.) Also called **Global condition.** (Chomsky and Halle, 1968, 257, 259.) See also GLOBAL OPERATION.

Global operation. *G–2.* An operation, such as a transformation, which affects an entire string throughout the course of its derivation. (Chomsky, 1966a, 42.) See also GLOBAL CONSTRAINT.

Glottal stop. *G–2.* The glide [ʔ], which has the following distinctive feature specifications: [+sonorant], [−consonantal], [−vocalic]. (Chomsky and Halle, 1968, 303.) See also GLIDE.

Grammar. *G–1.* A hypothesis about the rules of sentence formation which underlie a collection of data, to be judged by its success in organizing and explaining and making generalizations about the data, and in accommodating new data (Chomsky, 1961b, 173); a theory of the sentences of a language; a device which enumerates the sentences of a language; a definition of the notion 'sentence of the language' (Chomsky, 1962, 223, 240–241, 245; Chomsky, 1961b, 173; Chomsky, 1961a, 120–121); a theory of sentencehood (Lees, 1960b, 150); a description of the structure of every sentence of a language (Fodor and Katz, 1964, 153); a finite set of rules which generate an infinite number of well-formed sentences of a language (Koutsoudas, 1966, 4); a description of the syntax, morphology, and phonology of a language (Katz and Fodor, 1963, 481). *G–2* The system of rules that account for the intuition of the native speaker (King, 1969, 32–33); the theory that concerns the mechanisms of sentence construction in language and the sound-meaning relation in a given language (Chomsky, 1964, 7); a description of the ideal speaker-hearer's linguistic competence

(Chomsky, 1965, 4); a theory of linguistic intuition (Chomsky, 1965, 19); a theory of language (Chomsky, 1965, 24) or of a particular language (Chomsky, 1966b, 6); a finite system that generates an infinite number of sentences (Postal, 1968b, 272); a systematic theory of linguistic structure (Katz and Postal, 1964, 4); one of the two major parts—syntax and phonology, as opposed to semantics—of a linguistic description (Katz and Postal, 1964, 4); the linguist's formal, explicit, written account of a speaker's competence (King, 1969, 14); a theory of linguistic competence (Chomsky and Halle, 1968, 372). *G–2S.* A theory of linguistic competence, as opposed to linguistics, the study of universal grammar. (Kiparsky, 1968, 188.) *Related terms:* A specialist in the study of grammar is most often referred to as a **Grammarian** (Chomsky, 1966a, 10), and a specialist in transformational grammar a **Transformational grammarian,** or **T-grammarian** (Lees, 1964b, xxxiii). A sentence that is correctly generated by the grammar is termed **Grammatical** (Rosenbaum, 1967a, 14), and one that is incorrectly generated, or not generated at all, is called **Ungrammatical** (Lees, 1960a, 56). The well-formedness of a sentence at various stages of its derivation is known as its **Grammaticality** (Rosenbaum, 1967a, 67) or its **Grammaticalness** (Chomsky, 1957, 13), and the ill-formedness its **Ungrammaticality** (Rosenbaum, 1967a, 61) or **Ungrammaticalness** (Lees, 1964b, xxxviii). See also TRANSFORMATIONAL GRAMMAR. Compare LINGUISTIC DESCRIPTION.

Grammar, analytic. See ANALYTIC GRAMMAR.

Grammar, case. See CASE GRAMMAR.

Grammar, competence-model. See COMPETENCE.

Grammar, constituent-structure. See CONSTITUENT-STRUCTURE GRAMMAR.

Grammar, descriptive. See DESCRIPTIVE GRAMMAR.

Grammar, first-generation transformational. See FIRST-GENERATION TRANSFORMATIONAL GRAMMAR.

Grammar, generative. See GENERATIVE GRAMMAR.

Grammar, generative-transformational. See GENERATIVE-TRANSFORMATIONAL GRAMMAR.

Grammarian. *G–2.* One who specializes in the study of grammar. (Postal, 1964b, 137; Chomsky, 1966a, 10; Jacobs and Rosenbaum, 1968, 41, 60; Fillmore, 1968, 88.) Compare LINGUIST. See also T-GRAMMARIAN.

Grammar, immediate-constituent. See IMMEDIATE-CONSTITUENT GRAMMAR.

Grammar, justification of a. See JUSTIFICATION OF A GRAMMAR.

Grammar, linguistic. See LINGUISTIC GRAMMAR.

Grammar, nongenerative transformational. See NONGENERATIVE TRANSFORMATIONAL GRAMMAR.

Grammar of embedded sentences. *G–2.* An explanatory description of the system of complementation. (Rosenbaum, 1967b, ix). See also COMPLEMENTATION.

Grammar, optimal. See OPTIMAL GRAMMAR.

Grammar, particular. See PARTICULAR GRAMMAR.

Grammar, pedagogic. See PEDAGOGIC GRAMMAR.

Grammar, phrase-structure. See PHRASE-STRUCTURE GRAMMAR.

Grammar, second-generation transformational. See SECOND-GENERATION TRANSFORMATIONAL GRAMMAR.

Grammar, semantic-based transformational. See SEMANTIC-BASED TRANSFORMATIONAL GRAMMAR.

Grammars, equivalent. See EQUIVALENT GRAMMARS.

Grammar, synthetic. See SYNTHETIC GRAMMAR.

Grammar, systematic. See SYSTEMATIC GRAMMAR.

Grammar, traditional. See TRADITIONAL GRAMMAR.

Grammar, transformation. See TRANSFORMATIONAL GRAMMAR.

Grammar, transformational. See TRANSFORMATIONAL GRAMMAR.

Grammar, transformational generative. See TRANSFORMATIONAL GENERATIVE GRAMMAR.

Grammar, universal. See UNIVERSAL GRAMMAR.

Grammatical. *G–1–2.* Correctly formed by the grammar as an acceptable sentence of the language; well-formed. (Rosenbaum, 1967a, 14.) Compare UNGRAMMATICAL. See also GRAMMATICALNESS.

Grammatical ambiguity. See AMBIGUITY.

Grammatical category. See CATEGORY.

Grammatical description. *G–1–2.* The derivational and transformational history which the grammar provides for each sentence that it generates (Koutsoudas, 1966, 28); a specification of the sentences of a language, along with the structure which each sentence has: viz., a grammar (Postal, 1964a, 3). See also GRAMMAR. Compare LINGUISTIC DESCRIPTION.

Grammatical formative. *G–2.* A member of the subclass of formatives which includes all of the items of the prephonological surface structure string except lexical items: auxiliary equipment, inflectional suffixes, transformational parts, boundary markers, etc. (Chomsky, 1965, 65.) Also called **Sentence trapping.** Compare LEXICAL FORMATIVE.

Grammatical function. *G–1–2.* One of the inherent notions, implied in the rewrite rules of the phrase-structure grammar (or categorial component in *G–2*), which characterizes certain relations between higher-level nodes and their descendants, as in: [NP, S] (subject or subject of); [VP, S] (predicate, or predicate of); [V, VP] (main verb, or main verb of); [NP, VP] (object, or object of). Each grammatical function is associated with a grammatical rule of the type A → XBY: "B has the grammatical function [B, A], or B of A." (Chomsky, 1965, 68, 73; Chomsky, 1966a, 56–58.) *G–2S.* The grammatical functions 'subject' and 'object' are not found on the deep structure level to which semantic rules apply. (Fillmore, 1966, 363.) Compare GRAMMATICAL RELATION.

Grammaticality. *G–1–2.* Well-formedness of a sentence at various stages of generation. A transformational grammar predicts and explains the grammaticality of well-formed sentences and the ungrammaticality of ill-formed sentences. (Rosenbaum, 1967a, 67, 89, 103.) Also called **Grammaticalness.** Compare UNGRAMMATICALITY.

Grammatical marker. *G–2.* A marker of the syntactic category of a dictionary entry, such as: noun, verb, adjective, etc. (Katz and Fodor, 1963, 497, 518.)

Grammatical morpheme. *G–1.* A symbol of the terminal grammatical string which is assigned a phonological representation by the morphophonemic rules, rather than by the earlier application of phonological rules, which apply to lexical morphemes. (Koutsoudas, 1966, 35, 119.) Compare GRAMMATICAL FORMATIVE.

Grammaticalness. *G–1.* Acceptability of a sentence to a native speaker as a grammatical sentence of his language, whether or not it is sensible, such as: "Colorless green ideas sleep furiously." (Chomsky, 1957, 13.) *G–2.*

Well-formedness, to a certain degree, of a sentence according to the rules of the grammar, which reflect the intuitive judgment of the native speaker. The scale of acceptability does not coincide with the scale of grammaticalness, which is only one of the factors interacting to determine acceptability; and, in fact, grammatical sentences are not necessarily acceptable or interpretable by the native speaker, nor are unacceptable sentences necessarily ungrammatical. There are no reliable operational criteria for judging grammaticalness. (Chomsky, 1965, 11, 19, 151.) Except in Chomsky, usually called **Grammaticality.** Compare ACCEPTABILITY, UNGRAMMATICALITY.

Grammaticalness, degree of. See DEGREE OF GRAMMATICALNESS.

Grammaticalness, scale of. See SCALE OF GRAMMATICALNESS.

Grammatical relation. *G–1.* The universal, nonsemantic function of a major constituent in its dominating phrase in an underlying phrase-marker, as defined in terms of the unique configuration of—and universal order of constituents in—a phrase structure branching diagram, such as:

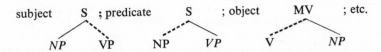

(Chomsky, 1957, 88; Postal, 1964, 111.) Grammatical relations are autonomous features of sentences and can be studied independently. (Lees, 1960a, xxiv.) Grammatical relations, such as subject-verb, can be defined in terms of grammatical relations. (Chomsky, 1966a, 58.) It is convenient to refer to grammatical relations when discussing structural change, but the grammar does not fully account for them. (Lees, 1960a, 27.) *G–2.* One of the uniform set of case-type relations among the words which make up the deep structure of a sentence. In *G–2,* the subject relation is: S   ;

NP   PredP

predicate is a category rather than a relation: PredP   ; and the

Aux   Pred

object relation is: Pred   . (Chomsky, 1966a, 45, 48.) The

V   NP

full set of deep structure relations can be categorized by a phrase-structure grammar. (Chomsky, 1966a, 40.) *G–2S.* The formal distinction between grammatical categories and grammatical functions, or relations, is unnecessary if grammatical cases are recognized as playing a role in the foundation of grammars. (Fillmore, 1966, 361–362.) Also called **Grammatical function.**

Grammatical rule. *G–1.* A rule of the grammar; one of the set of rules that represent the structural relations among members of a sentence. (Katz,

1964b, 407.) See also REWRITING RULE, PHRASE STRUCTURE RULE, TRANS-FORMATIONAL RULE.

Grammatical theory. *G–1.* That part of the theory of language which concerns itself with the nature of the syntactic and phonological components of a grammar and describes the language universals of these components. (Katz, 1966, 119.) Compare LINGUISTIC THEORY.

Grammatical transformation. *G–1.* An optional or obligatory set of syntactic rules which perform one or more of a limited set of operations—such as addition, subtraction, rearrangement, substitution—in mapping a single underlying phrase-marker into a derived phrase-marker (achieved by a singulary transformation) or embedding or conjoining a constituent phrase-marker to a matrix phrase-marker (achieved by a generalized transformation). (Chomsky, 1956, 149; Chomsky, 1961a, 128, 131; Chomsky, 1957, 44–45.) *G–2.* An obligatory syntactic rule which responds to a complex symbol in a generalized phrase-marker and performs one of a limited number of single operations—adjunction, deletion, substitution, and combinations of these—in relating the abstract deep structure of a sentence to its surface structure; one of the formal operations that relate a system of mental propositions, which express the meaning of the sentence, to the realization of the sentence as a physical signal. (Chomsky, 1965, 89–90, 146–147; Chomsky, 1966b, 5; Chomsky, 1968, 15, 25; Chomsky and Halle, 1968, 20.) See also TRANSFORMATION.

Grave. *G–1.* The phonetic distinctive feature which is positively specified for sounds that are produced with narrowing at the extreme front—the lips—or back—the velum—of the oral cavity, and which is negatively specified—nongrave, or acute—for sounds that are articulated with narrowing in the central region. (Halle, 1959, 326.) *G–2.* The oral-articulator feature which is positively specified for sounds that have their primary area of articulation in the back of the oral cavity—for vowels—or on the periphery of the oral cavity—for consonants. (Harms, 1968, 22, 26–27.)

Greek-letter variable. See ALPHA-TYPE VARIABLE.

H

'Have'. *G–1.* The middle verb *have,* which does not take manner adverbials freely (e.g., *"The raft *had* a leak easily"), cannot be transformed into an action nominal (*"The raft's *having* of a leak"), and does not undergo the passive transformation (*"A leak *was had* by the raft"). (Thomas, 1965, 122.) *G–2.* The nontransitive, nonmiddle verb *have,* which does not undergo the passive transformation except in a few marginal cases, as in: "A good time *was had* by all." (Chomsky, 1965, 103–104.) *G–2S.* The copula form *have,* which is not present in the lexicon of the base but is introduced by transformational rule. Another mechanism accounts for the empty, or auxiliary, use of *have.* (Fillmore, 1968, 47.) See also MIDDLE VERB.

Head. *G–1.* The final member—the modified noun—of a nominal compound or nominal phrase, such as: "hóuse *guest*"; "gúest *house.*" (Lees, 1960a, 128.) *G–2.* The noun constituent of a noun phrase complement construction: NP → N+S. (Rosenbaum, 1967a, 29, 35.)

Hierarchic semantic feature. *G–2.* A semantic feature which automatically specifies the features that are below it in the hierarchy, as when [+human] implies [+animate] and [−abstract]. (Langendoen, 1969, 36–37.) See also SEMANTIC FEATURE.

Hierarchy, binary feature. See BINARY FEATURE HIERARCHY.

High. *G–2.* The phonological distinctive feature which is positively specified for sounds whose production involves a raising of the body of the tongue above its neutral position. Earlier, it was called **Diffuse** for vowels and **Palatalization** for consonants. The [+high] sounds are high vowels, liquids, glides, and palatal and velar consonants. The negative specification is called **Nonhigh.** (Chomsky and Halle, 1968, 304–307.) Compare LOW, DIFFUSE.

High(er)-level. *G–1–2.* In the upper part of the hierarchy or order of components, rules, categories, or features. 'High(er)-level' generalizations appear earlier in the hierarchy or order than 'low(er)-level' generalizations, and are consequently more abstract. (Bach, 1964, 59; Chomsky, 1965, 69, 150; Chomsky and Halle, 1968, 43, 59.) Compare LOW(ER)-LEVEL, LOW-LEVEL RULE. See also HIGH-LEVEL RULE.

Higher-level rule. See HIGH-LEVEL RULE.

High-level rule. *G–1–2.* A rule at or near the beginning of an ordered set of rules within a single level—phrase structure, transformational, phonological; a rule—a 'higher-level' rule—that is placed earlier in an ordered set of rules than another, 'lower-level' rule in the same set; a phrase structure rule as contrasted with a transformational rule or a phonological rule; a transformational rule as contrasted with a phonological rule. (Bach, 1964, 59.) See also EARLY RULE.

Historical linguistics. *G–2.* The study of all aspects of language change as changes in the grammar, or rules, of the language, and in the competence of its speakers, rather than as a history of the development of its sounds or grammatical forms. The generative historical linguist assumes at every stage of comparison that the universals of language hold throughout time, and that a reconstruction must not violate what is known to be true of natural languages generally. (King, 1969, 15, 102–104, 125–128, 176–177.) Compare DESCRIPTIVE LINGUISTICS.

History, derivational. See DERIVATIONAL HISTORY.

History, transformational. See TRANSFORMATIONAL HISTORY.

Homomorph. *G–1.* A morph that is identical in form to another morph, although not necessarily identical to it in function, such as the nominalization morpheme *for* as opposed to the preposition *for*. (Lees, 1960a, 30). Compare HOMONYM.

Homonym. *G–1–2.* An utterance which is phonemically identical to, but different in meaning from, another utterance, as in the instance of *look over* (examine) vs. *look over* (look across the top of) (Chomsky, 1957, 95); a word which has two or more different combinations of semantic features—has different meanings (Langendoen, 1969, 34). Compare HOMOMORPH.

Homonymous. *G–1–2.* Having the same form in sound and spelling but different function and meaning from another morpheme. For example, "*tend* to rust" (intransitive) and "*tend* the flocks" (transitive) are hononymous verbs. (Rosenbaum, 1967a, 22.) Also called **Homophonous.**

Homophonous. *G–1.* Identical in all phonological respects, though not necessarily syntactically or semantically equivalent, as in: "Huck *looked* *over* the raft" (examined it); "Huck *looked over* the raft" (looked across the top of it). (Lees, 1960a, 30.) Also called **Homonymous.**

Hypercorrection. *G–2.* The addition, but incorrect use, by an adult of a set of prestige-bearing rules which form an overlay on his native-acquired grammar, rather than a restructuring of that grammar. (King, 1969, 68–71.) See also RULE ADDITION.

Hypothesis, left-identity. See LEFT-IDENTITY HYPOTHESIS.

Hypothesis, nontrivial. See NONTRIVIAL HYPOTHESIS.

I

Ideal pronunciation. *G–2.* The instructions which specify how the vocal apparatus must behave in order to produce the phonetic representation of an utterance; the knowledge which the phonological component of a grammar attempts to account for. (Postal, 1968a, 293.) Compare PERFORMANCE.

Ideal speaker-hearer. *G–2.* A hypothetical native speaker whose fluency of performance is unaffected by psychological limitations or by variations in situations or speakers. (Chomsky, 1965, 4; Katz, 1966, 117.) See also NORMAL SPEAKER.

Identical. *G–2.* Having the same origin, form, and meaning as another constituent. For example, the erasure principle demands that the erasing noun phrase in the main sentence and the erased noun phrase in the complement sentence be 'identical', as in: "*Huck* wanted (for *Huck*) to sleep." (Rosenbaum, 1967a, 6, 68.) See also IDENTICAL REFERENCE.

Identical conjunct reduction. *G–2.* The transformation which deletes one of two identical conjuncts with identical reference in the same phrase, as when: "(*Huck* and *Huck*) poled and steered" ⇒ "*Huck* poled and steered"; "Tom and Becky (*laughed* and *laughed*)" ⇒ "Tom and Becky *laughed.*" (Jacobs and Rosenbaum, 1968, 257–258.) See also CONJUNCTION REDUCTION TRANSFORMATION.

Identical noun phrase deletion. *G–2.* The transformation which deletes a noun phrase, in an embedding, which is identical to a noun phrase in the matrix, as when: "*Twain* is suitable (for anyone to read *Twain*)" ⇒ "*Twain* is suitable for anyone to read." The indefinite pronoun *anyone* is then optionally deleted by indefinite noun phrase deletion, along with the first part of the complementizer, *for* (to): "Twain is suitable to read." (Jacobs and Rosenbaum, 1968, 27, 166.) Also called **Noun phrase deletion rule,** in such cases as: "*Tom* wants (*Tom* to run away)" ⇒ "Tom wants to run away." (Langacker, 1968, 127.) Also called **Equi-NP-deletion** (Ross, 1967, 194–195) and **Erasure** (Rosenbaum, 1967a, 50). See also IDENTITY ERASURE TRANSFORMATION.

Identical reference. *G–2.* Reference by two linguistic objects to the same physical object (e.g., "*Huck* poled and *Huck* steered"; "*Huck* and *Huck* poled and steered"), permitting their reduction to a single constituent ("*Huck* poled and steered"). Two identical constituents that have identical reference are said to be strongly identical; two identical constituents that do not have identical reference are said to be weakly identical, as for: *"The King* died and *the King* succeeded." (Jacobs and Rosenbaum, 1968, 258.) See also STRONGLY IDENTICAL, WEAKLY IDENTICAL, IDENTICAL.

Identical, strongly.   See STRONGLY IDENTICAL.

Identical verb phrase deletion.   *G–2.* The transformation which deletes the main verb and complements of the second of two identical verb phrases, as when: "Tom can *paint fences,* and Huck can *paint fences* too" ⇒ "Tom can paint fences, and Huck can . . . too"; "Tom *worked hard* because Aunt Polly wanted him to *work hard"* ⇒ "Tom worked hard because Aunt Polly wanted him to. . . ." (Jacobs and Rosenbaum, 1968, 27, 41–42.) See also DELETION.

Identical, weakly.   See WEAKLY IDENTICAL.

Identity.   *G–2.* Sameness of referent and underlying features of two or more constituents. For example, the erasure principle operates on the identity of the erasing noun phrase in the main sentence and the erased noun phrase in the complement sentence, as in: *"Huck* wanted (for *Huck*) to sleep." (Rosenbaum, 1967a, 50.) Compare SYNONYMY, RELATEDNESS. *Related terms:* Constituents which have the same origin, form, and meaning are said to be **Identical.** (Rosenbaum, 1967a, 6, 68.) Two identical constituents which refer to the same physical object are said to have **Identical reference.** Two identical constituents which have identical reference are said to be **Strongly identical**—or, if not, **Weakly identical.** (Jacobs and Rosenbaum, 1968, 258.) The principle which governs the deletion of an identical noun phrase is called **Identity erasure.** (Rosenbaum, 1967a, 6, 18, 49.) The restraint which prevents identity erasure from occurring unless the relevant noun phrases are identical is the **Identity restriction.** (Rosenbaum, 1967a, 68.)

Identity erasure.   *G–2.* The operations performed by the Identity Erasure Transformation. (Rosenbaum, 1967a, 50.)

Identity erasure transformation.   *G–2.* The transformation which, governed by the erasure principle, achieves identity erasure by erasing the noun phrase of an embedded complement construction, provided that this noun phrase follows either the complementizing morpheme POSS or the complementizing morpheme *for* and is identical to a noun phrase of the main sentence, as in: *"Huck* wanted (for *Huck*) to sleep"; *"Tom* liked (POSS-*Tom*) steering the raft." (Rosenbaum, 1967a, 6, 18, 49.) See also ERASURE PRINCIPLE.

Identity restriction.   *G–2.* The restriction on noun phrases, stated in the erasure principle, which permits identity erasure of a noun phrase of the complement sentence by identity erasure transformation, provided that it is identical to a noun phrase of the main sentence and follows the complementizing morpheme *for* or POSS). (Rosenbaum, 1967a, 68.) See also ERASURE PRINCIPLE, IDENTITY ERASURE TRANSFORMATION.

Idiolect.   *G–2.* The language of a single fluent speaker. (Langendoen, 1969, 2.) Compare DIALECT.

Idiom.   *G–2a.* A single lexical item which, though it consists of more than one morpheme, cannot be derived syntactically, such as: *re-ceive,* a multimorpheme idiom. (Postal, 1964c, 31.) *G–2b.* A phrase, often with special syntactic properties, whose meaning is not predictable from the meanings of its individual morphemes, such as: "to rain *cats and dogs."* (Langacker, 1968, 79; Gleitman, 1965, 112.) See also DERIVED WORD.

Ill-formed. See WELL-FORMED.

Ill-formedness. See WELL-FORMED.

Immediate-constituent analysis. *G–1*. An unlabeled hierarchical bracketing of the string of morphemes in an utterance. (Chomsky, 1962, 211; Postal, 1964a, 23; Bach, 1964, 33–34.) Compare PHRASE-MARKER, LABELED BRACKETING.

Immediate-constituent grammmar. *G–2*. A phrase-structure grammar. Also called **IC-grammar.** (Lees, 1964b, xxxiv.) See also PHRASE STRUCTURE GRAMMAR.

Immediate constituent rule. See PHRASE STRUCTURE RULE.

Immediate domination. *G–2*. Domination in the same branching of a tree diagram. For example, S and V are 'immediately dominated' by VP in the diagram: VP , and VP 'immediately dominates' both S and V—an

example of verb phrase complementation. (Rosenbaum, 1967a, 9, 12.) See also DOMINATION.

Imperative. *G–1*. A sentence with the underlying form "You will V" which has been transformed, by imperative transformation, into a sentence of the type "You V" (e.g., "You bring the coffee!") or "V" (e.g., "Bring the coffee!") or, with reflexive, "V yourself" (e.g., "Watch yourself!") or, with a tag question, "V, won't you?" (e.g., "Come in, won't you?") (Katz and Postal, 1964, 43–76); a sentence derived from an underlying sentence of the type "You close the door" (no *will*) (Lees, 1964a, 142). *G–2*. An elliptical transform of an underlying sentence of the type "I order (or request) you S" (Chomsky, 1966c, 46); a sentence derived syntactically from a sentence of the form "I request that you will V" by deleting the first five morphemes, or the first three, plus *will*. The imperative morpheme I, which is assigned to all phrase-markers that underlie imperative sentences, has as a dictionary entry: "The speaker requests or asks or demands. . . ." Imperatives cannot be embedded, except quotationally, as in: "I said, 'Forget it!' " (Katz and Postal, 1964, 43, 78, 149.) The first person plural imperative with *let's* (e.g., "Let's go fishing") requires an inclusive first person and does not have an underlying *you will*, as in: "Let's (you and I/me) go fishing." (McCawley, 1968, 160–161.)

Imperative transformation. See IMPERATIVE.

Impersonal inversion. *G–2*. A transformation of the type "It is fortunate that Huck swims" ⇒ "That Huck swims is fortunate." (Lees, 1964b, xlii.) See also IMPERSONAL SUBJECT. Compare EXTRAPOSITION.

Impersonal subject. *G–1–2*. The expletive *it* (e.g., "*It* is easy to build a raft") or the expletive *there* (e.g., "*There* are many ways to build a raft"). Impersonal subjects are probably present in the underlying trees of impersonal sentences. (Lees, 1960a, 77; Lees, 1964b, xliii.) See also EXPLETIVE.

Implicit subject. *G–2*. The subject of a predicate complement construction, though not present in the surface structure. The presence of the subject in the underlying structure is 'implied' by the fact that the identity erasure transformation has been permitted to apply, as in: "Huck prevailed upon Tom (for *Tom*) to remain." (Rosenbaum, 1967a, 20, 68.) Compare UNDERLYING SUBJECT.

Impossible. *G–2*. Ungrammatical (*); filtered out by a transformation which is not defined on the environment of that derivation. For example, a sentence such as *"It annoyed Tom Huck's smoking" is 'impossible,' because the extraposition transformation is not defined on POSS-ing complements. (Rosenbaum, 1967a, 76, 78, 80, 95.) See also UNGRAMMATICAL.

Impossible morpheme. See POSSIBLE MORPHEME.

Inchoative. *G–2S.* A syntactic feature of a predicate which specifies that the concept in the argument is "getting" or "becoming" or "growing" to have or be of a certain quality, as when: "The room is getting warm" ⇒ "The room is warming up"; "The leather is becoming soft" ⇒ "The leather is softening up"; "The sky is growing dark" ⇒ "The sky is darkening." Inchoative is sometimes combined with 'causative,' as when: "The cook is causing the potatoes to become warm" ⇒ "The cook is warming up the potatoes." Inchoative is a feature of a one-place predicate, called an **Abstract inchoative predicate.** (Langendoen, 1969, 107–108.)

Inchoative predicate, abstract. See INCHOATIVE.

Including sentence. See MAIN SENTENCE.

Inclusion, mutual. See MUTUAL INCLUSION.

Inclusion relation, category. See CATEGORY INCLUSION RELATION.

Incorporation transformation, auxiliary. See AUXILIARY INCORPORATION TRANSFORMATION.

Indefinite. See INDEFINITE PRONOUN.

Indefinite, negative. See NEGATIVE INDEFINITE.

Indefinite noun phrase deletion. See IDENTICAL NOUN PHRASE DELETION.

Indefinite pronoun. *G–1–2.* A pronoun of the type *someone, somebody,* which, in some dialects, prevents the deletion of the 'that' complementizer, as in: "It was clear to *someone* (*that*) Tom had survived." Also called an **Indefinite.** (Rosenbaum, 1967a, 39–40.)

Indefinite pronoun deletion transformation. *G–2.* The transformation which optionally deletes an indefinite pronoun in a complex sentence containing a predicate complement, as in: "It was clear (to *someone*) that Tom had survived." (Rosenbaum, 1967a, 40.) See also INDEFINITE PRONOUN.

Independent justification. See INDEPENDENT MOTIVATION.

Independently motivated. *G–2.* Justified for application in one system of the grammar because of a rule's ability to explain derivations in another, separate, system. (Rosenbaum, 1967a, 13, 64.) See also INDEPENDENT MOTIVATION.

Independent motivation. *G–2.* Justification for the application of a transformation in one system of rules because of its ability to explain derivations in another, separate, system. Such a transformation is said to have 'independent motivation,' or to be 'independently motivated,' in the other system. For example, the pronoun replacement transformation is justified for the object complement system because it has 'independent motivation' in the subject complement system, and vice versa. Also called **Independent justification.** (Rosenbaum, 1967a, 61, 91). Compare AD HOC RULE.

Index, referential. See REFERENTIAL INDEX.

Index, structural. See STRUCTURAL INDEX.

Index, structure. See STRUCTURE INDEX.

Indirect object. *G–2.* The animate noun phrase object which appears with the preposition *to* at the left of another noun phrase object—the direct object—in the underlying structure of a sentence, as in: "Huck gave *to Tom* a knife." If the preposition *to* is not optionally deleted, the indirect object (plus *to*) is moved to the right of the direct object by a separation rule, as in: "Huck gave a knife *to Tom.*" (Lees and Klima, 1963, 154.) If the preposition *to* is deleted, the indirect object remains to the left of the direct object, as in: "Huck gave *Tom* a knife." (Lees, 1964b, xlii.) The indirect object inversion transformation reverses the order of the underlying direct object noun phrase and a following animate indirect object noun phrase when the preposition *to* is deleted from the latter, as when: "Huck gave a knife *to Tom*" ⇒ *"Huck gave a knife *Tom*" ⇒ "Huck gave *Tom* a knife." (Jacobs and Rosenbaum, 1968, 143–145.)

Indirect object inversion transformation. See INDIRECT OBJECT.

Indirect question. *G–2.* An embedded simple question which does not undergo inversion but has the question marker replaced by *whether* or *if,* as in: "Tom wanted to know *whether Becky could swim*"; "Huck asked Jim *if he would steer the raft for a while.*" (Jacobs and Rosenbaum, 1968, 180.) See also QUESTION.

Infinite. *G–1.* Not finite; without limit. Languages are said to be infinite in the number of their sentences and in the length of those sentences. (Chomsky, 1957, 23.) *G–2.* Languages are infinite only in respect to the competence of their speakers, not in respect to the performance of their speakers, which is restricted by physical, psychological, and social factors. (Katz, 1966, 121, 152.) Compare FINITE.

Infinitival clause. See INFINITIVE.

Infinitival clause separation transformation. *G–2.* The transformation which moves the infinitival clause from its verb phrase position in an embedded noun phrase to a position in the predicate verb phrase, as when: "(Huck *to swim*) started" ⇒ "Huck started *to swim.*" The infinitival clause separation transformation can also be applied to an infinitival clause in a verb phrase of an object noun phrase, positioning it under the verb phrase of the sentence; but in that case there is no change in the order of constituents, as seen when: "Tom expected (Huck *to swim*)" ⇒ "Tom expected Huck *to swim.*" (Langendoen, 1969, 56–64.)

Infinitive. *G–1.* The product of a generalized nominalizing transformation, which derives transforms of the type *to-VP* from kernel sentences and then inserts the infinitive nominal in a noun phrase position of another sentence, as when: "(INF-NOM-Huck steered the raft) was impossible" ⇒ "*To steer the raft* was impossible." (Chomsky, 1957, 72, 113.) *G–2.* The form of the verb which is indicated by an immediately preceding *to.* An **Infinitival clause** is one which contains an infinitive. (Langendoen, 1969, 57.)

Infinitive complementizer. *G–2.* The morphemes *for . . . to,* which are inserted into a sentence by complementizer transformation and then obligatorily reduced by complementizer deletion when the infinitive is not the subject of the sentence or does not follow a verb like *ask,* as when: "(*For . . . to* you go) is impossible" ⇒ "For you to go is impossible"; "I asked (*for . . . to* you go)" ⇒ "I asked (for) you to go"; "I want (*for . . . to* I go)" ⇒ "I want (for me) to go." (Jacobs, 1968, 51.) See also FOR-TO COMPLEMENTIZER.

Infinitive nominal. *G–1.* The infinitive transform which functions as the nominal object of the preposition *for,* as when: "Huck fishes" ⇒ "For *Huck to fish.* . . ." (Lees, 1960a, 32.) Compare INFINITIVE.

Inflect. See INFLECTION.

Inflection. *G–1.* A grammatical morpheme, usually called an 'affix' or a 'suffix,' which is introduced either by the phrase structure rules to express number, tense, or aspect, or else by the transformational rules to express possession, degree, or nominalization (Bach, 1964, 115, 118–119); an inflectional ending (Thomas, 1965, 49). A lexical item to which an inflection has been attached is said to be inflected. (Thomas, 1965, 54.) *G–2.* One of the unordered syntactic features—some inherent, some introduced by grammatical rule—which assign to nodes in the deep structure the properties that were regarded as underlying morphemes in *G–1:* number (singular or plural) and possession for nouns; case (possessive or objective) for pronouns; tense (present or past) and aspect (perfective or progressive) and gerund for verbs; degree (comparative or superlative) for adjectives and adverbs. (Chomsky, 1965, 170–176.) See also AFFIX.

Inflectional ending. See INFLECTION.

Inflectional morphology. See MORPHOLOGY.

Informant. *G–1–2.* A fluent, often native, speaker of a language—usually the linguist himself—who is appealed to for introspective judgments about the acceptability, grammaticality, expansion, meaning, etc., of linguistic objects. Generativists do not usually identify their informant, since their description is based on the entire language rather than on a restricted corpus of utterances in that language. (Chomsky, 1965, 194; Langendoen, 1969, 3.) See also IDEAL SPEAKER-HEARER.

Information, functional. See FUNCTIONAL INFORMATION.

Ing-affix. *G–1.* The affix *ing,* in the auxiliary, which indicates progressive aspect. (Lees, 1960a, 19.) See also PROGRESSIVE MORPHEME. Compare ING-MORPHEME.

Ing insertion. *G–2.* The replacement of the tense morpheme in a subordinate clause by *ing* (one of the *sentence trappings*), which changes the subject of the clause to a possessive, as when: "Tom envied (Huck smoke-*ed*)" ⇒ "Tom envied Huck's smoke-*ing*." (Langacker, 1968, 126–127.) See also GERUND.

Ing-morpheme. *G–1.* The gerund *ing,* or gerund form *ing,* which is part of the transformational machinery for deriving gerunds, as in: "The machine washes clothes" ⇒ "The machine for wash*ing* clothes. . . ." (Lees, 1960a, 93, 108.) See also GERUND.

Inherent feature. *G–2a.* A syntactic, semantic, or phonological feature which is inherent to a lexical item, irrespective of context, as opposed to a contextual feature, which refers to a particular context. (Chomsky, 1965, 176–177.) *G–2b.* A syntactic feature, such as number, which is inherent to a phrase-marker rather than to a lexical item that is inserted into that phrase-marker. (Chomsky, 1965, 177.) Compare CONTEXTUAL FEATURE.

Initial category. *G–1.* The initial symbol S of a derivation, representing 'sentence.' (Chomsky, 1966a, 52.) See also INITIAL STRING.

Initial string. *G–1.* One of the finite set, Σ, of single symbols—consisting at least of the 'initial symbol' #Sentence#—which are given in the phrase structure, rather than rewritten from another symbol, and which initiate all phrase structure derivations, such as: Sentence → NP+VP. (Chomsky, 1957, 26–29.) *G–2.* The single initial symbol #S#. (Bach, 1964, 45.) Also called **Initial category.**

Initial symbol. See INITIAL STRING.

Innovation. *G–2.* The addition, by a child, of a phonological rule to his grammar. (King, 1969, 123.) See also RULE ADDITION.

Insert. See EMBEDDING.

Insertion. See EMBEDDING.

Insertion, complementizer. See COMPLEMENTIZER INTRODUCTION.

Insertion, ing. See ING INSERTION.

Insertion, lexical. See LEXICAL INSERTION.

Insertion rule, boundary. See BOUNDARY.

Insertion, 'that'. See 'THAT' INSERTION.

Insertion, 'to'. See 'TO' INSERTION.

Insertion transformation. See EMBEDDING.

Instruction. *G–2.* A marker in the lexical entry of a formative which stipulates that a particular transformation must apply if its structural conditions are met. (Rosenbaum, 1967a, 72.) See also VERBAL MARKER.

Instruction formula. *G–1.* One of a finite set of rules (F) of the type X → Y (rewrite X as Y), which, with the finite set (Σ) of initial strings (e.g., #Sentence#), make up the basis for a constituent structure grammar: [Σ, F]. (Chomsky, 1957, 29, 111.) Also called **Rewriting rule.**

Instrumental. *G–2S.* The case—identified with the preposition *with*—of the inanimate instrument which is the cause of an action or state expressed by the verb, as in: "Huck opened the drawer *with the key*"; "The drawer was opened *with the key* by Huck"; "*The key* opened the drawer"; etc. (Fillmore, 1968, 24–25.) See also CASE.

Intensive pronoun. *G–1.* A pro-form which replaces a constituent sentence that is a duplicate of the matrix sentence, as when: "Huck (Huck built the raft) built the raft" ⇒ "Huck *himself* built the raft." Because the intensive pronoun intensifies the entire matrix sentence, it can be moved about rather freely, as in: "Huck built the raft *himself*." Also called **Intensifying pronoun, Intensifier pronoun, Intensifier.** (Thomas, 1965, 96–97.) Compare REFLEXIVE PRONOUN.

Interesting. *G–1–2.* Revealing to the theory, significant to the description, and satisfying to the analyst—nontrivial, nonobvious, not self-evident, abstract. An 'interesting' procedure is one which focuses on crucial problems of linguistic analysis and provides satisfying answers about the nature of linguistic theory. (Chomsky, 1957, 52–53.) Compare TRIVIAL.

Intermediate stage. *G–2.* The stage in the derivation of a sentence at which the string is neither an underlying structure nor a final derived structure—that is, the stage at which at least one transformation has applied to the base and at least one more transformation will apply to yield the surface structure. (Rosenbaum, 1967a, 35–36.) See also INTERMEDIATE STRUCTURE.

Intermediate string. See INTERMEDIATE STRUCTURE.

Intermediate structure. *G–2.* The constituent structure which is formed by one or more transformations between the deep structure and the surface structure—that is, one which is intermediate between a generalized phrase-marker and a final derived phrase-marker. The string of an intermediate structure is called an **Intermediate string.** (Jacobs and Rosenbaum, 1968, 21.) See also INTERMEDIATE STAGE.

Internal condition of adequacy. See JUSTIFICATION OF A GRAMMAR.

Internal constituency. *G–2.* The make-up of a phrase structure, consisting of the constituents that are immediately dominated by a single node. (Rosenbaum, 1967a, 69.) See also PHRASE STRUCTURE.

Internal contradiction. *G–2.* A violation of semantic selection restrictions of the type *"Becky is the nephew of Aunt Polly." (Langendoen, 1969, 7.) See also SELECTION RESTRICTION.

Internalization.   See INTERNALIZE.

Internalize.   *G–2.* To learn a language natively; to master a system of rules perfectly; to acquire native-speaker competence in a grammar. **Internalization** of a language means that the grammar of the language—the system of rules of the language—has been learned natively or mastered perfectly, or has been 'internalized.' (King, 1969, 71–72, 113.) Internalized rules cannot be brought to consciousness. (Chomsky, 1966a, 10.)

Internalized rule.   See INTERNALIZE.

Interpretation.   *G–2.* The mapping of a syntactically generated structure onto a concrete representation. Interpretation can be either semantic, by the semantic component—a semantic interpretation, or phonetic, by the phonological component—a phonetic interpretation. (Chomsky, 1964, 52.) See also SEMANTIC INTERPRETATION, PHONOLOGICAL COMPONENT.

Interpretation, phonetic.   See PHONOLOGICAL COMPONENT.

Interpretation, phonological.   See PHONOLOGICAL COMPONENT.

Interpretation, semantic.   See SEMANTIC INTERPRETATION.

Interrogative transformation.   See QUESTION.

Interrupted.   See CONTINUANT.

Intonation.   *G–1–2.* The pitch contour of a sentence. All sentences have the falling, or declarative, intonation pattern; special rules then assign rising intonation to simple questions (e.g., "Does Becky know how to paint?") and comma intonation to conjoined morphemes in a series (e.g., "Tom, Huck, and Jim were on the raft"). (Katz and Postal, 1964, 111; Gleitman, 1965, 95.) The prosodic contour of a sentence is determined by its surface structure. Pitch, or intonation, is one of the three universal prosodic features: pitch, stress, length. (Chomsky and Halle, 1968, 15, 300.) Intonation is the least investigated aspect of transformational phonological theory. (Bach, 1964, 138–139.) See also COMMA INTONATION. Compare STRESS.

Intonation, comma.   See COMMA INTONATION.

Intonation, parenthetic-type.   See COMMA INTONATION.

Intonation pattern.   See INTONATION.

Intransitive.   See INTRANSITIVE VERBAL.

Intransitive adjective.   *G–2.* A predicate adjective which is not followed by a noun phrase (e.g., "The box is *open*"), as opposed to transitive adjectives, which are followed by a noun phrase (e.g., "The box is *open at the top*"). (Jacobs and Rosenbaum, 1968, 65.) See also INTRANSITIVE VERBAL. Compare TRANSITIVE ADJECTIVE.

Intransitive oblique noun phrase complementation.   *G–2a.* A noun phrase complement of an object of a preposition following an intransitive verb, as in: "Huck thought about the fact *that spring was late*." (Rosenbaum, 1967c, 320–321.) *G–2b.* The embedding of a sentence as a complement of a noun in a prepositional phrase within a verb phrase:

For example: "Huck thought about (it) *hiding the raft.*" (Rosenbaum, 1967a, 4.) Compare TRANSITIVE OBLIQUE COMPLEMENTATION.

Intransitive verb. *G–1–2.* A verb which can optionally be followed by an adverb but not by a nominal or adjective: VP → V (ADV). (Langendoen, 1969, 25.) 'Intransitive' is one of the four classes of verbs: *be,* copulative, transitive, and intransitive. (Thomas, 1965, 120–121.) See also INTRANSITIVE VERBAL. Compare TRANSITIVE VERB.

Intransitive verbal. *G–2.* A verbal—that is, a verb or an adjective—which is the only constituent of a verb phrase: VP → VB. The intransitive adjective verbal contains features which specify a particular copula in the surface structure introduced by copula transformation. (Jacobs, 1968, 22–24; Jacobs and Rosenbaum, 1968, 52–53.) Compare TRANSITIVE VERBAL.

Intransitive verb phrase complementation. *G–2a.* An infinitivalized sentence complement of a verb within a verb phrase to which the passive transformation and the pseudo-cleft sentence transformation cannot apply, as in: "Huck tended *to like the job*"; *"The job was tended to like by Huck"; *"To like the job was tended by Huck"; *"What Huck tended was to like the job." (Rosenbaum, 1967c, 322.) *G–2b.* The embedding of a sentence as a complement of a verb in the verb phrase of a main sentence:

For example, "Huck proceeded *(for Huck)* *to launch the raft.*" Either the for-to or the POSS-ing complementizer can occur, depending on the verb. (Rosenbaum, 1967a, 2.) Compare TRANSITIVE VERB PHRASE COMPLEMENTATION.

Introduction, comparative. See COMPARATIVE TRANSFORMATION.

Introduction, complementizer. See COMPLEMENTIZER INTRODUCTION.

Introductory 'there'. *G–2.* The morpheme *there,* which can be introduced into the subject position of a sentence of the type "A girl was in Tom's soup" ("*There* was a girl in Tom's soup") and then treated as the subject of that sentence by all transformations which subsequently apply to it. For example, passive: "Tom believed *there* to be a girl in his soup" ⇒ "*There* was believed by Tom to be a girl in his soup." (Rosenbaum, 1967a, 64.) See also EXPLETIVE, IMPERSONAL SUBJECT.

Introspection. *G–2.* Self-inquiry into one's judgments regarding the status of a linguistic object (e.g., as to acceptability, grammaticality, etc.)—the most common form of elicitation in generative grammar. (Langendoen, 1969, 3.) Introspective judgment of the informant, often the linguist himself, is vital to the study of language. (Chomsky, 1965, 194.) Compare INTUITION.

Intuition. *G–1–2.* The native speaker's knowledge of his language, as opposed to his knowledge *about* his language (Thomas, 1965, 45); the judgments of the native speaker about the physical events of his language, about what he says and hears (his *Sprachgefühl*); what a linguistic analysis tries to account for, and what the native-speaker linguist knows ahead of time that he wants to come up with (Bach, 1964, 3–4, 151); the tacit competence of the native speaker—his knowledge of his language (Chomsky, 1965, 24–27). The native speaker's intuition is the ultimate standard for determining the accuracy of a grammar or a theory of grammar. (Chomsky, 1965, 19, 21.) Reliance on the intuition of a fluent speaker is essential to the study of language (Thomas, 1965, 10), but intuition is not *required* in the determination of what a grammar states about a sentence (Chomsky, 1961a, 120). The major goal of grammar is to substitute rigor and objectivity for reliance on intuition. (Chomsky, 1957, 94.) Intuition about linguistic form—the usual sense of the word— is not to be confused with intuition about meaning. (Chomsky, 1957, 94.) Intuitions about surface structures are not very reliable. (Jacobs and Rosenbaum, 1968, 37.) See also COMPETENCE, LINGUISTIC INTUITION. Compare INTROSPECTION.

Intuition, linguistic. See LINGUISTIC INTUITION.

Inversion. *G–1–2.* The process by which the subject and the finite verb (or *be*) of a sentence are rearranged from the order subject-verb to the order verb-subject in simple questions, information questions, and tag questions (e.g., *"Has he* left?"; "Why *has he* left?"; "He hasn't left, *has he?"*) or with an initial adverb or expletive (e.g., "Here *is a book"*; "There *is a book* here"). (Chomsky, 1968, 41.) Another type of rearrangement, called **Stylistic inversion,** a form of stylistic reordering, moves an object to the front of the sentence by stylistic transformation but does not reorder the subject and the verb, as seen in: *"Her* I would never invite to another party." (Chomsky, 1965, 222–223.) See also INVERT, 'IT' IN-VERSION, PARTICLE INVERSION TRANSFORMATION, ABSTRACT PREDICATE IN-VERSION, ADJECTIVE INVERSION, IMPERSONAL INVERSION, INVERSION RULE.

Inversion, abstract predicate. See ABSTRACT PREDICATE INVERSION.

Inversion, adjective. See ADJECTIVE INVERSION.

Inversion, impersonal. See IMPERSONAL INVERSION.

Inversion, 'it'-. See 'IT'-INVERSION.

Inversion rule. *G–2.* The transformation which inverts two constituents of a string, such as the subject of the main sentence and an adjective complement, as in: *"Huck* was smart *to retreat"* ⇒ *"To retreat* was smart of *Huck."* (Rosenbaum, 1967a, 107.) See also INVERSION, INVERT.

Inversion, stylistic. See STYLISTIC INVERSION.

Inversion transformation, particle. See PARTICLE INVERSION TRANSFORMA-TION.

Inversion transformation, subject-object. See SUBJECT-OBJECT INVERSION TRANSFORMATION.

Invert. *G–1–2.* To reposition two constituents of a string so that each of the constituents occupies the original position of the other constituent: XAYBZ ⇒ XBYAZ. Constituents A and B are then said to be 'inverted.' (Rosenbaum, 1967a, 98.) See also INVERSION, INVERSION RULE.

Irrecoverable. *G–1.* Not capable of being understood as having been deleted from a grammatical sentence, as in: *"Huck caught more fish than. . . ."* (Thomas, 1965, 87–88.) Compare RECOVERABLE.

Irreflexive. *G–1–2.* Not permitting identity in two members of a construc-tion. For example, the symmetric predicates *similar* and *resemble,* which are grammatically irreflexive, prohibit identity of conjoined noun phrases in their sentences: *"Huck* is *similar* to *Huck"* ⇒ *"Huck* and *Huck* are *similar*"; *"*Huck resembles Huck*" ⇒ *"*Huck* and *Huck resemble.*" (Bach, 1964, 155; Lakoff and Peters, 1966, 124, 133.) See also IDENTITY, SYMMETRIC PREDICATE. Compare REFLEXIVE VERB.

Irregular verb. *G–1.* A verb which violates the phrase structure constraints for the formation of its past tense form: a strong verb. (Halle, 1959, R&S, 50.) *G–2.* A verb that is specified for an exception feature which blocks the application of the verb suffix transformation and substitutes for the verbal segment an appropriate past tense form. (Jacobs and Rosenbaum, 1968, 134.) See also PAST TENSE.

Is-a relation. *G–1–2.* The relation which holds between the right-hand side—the expansion—and the left-hand side—the category symbol—of a context-free rewriting rule. For example, in the rule $A \rightarrow B + C$, $B + C$ *is an* A—that is, $B + C$ is derived from A, or is analyzable as A. (Bach, 1964, 73; Chomsky, 1965, 143.) See also ANALYZABILITY, BOOLEAN CONDITION.

Isogloss. *G–2.* One of a bundle of feature boundaries which establish a dialect boundary between two grammars of the same language—that is, each dialect has a rule that the other one lacks. (King, 1969, 36.) See also DIALECT.

It. See PRONOUN 'IT'.

'It' deletion transformation. *G–2a.* The local transformation which substitutes a sentence complement of the 'that'-type for the impersonal 'it' which precedes it in the noun phrase of an underlying string, as when: "(*It—that Huck left*) surprised Tom" ⇒ "*That Huck left* surprised Tom." (Chomsky, 1965, 100–101.) *G–2b.* The obligatory transformation which deletes the abstract pronoun 'it' from a subject noun phrase containing a complement when optional extraposition is not applied, as when: "(*It—for Huck to leave*) surprised Tom" ⇒ "*For Huck to leave* surprised Tom." (Jacobs, 1968, 50; Ross, 1967, 192.) *G–2c.* The syntactic process by which the pronoun 'it' is deleted by optional transformation from before a complement in a sentence of the type "Tom can prove *it that this is false*": "Tom can prove *that this is false.*" (Rosenbaum, 1967c, 327.) Compare 'IT' REPLACEMENT TRANSFORMATION.

Item, lexical. See LEXICAL ITEM.

Iterative. *G–1.* Recursive—permitting increasingly more complex constructions to be built up from simpler constructions or constituents. (Lees, 1960a, xviii.) See also RECURSION.

Iterative cycle. *G–2.* A recursive cycle, in which certain rules must precede or follow certain others. (Lees, 1964b, xxxvi.) See also CYCLE, RECURSION.

'It'-inversion. *G–1.* The extraposition of a subject nominalization to the end of the sentence, with the subject pronominal 'it' standing in the subject position, as when: "*To leave* was difficult" ⇒ "*It* was difficult *to leave.*" (Lees, 1960a, 32; Lees, 1961, 314.) See also EXTRAPOSITION.

'It', pronoun. See PRONOUN 'IT'.

'It' replacement transformation. *G–2a.* The optional rule which replaces the sentence-initial pronoun 'it' with the object noun phrase of an embedded infinitival complement of a predicate adjective, as when: "*It* was hard for Huck to steer *the raft*" ⇒ "*The raft* was hard for Huck to steer." (Jacobs, 1968, 52.) *G–2b.* The obligatory rule which applies to a noun phrase complement of 'it' that contains an infinitival or gerundive complementizer. The 'it' replacement transformation replaces the pronoun 'it' with the subject of the complement sentence, followed by reflexivization, as when: "Huck believed *it* for-to he capable" ⇒ "Huck believed for-to he capable" ⇒ "Huck believed for he to be capable" ⇒ "Huck believed (for) himself to be capable." (Jacobs and Rosenbaum, 1968, 184–189.) Compare 'IT' DELETION TRANSFORMATION.

J

Jakobsonian distinctive feature. *G–1.* A binary phonetic property of sounds, one of a dozen or so developed by Roman Jakobson in the 1920's. The Jakobsonian distinctive features were based on both articulatory and acoustic properties, but the articulatory features are more widely referred to now than the acoustic ones. (Harms, 1968, 7.) See also DISTINCTIVE FEATURE, PHONETIC FEATURE, PHONOLOGICAL DISTINCTIVE FEATURE.

Juncture. See BOUNDARY.

Justification. See MOTIVATION.

Justification, independent. See INDEPENDENT MOTIVATION.

Justification of a grammar. *G–1–2.* The evaluation of a grammar, or linguistic theory, on the basis of external and internal adequacy. A grammar is 'justified' on the level of external or descriptive adequacy if it correctly describes the competence of the native speaker; it is 'justified' on the level of internal or explanatory adequacy if it provides a principled basis for selecting the correct descriptively adequate grammar. (Reibel and Schane, 1969, 2.) See also ADEQUACY, DESCRIPTIVE ADEQUACY, EXPLANATORY ADEQUACY, EXTERNAL CONDITION OF ADEQUACY.

K

Kernel. *G–1a.* The small, probably finite, set of basic—simple, active, declarative, affirmative—sentences, called 'kernel' sentences, that are derived from terminal phrase structure strings by obligatory transformations only. (Chomsky, 1956, 150.) Every sentence of the language belongs either to the 'kernel' or to the infinite set of derived sentences, called transforms. (Chomsky, 1957, 45.) *G–1b.* A kernel sentence. A sentence that has the characteristics of a kernel sentence is said to be a 'kernel,' or to be 'kernel.' A sentence is 'kernel' if it yields a simpler derivation than the other source sentence in a complex string. (Koutsoudas, 1966, 201, 256.) See also KERNEL SENTENCE.

Kernel noun. *G–1.* A noun that is free of derivational affixes; a noun that is not agentive or gerundive. (Lees, 1960a, 127.) Compare DERIVED WORD.

Kernel sentence. *G–1.* A sentence that is generated from a basic string—a kernel string: simple, declarative, active, affirmative—to which only phrase structure rules and obligatory singulary transformations have applied, as opposed to a nonkernel or derived sentence, which is generated by applying optional singulary and/or generalized transformations to underlying kernel strings. (Chomsky, 1956, 150.) A kernel 'sentence' should not be confused with its underlying kernel 'string.' (Chomsky, 1966a, 52.) Also called **Simplex sentence** (Lees and Klima, 1963, 148), **Kernel** (Koutsoudas, 1966, 256), **K-string** (Katz and Postal, 1964, 56). *G–2.* The basic nature of kernel sentences, and the usefulness of the distinction between kernel and derived sentences, is questioned. (Bach, 1964, 69.) Although the notion 'kernel sentence'—that is, a sentence with a minimum of transformations—has intuitive importance, kernel sentences play no significant role in the generation or interpretation of sentences. (Chomsky, 1965, 17–18.) Kernel sentences are no longer distinguished from derived sentences by optional transformations, most of which are regarded as obligatory in *G–2.* (Koutsoudas, 1966, 322.) There probably are no kernel sentences. (Lees, 1964b, xxxvi.) Compare DERIVED SENTENCE.

Kernel sentence rule. *G–1.* A constituent-structure rule. (Lees, 1960a, 3.) See also PHRASE STRUCTURE RULE.

Kernel string. See KERNEL SENTENCE.

K-string. See KERNEL SENTENCE.

L

Labeled bracketing. *G–1–2.* A phrase-marker formula for a string of words in which paired brackets are labeled with pairs of category symbols, the labels being either both outside the brackets or the right-hand label outside and the left-hand label inside (or omitted entirely), as in:

$$_S[_{NP}[_{ADJ}[green]_{ADJ}\ _N[ideas]_N]_{NP}\ _{VP}[_V[sleep]_V\ _{ADV}[furiously]_{ADV}]_{VP}]_S$$

(Chomsky, 1965, 17, 64; Chomsky, 1968, 25); a phrase-analysis, or correct analysis, of a transform into immediate constituents (Lees, 1960a, 114); a parsing; an immediate constituent analysis; a hierarchical categorization. A labeled bracketing is exactly equivalent to a labeled tree diagram, a labeled parenthesization, or a labeled box diagram. (Postal, 1964a, 6–7, 20, 82; Postal, 1964c, 21–22.) A categorially labeled bracketing of an actual sentence is inadequate to represent the deep structure of that sentence. (Chomsky, 1966a, 40.) See also PHRASE-MARKER, BRANCHING DIAGRAM.

Language. *G–1–2.* An infinite set of sentences constructed out of a finite set of symbols by a finite set of rules (Chomsky, 1956, 142; Chomsky, 1957, 13); a subset of a set of possible strings of objects constructed out of a set of elements by concatenation (Bach, 1964, 12); all of the sentences generated by a particular grammar (Langendoen, 1969, 1, 21). *G–2.* An instrument of communication which enables its users to pair meanings with sounds (Katz, 1966, 176); the mental reality which underlies speech and constitutes a speaker's competence (Katz, 1966, 116–117); an abstract object represented in neural tissues (Postal, 1968a, 295); a set of psychological principles that constitute a speaker's linguistic competence (Langacker, 1968, 35). Compare GRAMMAR.

Language acquisition. *G–2.* The process by which the child matches a succession of increasingly complex hypotheses, or potential theories, to the utterances of its parents until it selects, on the basis of an evaluation measure, the optimal, or simplest, grammar of the language. (Kiparsky, 1968, 194.) The child takes a fresh look at the facts of the language that he is learning by viewing the original grammar of his parents, and the innovations that they have made, as a single grammar. He then constructs a new, simplified grammar with innovations of its own. (King, 1969, 80–81.) Language acquisition is both species uniform, in that all humans learn one, and species specific, in that only humans learn one. (Langacker, 1968, 14.) See also ACQUISITION MODEL, LANGUAGE-ACQUISITION DEVICE.

Language-acquisition device. *G–2.* A hypothetical device—an AD, or acquisition device—which, on the basis of an input of primary linguistic data from a language, produces an output consisting of a descriptively adequate grammar for that language: primary linguistic data → AD → grammar of the language. The language-acquisition device must be language-independent—that is, capable of learning any human language—and must provide a definition of the notion 'human language.' (Chomsky, 1966a, 20–21.) A language-acquisition device, or LAD, is a kind of 'black box.' (King, 1969, 85.) See also ACQUISITION MODEL, LANGUAGE ACQUISITION.

Language-independent. *G–2.* Universal, as opposed to language-particular. For example, the universal phonetic alphabet provides a language-independent system for representing phonetic segments. (Chomsky and Halle, 1968, 28.) Compare LANGUAGE-PARTICULAR.

Language-particular. *G–2.* Required by a particular language, as opposed to language-independent. For example, the phonetic rules of English are language-particular. (Postal, 1968a, 65–66.) Compare LANGUAGE-INDEPENDENT.

Language universal. See LINGUISTIC UNIVERSAL.

Langue. *G–2.* The generative grammar that has been internalized by a native or fluent speaker of a language (Chomsky, 1964, 52, 60); the underlying linguistic competence of a fluent speaker, as opposed to parole, the speaker's performance (Lyons, 1968, 51–52). Compare PAROLE.

Lateral. *G–2.* The phonological distinctive feature which is positively specified for sounds that are articulated with a lowering of the midsection of the tongue at one or both sides, allowing the air to escape around the raised tip: English [1]. The negative specification is called **Nonlateral.** (Chomsky and Halle, 1968, 317.) See also LIQUID.

Late rule. *G–2.* A rule which is located close to the end of the set of ordered rules comprising a given component of the grammar; a rule at the end of the phonology which has relatively minor effect on the phonetic output of the grammar. Changes in adult grammars consist mostly of additions of late rules in the phonological component, often resulting in hypercorrection. (King, 1969, 26, 65, 68, 78–79.) Compare EARLY RULE.

Left-branching. *G–2.* Permitting embedding in the left branch of successive phrase structures—[[[A] A] A], as in: "John's wife's father." All languages are said to permit left-branching as well as right-branching and self-embedding. (Chomsky, 1965, 13.) Earlier, called **Left-recursive.** (Chomsky, 1961a, 123.) Compare RIGHT-BRANCHING CONSTRUCTION.

Left-identity hypothesis. *G–2*. The untenable formulation of the identity erasure transformation as obligatorily deleting the subject of the complement sentence simply if it is identical to the first noun phrase to its left in the main sentence. (Rosenbaum, 1967a, 16–17.) See also IDENTITY ERASURE TRANSFORMATION.

Left-recursive. See LEFT-BRANCHING.

Length. *G–2*. Duration, which is one of the three types of prosodic or suprasegmental features, the other two being stress and pitch. Length is a feature of both vowels and consonants in English. Vowels are of slightly longer duration before voiced consonants than before voiceless consonants (e.g., *had* vs. *hat*); consonants are of slightly longer duration when doubled (e.g., *illegal* vs. *legal*). (Chomsky and Halle, 1968, 300; Langacker, 1968, 151.) See also PROSODIC FEATURE.

Level. See LINGUISTIC LEVEL.

Level, deep. See DEEP LEVEL.

Leveling. See SIMPLIFICATION.

Level, linguistic. See LINGUISTIC LEVEL.

Level, phonemic. See PHONEMIC LEVEL.

Level, surface. See SURFACE LEVEL.

Lexical. See LEXICON.

Lexical category. *G–2*. A syntactic category that appears on the left of a lexical rule, which is a rule that replaces a category with a lexical formative. For example: N → *idea*; V → *sleep*; ADJ → *green*; etc. Noun is the selectionally dominant lexical category, because its features are carried over to other lexical categories (e.g., to verb and adjective) by selectional rules. A 'major' category is one that dominates a lexical category (e.g., NP, VP, etc.). (Chomsky, 1965, 74, 115–116.) See also CATEGORY. Compare LEXICAL FORMATIVE, LEXICAL ITEM.

Lexical component. *G–2*. The lexicon, in the base component of a second-generation transformational grammar, which adds phonological, semantic, and syntactic features to complex symbols in deep structures. The lexical component has taken over the subcategorization rules from the earlier phrase structure grammar, which is now the categorial component of the base component. (Chomsky, 1965, 120–122.) *G–2S*. The lexical component is excluded from a universal base because of its arbitrariness. Also, in a particular grammar, the lexical component does not provide phonological representations to complex symbols in the deep structure. (Bach, 1968, 117.) See also LEXICON, BASE COMPONENT.

Lexical entry. *G–1–2*. A phonological distinctive feature matrix—the spelling of the lexical item (Lees, 1960a, 21)—and a collection of the syntactic feature specifications, or complex symbol, of a formative (Chomsky, 1965, 84); a list of the idiosyncratic categories—or inherent features: phonological, semantic, syntactic—to which a formative belongs (Chomsky and Halle, 1968, 7). Also called **Lexical representation.** (Rosenbaum, 1967a, 81, 88.) Compare DICTIONARY ENTRY.

Lexical formative. *G–2*. A lexical item, such as *green* or *idea,* which is selected from a universal set of vocabulary symbols; a member of one of the two subdivisions of formatives, the other being grammatical formatives such as determiners and inflections. (Chomsky, 1965, 65.) Compare GRAMMATICAL FORMATIVE, LEXICAL CATEGORY. See also LEXICAL ITEM.

Lexical insertion. *G–2*. The insertion of lexical items into the positions of a preterminal string marked by the fixed dummy symbol △, thereby converting the string into a terminal string. (Chomsky, 1966a, 70.) See also LEXICAL PASS.

Lexical item. *G–1.* A single terminal symbol, or word, such as *green* or *idea,* which appears on the right of a morphophonemic rule, as in: N → *idea*; ADJ → *green.* (Bach, 1964, 115.) *G–2.* The morpheme or word which is specified by the features of a lexical entry and marked in some fashion for the application of certain transformations (Rosenbaum, 1967a, 108); a set of inherent syntactic, semantic, and phonological features which, when inserted into a phrase-marker by lexical rule to replace a complex symbol, acquires the inherent features of the phrase-marker, such as number, of certain transformations, such as case, and of certain dominant nouns if the formative is a verb or adjective. Some lexical items appear in the lexicon even though they have a complex internal structure, as in the case of idioms such as *catch on* or *take issue with.* The lexicon may require some kind of internal computation to handle these items. (Chomsky, 1965, 84, 177, 190–191.) *G–2S.* A lexical item need not necessarily appear in the lexicon of the language; the existence of one item can predict the existence of another, which need not be listed, as when *warm* (temperature) implies *warm* (feeling). (McCawley, 1968, 168.) Also called LEXICAL FORMATIVE. Compare LEXICAL ENTRY, LEXICAL CATEGORY.

Lexical marker. *G–2.* An instruction, accompanying a lexical item, which governs the application or nonapplication of certain transformations to that lexical item. (Rosenbaum, 1967a, 108.) See also INSTRUCTION, VERBAL MARKER.

Lexical morpheme. *G–1.* A morpheme symbol, introduced by phrase structure rule or transformational rule, which is assigned a phonological representation by the first set of rules of the phonological component— that is, before morphophonemic representation. (Koutsoudas, 1966, 35.) Compare LEXICAL ITEM, LEXICAL FORMATIVE.

Lexical pass. *G–2.* The insertion of lexical segments—i.e., lexical items or bundles of semantic features—into the deep structure of a sentence before transformations apply (in the 'first lexical pass'), or the insertion of phonological segments, or words, into the transformed structure before phonological rules apply (in the 'second lexical pass'). (Jacobs and Rosenbaum, 1968, 84.) See also FIRST LEXICAL PASS, SECOND LEXICAL PASS, LEXICAL INSERTION.

Lexical pass, first. See FIRST LEXICAL PASS.

Lexical pass, second. See SECOND LEXICAL PASS.

Lexical reading. *G–2.* The semantic interpretation of one of the branches— senses, or meanings—of the dictionary entry of a single lexical item, as opposed to the derived reading of an amalgamation of such 'lexical readings' for a phrase or for the entire sentence. (Katz, 1966, 156–157.) See also SEMANTIC INTERPRETATION.

Lexical redundancy rule. *G–2.* One of the unordered readjustment rules —or morpheme structure rules, or conditions on the lexicon—which act as filters within single lexical entries, accepting or rejecting proposed phonological matrices without modifying the feature composition of those matrices—that is, not functioning as phonological rules. Lexical redundancy rules fill in unspecified (O, U) squares, or cells, of the phonological matrix and thereby convert that matrix into a phonetic matrix. (Chomsky and Halle, 1968, 171, 382, 388.) Also called **Blank-filling rule, Morpheme structure rule, Phonological redundancy rule, Morphophonemic rule.** Compare LEXICAL RULE.

Lexical representation. *G–2.* The phonological matrix of a lexical or grammatical formative which is provided directly to the syntax by the lexicon rather than introduced by the syntactic rules themselves. (Chomsky and Halle, 1968, 9, 165.) See also LEXICAL ENTRY.

Lexical rule. *G–1.* A rule at the end of the constituent-structure grammar which expands one of the lowest-level grammatical categories in the constituent-structure string into an individual morpheme, such as: N → *idea.* (Lees, 1960a, 20.) *G–2.* A universal convention of the base component which introduces lexical formatives into the deep structure to replace complex symbols (Chomsky, 1965, 74, 86, 112); a lexical substitution rule, which substitutes lexical items for complex symbols in the deep structure but is outside the grammar proper (Lyons, 1968, 243); a lexical pass, which introduces segments into the deep structure—the first lexical pass—and words into the surface structure—the second lexical pass (Jacobs and Rosenbaum, 1968, 83–84). *G–2S.* Some lexical items are predicted by rules which precede lexical insertion (e.g., *buy/sell*) while other items must be inserted after certain transformations, such as nominalization, have applied (e.g., *former/latter*). (McCawley, 1968, 169.) See also LEXICAL INSERTION, LEXICAL PASS. Compare LEXICAL REDUNDANCY RULE.

Lexical segment. See LEXICAL PASS.

Lexicon. *G–2.* A set of lexical entries, each of which consists of a phonological distinctive feature matrix, which spells a lexical formative, and a complex symbol of syntactic, semantic, morphological, transformational, and exceptional features (Chomsky, 1965, 166); a subcomponent, along with the categorial subcomponent, of the base component of the syntactic component of a generative grammar (Chomsky, 1965, 84); an unordered list of all of the lexical formatives of the language, each of which is positively specified for strict subcategorizational features and negatively specified for selectional features (Chomsky, 1965, 164); a set of lexical entries plus a set of lexical substitution transformations for introducing the lexical items into preterminal strings (Chomsky, 1965, 122); a list of the morphemes of the language, along with the information characterizing each morpheme's behavior at each of the levels of the grammar (King, 1969, 18–19); the vocabulary of morphemes of a language, along with their unpredictable, or nonredundant, associations with semantic, syntactic, and phonological properties (Postal, 1968a, 153–154); an internalized dictionary: an inventory of lexical entries, each of which represents, in features, the sound and meaning of a morpheme (Jacobs and Rosenbaum, 1968, 59–60). The lexicon does not designate the lexical category of an item. (Chomsky, 1965, 166.) The lexicon lists both morphemes and idioms. (Postal, 1968a, 153–154.) Formally speaking, the lexicon is the most static component of a grammar. (King, 1969, 67.) The lexicon is subdivided phonologically and morphologically into foreign and nonforeign classes. (Chomsky and Halle, 1968, 174.) The lexicon is partly identifiable with the traditional notion of dictionary. (King, 1969, 18–19.) The lexicon is not to be confused with the dictionary of the semantic component; the lexicon is a part of the syntactic component. (Katz and Postal, 1964, 161.) The question of how to enter lexical items in the lexicon is not settled. (Chomsky, 1965, 119–120.) *G–2S*. A component with two divisions: a major-category lexicon, which inserts semantically relevant items, and a minor-category lexicon, which inserts function words (Fillmore, 1966, 371); a set of transformational mappings of parts of strings into phonological representations (Bach, 1968, 120–121). Compare DICTIONARY. See also LEXICAL COMPONENT, BASE COMPONENT.

Linear ordering. *G–1*. The linear succession of morphemes in a string. (Bach, 1964, 103–108.) *G–2*. The linear succession of formatives in a surface structure string. Order helps to determine the grammatical relations of surface structures (basically topic—comment), but it plays no part in determining the grammatical relations of deep structures (fundamentally subject—predicate). (Chomsky, 1965, 221.) *G–2S*. Linear ordering of constituents is relevant to syntactic description but not to semantic description. Transformations account for the linear order of structures. (Langacker, 1969, 170.) Compare RULE ORDERING.

Linguist. *G–1*. A student of human language, of the theory of language, of the theory of linguistic structure, of grammar, of syntax. (Chomsky, 1957, 11.) *G–2*. A grammarian. (Jacobs and Rosenbaum, 1968, 41.) Seldom used in *G–2*. See also GRAMMARIAN.

Linguistic. See LINGUISTICS.

Linguistic analysis. *G–1*. The separation of the sentences of a language from the ungrammatical sequences, and the study of the structure of the sentences. (Chomsky, 1957, 13.) See also ANALYSIS. Compare LINGUISTIC DESCRIPTION.

Linguistic change. *G–1*. The addition or elimination of one or more phonological rules in the grammar of an adult, or the wholesale restructuring of his phonology by the child. (Halle, 1959, 344, 347.) *G–2a*. Change in a language through a series of individual innovations, consisting primarily of the addition of single rules to the grammar by adult speakers and the simplification of the adult grammar by the child, causing a minimal discontinuity in transmission from generation to generation (Closs, 1965, 395); change in a language resulting from innovations during the child's acquisition of language (Gruber, 1967, 444); change in an adult speaker's competence, but not necessarily in his performance, because of the addition of one or more rules to a given component of his grammar (King, 1969, 66); addition by the adult, or simplification (by analogy) by the child, of the rules of a grammar, resulting in discontinuous transmission of language and its re-creation or restructuring by each child who learns it (Kiparsky, 1968, 174–177). The grammars of adult speakers change by minor alterations occurring late in the rules of a given component. Such alterations are the addition of lexical items, addition of a few rules, and slight modification of rules. (King, 1969, 66.) The order of grammatical rules is also subject to historical change. (Kiparsky, 1968, 174–177.) There are two types of linguistic change: primary change (rule addition, loss, reordering, and simplification) and restructuring (change in the deep structure). (King, 1969, 39.) Simplification occurs, rarely, when a feature of the child's grammar survives into adulthood and is adopted by the community. (Kiparsky, 1968, 195.) A model of linguistic change describes the process by which the speech output from the adult grammar of the first generation is inputted into the language acquisition device (LAD) of the child of the second generation. The child then constructs an optimal grammar, incorporating innovations into it as he matures, and outputs to the child of the third generation a grammar which is changed from that of his grandfather. (King, 1969, 85.) *G–2b.* The grammatical result of two dialects having become different. All historical change can be traced to dialect differentiation. (King, 1969, 28, 39.) See also RULE ADDITION, RULE LOSS, RESTRUCTURING, SOUND CHANGE, SIMPLIFICATION, REORDERING.

Linguistic data, primary. See PRIMARY LINGUISTIC DATA.

Linguistic description. *G–1.* A description of the systems of levels of representation of the sentences of a language: the phonemic level, the morphological level, the phrase structure level, and the transformational level. (Chomsky, 1957, 11, 18.) *G–2a.* An integrated description of both the grammar of a natural language—the syntax and phonology of *G–1*—and the semantic system of that language. (Katz and Postal, 1964, 10.) *G–2b.* A scientific theory from which the syntactic, phonological, and semantic facts of the language can be derived; a reconstruction of the principles which underlie the human's ability to master a language and communicate with others in it (Katz and Postal, 1964, ix, 1, 150, 166); an explication of the linguistic competence of a fluent speaker and the contribution of that competence to his linguistic performance (Katz, 1966, 115–116); a description of the sentences which define a language and underlie the behavior of its speakers (Postal, 1964c, 35); a grammatical analysis; a descriptive analysis of a syntactic problem (Rosenbaum, 1967b, ix). Compare GRAMMAR.

Linguistic grammar. *G–2.* A theory of grammar whose aim is to discover and describe the apparatus which permits a speaker to understand and produce the sentences of his language. (Chomsky, 1966a, 10.) See also GRAMMAR, LINGUISTIC DESCRIPTION.

Linguistic intuition. *G–1–2.* Knowledge of a language which comes without instruction and is outside of awareness (Chomsky, 1968, 42); the basis of a speaker's subconscious ability to speak and understand his language fluently and to make judgments regarding the structure or meaning of sentences (Langendoen, 1969, 3–4, 6). Linguistic intuition is one of the bases on which a grammar can be constructed but should not be evaluated. (Chomsky, 1957, 56.) See also INTUITION. Compare INTROSPECTION.

Linguistic level. *G–1.* One of the four or more necessary levels of representation of a linguistic theory: phonemic, morphological, phrase structure, transformational. (Chomsky, 1957, 11, 47.) There is no fixed set of levels in the phrase structure grammar itself, but rather higher-level rules and lower-level rules. (Bach, 1964, 59.) In a general theory of linguistic levels, phrase structures and transformations each constitute a linguistic level. On each of these levels, the sentence is represented by markers: a derived phrase-marker on the phrase structure level, and a T-marker, or transformation-marker, on the transformational level. Each level represents the sentence in terms of certain elementary atomic symbols called **Primes.** The levels are organized in a hierarchy, with the markers of one level being mapped into the markers of the next lowest level. (Chomsky,

1966a, 54.) *G–2.* One of the systems of the linguistic hierarchy: phonetic, phonological, morphological, word, phrase structure, transformational. (Chomsky, 1965, 222–223.) Each level, or system, of a linguistic theory consists of a set of primes (viz., an alphabet), a set of markers or representations, and a set of relations among the representations on one level and between those on that level and those on other levels. (Bach, 1964, 58.) See also DEEP LEVEL, SURFACE LEVEL.

Linguistics. *G–1.* The study of human language and the theory of language; the study of individual natural languages and the construction of their grammars. (Postal, 1964b, 137.) *G–2.* The study of language universals and native speaker competence. (Postal, 1968b, 282–283.) *G–2S.* The study of 'universal' grammar, as opposed to 'grammar,' which is a theory of linguistic competence. (Kiparsky, 1968, 188.) Linguistics is classified variously as an empirical science (Bach, 1964, 97); as a branch of cognitive psychology (Chomsky, 1968, 1); as a social science (Langacker, 1968, 5); and as a combination of science and the humanities (Lyons, 1968, i). Compare GRAMMAR. See also CARTESIAN LINGUISTICS, TRANSFORMATIONAL GRAMMAR, GENERATIVE GRAMMAR, TRADITIONAL GRAMMAR, STRUCTURAL LINGUISTICS.

Linguistics, Cartesian. See CARTESIAN LINGUISTICS.

Linguistic science. *G–1.* The study of the formal properties of sentences: linguistics. (Lees, 1960a, 1.) See also LINGUISTICS.

Linguistics, descriptive. See DESCRIPTIVE LINGUISTICS.

Linguistics, formal. See FORMAL THEORY.

Linguistics, general. See GENERAL LINGUISTICS.

Linguistics, historical. See HISTORICAL LINGUISTICS.

Linguistics, mentalistic. See MENTALISTIC LINGUISTICS.

Linguistics, modern. See STRUCTURAL LINGUISTICS.

Linguistics, structural. See STRUCTURAL LINGUISTICS.

Linguistics, taxonomic. See STRUCTURAL LINGUISTICS.

Linguistics, traditional. See TRADITIONAL GRAMMAR.

Linguistic theory. *G–1.* A theory of linguistic structure; a schema for linguistic description which characterizes the form of grammars and provides a method for selecting among grammars (Chomsky, 1961b, 173–174); a precise characterization of the possible kinds of rules and structures and the mechanical methods for associating them with sentences (Postal, 1964b, 138); the product of linguistic study, which is a formal, explicit, complete, and simple set of statements about language; a theory of a specific language, which predicts all and only the sentences of the language and assigns a structural description to each (Bach, 1964, 2, 6, 11). *G–1–2.* A hypothesis about linguistic universals which asserts that the grammars of all languages are constructed according to a certain plan (Chomsky, 1961b, 173–174); a general theory of linguistic structure which provides a partial definition of 'language' (Chomsky, 1962, 224); a general linguistic theory, about language in general (Bach, 1964, 2, 6, 11); a theory about the nature of language (Postal, 1964a, 3); a theory of linguistic universals, or a theory of a particular language (Katz, 1966, 108); a system of hypotheses about the essential, general characteristics of human language (Chomsky, 1964, 50); a metatheory dealing with universal properties of linguistic descriptions of natural languages (Fodor and Katz, 1964, 19); a theory of linguistic description, specifying linguistic universals, the components of the description, and the inter-connections between the components (Katz and Postal, 1964, 161); a general theory of linguistic description which specifies the common features of all correct individual linguistic descriptions; a theory of the nature of language which represents the structure common to all natural languages (Katz and Postal, 1964, ix, 2); a statement of linguistic universals and a definition of the notion 'natural language' (Katz, 1966, x). *G–2.* An attempt to match the linguistic behavior of fluent speakers and to reconstruct the mechanisms underlying human language (Fodor and Katz, 1964, 17); an explanation for the linguistic intuition of native speakers (Chomsky, 1964, 63); a theory which is concerned with the discovery of mental reality underlying verbal behavior; a specific hypothesis about the nature of mental structures and processes: a general linguistic theory (Chomsky, 1965, 4, 53). See also TRANSFORMATIONAL GRAMMAR, GENERATIVE GRAMMAR, GRAMMATICAL THEORY, SYNTACTIC THEORY.

Linguistic universal. *G–2.* One of the descriptive statements which can be eliminated from the grammar of a particular language because it is attributable to the general theory of grammar (Chomsky, 1965, 35); one of the properties which define 'possible natural language' and 'potential grammar for a natural language' (Chomsky and Halle, 1968, 4); one of the general principles that are compatible with the facts of human languages and act as preconditions on language acquisition (Chomsky and Halle, 1968, 25); one of the formal statements—a formal universal—or substantive elements—a substantive universal—of a general linguistic theory (Katz and Postal, 1964, 160); one of the integral parts of an evaluation measure which allows the child to select the best grammar of his language (King, 1969, 15); one of the biologically determined, or innate, linguistic structures of the human organism (Postal, 1968b, 284). The account of linguistic universals is the main task of linguistic theory. (Chomsky, 1965, 28, 36.) Also called **Universal of language** (Katz and Postal, 1964, 160) and **Language universal** (Langacker, 1968, 241). See also FORMAL UNIVERSAL, SUBSTANTIVE UNIVERSAL.

Liquid. *G–1–2.* A phonological natural class of segments which are specified as [+vocalic] and [+consonantal]. They are the lateral consonant [1] and the retroflex consonant [r]. (Halle, 1959, 327; Chomsky and Halle, 1968, 177.) See also LATERAL. Compare CONSONANT, GLIDE.

Local transformation. *G–2.* Any rule of the transformational cycle which affects only a substring of a category, such as the nominalization rule, which replaces the dummy symbol △ in the deep structure with S, in a 'strictly local' transformation. (Chomsky, 1965, 89, 214.) See also TRANSFORMATION.

Locative. *G–2S.* The case category which characterizes the location of the action or state expressed by the verb. (Fillmore, 1968, 25.) See also CASE.

Loop. *G–1a.* Recursion in a derivation. (Chomsky, 1957, 24; Lees, 1960a, 55.) *G–1b.* To recur in a derivation. (Lees, 1964a, 151.) See also RECURSION.

Loss, rule. See RULE LOSS.

Low. *G–2.* The phonological distinctive feature which is positively specified for sounds that are articulated with the body of the tongue lowered below the neutral position: English [æ], [a], [ɔ], [h], [ʔ]. The feature 'low' is equivalent to the earlier **Compact** for vowels and **Velarization** for consonants. The negative specification is called **Nonlow.** (Chomsky and Halle, 1968, 305.) Compare HIGH, COMPACT.

Low(er)-level. *G–1–2.* In the lower part of the hierarchy or order of components, rules, categories, or features. 'Low(er)-level' generalizations appear later in the hierarchy or order than 'high(er)-level' generalizations and are consequently less abstract. (Bach, 1964, 53, 59; Chomsky, 1965, 150; Chomsky and Halle, 1968, 43, 59.) Compare HIGH(ER)-LEVEL.

Lower-level rule. See LOW-LEVEL RULE.

Low-level rule. *G–1.* A rule at or near the end of an ordered set of rules on a single level: phrase structure, transformational, phonological; a rule that is placed later in an ordered set of rules than another, higher-level rule in the same set; a phonological rule as contrasted with a transformational rule; a transformational rule as contrasted with a phrase structure rule; a phonological or morphological rule. (Bach, 1964, 53–59.) See also LATE RULE. Compare HIGH-LEVEL RULE.

M

Machinery, transformational. See TRANSFORMATIONAL MACHINERY.

Main clause. *G–1.* The clause in a complex sentence that is not subordinate to another clause. (Lees, 1960a, 2.) See also MAIN SENTENCE, MATRIX SENTENCE.

Main sentence. *G–2.* A sentence that is not an embedding or a conjunct (Jacobs and Rosenbaum, 1968, 77); a matrix sentence (Reibel and Schane, 1969, ix); a main structure (Chomsky, 1966a, 53); an including sentence (Rosenbaum, 1967a, 16, 27, 34). See also MATRIX SENTENCE.

Main stress rule. *G–2* The set of phonological rules which, operating cyclically on a labeled bracketing not restricted to the word level, place primary stress on the proper vowel. (Chomsky and Halle, 1968, 41, 240.) See also STRESS PLACEMENT RULE, NUCLEAR STRESS RULE.

Main verb. *G–1.* A major category (MV) of the verb phrase, codominated with AUX and dominating V and COMP (i.e., NP or ADJ): VP $\rightarrow$ AUX+MV; MV $\rightarrow$ V+NP/ADJ. (Lees, 1960a, 44; Bach, 1964, 63.) *G–2a.* The grammatical relation which holds between a verb (V) and the verb phrase (VP) which dominates it: [V, VP], V is the main-verb-of VP. Not a major category in *G–2.* (Chomsky, 1965, 71.) *G–2b.* The verb of the main sentence in a complex sentence. (Rosenbaum, 1967a, 33.) See also VERB PHRASE.

Major class feature. *G–2.* One of the universal phonetic features [sonorant], [vocalic], or [consonantal], which are used to define the categories of speech sounds as vowels, glides, liquids, nasal consonants, and nonnasal consonants (that is, stops, fricatives, and affricates). (Chomsky and Halle, 1968, 299, 301–303.)

Major rule. *G–2.* A phonological rule which applies automatically to every form that has not been marked [−rule] (as foreign words are), as opposed to a 'minor' rule, which applies only to forms specifically marked for it. (King, 1969, 137–138.) Compare MINOR RULE.

91

Manner adverbial. *G–1.* An adverb, or complex adverb or adverbial, which expresses the manner in which a verb achieves an action, such as: *slowly.* (Lees, 1960a, 7.) *G–2a.* An optional constituent of the verb phrase: VP → V+NP (PP) (manner). Manner adverbials participate in verb subcategorization; hence, for example, all transitive verbs take manner adverbials freely except middle verbs like *cost, weigh,* etc. Manner adverbial can be rewritten as *by-passive* to signify that the passive transformation must apply: NP+AUX+V+NP+*by-passive*. A verb will undergo the passive transformation, and take manner adverbials freely, only if it is positively specified for the feature [___NP+manner]. (Chomsky, 1965, 103–105.) As a constituent of a passive sentence, manner adverbial can be symbolized as MAN. (Rosenbaum, 1967a, 37.) *G–2b.* The result of a manner adverbial transformation, which converts an adjective such as *correct,* in the verb phrase of a sentence with a noun phrase complement as subject, into an adverbial of manner (*correctly*) if a nominalization transformation does not apply, as when: "It (Tom solved the problem) was *correct*" ⇒ "Tom solved the problem *correctly.*" (Jacobs and Rosenbaum, 1968, 228–231.) See also PASSIVE TRANSFORMATION.

Manner adverbial transformation. See MANNER ADVERBIAL.

Manner feature. *G–2.* One of the phonological distinctive features which relate primarily to manner of articulation: for English, [continuant], [strident] (or [abrupt offset]), and [tense]. (Harms, 1968, 23, 33–36.) See also DISTINCTIVE FEATURE.

Map. *G–1.* To carry an object on the level of phrase structure into a string of words, or a mapping (Chomsky, 1957, 39); to convert phrase-markers into phrase-markers and strings into strings (Postal, 1964a, 79). *G–2.* To transform a structure generated by the base into an actual sentence (Chomsky, 1965, vi); to project an infinite set of deep structures onto an associated set of surface structures (Chomsky, 1968, 26–27). A transformation maps an underlying structure onto a new derived structure. (Rosenbaum, 1967a, 1.) See also TRANSFORM.

Mapping. See MAP.

Mark. *G–2.* To assign an instruction or marker to. For example, nouns can be marked for the application of the pronoun replacement transformation, and verbs can be marked for the application of the passive transformation. (Rosenbaum, 1967a, 15, 108.) See also INSTRUCTION, MARKER.

Marked. See MARK.

Markedness. *G–2.* The notion, in systematic phonemics, of the normal state of a segment—natural, unmarked, U—as opposed to the exceptional state of a segment—unnatural, marked, M. The rules that apply to marked/unmarked representations in a phonological matrix, specifying them as plus (+) or minus (−), are universal; language-particular rules apply only to +/− specified values. The theory of markedness eliminates most of the morpheme structure rules of early *G–2* and accounts for the order of acquisition of sounds by the child: completely unmarked first (e.g., [m], [a]). (Postal, 1968a, 166–167, 172.) See also SYSTEMATIC PHONEMICS.

Marker. *G–2a.* A syntactic, i.e., grammatical, or semantic feature in the dictionary entry of a lexical item. The grammatical marker specifies the syntactic relations of the item, such as noun, count, masculine, etc., and the semantic marker provides the semantic relations between that item and the rest of the vocabulary: (human), (male), (young), etc. Although syntactic markers and semantic markers have different selectional functions and a different theoretical basis, the names of the markers are in some cases the same or similar, as in: human vs. (human); masculine vs. (male). (Katz and Fodor, 1963, 500, 518.) *G–2b.* An instruction on a lexical item which regulates the application of certain transformations to structures containing that item—as 'optional,' 'obligatory,' 'not applicable.' For example, a verb must have a marker to regulate the application of the extraposition transformation. (Rosenbaum, 1967a, 69, 72.) See also INSTRUCTION, VERBAL MARKER, SEMANTIC MARKER, SYNTACTIC MARKER.

Marker, analysis.   See ANALYSIS-MARKER.

Marker, complement sentence.   See COMPLEMENT SENTENCE MARKER.

Marker, grammatical.   See GRAMMATICAL MARKER.

Marker, lexical.   See LEXICAL MARKER.

Marker, question.   See QUESTION MARKER.

Marker, scope.   See SCOPE MARKER.

Marker, semantic.   See SEMANTIC MARKER.

Marker, strict subcategorization.   See STRICT SUBCATEGORIZATION MARKER.

Marker system.   *G–2a.* A set of features which distinguish the properties of a set of morphemes. For example, the complementizing markers characterize the set of complementizing morphemes, also called **Complementizers:** *that, for, to,* POSS, *ing,* etc. (Rosenbaum, 1967a, 24.) *G–2b.* A set of instructions on lexical items which determine the applicability of certain transformations—as 'optional,' 'obligatory,' 'not applicable.' For example, the verb *tend,* as in "The raft *tends* to leak," is marked for the nonapplicability of the passive transformation: *"To leak is tended by the raft." (Rosenbaum, 1967a, 69, 72.) See also MARKER.

Marker, transformation.   See TRANSFORMATION-MARKER.

Marker, verbal.   See VERBAL MARKER.

Mass noun.   See ABSTRACT.

Matrix.   *G–1a.* A matrix sentence. (Thomas, 1965, 93.) *G–1b.* A representation of the distinctive syntactic features of a lexical item. (Lees, 1963, xxviii.) *G–1c.* A chart of the distinctive feature classifications of the phonemes of a language. (Halle, 1959, 331.) Each column represents a phonemic segment, and each row represents a phonetic feature. (Lees, 1960a, 21.) *G–2.* A description, in the lexicon, of the phonological distinctive feature structure of a lexical item, with the columns representing phonological segments and the rows representing the binary specifications of individual phonological features (Chomsky, 1965, 213); a representation at the systematic phonemic level of the binary distinctive feature specifications of the morphemes of a language; a representation at the systematic phonetic level of the binary or nonbinary specifications of the distinctive and nondistinctive features of the morphemes of a language (Harms, 1968, 14). See also PHONOLOGICAL MATRIX, PHONETIC MATRIX.

Matrix, classificatory.   See CLASSIFICATORY FEATURE.

Matrix, phonetic.   See PHONETIC MATRIX.

Matrix, phonological.   See PHONOLOGICAL MATRIX.

Matrix phrase-marker.   *G–2.* A phrase-marker which has a matrix dummy (md) element embedded in one of its terminal nodes. Also called **Matrix P-marker.** (Katz and Postal, 1964, 48.) See also PHRASE-MARKER.

Matrix sentence.   *G–1.* The first source-sentence of a transformational rule —as opposed to the 'constituent sentence,' which is the second source-sentence (Lees, 1961, 309); the embedding sentence, as opposed to the embedded sentence (Bach, 1964, 75); the basic or independent sentence: the matrix (Thomas, 1965, 93); the sentence into which a constituent sentence is inserted by a generalized transformation (Chomsky, 1966a, 62). By general convention, the 'matrix-sentence' never has a generalized transformation in its history. (Lees, 1960a, 108.) Also called **Main sentence, Main clause, Receiver sentence, Receiver, Matrix structure, Matrix.** See also MAIN SENTENCE, MATRIX PHRASE-MARKER.

Maximal sentence. *G–1.* The source sentence from which an elliptic sentence is derived, such as: *"You will report!"* ⇒ "Report!" (Lees, 1960a, 53.) See also SOURCE SENTENCE.

Meaning. *G–1.* The semantic relation which holds between a sentence and the interpretation of that sentence. (Chomsky, 1957, 103; Chomsky, 1964, 68.) *G–2.* The combination of the references of the lexical items of a sentence with the grammatical relations that hold between them. (Katz and Postal, 1964, 39.) Meaning plays no role in the form of the syntactic and phonological components of a grammar. (Chomsky, 1965, 226.) 'Meaning' in the sense of linguistic meaning must be distinguished from 'meaning' in the sense of intention. (Chomsky, 1966a, 29.) Compare READING, SEMANTIC INTERPRETATION.

Measure, simplicity. See SIMPLICITY METRIC.

Mellow. See STRIDENT.

Membership rule, constituent-. See CONSTITUENT-MEMBERSHIP RULE.

Mentalistic linguistics. *G–2.* Theoretical linguistics, the primary object of which is the investigation of the internalized linguistic knowledge, or competence, of the native or fluent speaker, using his performance, among other things, as data (Chomsky, 1965, 193); an attempt to develop a theory of mental processes by defining the notion 'form in language' and investigating the implications of that definition for cognitive psychology (Chomsky, 1966a, 9). See also CARTESIAN LINGUISTICS. Compare STRUCTURAL LINGUISTICS.

Metalanguage. *G–1.* The language of a linguistic theory in relation to the language of the grammars that employ that theory; the language of a grammar in relation to the language for which that grammar is constructed. The language of a linguistic theory is thus a **Metametalanguage** in relation to the language that is described in one of its grammars. (Chomsky, 1957, 54.) Compare METATHEORY.

Metalinguistic. *G–2S.* Concerning such matters as the social value of different forms of speech—an important part of a speaker's competence. (Kiparsky, 1968, 175.)

Metametalanguage. See METALANGUAGE.

Metarule. *G–2.* A convention, such as 'tree-pruning'; a universal rule, not entered in any particular grammar. (Ross, 1966, 289.) See also CONVENTION.

Metatheory. *G–1.* The theory that deals with the points of connection of grammar and semantics (Chomsky, 1957, 102); the theory about theories about languages: general linguistic theory (Bach, 1964, 14); the general theory of grammars (Lees, 1960a, 55, 111). Also: **Meta-theory.** (Lees, 1960a, 111.) Compare METALANGUAGE. See also LINGUISTIC THEORY.

Metric, simplicity. See SIMPLICITY METRIC.

Middle object. *G–1.* The object of a middle verb (or *have*), as in:

"Tom has *a knife.*" All genitives mirror the relation of a subject and an object of a middle verb (e.g., "Tom's knife"), except for certain nominalizations like "Tom's tricking of Huck." (Lees, 1960a, 130–131.) See also MIDDLE VERB, 'HAVE'. Compare DIRECT OBJECT.

Middle verb. *G–1–2.* A verb which, like a transitive verb, is followed by a noun phrase object with a referent different from the subject noun phrase, but which, unlike a transitive verb, cannot accept manner adverbs freely or be transformed into an action nominal or undergo the passive transformation, as in: **"The suit *cost* fifty dollars satisfactorily"; **"The suit's *costing* of fifty dollars was satisfactory"; **"Fifty dollars *was cost* by the suit satisfactorily." Other 'middle verbs' besides *cost* are *weigh, resemble, mean,* and *have.* (Lees, 1960a, 8; Thomas, 1965, 122; Chomsky, 1965, 103.) Compare TRANSITIVE VERB.

Minor rule. *G–2.* A phonological rule which applies to a form only if it is specifically marked for that rule. A 'minor rule' in a language is simply a collection of exceptions, marked 'minus the rule,' to a contemporary 'major rule,' which may have started out as a collection of exceptions itself—that is, the current exceptions may be the residue of earlier regularities. (King, 1969, 38.) Compare MAJOR RULE. See also EXCEPTION, EXCEPTION FEATURE, MINUS-NEXT-RULE CONVENTION.

Minus-next-rule convention. *G–2.* A universal phonological rule which automatically assigns the feature minus-next-rule to a form which is marked as being unable to undergo an immediately following rule in a conjunctive ordering. (Harms, 1968, 73.) For example, the minus-rule feature is positively specified (as $+[-\text{rule } n]$) for foreign vocabulary in English which undergo vowel laxing and are therefore exceptions to the general rule, as in: *serene* $[+\text{foreign}] +[-\text{rule } n] \rightarrow$ *serenity*. (King, 1969, 135–136.) See also EXCEPTION.

Minus rule feature. See MINUS-NEXT-RULE CONVENTION.

Modal. *G–1.* The optional constituent M of the auxiliary system of a transformational grammar: AUX $\rightarrow$ C (M) *(have+en) (be+ing).* M can be replaced by the elements *will, shall, can, may,* or *must,* which are also called modals. (Chomsky, 1957, 39.) *G–2a.* The optional constituent M, or modal, of the auxiliary phrase of a generative grammar: AUX $\rightarrow$ Tense (modal) (perfect) (progressive). (Chomsky, 1965, 43, 85; Rosenbaum, 1967a, 30.) *G–2b.* A lexical item which is marked [+M] in the lexicon. (Chomsky, 1965, 43, 85.) A modal can appear in both declarative and interrogative sentences—it is not deleted in declarative sentences the way *do* is. (Jacobs and Rosenbaum, 1968, 41, 120–121.) *G–2S.* A predicate which contains a modal is called a **Modal predicate.** (Langendoen, 1969, 117.) See also MODAL PREDICATE.

Modality. *G–2Sa.* The constituent M (or Mod: S $\rightarrow$ Mod+AUX+Prop), which contains various adverbial elements, including interrogative and negative elements, that are 'modalities' of the sentence as a whole; an adverbial element of the Mod constituent. (Fillmore, 1966, 365.) *G–2Sb.* The constituent M of the basic structure of a sentence (S $\rightarrow$ M+P), which contains various elements—including negation, tense, mood, and some sentence adverbials—that are associated directly with the sentence as a whole. Other sentence adverbs are introduced from included sentences by transformation. (Fillmore, 1968, 23.) Compare PROPOSITION, MODAL PREDICATE.

Modal predicate. *G–2S.* A predicate (P), S → P+NP, which consists of one of the class of modal auxiliaries: *can, will, shall, may, ought, must.* The argument (NP) of a modal predicate cannot contain another modal predicate, thus: "Tom could have painted the fence"; *"Tom might could have painted the fence." (Langendoen, 1969, 117.) Compare MODALITY. See also MODAL.

Modal sentence. *G–2S.* A sentence whose main predicate states the necessity, possibility, certainty, or truth of the content of the subordinate sentence, as in: "It was necessary that Huck find the raft"; "It was possible that the raft had been stolen"; "It was certain that the raft was missing"; "It was true that the rope had been cut." (Langendoen, 1969, 115.) See also MODAL, MODAL PREDICATE.

Model. *G–1.* A linguistic theory; a conception of language; a conception of linguistic structure; a conception of grammar, such as a phrase structure model based on immediate constituent analysis, or a transformational model based on transformational analysis. (Chomsky, 1957, 20–21.) *G–2.* A linguistic theory, such as: a competence model, which is a theory of the speaker's knowledge of his language; a performance model, which is a theory of speech production and language use; a perceptual model, which is a theory of speech recognition and reception; or an acquisition model, which is a theory of language learning and grammar construction. (Chomsky, 1965, 9, 25.) See also COMPETENCE MODEL, PERFORMANCE MODEL, PERCEPTUAL MODEL, ACQUISITION MODEL, *etc.*

Model, acquisition. See ACQUISITION MODEL.

Model, cognitive. See COGNITIVE MODEL.

Model, perceptual. See PERCEPTUAL MODEL.

Model, performance. See PERFORMANCE MODEL.

Model, speech production. See SPEECH PRODUCTION MODEL.

Model, speech recognition. See SPEECH RECOGNITION MODEL.

Modern linguistics. See STRUCTURAL LINGUISTICS.

Modern structuralism. See STRUCTURAL LINGUISTICS.

Modifier. *G–1.* A word or phrase which alters the meaning of another word or phrase in the same construction, such as *sleeping* in "the *sleeping* child." (Chomsky, 1957, 74; Lees, 1960a, xvii.) The modifier is said to 'modify' the head of the construction. (Chomsky, 1957, 74.) See also NOUN MODIFIER, NOMINAL MODIFIER.

Modifier, nominal. See NOMINAL MODIFIER.

Modifier, noun. See NOUN MODIFIER.

Modifier, post-nominal-. See POST-NOMINAL-MODIFIER.

Modify. See MODIFIER.

Morpheme. *G–1.* A terminal unit of the syntax, whether meaning-bearing or not. Meaning is a relatively useless basis for 'morphemic' analysis, since combinations such as *gl-* have meaning but are not regarded as morphemes, and words such as *to* (go) and *do* (go) are morphemes but have no meaning. (Chomsky, 1957, 100.) *G–2a.* A terminal element of the deep syntactic structure, as opposed to a 'formative,' which is the terminal element of the surface syntactic structure (Postal, 1968a, 156); a distinctive feature matrix which is in harmony with the features of the terminal node of the base rules to which it is attached; the basic unit of the syntactic component (Harms, 1968, 4–5). Morphemes can be deleted from the deep structure and thus not appear in the surface structure; formatives can be added to the deep structure and thus appear only in the surface structure. (Postal, 1968a, 156.) *G–2b*. A simple lexical item, whether inserted in the underlying structure or introduced by transformation, like the preposition *for* or the complementizer *for* (to) (Rosenbaum, 1967a, 24, 86, 90); a bundle of syntactic, semantic, and phonological features (Langacker, 1968, 81). Compare FORMATIVE.

Morpheme, adjectivalization. See ADJECTIVALIZATION MORPHEME.

Morpheme, bound. See BOUND MORPHEME.

Morpheme, complementizing. See COMPLEMENTIZING MORPHEME.

Morpheme, derivative. See DERIVATIVE MORPHEME.

Morpheme, emphasis-. See EMPHATIC AFFIRMATIVE.

Morpheme, empty. See EMPTY MORPHEME.

Morpheme feature. *G–2*. An exception feature, not contained in the phonological feature matrix, which is applied to morphemes which do not undergo certain general phonological rules: e.g., [+foreign], for nonnative vocabulary, which is automatically specified as $+[-$ rule n$]$ by the minus-next-rule convention. (Harms, 1968, 119.) Also called **Morphological feature, Exception feature.** See also MINUS-NEXT-RULE CONVENTION.

Morpheme, free. See FREE MORPHEME.

Morpheme, grammatical. See GRAMMATICAL MORPHEME.

Morpheme, impossible. See POSSIBLE MORPHEME.

Morpheme, ing-. See ING-MORPHEME.

Morpheme, lexical. See LEXICAL MORPHEME.

Morpheme, native. See NATIVE MORPHEME.

Morpheme, nominal affix. See NOMINAL AFFIX MORPHEME.

Morpheme, nominalizing. See NOMINALIZING MORPHEME.

Morpheme, nonnative. See NONNATIVE MORPHEME.

Morpheme, number. See NUMBER MORPHEME.

Morpheme, passive. See PASSIVE MORPHEME.

Morpheme, possessive. See POSSESSIVE MORPHEME.

Morpheme, possible. See POSSIBLE MORPHEME.

Morpheme, progressive. See PROGRESSIVE MORPHEME.

Morpheme, pro-nominalizing. See PRO-NOMINALIZING MORPHEME.

Morpheme, root. See ROOT MORPHEME.

Morphemes, paired. See PAIRED MORPHEMES.

Morpheme structure component. *G–2*. The component which deals with phonological constraints, including admissibility and inadmissibility, of single morphemes. **Morpheme structure rules,** also called **Phonological redundancy rules** and **Feature-switching rules,** operate on lexical entries before the phonological, or morphophonemic, rules, inserting plus and minus specifications for unspecified, or redundant, features. The two types of rules contained in the morpheme structure component are **Sequential constraint rules** and **Blank-filling rules.** (Harms, 1968, 84–91, 112.) See also PHONOLOGICAL COMPONENT, MORPHEME STRUCTURE RULE, PHONOLOGICAL REDUNDANCY RULE, SEQUENTIAL CONSTRAINT RULE, BLANK-FILLING RULE.

Morpheme structure rule. *G–2*. One of the later rules of a grammar which supply redundant, or nondistinctive, features to the phonological distinctive feature matrix of a lexical or grammatical morpheme. (Bach, 1964, 135–136.) Morpheme structure (MS) rules of the morpheme structure component are the basis for the agreement among native speakers concerning admissibility or inadmissibility of new morphemes. They generally can be regarded as feature-addition rules—as opposed to phonological rules, which are feature-switching rules—although MS rules sometimes switch redundant features. (Harms, 1968, 88–89, 112.) Also called **Phonological redundancy rule, Lexical redundancy rule.** (Chomsky and Halle, 1968, 382.) Compare MORPHOPHONEMIC RULE.

Morphemic. See MORPHEME.

Morphographemic rule. *G–1.* A rule, of the final section of the grammar, which converts the morphemes of a terminal string into their graphic representations as written words; a spelling rule. (Thomas, 1965, 59; Lyons, 1968, 265.) Compare MORPHOPHONEMIC RULE.

Morphological feature. *G–2.* A feature of a whole morpheme, rather than of a phonological segment, which assigns that morpheme to an arbitrary class which behaves unpredictably under certain syntactic rules, such as 'derivation'; e.g., some verbs nominalize with *-ment,* some with *-tion,* etc. Morphological features that mark unique treatment for single morphemes, as unique exceptions, are called **Exception features;** they are determined completely by the phonological rules of the language. (Postal, 1968a, 120–127, 131–134.) Also called MORPHEME FEATURE, EXCEPTION FEATURE.

Morphology. *G–1.* The word level of a linguistic theory—that is, the morphological level, on which, for example, *wrote* is represented as *write +* Past (Chomsky, 1957, 11, 58); the level of word-construction, which is a relatively fixed, relatively compact subpart of the grammar, with a finite output and no recursion (Bach, 1964, 105, 114). Morphology can be subdivided into three types: **Inflectional morphology,** which is developed by the constituent-structure grammar, **Derivative morphology,** which develops idioms within the lexicon, and **Transformational morphology,** which develops bound morphemes by generalized transformations in complex sentences, as with *-ness, -ish, -ize.* (Lees, 1960a, 109.) *G–2.* The study of the rules which govern the spoken or written form of the sentences of a language; the study of the way in which the categories and feature specifications underlying sentences are realized as phonetic elements (Langendoen, 1969, 128, 152); the aspects of the phonological system that account for variations in the phonetic realization of morphemes (Langacker, 1968, 167).

Morphology, derivative. See DERIVATIVE MORPHOLOGY.

Morphology, inflectional. See MORPHOLOGY.

Morphology, transformational. See MORPHOLOGY.

Morphophoneme. *G–1.* An element on the level between phonemes and morphemes (Chomsky, 1957, 33); a nonterminal symbol in the lexical representation of a morpheme: e.g. /F/ in /wayF/ (*wife*), which will appear as [f] in word-final position, [wayf], but will appear as [v] when combined with /Z/ 'Plural' (also a morphophoneme)—/wayF//Z/ ⇒ [wayv]/Z/ ⇒ [wayvz] (*wives*) (Bach, 1964, 25–26). *G–2.* A class of systematic phonemic segments whose phonetic realizations form a natural class in regard to phonetic features; a combination of features, each of which is the reflex of a phonetic property or the representative of a universal kind of boundary. (Postal, 1968a, 114.) Compare PHONEME, ARCHIPHONEME.

Morphophonemic rule. *G–1.* One of the set of unordered, lower-level rules which convert a string of morphemes into a string of phonemes (Chomsky, 1957, 32–33); one of a set of morphophonemic transformations (Lees, 1960a, 57). **G–2.** One of the set of ordered spelling rules (M) which introduce phonological matrices for lexical items in the terminal string of a derivation—occurring in the post cycle, following the application of syntactic transformations (Rosenbaum, 1967a, 22, 38, 91); a phonological rule (Chomsky, 1966a, 79–80). Also called **Morphophonetic rule.** (Thomas, 1965, 59). Compare MORPHEME STRUCTURE RULE, PHONOLOGICAL REDUNDANCY RULE, MORPHOPHONOTACTIC RULE.

Morphophonetic rule. *G–1.* A rule of pronunciation, or a morphophonemic rule, as opposed to a rule of spelling, or a morphographemic rule. (Thomas, 1965, 59.) See also MORPHOPHONEMIC RULE.

Morphophonotactic rule. *G–2.* One of the set of rules which describe the potential combinations of morphophonemes in morphemes. (Postal, 1968a, 209.) Compare MORPHOPHONEMIC RULE.

Motivated. *G–2.* Justified as a rule of one system, or one part of a system, of the grammar, beyond its mere ad hoc requirement. (Rosenbaum, 1967a, 75, 79, 94, 107.) See also INDEPENDENTLY MOTIVATED, MOTIVATED SYSTEM.

Motivated, independently. See INDEPENDENTLY MOTIVATED.

Motivated system. *G–2.* A set of rules which are justified by more than ad hoc requirement for explaining a set of linguistic data. (Rosenbaum, 1967a, 69.) Compare AD HOC RULE.

Motivation. *G–2.* Justification of a transformation in one system, or one part of a system, of the grammar beyond its mere requirement as an ad hoc rule. Also called **Justification.** (Rosenbaum, 1967a, 52, 69.) See also INDEPENDENT MOTIVATION.

Motivation, independent. See INDEPENDENT MOTIVATION.

Movement, conjunct. See CONJUNCTION.

Multimorpheme idiom. See IDIOM.

Multinary branching. *G–2.* Multiple (n-ary), as opposed to binary, branching from a single node. Transformations increase the number of branches but decrease the number of nodes. (Lees, 1964b, xxxvii.) See also MULTIPLE-BRANCHING CONSTRUCTION.

Multiple-branching construction. *G–2.* A construction with no internal structure, such as a compound noun phrase like "Huck, Tom, and Jim. . . ." Multiple-branching constructions are optimally acceptable in performance. (Chomsky, 1965, 12–14.) See also MULTINARY BRANCHING.

Multiple embedding. *G–2.* The embedding of a sentence within another embedded sentence without the application of certain required transformations, resulting in quasi-grammatical sentences such as *"Huck believed that that Tom was safe was true" ("Huck believed that it was true that Tom was safe".) (Rosenbaum, 1967a, 66.) See also NESTING, SELF-EMBEDDING.

Mutual block. See BLOCK.

Mutual exclusion. *G–1–2.* The condition under which two items of a set must occur separately, not with the other member of the set. For example, in the complementizer system, the complementizing morpheme *that* must occur alone, without another complementizer such as *for-to.* (Rosenbaum, 1967a, 24.) Compare MUTUAL INCLUSION.

Mutual inclusion. *G–1–2.* Co-occurrence, which is the condition under which one member of a set occurs only with another member of the set, and vice versa. For example, the complementizing morpheme *for* occurs only with the complementizing morpheme *to,* and vice versa, although *for* can be deleted in some cases; and POSS occurs only with *ing,* and vice versa, although POSS can be deleted in some cases. (Rosenbaum, 1967a, 24.) Compare MUTUAL EXCLUSION.

N

Name. *G–1.* A noun. The number and length of names is infinite. (Lees, 1960a, xviii.) See also NOUN.

Narrowing. *G–1.* The approximation of upper and lower articulators in the vocal tract, measured in four degrees: contact, the most extreme degree of narrowing, as in stops; occlusion, capable of creating turbulence, as with fricatives; obstruction, as in the articulation of glides; and constriction, the least extreme degree of narrowing, as in the articulation of high vowels. Not a distinctive feature. (Halle, 1959, 324.)

Nasal. *G–1–2.* The phonological distinctive feature which is positively specified for nasal consonant sounds that are articulated with a lowered velum, allowing air to pass through the nose: [m], [n], [ŋ]. The feature is negatively specified, or nonnasal, for sounds produced with a raised velum, which prevents air from escaping through the nose. (Halle, 1959, 327; Chomsky and Halle, 1968, 316.)

Nasal consonant. See NASAL.

Native morpheme. *G–2.* A morpheme which is not marked [+foreign] in the lexicon as being an exception to one or more general, or major, phonological or morphological rules and thus requiring one or more redundancy rules of the type [−rule n], as in *bus* (plural *buses*), as opposed to *phenomenon* (plural *phenomena*). Both are borrowed morphemes, however. (King, 1969, 136.) See also EXCEPTION. Compare NONNATIVE MORPHEME.

Natural. See NATURAL CLASS.

Natural categorial segment. *G–2.* A phonological segment, containing only binary values, which corresponds to a phonetic segment in an actual representation, the difference between the two being the minimal necessary to account for the regularities of the language. Phonetic properties directly determine a large proportion of phonological properties. (Postal, 1968a, 73.) See also NATURAL CATEGORIAL SEQUENCE.

Natural categorial sequence. *G–2.* The sequence of natural categorial segments which corresponds, in the same order, to a sequence of phonetic segments in a phonetic representation. (Postal, 1968a, 74–75.) See also NATURAL CATEGORIAL SEGMENT.

Natural class. *G–1.* A set of speech sounds that can be designated by fewer features than any individual sound in the class. (Halle, 1959, 328.) *G–2.* A general set of systematic phonemes which share features that have a certain degree of phonetic plausibility and which can be specified with fewer features than any of the individual phonemes in the class (Harms, 1968, 26); a set of phonological segments that have more features in common—are more 'natural'—than randomly selected sets: stops, continuants, vowels, etc. Judgments of naturalness are supported by the fact that it is the 'natural' classes that are the most relevant for phonological processes in all languages. (Chomsky, and Halle, 1968, 335.) See also NATURALNESS CONDITION, MAJOR CLASS FEATURE.

Naturalness condition. *G–2a.* The fundamental constraint which governs the natural-class relations between phonological—systematic phonemic—and phonetic structures; the condition by which every phonological segment is assigned a phonetic reflex by virtue of universal principles. (Postal, 1968a, xiv, 73, 92.) The consequence of the 'naturalness condition' is that only those aspects of systematic phonemic structure having arbitrary phonetic realizations need special, or language-particular, rules, and when a child has determined the phonetic realization of a form, he has determined a large part of its phonological structure. (Postal, 1968a, 56, 102.) *G–2b.* The fundamental constraint which governs the deep structure/surface structure relations in the syntax, but to a lesser degree than in phonology. Differences between deep and surface structure are the minimum required to state the actually existing regularities of the language without the use of ad hoc rules. (Postal, 1968a, 202–203.)

Necessary condition. *G–2.* An obligatory context. For example, identity of erasing and erased noun phrases is a 'necessary condition' for the derivation of noun phrase complements in some cases, while nonidentity is a 'necessary condition' in other cases. The necessary conditions make up a **Necessary environment.** (Rosenbaum, 1967a, 95.) See also ENVIRONMENT, STRUCTURAL DESCRIPTION.

Necessary environment. See NECESSARY CONDITION.

Negation. *G–1.* The transformation which introduces *not* after the second element of the auxiliary before affix transformation: C+M+*not;* C+*have*+ *not;* C+*be*+*not.* If the auxiliary contains only the concord marker C, C is rewritten as C+*do,* which, after affix transformation, gives *doesn't* or *don't.* (Chomsky, 1957, 61–62.) Negation is the denial of a predicate by the introduction of *not,* or the denial of an entire sentence by the use of an impersonal construction, such as "It is not the case that S." (Smith, 1964, 258.) *G–2.* The attachment of an S-dominated negative marker to one of the constituents of a sentence, rather than the introduction of negative into the auxiliary of a positive sentence (Kuroda, 1969, 333); the combination of the formant Neg with various parts of the sentence—realized as the negative particle *not* or *n't,* the negative pronouns *nobody* and *nothing,* the negative adverbs *never* and *nowhere,* and the negative determiner *no* (Klima and Bellugi-Klima, 1966, 450); the attachment of Neg to a sentence, whether the main sentence—a sentence negation—or a sentence dominated by a noun phrase—an element negation (Bach, 1968, 97). The negative element is introduced by the rewrite rules of the base; a transformation then places it in the correct position in the sentence. (Chomsky, 1966a, 59.) See also SENTENCE NEGATION, CONSTITUENT NEGATION.

Negation, constituent. See CONSTITUENT NEGATION.

Negation, covert. See COVERT NEGATION.

Negation, overt. See OVERT NEGATION.

Negation, sentence. See SENTENCE NEGATION.

Negative. *G–1–2.* Having undergone negation through the introduction of *not* into the auxiliary of the sentence by negation transformation (Chomsky, 1957, 61–62) or through the introduction of Neg under the domination of S by phrase structure rule and its subsequent positioning within the sentence by attachment transformation (Kuroda, 1969, 333). *G–2.* The grammatical element Neg, which is introduced into the base of a sentence by phrase structure rule and then placed in the proper position for sentence negation (e.g., "Huck couldn*'t* decide") or for constituent negation (e.g., "Huck was *un*decided") by attachment transformation. (Klima, 1964a, 300.) *G–2S.* The element 'negative' of the obligatory sub-constituent 'negative/affirmative' of the modality constituent of a sentence. (Fillmore, 1966, 365.) See also NEGATION.

Negative adjunction transformation. *G–2.* The optional transformation which adjoins the sentence constituent 'negative' to the auxiliary segment of AUX, rather than placing it after the AUX by negative placement transformation. It then replaces the negative element with the contraction *n't*: NEG + NP + AUX + VP ⇒ NP + AUX + NEG + VP, as when: "NEG Tom should leave" ⇒ "Tom shouldn*'t* leave." (Jacobs and Rosenbaum, 1968, 125–126.) Compare NEGATIVE PLACEMENT TRANSFORMATION. See also CONTRACTION.

Negative affix. *G–2.* One of the negative prefixes (*un-, in-, dis-,* etc.) or negative suffixes (*-less, -free,* etc.) which participate in constituent negation (i.e., *unhappy, insecure, disapprove, careless, carefree,* etc.)—as opposed to the pre-verbal particle Neg, which negates an entire sentence (e.g., "Huck wasn*'t un*happy"). (Klima, 1964a, 308.) See also CONSTITUENT NEGATION.

Negative indefinite. *G–2.* An indefinite form which is the result of the combination Neg + *any* + *one/body/thing*: *no one, nobody, nothing.* (Klima, 1964a, 274.) See also CONSTITUENT NEGATION.

Negative placement transformation. *G–2.* The transformation which places the S-constituent 'negative' immediately after the auxiliary constituent and, if no other transformations apply, such as the negative adjunction transformation for contractions, replaces 'negative' by *not*: NEG + NP + AUX + VP ⇒ NP + AUX + NEG + VP. (Jacobs and Rosenbaum, 1968, 125–126.) Compare NEGATIVE ADJUNCTION TRANSFORMATION.

Negative pre-verb. *G–2.* The negative particle *not*—in pre-sentential position: S → *not* + NP + VP—and the negative pre-verbal adverbs—*hardly, scarcely.* (Klima, 1964a, 262, 301.) See also NEGATIVE PRE-VERBAL ADVERB.

Negative pre-verbal adverb. *G–2.* One of the adverb subclass of negative pre-verbs, which are formed by the combination of Neg + time/manner/quantity/etc.: Neg + *ever* ⇒ *never*; Neg + *usually* ⇒ *rarely*; Neg + *often* ⇒ *seldom*; etc. Some, but not most, pre-verbal adverbs cause sentence negation. (Klima, 1964a, 254, 270, 281.) See also CONSTITUENT NEGATION, SENTENCE NEGATION.

Negative sentence. *G–1.* A sentence containing *not* or a negative adverb like *scarcely* or *hardly.* A sentence which contains only a word with a negative prefix, however, is not a negative sentence. (Lees, 1960a, 24.) See also SENTENCE NEGATION.

Negative specification. *G–2a.* The assignment, in a lexical entry, of a minus value to a syntactic feature which corresponds to a context in which that lexical item may not occur. For example, *Tom* and *cave* must be specified as [−V] in order to exclude them from the position of *explored* in "Tom explored the cave"; and *explored* must be specified as [−N] for the position of *Tom* and *cave*. (Chomsky, 1965, 110–111.) *G–2b.* The assignment of a minus value in the phonological or phonetic matrix of a lexical entry to indicate that a segment of the formative is not a member of the distinctive category in question—thus, the *i* of *in* is [−consonantal] and [+vocalic], while the *n* is [+consonantal] and [−vocalic]. (Chomsky and Halle, 1968, 165.) Marking theory has replaced most of the earlier plus, minus, and zero specifications for phonological segments with the values of U, for unmarked, and M, for marked, which are then replaced by the symbols + and − by universal interpretation rules. The phonological matrix for the formative *in* would be unmarked for both [consonantal] and [vocalic] for both *i* and *n*. (Chomsky and Halle, 1968, 415.) See also MARKEDNESS, FEATURE COEFFICIENT.

Negative transformation. See NEGATION.

Nesting. *G–1–2.* Self-embedding, which is the embedding of a category within a phrase which is dominated by the same category symbol; the embedding of a sentence within another, perhaps embedded, sentence, as in: "The report that the medicine that Mark Twain took killed him was greatly exaggerated." Each of the nested embeddings is called a **Nested dependency.** The nesting of dependencies is common to all human languages and is one of the bases for recursion in a grammar. The depth of the nesting, which is determined by the number of self-embeddings—two in the illustration above—is restricted by finiteness of memory and other factors to only two or three in any one sentence. Nesting is handled with embedding transformations in *G–1* but is achieved by the base rules, before transformations, in *G–2*. (Chomsky, 1961a, 123; Chomsky, 1965, 197–198; Langacker, 1968, 183.) See also SELF-EMBEDDING, MULTIPLE EMBEDDING.

Neutral affix. *G–2.* A derivational or inflectional suffix which plays no role in stress placement within the word and is separated from the rest of the word by the boundary #, as opposed to the affixes *-ity, -ion, -ical,* and *-ify,* which *do* affect stress placement and are separated by no boundary except the bracket. (Chomsky and Halle, 1968, 84–89.) Compare PREFIX.

Neutralization. *G–1–2.* The phenomenon in which only one of the possible values of a set of features can occur in a certain context. For example, the systematic phonemes /t/ and /d/ are 'neutralized' in intervocalic position for many English speakers and can be represented in a phonological description as the archiphoneme /D/, as in: *bit her* /bíDer/; *bid her* /bíDer/, both phonetically [bídər]. (Postal, 1968a, 167–168, 172.) See also ARCHIPHONEME.

Neutral position. *G–2.* The characteristic position of the vocal tract just before articulation. The velum is raised; the body of the tongue is raised to the position for [ε]; the glottis is narrowed; and the subglottal air pressure is increased. (Chomsky and Halle, 1968, 300.)

Neutral vowel. *G–2.* The mid central vowel 'schwa' [ə]—or the high central vowel 'barred I' [ɨ]—to which insufficiently stressed vowels are reduced by phonological rule, as in: *Jakobsonian* [yakəbsónian]; *Jakobson* [yákəbsən]. (Chomsky and Halle, 1968, 59.)

Node. *G–1.* A point, or dot, in a branching diagram at which a branching occurs. For example, in the diagram   S   the S labels the sentence

node, the NP labels the noun phrase node, and the VP labels the verb phrase node. (Katz, 1964a, 526; Thomas, 1965, 31.) Also called **Node**

point. (Chomsky, 1957, 68.) $G-2$. The labeled intersection of two or more branches in a tree diagram. For example, in the diagram

$$
\begin{array}{ccc}
 & S & \\
\diagup & & \diagdown \\
NP & & VP \\
| & & | \\
X & & Y
\end{array}
$$

the S node is the intersection of the branches S-NP and S-VP; NP is the intersection of the branches of S-NP and NP-X; and VP is the intersection of the branches S-VP and VP-Y. (Rosenbaum, 1967a, 6.) See also BRANCHING DIAGRAM.

Node deletion. $G-2$. Tree pruning, which is the convention, or metarule, by which a nonterminal node is deleted if it does not dominate any lexical item, or by which an S node is deleted if it does not immediately dominate VP plus some other constituent. (Ross, 1966, 297–299.) See also TREE PRUNING, METARULE.

Node, nonterminal. See NONTERMINAL NODE.

Nominal. $G-1-2a$. A noun phrase plus a number affix: Nom $\rightarrow$ NP+N° (Lees, 1960a, 14); a noun, or a noun derived from a verb (e.g., *determination*) (Lyons, 1968, 347); a noun-like version of a sentence which occurs inside another sentence in the place of an abstract noun (Lees, 1960a, 54); a nominalization transform of one of various types: a factive nominal (*that*+S), an action nominal (N's ADJ V-*ing* of N), an agentive nominal (N-*er*), a gerundive nominal (N's havi*ng* V-*en*), or an infinitival nominal (*for* N *to* V) (Thomas, 1965, 106–114). $G-1-2b$. Having the properties of a noun: noun-like; dominated by N, such as a 'nominal' compound, a 'nominal' phrase, a 'nominal' transform. (Thomas, 1965, 106–114.) $G-2$. The noun or adjective subset of the category noun phrase in the deep structure of a sentence. Nouns and adjectives are categorized together as 'nominals' because they are affected alike by several transformational processes, such as question formation, relativization, equation, topicalization, pseudo-cleft construction, and pro-formation. (Ross, 1969, 357.) Compare ADJECTIVAL, ADVERBIAL, VERBAL. See also FACTIVE NOMINAL, ACTION NOMINAL, GERUNDIVE NOMINAL, INFINITIVE NOMINAL, ABSTRACTIVE NOMINAL.

Nominal, abstractive. See ABSTRACTIVE NOMINAL.

Nominal, action. See ACTION NOMINAL.

Nominal affix morpheme. $G-1$. The number morpheme N° in the expansion of a Nominal: Nom $\rightarrow$ NP+N°. (Lees, 1960a, 4.) See also NUMBER MORPHEME.

Nominal, agentive. See AGENTIVE NOMINAL.

Nominal compound. $G-1-2$. A compound word that functions as a nominal, such as *wáshing machine, bóokstore, phráse-marker*. Nominal compounds are interpreted according to certain fixed syntactic relations among the constituents of the sentences that underlie them. They are multiply ambiguous. (Lees, 1964b, xxxix.) See also COMPOUND.

Nominal compound, complex. See COMPLEX NOMINAL COMPOUND.

Nominal, factive. See FACTIVE NOMINAL.

Nominal, gerundive. See GERUNDIVE NOMINAL.

Nominal, infinitive. See INFINITIVE NOMINAL.

Nominalization. $G-1-2a$. An embedded expression which replaces a nominal constituent in an underlying matrix sentence (Lees, 1960b, 153;

Bach, 1964, 82); a construction which is derived from a sentence by the application of a set of rules called the nominalization transformation (Jacobs and Rosenbaum, 1968, 226); a word, such as *refusal,* which is the surface structure realization of a lexical entry that is introduced under the domination of a noun (Jacobs and Rosenbaum, 1968, 226–228). *G–1–2b.* The process of creating a nominal to perform the function of a noun phrase in a sentence, as when: "The fish is slippery" ⇒ "The slippery fish . . ."; the process which transforms sentences into noun phrases, as when: "Tom insisted on going" ⇒ "Tom's insistence on going . . ." (Thomas, 1965, 74–76, 106; Jacobs and Rosenbaum, 1968, 53); the process of introducing a lexical entry, unspecified as to class, under the domination of N in the base rules (Jacobs and Rosenbaum, 1968, 228). See also NOUN PHRASE, COMPLEMENTATION.

Nominalization transformation. *G–2.* The set of rules which derive nominalizations from sentences. (Jacobs and Rosenbaum, 1968, 226.) Also called **Nominalizing transformation.** See also NOMINALIZATION, COMPLEMENTATION.

Nominalize. *G–1–2.* To transform into a nominal by means of a nominalization transformation, as when: "Huck arrived early" ⇒ "Huck's early arrival. . . ." (Jacobs and Rosenbaum, 1968, 227–228.)

Nominalizer. See COMPLEMENTIZER.

Nominalizing morpheme. *G–1.* One of the nominalizers, or complementizers, *that, 's . . . ing,* and *(for)to.* (Lees, 1960a, 68.) Also called **Complementizing morpheme.**

Nominalizing transformation. *G–1.* A generalized transformation which operates on a pair of sentences, converting one of them into a noun phrase of the form *to+*VP or *ing+*VP or ADJ-NP and substituting it for an NP in the other, as when: "(The girl is beautiful) entered" ⇒ "The beautiful girl entered." (Chomsky, 1957, 72, 114; Bach, 1964, 82, 106.) Also called **Nominalization transformation.** See also NOMINALIZATION. Compare COMPLEMENTATION.

Nominal modifier. *G–2.* A modifier of a nominal. Nominal modifiers inherently follow the nominal that they modify, but some types, such as single-word adjectives, can be shifted to pre-nominal position. (Lees, 1964b, xlii.) See also ADJECTIVE, ADJECTIVAL, ATTRIBUTIVE. Compare NOUN MODIFIER.

Nominal phrase. *G–1.* An attributive-plus-noun sequence consisting of an adjectival modifier shifted transformationally from post-nominal position, followed by a noun head—the entire phrase appearing under a ∧+/ stress-superfix, as in: *blînd álley, Dûtch tréat, góld wátch.* (Lees, 1960a, 181.) Compare NOMINAL COMPOUND.

Nominal, predicate. See PREDICATE NOMINAL.

Nominal, subject. See SUBJECT NOMINAL.

Nominative, predicate. See PREDICATE NOMINATIVE.

Nonapplication. *G–2.* Failure of application of a transformation, either because a lexical item in the string is marked against it or because the necessary environment is not satisfied. For example, the passive transformation cannot apply following the subject-object inversion transformation, since the subject noun phrase is to the right of the verb phrase complement sentence. (Rosenbaum, 1967a, 15, 41, 79, 99.) Compare VACUOUS APPLICATION.

Noncleft sentence. *G–2.* A sentence which has not undergone the pseudo-cleft sentence transformation, but which appears to contain the necessary environment for that transformation, such as the 'noncleft' sentence "Huck liked to fish," as opposed to the 'pseudocleft' sentence "What Huck liked was to fish." (Rosenbaum, 1967a, 13.) Compare PSEUDOCLEFT SENTENCE.

Noncyclical phonology. *G–2.* The phonological rules which apply only at word boundaries and do not reapply at successive stages of the transformational cycle. (Chomsky and Halle, 1968, 60.) See also CYCLE.

Nonextraposition. *G–2.* The nonapplication of the extraposition transformation because of the absence of a necessary environment (e.g., because of the presence of a POSS-ing complementizer). (Rosenbaum, 1967a, 45.) Compare EXTRAPOSITION.

Nongenerative transformational grammar. *G–1.* The theory of transformations as relations among actual sentences, developed originally by Zellig S. Harris outside of the theory of generative grammar. (Chomsky, 1966c, 107.) Compare GENERATIVE-TRANSFORMATIONAL GRAMMAR.

Nonidentity. *G–2.* The condition under which two noun phrases have different referents, or one noun phrase lacks an identical antecedent. For example, 'nonidentity' of the noun phrase object in the main sentence with the underlying noun phrase subject of the predicate complement sentence blocks the erasure transformation in most cases (e.g., "Huck hated for Tom to go"), but with some main verbs it is a necessary condition for erasure (e.g., "Huck said (for Tom) to go"). (Rosenbaum, 1967a, 68, 95.) Compare IDENTITY.

Noniterative rule convention. *G–2.* The universal constraint on grammars that prevents a phonological rule from reapplying to its own output—that is, the output of a phonological rule cannot be a subsequent input to the same rule. The alpha-switching rule is one of the types of phonological rules affected by this convention. (Harms, 1968, 62, 64.) Compare ITERATIVE CYCLE.

Nonnative morpheme. *G–2.* A morpheme which is marked [+foreign] in the lexicon as being an exception to one or more general, or major, phonological or morphological rules and thus requiring one or more redundancy rules of the type [−rule n], such as *phenomenon* (plural, *phenomena*), as opposed to *bus* (plural, *buses*)—both borrowed morphemes, however. (King, 1969, 136.) Compare NATIVE MORPHEME.

Non-null. *G–1–2.* Representing one or more constituents: not empty. This is said of a variable symbol in a string. (Koutsoudas, 1966, 19.) Compare NULL.

Nonoccurrence. *G–2.* Failure to be generated, or to occur, as a grammatical sentence of the language. For example, the 'nonoccurrence' of the sentence *"It was fortunate Tom's escaping" is explained by the fact that the extraposition transformation is blocked if the complementizer is POSS-ing. (Rosenbaum, 1967a, 38–39, 67, 75, 90, 96, 104.) Compare UNGRAMMATICALITY.

Nonoral-articulator feature. *G–2.* One of the phonological distinctive features which refer to articulators other than in the oral cavity, such as: [voiced] (voicing, in the glottis); [nasal] (nasalization, in the nasal cavity); [checked] (glottalization, in the glottis). (Harms, 1968, 23, 36.) Compare ORAL-ARTICULATOR FEATURE.

Nonrestrictive clause. *G–2.* A sentence which has been introduced, by nonrestrictive clause transformation, from its position as the second of two conjoined sentences into the first conjoined sentence under the domination of S (or NP), as when: "Huck steered the raft, *and Huck was a good navigator*" ⇒ "Huck, *and Huck was a good navigator,* steered the raft." After the application of the pronoun transformation, the sentence can surface as "Huck, and *he* was a good navigator, steered the raft"; or the relative clause transformation can produce a nonrestrictive relative clause: "Huck, *who* was a good navigator, steered the raft." (Jacobs and Rosenbaum, 1968, 259–263.) Compare NONRESTRICTIVE RELATIVE CLAUSE.

Nonrestrictive clause transformation. See NONRESTRICTIVE CLAUSE.

Nonrestrictive relative clause. *G–1.* An appositive clause, one which follows a noun with a specified determiner, such as *the,* or no determiner at all, as in: "Huck, *who was a good navigator,* steered the raft"; "The raft, *which was falling apart,* floated downstream." Appositive clauses can be reduced, as in: "Huck, *a good navigator,* steered the raft"; "The raft, *falling apart,* floated downstream." (Thomas, 1965, 156–157.) The relative pronoun in a nonrestrictive relative clause is not ordinarily reducible to *that.* (Lees, 1960a, 86.) *G–2.* An S complement of the full NP (NP → DET+N+S: "The raft, *which was falling apart,* . . .") or of the entire sentence (S → NP+VP+S: "Tom returned alive, *which surprised everyone*") (Chomsky, 1965, 217); an independent conjoined sentence which is adjoined to a noun phrase by the nonrestrictive clause transformation and then relativized (Jacobs and Rosenbaum, 1968, 260–261). If a nonrestrictive, or appositive, relative clause is reduced to an adjective, the noun head is stressed, as when: "The raft, *which was made of logs,* . . . ⇒ "The *log* ráft. . . ." (Langendoen, 1969, 93.) Compare RESTRICTIVE RELATIVE CLAUSE. See also NONRESTRICTIVE CLAUSE.

Nonsense string. *G–2.* A string which departs so far from grammaticality that it is incomprehensible—it cannot be paraphrased or understood—or is comprehensible only by virtue of nonlinguistic knowledge. It becomes 'word salad,' like *"world round go the love makes." (Katz, 1964b, 402–403.) Compare NONSENTENCE. See also DEVIATION, GRAMMATICALITY.

Nonsentence. *G–1–2.* An utterance that neither is nor could be a sentence of the language (Chomsky, 1957, 14; Lees, 1960a, 26; Lees, 1964b, xxxii); an ungrammatical string (Postal, 1964c, 19). Compare NONSENSE STRING. See also DEVIATION, GRAMMATICALITY.

Nonstative verbal. *G–2.* A verb or adjective, plus copula, which can take the progressive aspect, participate in the imperative and DO-SO transformations, and appear in the frame "He persuaded NP to _____": *"slice* the bread" (a nonstative verb); "be *careful*" (a nonstative adjective). (Lakoff and Peters, 1966, 115.) Compare STATIVE VERBAL.

Nonsynonymy. *G–2.* The condition under which two sentences have different semantic interpretations because of the differences in their underlying structures. For example, the nonsynonymy of the sentences "Tom forced Huck to help Jim" and "Tom forced Jim to be helped by Huck" is predicted from the differences in their underlying structures: "Tom forced Huck for Huck to help Jim"; "Tom forced Jim for Jim to be helped by Huck." (Rosenbaum, 1967a, 118.) Compare SYNONYMY.

Nonterminal node. *G–2.* A node, in a deep structure, which is deleted by the automatic conventions of tree pruning, that is, it will not appear in the surface structure. (Ross, 1969, 354–355.) Compare NONTERMINAL SYMBOL.

Nonterminal symbol. *G–1.* A grammatical symbol which can be developed further by grammatical rules; a non-lowest order symbol. (Lees, 1960a, 50.) Compare NONTERMINAL NODE.

Nontrivial. *G–1.* Interesting; revealing; significant; not obvious; not self-evident; abstract. Said of a linguistic hypothesis. (Chomsky, 1957, 85.) See also INTERESTING. Compare TRIVIAL.

Nontrivial hypothesis. *G–2.* A hypothesis whose truth is not obvious, such as the hypothesis that deep structures are basically the same for all languages, though surface structures are quite diverse. (Chomsky, 1966c, 45.) See also NONTRIVIAL.

Normal speaker. *G–2.* A native, or fluent, speaker of a natural language whose linguistic abilities are explained by a general theory of language. (Rosenbaum, 1967a, 10.) See also IDEAL SPEAKER-HEARER.

Notation. See FEATURE SPECIFICATION.

Notation, abbreviatory. See ABBREVIATOR.

Notational convention. *G–1.* One of the formal syntactic devices for symbolizing strings and rules. (Chomsky, 1957, 26, 109.) *G–2.* One of the universal abbreviatory devices used in the statement of phonological rules. **Square brackets** designate a single segment: $\begin{bmatrix} +\text{consonantal} \\ -\text{vocalic} \end{bmatrix}$

Parentheses indicate an optional segment: $\left(\begin{bmatrix} +\text{consonantal} \\ -\text{vocalic} \end{bmatrix} \right)$. **Braces,** sometimes numbered, abbreviate sequences of partially similar rules, possibly ordered: $\begin{bmatrix} \left\{ \begin{matrix} +\text{consonantal} \\ -\text{vocalic} \end{matrix} \right\} \end{bmatrix} \rightarrow [-\text{stress}]$; that is, "a consonantal segment is unstressed; a nonvocalic segment is unstressed." **Greek letter variables,** also called **Alpha variables,** stand for plus and minus values of features of a segment to indicate agreement or disagreement of values in different parts of a rule: $\begin{bmatrix} \alpha \text{ consonantal} \\ \alpha \text{ vocalic} \end{bmatrix} \rightarrow [+\text{syllabic}]/\text{C}\_\_\_\_\_\text{C}$; that is, "a segment that is either [+consonantal] and [+vocalic] (liquids) or [−consonantal] and [−vocalic] (glides) is syllabic between consonants." **X-type variables** (X, Y, Z) stand for arbitrary environments, possibly null, in a rule, as in: X_____ "in an environment following anything." **Cover symbols** (C,V) are used for the universal classes 'consonant' and 'vowel' in place of the full feature specifications, as in: _____C "in the environment preceding a consonant." **Angled parentheses,** also called **Angle brackets** or **Angles** (< >), indicate elements in one part of a rule that require the presence of elements, also in angles, in another part. (Harms, 1968, 57–66.) See also ABBREVIATOR.

Notation, feature. See FEATURE NOTATION.

'Not' promotion. *G–2.* A permutation rule which moves *not* from the embedded sentence into the main sentence, as when: "Huck believed (that Tom had *not* drowned)" ⇒ "Huck did*n't* believe (that Tom had drowned)." (Langacker, 1968, 128.) See also NEGATION.

Noun. *G–1.* The obligatory category N in a noun phrase: NP → T+*N*; the replacement for the N category, as in: N → *color, idea,* etc. (Chomsky, 1957, 27.) *G–2.* The obligatory N category in a noun phrase: NP → (DET) *N* (S'); the single-word replacement for the N category, as in:

N → *color, idea,* etc.; a lexical entry marked [+N] (Chomsky, 1965, 129); a word that can have an adjective preposed before it, as in: "Huck's masterful *steering* of the raft" (Lakoff and Peters, 1966, 132). *Related terms:* A **Noun phrase** is a major category of the sentence which can dominate the category Noun. (Chomsky, 1957, 111.) A **Nominal** is a noun-like version of a sentence that is dominated by a noun phrase (Lees, 1960a, 54), or a noun or adjective subset of the category noun phrase (Ross, 1969, 357). **Nominalization** is the process of creating a nominal to perform the function of a noun phrase in a sentence (Thomas, 1965, 74–76, 106), or is the name of the construction resulting from that process (Jacobs and Rosenbaum, 1968, 226-228). A **Nominalizer,** or **Nominalizing morpheme,** is the marker of an embedded sentence which is to undergo nominalization. (Lees, 1960a, 68.) A **Nominalizing transformation,** or **Nominalization transformation,** is the set of rules which derive nominalizations from embedded sentences. (Chomsky, 1957, 72, 114.)

Noun, common.　See COMMON NOUN.

Noun, generic.　See GENERIC DETERMINER.

Noun, kernel.　See KERNEL NOUN.

Noun, mass.　See ABSTRACT.

Noun modifier.　*G–2.* A prenominal or postnominal single-word modifier of a noun head which is introduced into a definite noun phrase by way of relative clause embedding, deletion of the Wh-word and *be,* and order change with the head. (Smith, 1964, 247.) Compare NOMINAL MODIFIER.

Noun phrase.　*G–1.* One of the major categories (NP) of the sentence: $NP_{sing} \rightarrow T+N+\emptyset$ or $NP_{pl} \rightarrow T+N+S$. (Chomsky, 1957, 111; Bach, 1964, 76; Postal, 1964a, 65.) *G–2.* One of the major categories (NP) of the sentence, rewritten variously as determiner+noun (Katz and Postal, 1964, 104); (DET) $N+N^o(S)$ (Thomas, 1965, 146); (article) (sentence) noun (Katz, 1966, 146); (DET) N (S') (Chomsky, 1965, 129); (ART) N (S), or NP+S (Jacobs and Rosenbaum, 1968, 47; Langacker, 1968, 131). *G–2S.* One of the major categories (NP) of a case category of the proposition of a sentence, rewritten as Prep (DET) (S) N (Fillmore, 1966, 367) or NP+Case (Fillmore, 1968, 83); one of the arguments of a sentence, $S \rightarrow Pred+NP$ (NP) (NP), as opposed to the predicate (Langendoen, 1969, 137). Noun phrases are typed as joint or nonjoint, according to whether they allow adjuncts such as *together* (joint) or *each* (nonjoint). (McCawley, 1968, 152.)

Noun phrase advancement.　*G–2.* The rule which moves the identical noun phrase of a relative clause to the front of that clause, optionally moving an associated preposition also, as when: "Huck steered the raft *with a pole*" ⇒ *"a pole* Huck steered the raft *with*" or *"with a pole* Huck steered the raft" (later to be relativized as "which Huck steered the raft with" or "with which Huck steered the raft"). (Langacker, 1968, 130–132.) See also RELATIVIZATION.

Noun phrase complement.　*G–2.* A sentence that is embedded by noun phrase complementation at the right of a noun in a noun phrase (NP → ART+N+S), as opposed to a relative clause, which is embedded after an NP in an NP (NP → NP+S). After a complementizer is introduced by complementizer transformation, the sentence can surface as, for example, "The report *that Mark Twain was dead* was greatly exaggerated" or "(It) *for Huck to steer the raft* was impossible" or "(It) *Tom's having* *escaped from the cave* was amazing." (Rosenbaum, 1967c, 327; Jacobs, 1968, 15; Jacobs and Rosenbaum, 1968, 163–169.) The head of the noun phrase complement is the constituent N of the noun phrase which specifies its features. Noun phrase complements are generally associated with the properties of passivization and pseudocleft formation in the main sentence. (Rosenbaum, 1967a, 3–5, 30, 114.) Questions can also be embedded as noun phrase complements. (Rosenbaum, 1967b, ix.) See also SUBJECT COMPLEMENT, OBJECT COMPLEMENT, OBLIQUE NOUN PHRASE COMPLEMENT.

Noun phrase complementation. *G–2.* The process which introduces a sentence as a complement to a noun head under the domination of a noun phrase: NP → DET+N+S. There are four types of noun phrase complementation: subject complementation; object complementation; intransitive oblique complementation, which generates a complement of the object of a preposition in the VP of an intransitive sentence; and transitive oblique complementation, which generates a complement of the object of a preposition in the VP of a transitive sentence. In all types of noun phrase complementation, the noun phrase functions as a single unit under passivization, and there is a corresponding pseudocleft formation. (Rosenbaum, 1967c, 316–322; Rosenbaum, 1967a, 1, 3–5, 14.) See also SUBJECT COMPLEMENTATION, OBJECT COMPLEMENTATION, OBLIQUE NOUN PHRASE COMPLEMENTATION.

Noun phrase complementation, intransitive oblique. See INTRANSITIVE OBLIQUE NOUN PHRASE COMPLEMENTATION.

Noun phrase complementation, object. See OBJECT COMPLEMENTATION.

Noun phrase complementation, oblique. See OBLIQUE NOUN PHRASE COMPLEMENTATION.

Noun phrase complementation, prepositional. See PREPOSITIONAL NOUN PHRASE COMPLEMENTATION.

Noun phrase complementation, subject. See SUBJECT COMPLEMENTATION.

Noun phrase complementation, transitive oblique. See TRANSITIVE OBLIQUE COMPLEMENTATION.

Noun phrase complement, oblique. See OBLIQUE NOUN PHRASE COMPLEMENT.

Noun phrase, connected. See CONNECTED NOUN PHRASE.

Noun phrase, definite. See DEFINITE NOUN PHRASE.

Noun phrase deletion, identical. See IDENTICAL NOUN PHRASE DELETION.

Noun phrase deletion, indefinite. See IDENTICAL NOUN PHRASE DELETION.

Noun phrase deletion rule. See IDENTICAL NOUN PHRASE DELETION.

Noun phrase, erased. See ERASED NOUN PHRASE.

Noun phrase, erasing. See ERASING NOUN PHRASE.

Noun phrase, underlying object. See UNDERLYING OBJECT NOUN PHRASE.

Noun phrase, underlying subject. See UNDERLYING SUBJECT NOUN PHRASE.

Noun, pivotal. See PIVOTAL NOUN.

Noun, predicate. See PREDICATE NOUN.

Noun, proper. See PROPER NOUN.

Noun segment deletion transformation. *G–2.* The set of rules which adjoin an article segment to a noun segment dominated by N, delete the noun segment, and then replace the article segment with a pronoun in the second lexical pass. (Jacobs and Rosenbaum, 1968, 95–96.) See also PRONOMINALIZATION.

Noun suffix transformation. *G–2.* The set of rules which introduce an affix segment into a noun segment which has the feature [−singular]. The affix segment assumes the number feature of the noun and becomes an actual suffix in the second lexical pass. (Jacobs and Rosenbaum, 1968, 83–84.) See also AFFIX SEGMENT.

Novel sentence. *G–2.* A sentence that has not been heard or uttered before; a novel utterance. (Thomas, 1965, 8; Langacker, 1968, 22.) See also NOVEL UTTERANCE.

Novel utterance. *G–2.* One of the infinite set of unique sentences; a novel sentence. (Lees, 1964b, xxx.) See also NOVEL SENTENCE.

NPN transformation. *G–1.* The nominalizing transformation which produces nominal compounds from noun phrases of the type noun-preposition-noun by deleting the preposition and reversing the order of the nouns. The result has the compound stress-superfix $/+\backslash$, as when: *"The man with the laundry"* ⇒ "the *láundry màn.* (Lees, 1960a, 174.) See also COMPOUND.

Nuclear stress rule. *G–2.* The phonological rule—part of the main stress rule—which assigns primary stress to a primary-stressed vowel which is preceded by another primary-stressed vowel in a noun phrase, as in: *bláck bóard* ⇒ *black bóard,* as opposed to *bláckboard,* to which stress is assigned by the compound rule. (Chomsky and Halle, 1968, 17.) Compare COMPOUND RULE. See also MAIN STRESS RULE.

Nucleus. *G–2.* The underlying phrase-marker of a sentence containing the element Q (question); Sentence → Q+Nucleus; Nucleus → Noun Phrase+Verb Phrase. (Katz and Postal, 1964, 104.) See also QUESTION.

Null. *G–1.* Lacking status as a morpheme or formative—that is, having no overt representation on any level of the grammar (Bach, 1964, 14–15); empty, void—said of a string, a null string, that is not a string at all. Phrase structure rules do not permit the rewriting of a symbol as a null string; that is, phrase structure rules cannot perform the operation of deletion. (Koutsoudas, 1966, 7.) *G–2a.* Empty, void, without constituents —said of a variable (X, Y, Z) in the structural description of a transformation. For example, the extraposition transformation can apply even if the variable Y (XNSY) is null, as when: "Huck thought it that Tom was lost . . ." ⇒ "Huck thought . . . that Tom was lost." (Rosenbaum, 1967a, 5, 41.) *G–2b.* Zero (∅), used in a phonological rule to delete a segment, as in: obstruent → null/#_____obstruent ("if two obstruents occur initially, the first is deleted"). (Harms, 1968, 44.) Compare NON-NULL, VACUOUS.

Null string. *G–1–2.* An empty string—that is, no string at all. (Koutsoudas, 1966, 7.) See also NULL.

Number. *G–1.* A constituent of the noun phrase (NP → DET+N+*Num*) or of the auxiliary (C → *Num*) which is realized as a singular morpheme (∅) or a plural morpheme (S) (Chomsky, 1957, 29); the constituent N° of the subject noun phrase which is adjusted to a predicate noun in a copula sentence by transformation (Lees, 1960a, 14); a constituent of the noun (N → N+*Num*) which is realized as a singular or plural morpheme: Num → Sg./Pl. (Koutsoudas, 1966, 155–157.) *G–2.* A syntactic feature, [+singular] or [−singular], which is generated in the noun segment by the segment structure rules and realized in the surface structure only if it is negatively specified—that is, if it is plural. (Jacobs and Rosenbaum, 1968, 82.) See also CONCORD, AGREEMENT.

Number adjustment. *G–1.* The transformation which adjusts the number of the verb and the predicate noun to the number of the subject. (Lees, 1960a, 14, 45.) Compare NUMBER TRANSFORMATION.

Number morpheme. *G–1.* One of the morphemes assigned to the verb and the predicate noun by number adjustment: singular (S for third person singular present verbs, Ø for predicate nouns), or plural (Ø for verbs, S for predicate nouns). (Lees, 1960a, 45.) See also CONCORD, AGREEMENT.

Number transformation. *G–1.* The obligatory transformation which converts the concord symbol C in the auxiliary into S, following a singular NP, or Ø, following any other NP, or Past (in any context). (Chomsky, 1957, 112.) Compare NUMBER ADJUSTMENT.

O

Object. *G–1–2.* A noun phrase that is immediately dominated by a verb phrase in the underlying structure: VP → V+*NP*. (Jacobs and Rosenbaum, 1968, 72.) Also called DIRECT OBJECT.

Object complement. *G–2.* The S in the expansion DET,N,S of an NP which is a constituent of a VP expanded as V,NP—that is, a sentence embedded as a noun phrase complement in an NP which is the direct object of a VP of a main sentence: Also called **Object**

noun phrase complement. (Rosenbaum, 1967a, 81.) Compare SUBJECT COMPLEMENT.

Object complementation. *G–2.* The process of embedding a sentence as an object complement in another (main) sentence—an instance of noun phrase complementation, as in: "Huck rejected the argument *that God is dead*." (Rosenbaum, 1967c, 320.) Also called **Object noun phrase complementation.** (Rosenbaum, 1967a, 3, 33.) See also OBJECT COMPLEMENT.

Object complement system. *G–2.* The set of rules necessary to explain object complementation. (Rosenbaum, 1967a, 36.) See also OBJECT COMPLEMENTATION, NOUN PHRASE COMPLEMENTATION.

Object, direct. See DIRECT OBJECT.

Object, indirect. See INDIRECT OBJECT.

Objectivalization. *G–2S.* The transformational process which brings a nominal element into a closer superficial relationship with the verb, as when: "Huck rubbed (with) liniment on *the bump*" ⇒ "Huck rubbed (on) *the bump* with liniment." (Fillmore, 1968, 47.) Compare SUBJECTIVALIZATION.

Objective. *G–2S.* The semantically neutral case of a thing whose role in the sentence is identified by the action or state of the verb. Earlier called **Ergative.** (Fillmore, 1968, 25.) See also CASE. Compare ERGATIVE.

Object, middle. See MIDDLE OBJECT.

Object noun phrase complementation. See OBJECT COMPLEMENTATION.

Object noun phrase, underlying. See UNDERLYING OBJECT NOUN PHRASE.

Object, reflexive. See REFLEXIVE PRONOUN.

Object, underlying. See UNDERLYING OBJECT NOUN PHRASE.

Obligatory. *G–1–2.* Required for application to a structure in order for the derivation to generate a grammatical sentence. Said of a transformational rule. For example, all of the transformational rules in the predicate complementation system are obligatory unless otherwise marked as optional. (Rosenbaum, 1967a, 5, 37, 61.) Compare OPTIONAL.

Obligatory complementizer deletion transformation. *G–2.* The transformation which obligatorily deletes the *for* of the *for-to* complementizer or the POSS of the POSS-ing complementizer from the predicate complement of a complex sentence at the instruction of the main verb, as in: "Huck trusted Tom (*for* Tom) to steer the raft"; "Huck preferred (Huck*'s*) smoking his pipe." The identical nouns are deleted by the erasure principle. (Rosenbaum, 1967a, 7, 52, 56.) Compare OPTIONAL COMPLEMENTIZER DELETION TRANSFORMATION.

Obligatory transformation. *G–1.* A transformation which does not affect the meaning of a kernel but must be applied if that string is to become a grammatical sentence (Chomsky, 1962, 223); a completely automatic transformation which appears at the end of the grammar and applies to all sentences that fit its conditions (Lees, 1960a, 32, 43). *G–2.* All transformations are obligatory, and singular, in second-generation transformational grammar. (Lyons, 1968, 268.) Compare OPTIONAL TRANSFORMATION.

Oblique complement, transitive. See TRANSITIVE OBLIQUE COMPLEMENTATION.

Oblique noun phrase complement. *G–2.* The S in the expansion DET,N,S of an NP which is a constituent of a prepositional phrase in a verb phrase expanded as V,PP or V,NP,PP—that is, the sentence embedded as a noun phrase complement in an NP object in a prepositional phrase in the VP of a main sentence:

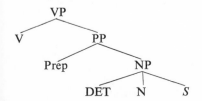

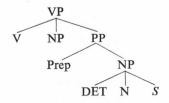

Intransitive oblique NP complementation.

Transitive oblique NP complementation.

(Rosenbaum, 1967a, 4, 81.) Compare OBJECT COMPLEMENT.

Oblique noun phrase complementation. *G–2.* The embedding of a sentence as an oblique noun phrase complement in another (main) sentence—an instance of noun phrase complementation. (Rosenbaum, 1967a, 4, 81.) See also OBLIQUE NOUN PHRASE COMPLEMENT, INTRANSITIVE OBLIQUE NOUN PHRASE COMPLEMENTATION, TRANSITIVE OBLIQUE COMPLEMENTATION. Compare OBLIQUE VERB PHRASE COMPLEMENTATION, OBJECT COMPLEMENTATION.

Oblique noun phrase complementation, intransitive. See INTRANSITIVE OBLIQUE NOUN PHRASE COMPLEMENTATION.

Oblique noun phrase complementation, transitive. See TRANSITIVE OBLIQUE COMPLEMENTATION.

Oblique verb phrase complementation. G–2. The expansion of a VP as V,PP,S—that is, the embedding of a sentence as a complement in the verb phrase of another (main) sentence containing a prepositional phrase as a constituent: VP   , as in: "Tom relied on Huck *to do*

$$
\begin{array}{ccc}
 & \text{VP} & \\
\diagup & | & \diagdown \\
\text{V} & \text{PP} & S
\end{array}
$$

the cooking." (Rosenbaum, 1967a, 3, 97, 125.) See also VERB PHRASE COMPLEMENTATION. Compare OBLIQUE NOUN PHRASE COMPLEMENTATION, OBJECT COMPLEMENTATION.

Observational adequacy. G–1. The level of justification of a grammar which accounts for the primary linguistic data of a corpus—that is, for the input to the language acquisition device. This is the level of adequacy of a structural grammar. (Chomsky, 1964, 64.) See also EMPIRICAL ADEQUACY.

Obstruction. G–1. The degree of narrowing in the vocal tract which characterizes the articulation of the glides [w] and [y]. (Halle, 1959, 326.) See also NARROWING.

Obstruent. G–2. A nonsonorant, which can be a stop, a fricative, or an affricate. (Chomsky and Halle, 1968, 302.) Compare SONORANT.

Occlusion. G–1. The degree of narrowing of articulators in the vocal tract which is capable of producing turbulence, as in the fricatives. (Halle, 1959, 326.) See also NARROWING.

One-grammatical. G–1. Needing no special interpretation in order to be understood, such as "Tom likes Huck," which is a one-grammatical sentence. (Katz, 1964b, 405.) Compare TWO-GRAMMATICAL.

One-many rule. See EXPANSION RULE.

One-place predicate. G–2S. A predicate which contains an intransitive verb and occurs with only one argument, or noun phrase, as in: "Huck disappeared." (Langendoen, 1969, 97.) Compare TWO-PLACE PREDICATE, THREE-PLACE PREDICATE.

Operation. G–1–2. The type of structural change which a singulary transformation effects in an underlying phrase-marker. It can be reordering (permutation, rearrangement, juxtaposition, inversion: $A+B \Rightarrow B+A$), or addition (adjunction: $A+B \Rightarrow A+B+C$), or deletion (reduction: $A+B+C \Rightarrow A+B$). (Chomsky, 1962, 222; Katz and Postal, 1964, 40.) Other types of operations that have been posited are combining, incorporating, restructuring (Klima, 1964a, 252, 295), and substitution or replacement: $A+B \Rightarrow A+C$ (Koutsoudas, 1966, 27). See also SINGULARY TRANSFORMATION, ELEMENTARY TRANSFORMATION, GRAMMATICAL TRANSFORMATION.

Operation, global. See GLOBAL OPERATION.

Operator. G–1. A vocabulary symbol in the syntactic rules which indicates one of two types of grammatical operations, either concatenation of elements in a string (e.g., $A+B$) or rewriting or transforming a string as a different string (e.g., $A \rightarrow B$). (Koutsoudas, 1966, 8–9.) See also ABBREVIATOR, NOTATIONAL CONVENTION.

Optimal. G–1–2. Simplest; involving no more mechanism than the facts demand. Said of a grammar, or of a rule of the grammar. (Halle, 1959, 344; Chomsky, 1965, 115.) See also OPTIMAL GRAMMAR.

Optimal grammar. *G–1–2.* The simplest grammar, which is the one that the child constructs from a finite set of utterances. The child 'optimizes,' or simplifies, the adult grammar. The adult constructs a **Nonoptimal grammar** under the same circumstances. (Halle, 1959, 344; King, 1969, 65, 84.) See also LANGUAGE ACQUISITION.

Optimize. See OPTIMAL GRAMMAR.

Optional. *G–1–2.* Not required for, and not prevented from, application to a structure in order for the derivation to generate a grammatical sentence. Said of a transformational rule. For example, the passive transformation is (usually) optional. (Rosenbaum, 1967a, 37.) Compare OBLIGATORY.

Optional complementizer deletion transformation. *G–2.* The transformation which optionally deletes the *that* complementizer, or the *for* of the *for-to* complementizer, or the POSS of the POSS-ing complementizer from the predicate complement of a complex sentence, as in: "Tom knew (*that*) Becky was lost"; "Huck expected (*for*) Tom to return"; "Becky appreciated Tom(*'s*) rescuing her." (Rosenbaum, 1967a, 6.) Compare OBLIGATORY COMPLEMENTIZER DELETION TRANSFORMATION.

Optional transformation. *G–1.* A single-base or double-base transformation which is not required of a string for it to become a grammatical sentence. The optional part of the grammar specifies the choices available to the speaker for the production of a sentence. (Chomsky, 1962, 242.) *G–2.* In second-generation transformational grammar, all transformations are singulary and obligatory, though there are still some optional rules in the categorial component. (Lyons, 1968, 268.) Compare OBLIGATORY TRANSFORMATION.

Oral-articulator feature. *G–2.* One of the phonological distinctive features which help to subclassify consonants and vowels in respect to primary (relative) place of articulation. The polar dimensions are: *diffuse*—high vowel, front consonant—vs. *compact*—low vowel, back consonant; *grave* or *low tonality*—back rounded flat vowel, peripheral consonant—vs. *acute* —front vowel, central consonant; *high*—high vowel, post-alveolar consonant—vs. *buccal*—mid and low vowel, pre-palatal consonant; and *peripheral*—front and back vowel—vs. *nonperipheral*—central vowel. (Harms, 1968, 26–31.) Compare NONORAL-ARTICULATOR FEATURE.

Order-change transformation. See ADJECTIVE INVERSION.

Ordered. *G–2.* Applied in a strict or partial order within a transformational cycle. For example, the transformations in the predicate complementation system make up an ordered set, some of which are strictly ordered and some partially ordered in relation to each other. (Rosenbaum, 1967a, 35, 47, 51–52.) See also RULE ORDERING. Compare LINEAR ORDERING.

Ordered, critically. See CRITICALLY ORDERED.

Ordered, partially. See PARTIALLY ORDERED.

Ordered, strictly. See STRICTLY ORDERED.

Ordering. See RULE ORDERING.

Ordering, conjunctive. See CONJUNCTIVE ORDERING.

Ordering, disjunctive. See DISJUNCTIVE ORDERING.

Ordering, linear. See LINEAR ORDERING.

Ordering relation. See RULE ORDERING.

Ordering, relative.   See RELATIVE ORDERING.

Ordering, rule.   See RULE ORDERING.

Order of acquisition.   *G–1–2.* The largely fixed order in which the child learns the segments and rules of his language as his hypotheses become more and more complex. The order of acquisition is governed not by the order of presentation or the frequency of occurrence but by universal relative linguistic complexity. In phonology, for example, the child first produces unvoiced, unaspirated stops, which are not even phonemes in English. (Kiparsky, 1968, 194.) See also LANGUAGE ACQUISITION.

Order, word.   See WORD ORDER.

Orthography, conventional.   See CONVENTIONAL ORTHOGRAPHY.

Overt negation.   *G–2.* The negation of a sentence or one of its constituents by means of *not* or some other formative, as in: "It is *not* true that *no* one is *un*happy." (Langendoen, 1969, 127.) Compare COVERT NEGATION.

P

Paired morphemes.   *G–2.* A pair of morphemes which feature mutual inclusion, such as the perfective morphemes *have*+*en,* the passive morphemes *be*+*en,* the progressive morphemes *be*+*ing,* and the complementizing morphemes *for*+*to* and POSS+*ing.* (Rosenbaum, 1967a, 24.) See also AUXILIARY, COMPLEMENTIZER.

Pair test.   *G–1.* An operational test for determining phonemic distinctness on the basis of an informant's judgment as to whether two semantically different items are recognized as having the same or different pronunciation. Using pronunciation as a criterion for phonemic distinctness results in such conclusions as "[t] and [d] are allophones of different phonemes if *metal* and *medal* are recognized as having different pronunciations." (Chomsky, 1957, 96–97.)

Paradigm.   *G–2a.* A set of different sentences whose relatedness can be attributed to their common underlying structure, which can be specified in a single branching diagram, as in: "Huck preferred to fish"; "To fish was preferred by Huck"; "What Huck preferred was to fish":

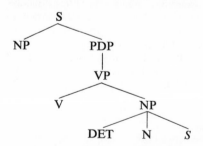

(Rosenbaum, 1967a, 14, 34.) *G–2b.* A single model sentence whose structure exemplifies the type of construction generated by one of the transformational systems of the grammar. For example, the sentence "Huck condescended to rescue Jim" is a paradigm, or example, of intransitive verb phrase complementation. Also called **Paradigm case.** (Rosenbaum, 1967a, 73.) See also RELATEDNESS, RELATED SENTENCES.

Paradigm case. *G–2.* An example, or model, of a construction type. (Rosenbaum, 1967a, 59.) See also PARADIGM.

Paraphrase. *G–1–2a.* The relation which holds between a pair of sentences that are either transformationally related—that is, they have the same set of underlying phrase-markers—or semantically related—they contain synonymous expressions. (Lees, 1960a, 78.) *G–1–2b.* A heuristic, rule of thumb device for reconstructing the derivation of a sentence, by seeking syntactic equivalents and constructing rules that relate the given sentence to the equivalents through the same set of underlying phrase-markers. (Katz and Postal, 1964, 157.) *G–1–2c.* To decompose a complex sentence as a set of simple sentences. (Kuroda, 1969, 340.) Also called **Discourse paraphrase.** See also RELATED SENTENCES.

Paraphrase, discourse. See DISCOURSE PARAPHRASE.

Parenthetical verb. *G–2.* A verb which is a member of a class of verbs which can shift their subject and auxiliary to the end of the sentence, as when: *"I wonder* how Tom escaped from the cave" ⇒ "How did Tom escape from the cave, *I wonder?";* *"I think* Tom escaped from the cave" ⇒ "Tom escaped from the cave, *I think";* *"I notice* that Tom escaped from the cave" ⇒ "Tom escaped from the cave, *I notice."* (Katz and Postal, 1964, 110.)

Parenthetic-type intonation. See COMMA INTONATION.

Parole. *G–1–2.* The performance of a native or fluent speaker, as opposed to *langue,* his linguistic competence. (Chomsky, 1964, 59, 92; Chomsky, 1968, 17.) Compare LANGUE.

Parse. *G–1–2.* To analyze a sentence into a linear sequence of hierarchically bracketed constituents. (Postal, 1964a, 2; Postal, 1964c, 21; Langendoen, 1969, 11.) See also PARSING.

Parsing. *G–1–2.* An immediate constituent analysis (Chomsky, 1957, 26; Chomsky, 1962, 211); a bracketing structure (Lees, 1960b, 150); a phrase structure (Postal, 1964a, 2); an analysis of a sentence into its constituents (Langendoen, 1969, 11). See also ANALYSIS.

Partially ordered. *G–2.* Applied in a relative order—as opposed to a strict order—within a transformational cycle. For example, in the predicate complementation system, the 'partially ordered' pronoun deletion transformation sometimes precedes the 'strictly ordered' passive transformation and sometimes follows it—in which case pronoun deletion does not apply: "(It) that Tom would return was not doubted by Huck" vs. "It was not doubted by Huck that Tom would return." (Rosenbaum, 1967a, 7, 35.) Compare STRICTLY ORDERED.

Participle. *G–1–2.* A verb which follows an auxiliary and ends in *ing*—a present participle (e.g., "is *going"*) or in *ed/en*—a past participle (e.g., "has *gone");* a verbal adjective that is derived from a verb in *ing* or *ed/en* and modifies a noun (e.g., *"flying* planes"; *"deserted* villages") (Lyons, 1968, 250); one of the two non-tense inflectional forms of the verb: the present participle in *ing,* which indicates progressive aspect, and the past participle in *ed/en,* which indicates perfect aspect or passive voice (Langendoen, 1969, 118–119, 134). *G–2S.* An adjective which occurs as the predicate of a passive sentence in a sentential argument of *be*—a past participle (e.g., "was *frightened*")—or which occurs as an adjectival predicate with the suffix *ing* in a sentence which selects a dative argument—a present participle (e.g., "were *frightening*"). (Langendoen, 1969, 118–119, 134.) See also PRESENT PARTICIPLE.

Participle affix. *G–1*. The participial ending *en* (e.g., "have walk*ed*"; "have driv*en*"; "have go*ne*"), as opposed to the ing-affix—the gerundive ending *ing,* as in "are walk*ing*." (Lees, 1960a, 19–20.) See also PARTICIPLE.

Participle, past. See PARTICIPLE.

Participle, present. See PRESENT PARTICIPLE.

Particle. *G–1*. The constituent in a V+Prt construction which can be separated from the verb by an optional separation transformation, which is obligatory if Prt is a pronoun: "Tom looked *up* the meaning" ⇒ "Tom looked the meaning *up*" (Chomsky, 1957, 75–76); the constituent of a set of complex verbs which is inverted with the following noun phrase by a particle inversion transformation (Katz and Postal, 1964, 41) or by particle permutation (Katz, 1966, 139). *G–2*. The verb particle is introduced into a verbal containing the specification [+particle] by particle segment transformation and moved to the right of the object noun phrase by particle movement transformation. (Jacobs and Rosenbaum, 1968, 104.) The particle separation rule is blocked if the following noun phrase is complex. (Ross, 1966, 291.) *G–2S*. The sentence to which the particle shift rule has applied and the sentence to which it has not applied are both derived from the same underlying intermediate conceptual structure, not one from the other. (Langacker, 1968, 119.) See also VERB PARTICLE, SEPARABLE VERB.

Particle inversion transformation. *G–1*. The transformation which inverts the particle of certain complex verbs with their noun phrase object. (Katz and Postal, 1964, 41.) Also called **Particle separation, Particle permutation, Separation transformation, Particle movement transformation, Particle shift.** See also PARTICLE.

Particle movement transformation. *G–2*. The transformation which moves a particle segment from the verbal to the right of the object noun phrase:

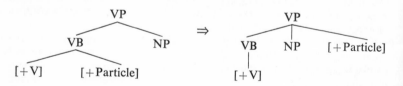

(Jacobs and Rosenbaum, 1968, 105.) Also called **Particle permutation, Particle separation, Separation transformation, Particle inversion transformation, Particle shift.** Compare PARTICLE SEGMENT TRANSFORMATION.

Particle permutation. See PARTICLE.

Particle segment transformation. *G–2*. The transformation which introduces a particle segment into a verbal which contains the specification [+particle]: VB → [+V]+[+particle]; the particle here is represented in the deep structure as a feature of the verb rather than as an actual constituent. The segment is then moved to the right of the object of the verb phrase by particle movement transformation. (Jacobs and Rosenbaum, 1968, 103–104.) Compare PARTICLE MOVEMENT TRANSFORMATION.

Particle separation. See PARTICLE.

Particle shift. *G–2.* The optional rule which permutes a verb particle and a following noun phrase object, as when: "Huck handed *over* the loot" ⇒ "Huck handed the loot *over*." (Langacker, 1968, 118.) Also called **Particle separation, Particle permutation, Separation transformation, Particle movement transformation, Particle inversion transformation.**

Particle, verb. See VERB PARTICLE.

Particular grammar. *G–2.* A compendium of specific and nonessential properties of a particular language, as opposed to a 'universal grammar,' which is a theory of the general and essential properties that characterize any human language. (Chomsky and Halle, 1968, 43.) Compare UNIVERSAL GRAMMAR.

Particular, language-. See LANGUAGE-PARTICULAR.

Part of speech. *G–1–2.* The grammatical class of a word (Langacker, 1968, 74); one of the traditional categories of words: noun, pronoun, verb, adjective, adverb, preposition, and conjunction (Langendoen, 1969, 10–12); one of the four morphological classes—noun, verb, adjective, adverb—or one of the bound morphemes—a prefix or suffix (Thomas, 1965, 48–49). *G–2S.* The three parts of speech—noun, verb, and adjective—exist only on the surface level; they are derived by transformation from a single base category—contentive. (Bach, 1968, 91, 114–115, 120.) Compare CATEGORY.

Pass. See LEXICAL PASS.

Pass, first lexical. See FIRST LEXICAL PASS.

Passive. *G–1–2.* Having undergone the passive transformation; a sentence whose underlying constituent structure contains the additional auxiliary element *be+en* and an optional agentive marker (*by* . . .). (Lees, 1960a, 34; Lees, 1964b, xlii.) Also called **Passive sentence.** See also PASSIVE TRANSFORMATION.

Passive morpheme. *G–2.* One of the morphemes *be, en, by* which are inserted into a sentence by the passive transformation. (Rosenbaum, 1967a, 9.) See also PASSIVE TRANSFORMATION.

Passive predicate. *G–2S.* A predicate, corresponding to an active two-place predicate with an agent or instrumental argument, which consists of a past participle occurring in a sentential argument of *be,* as in: "Huck was *scared by Aunt Polly.*" The passive predicate is also permitted to occur without the agent argument, thereby expressing a state rather than an activity, as in: "Huck was *scared.*" (Langendoen, 1969, 117–119.)

Passive, second. See SECOND PASSIVE.

Passive sentence. *G–2.* A sentence to which the passive transformation has applied. (Rosenbaum, 1967a, 37, 60.) Also called **Passive.** Compare ACTIVE SENTENCE.

Passive test. *G–2.* A test for noun phrase status, which says that if a pair of phrases can be inverted by the passive transformation, then they are both noun phrases—for example: "*Tom* painted *the fence*" ⇒ "*The fence* was painted by *Tom.*" (Jacobs and Rosenbaum, 1968, 38.) See also PASSIVE TRANSFORMATION.

Passive transformation. *G–1.* The optional singulary transformation which operates on a sentence of the type $NP_1 + AUX + V + NP_2$ (where V is transitive), inverting the noun phrases and adding *be+en* after AUX, and *by* after V, as when: "*Huck* built a *raft*" ⇒ "*The raft* was buil*t by Huck.*" (Chomsky, 1957, 43, 79.) Passive precedes reflexive (Lees and

Klima, 1963, 151) and agreement (Thomas, 1965, 193). *G–2.* The elementary substitution transformation which applies obligatorily to a base phrase-marker which contains a manner adverbial with the dummy element *by+passive,* substituting the first NP for *passive* and placing the second NP in first position. The verb, which is subcategorized as [——NP+ manner], can be either transitive or intransitive—the latter in pseudo-passives, as in: "Huck was looked up to by Tom." (Chomsky, 1965, 104–105.) Passivization is restricted to verbs that can occur freely with manner adverbials. (Katz, 1966, 143.) Passives are not derived from actives. (Katz and Postal, 1964, 72.)

Passive transformation, second. See SECOND PASSIVE.

Passivize. See PASSIVIZATION.

Passivization. *G–2.* The application of the passive transformation, by which the sentence is said to have been passivized (Rosenbaum, 1967a, 10, 14, 69.) See also PASSIVE TRANSFORMATION.

Pass, lexical. See LEXICAL PASS.

Pass, second lexical. See SECOND LEXICAL PASS.

Past participle. See PARTICIPLE.

Past tense. *G–1.* The concord morpheme *Past,* which is positioned first in the auxiliary and then attached to the right of the following base by auxiliary transformation. (Chomsky, 1957, 39.) *G–2.* The syntactic feature [−present] (i.e., syntactic past) of the auxiliary node of S in the deep structure which is copied on the verbal by verbal agreement transformation if the AUX is not realized as a copula or perfective form (Jacobs and Rosenbaum, 1968, 132–133); the underlying form [d], which is converted to [əd] by the schwa insertion rule, which inserts [ə] between obstruents of the same type (Langacker, 1968, 170). Some occurrences of the feature past tense are not introduced in the base rules but come from a second lexical pass following transformations governing such matters as sequence of tenses and indirect discourse. (Bach, 1968, 119.) *G–2S.* A feature of an abstract two-place predicate that occurs in every sentence type. One argument is a time expression, or time adverbial, and the other is a sentence, such as:

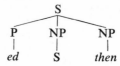

"Huck look*ed* for Tom *then*." (Langendoen, 1969, 121–122.) See also TENSE. Compare PRESENT TENSE.

Path. *G–2.* The branch(es) connecting two nodes in a tree diagram. For example, the two noun phrases in the following diagram have four branches in their path:

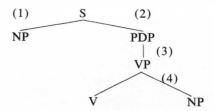

(Rosenbaum, 1967a, 6.) See also DERIVATIONAL PATH.

Path, derivational. See DERIVATIONAL PATH.

Pattern, compounding-stress-. See COMPOUNDING-STRESS-PATTERN.

Pattern, intonation. See INTONATION.

Pedagogic grammar. *G–2*. A grammar which attempts to provide the student with the ability to understand and produce the sentences of his language. (Chomsky, 1966a, 10.) Compare LINGUISTIC GRAMMAR.

Penetrable. *G–2*. A nonbinary semantic feature corresponding to the state of penetrability of physical objects, such as: gas [1-penetrable], liquid [2-penetrable], solid [3-penetrable]. (Langendoen, 1969, 40–41.) See also SEMANTIC FEATURE.

Perceptual model. *G–1–2*. A model of linguistic theory which assigns a structural description to a given utterance on the basis of an internalized generative grammar:

utterance → *perceptual model* → structural description.

The grammar of a particular language is an attempt to specify the information available to a perceptual model which permits it to understand an utterance. (Chomsky, 1964, 61.) Compare PERFORMANCE MODEL, SPEECH RECOGNITION MODEL, SPEECH PRODUCTION MODEL, COGNITIVE MODEL, ACQUISITION MODEL.

Perfect aspect. See ASPECT.

Perfective. See ASPECT.

Performance. *G–2*. The theory of language use; the actual use of language (Chomsky, 1965, 4, 9); what the speaker-hearer actually does on the basis of his knowledge of a language (Chomsky, 1964, 52); actual speech, as opposed to language; the subject of the psychological theory which deals with how linguistic competence is used in the production and comprehension of speech (Katz, 1966, 115, 119); linguistic behavior (Postal, 1968a, 269); the subject of a performance-model grammar, which includes a competence-model grammar within it (Chomsky and Halle, 1968, 3, 110); roughly, *parole* (King, 1969, 11). See also PAROLE. Compare COMPETENCE.

Performance model. *G–2*. A model for the speaker; a model of speech production; a model of the use of a generative grammar (Chomsky, 1965, 139–140); a specification of how a desired message is inputted into the grammar and outputted to the speech apparatus (Postal, 1964c, 36). Compare PERCEPTUAL MODEL, COGNITIVE MODEL, ACQUISITION MODEL, SPEECH PRODUCTION MODEL, SPEECH RECOGNITION MODEL.

Performative verb. *G–2*. A verb, or explicit performative, which can appear in the context "I hereby. . ." (Fodor and Katz, 1964, 14); a verb which specifies the illocutionary force, or performative relationship, between the speaker, *I*, and the person spoken to, *you*, such as: *order, declare, promise*, etc. Every sentence dominates a first person subject, a second person indirect object, and a performative verb, as in: "I order you (you close the door)" ⇒ "Close the door!" The loss of the subject in imperative sentences is a case of equi-NP-deletion and deletion of the performative verb and its subject. (McCawley, 1968, 155–156.)

Periphrasis, genitive. See GENITIVE PERIPHRASIS.

Permutation. *G–1–2*. One of the grammatical operations performed by grammatical transformations: reordering, as in the particle separation transformation (e.g., "Huck hauled *up the anchor*" ⇒ "Huck hauled *the anchor up*") (Chomsky, 1961a, 133–135); rearrangement, or juxtaposition, of two adjacent constituents, not necessarily attached to the same node (Koutsoudas, 1966, 32–34); a change in the linear order of constituents in a tree structure by permutation rule, whether or not the constituents are adjacent, as in not-promotion (e.g., "Huck *believed that Tom was not* serious" ⇒ "Huck did*n't believe that Tom was* serious") (Langacker, 1968, 127–128). Rearrangement of two nonadjacent constituents involves the operations of deletion and adjunction. (Koutsoudas, 1966, 32–34.) Permutation usually reduces the amount of structure in a sentence. (Chomsky, 1961a, 133–135.) See also OPERATION.

Permutation rule. See PERMUTATION.

Personal pronoun. *G–2.* A pronoun: NP → Pronoun (Chomsky, 1965, 221–222); one of the types of pro-forms (Langacker, 1968, 124–125). Pronouns are entered in the lexicon in their objective form. (King, 1969, 147.) The third person pronouns are definite articles assigned to nouns which have the features [+Pro] [+Def] [−Demon] [+III] [−II] [−I] and lack restrictive relative phrases. Plural nonthird person pronouns—in such expressions as *we/us men, you boys, you 'uns* (you ones)—are underlying nouns marked [−Pro] but [+I] or [+II]. (Postal, 1966, 215, 219, 222.) All personal pronouns are nominative ([−accusative]) in the deep structure but can receive the specification [+accusative] by case transformation. Personal pronouns are special types of nouns in the deep structure, with the feature [+N], [+Pro] and a number feature, a person feature, and a gender feature for third person; but in the surface structure they are definite articles. (Jacobs and Rosenbaum, 1968, 92–98, 220.) See also PRONOUN.

Phone. *G–2.* A phonetic segment in a systematic phonetic representation of a string (Chomsky, 1964, 87); a column in a phonetic matrix of a sentence (Chomsky, 1966a, 77). See also PHONETIC SEGMENT.

Phoneme. *G–1–2.* A basic, primitive phonological constituent developed in the phonological rules on the basis of a small set of universal phonetic features (Lees, 1960a, 21); a simultaneous actualization of a set of features, each of which is a pair of binary specifications (Halle, 1959, 324); an element of pronunciation and transcription; a bundle of feature specifications (Langendoen, 1969, 129); a systematic phoneme; a matrix of classificatory features that shows which features must be distinctively specified for a particular segment; an underlying segment in the spelling of a morpheme (written in slashes: e.g., /d/), as opposed to a phonetic segment (enclosed in brackets: e.g., [d]) (Harms, 1968, 2). See also SYSTEMATIC PHONEME.

Phoneme, systematic. See SYSTEMATIC PHONEME.

Phoneme, unit. See UNIT PHONEME.

Phonemic. *G–1–2.* Relating to the level of a linguistic theory which accounts for the way in which sentences are represented as sequences of phonemes by morphophonemic rules (Chomsky, 1957, 11, 13, 33); segmental (Chomsky, 1966a, 23). See also PHONEME.

Phonemic feature. *G–1.* One of the abstract binary features which serve to distinguish morphemes in their representation in the dictionary. (Halle, 1959, 330.) See also PHONOLOGICAL DISTINCTIVE FEATURE. Compare PHONETIC FEATURE.

Phonemic level. *G–1.* The level of representation of an utterance as a sequence of phonemes. (Chomsky, 1957, 11.) *G–2.* There is no reason for setting up a level of representation—a phonemic level—between the morphemic and phonetic levels. (Bach, 1964, 127). See also SYSTEMATIC PHONEMICS.

Phonemics, systematic. See SYSTEMATIC PHONEMICS.

Phonetic alphabet, universal. See UNIVERSAL PHONETIC ALPHABET.

Phonetic feature. *G–1–2.* One of the small number of fixed, universal phonetic properties which characterize the. elements of the output of the phonological component, each with acoustic and articulatory dimensions that are independent of a particular language (Chomsky, 1965, 28); one of the universal set of inherent properties which represent man's phonetic capabilities, each being a binary physical scale labeled with opposing qualities (e.g., high/nonhigh) (Chomsky and Halle, 1968, 299); a primitive of the system for describing ideal pronunciation, its values being not necessarily binary (Postal, 1968a, 110). See also PHONOLOGICAL DISTINCTIVE FEATURE. Compare PHONEMIC FEATURE.

Phonetic interpretation. See PHONOLOGICAL COMPONENT.

Phonetic matrix. *G–1–2.* A completely specified ($+$or$-$) representation of the phonetic distinctive features of a formative, such as:

	Segment$_1$	Segment$_2$	Segment$_3$.
Feature$_1$	$+$	$-$	$+$
Feature$_2$	$-$	$+$	$+$

(Chomsky, 1964, 86; Chomsky and Halle, 1968, 166, 169.) Compare PHONOLOGICAL MATRIX.

Phonetic representation. *G–2.* The output of the phonological component; a phonetic matrix, consisting of a sequence of phonetic segments, each a phonetic feature matrix. A phonetic representation describes a perceptual reality rather than a physical or acoustic reality. (Chomsky and Halle, 1968, 25, 164.) Compare PHONOLOGICAL REPRESENTATION.

Phonetic segment. *G–2.* One of the sequence of phonetic categories which make up the phonetic representation of a sentence, such as [p], [a], [t], etc. Each segment is a complex system of ideal instructions, or phonetic feature specifications, for the physical movement of the different parts of the speech apparatus, rather than an actual signal or articulation itself. (Postal, 1968a, 296; Postal, 1968b, 275–276.) Compare PHONOLOGICAL SEGMENT. See also SEGMENT.

Phonetic segment, universal. See UNIVERSAL PHONETIC SEGMENT.

Phonetics, systematic. See SYSTEMATIC PHONETICS.

Phonetic theory, universal. See UNIVERSAL PHONETIC THEORY.

Phonetic transcription. *G–1–2.* A direct graphic description of the acoustic signal produced by the articulation of speech (Postal, 1968a, 273); a representation of what the speaker of the language takes the phonetic properties of an utterance to be (Chomsky and Halle, 1968, 296); a designation of speech sounds by conventional alphabetic symbols which are abbreviations for feature complexes (Halle, 1959, 328); a sequence of instructions that indicate how the physical system of articulation is to operate (Postal, 1968a, 273). Compare CONVENTIONAL ORTHOGRAPHY.

Phonological admissibility. *G–2a.* The phonological possibility of the occurrence of a sequence in a particular language, as defined by the phonological redundancy—morpheme structure—rules of that language.

For example, in English, *bring* is phonologically admissible and occurring; *bling* is phonologically admissible but not occurring—it is an accidental gap; and *bning* is phonologically inadmissible, or impossible, and not occurring. (Chomsky, 1965, 168–169.) *G–2b*. The degree of phonological possibility of occurrence of a sequence in a particular language; the distance of a sequence from the lexicon, as defined by the markedness of its phonological matrices. The earlier tripartite theory of admissibility has been abandoned in favor of the multiple degrees of markedness. (Chomsky and Halle, 1968, 416–418.) See also ADMISSIBILITY.

Phonological alternation. *G–2*. Morphophonemic alternation, which is the chief source of evidence for deciding which rules to include in the phonological component. Phonological alternation can usually be accounted for by generalizing a common underlying form and positing a set of rules to relate this abstraction to the phonetic realizations, such as the alternation of [d], [t], and [ɪd] in English past tense formation, which can be related by a set of rules to the common underlying form /d/. (King, 1969, 25.)

Phonological ambiguity. See CONSTRUCTIONAL HOMONYMITY.

Phonological change. *G–2*. The addition of a rule to an idiolect, and the gradual spread of the innovation as it is borrowed among more and more speakers, until it becomes a major, obligatory rule. (King, 1969, 117, 119.) Underlying forms are much more resistant to change than late phonetic rules. (Chomsky, 1966a, 90.) Also called **Sound change.** Compare SYNTACTIC CHANGE. See also LINGUISTIC CHANGE.

Phonological component. *G–1*. One of the two major components of a grammar, the other being the syntax. The phonology maps each syntactic string into a representation of the most detailed phonetic features. That is, it provides each sentence with its pronunciation. (Lees, 1960b, 150.) *G–2a*. One of the two subcomponents of the grammatical component of a complete linguistic description, the other being the syntactic subcomponent. The phonological component is not related to the semantic component of a linguistic description, since these two components operate independently on the syntactic structure. (Katz and Postal, 1964, 2.) *G–2b*. The component of a generative grammar which converts the systematic phonemic representation of a syntactic string of formatives into a systematic phonetic representation (Harms, 1968, 14); the system of cyclic rules which map surface structures (i.e., labeled bracketings of strings of formatives) into phonetic representations (i.e., strings of universal phonetic segments) (Chomsky and Halle, 1968, 28); one of the three major components of a transformational generative grammar, the other two being the syntactic component and the semantic component. The phonological component converts a string of formatives into a phonetic representation, providing a bridge between syntax and phonetics. The rules of the phonological component are ordered transformational rules which apply in a cycle. (Chomsky, 1964, 52.) The phonological component operates only on the final derived phrase-markers from the syntax. (Postal, 1964c, 31.) It is purely interpretive. (Chomsky, 1965, 16).

Phonological distinctive feature. *G–2*. One of the features that label rows of a generally specified phonological matrix, as opposed to a phonetic distinctive feature, which is one of the universal physical scales that determine the rows of a fully specified phonetic matrix. (Chomsky and

Halle, 1968, 169.) Compare PHONETIC FEATURE. See also DISTINCTIVE
FEATURE, CLASSIFICATORY FEATURE, JAKOBSONIAN DISTINCTIVE FEATURE.

Phonological interpretation.   See PHONOLOGICAL RULE.

Phonological matrix.   *G–2a.* The spelling of a morpheme, which is introduced by morphophonemic rules following the final application of the
transformational rules. (Rosenbaum, 1967a, 22.) *G–2b.* A matrix of
phonological features that are not fully specified, in the sense that some
cells contain marked/unmarked specifications or blanks or 0's—that is,
they are archi-segments. (Chomsky and Halle, 1968, 166–169, 402–403.)
Compare PHONETIC MATRIX. See also MATRIX.

Phonological phrase.   *G–2.* One of the successive parts of a long or complex sentence. It is the maximal domain for phonological processes, as
determined by syntactic complexity or such physiological constraints as
breath capacity. (Chomsky and Halle, 1968, 10.)

Phonological realization rule.   *G–1.* A rule of the type *man+s → men,*
which rewrites more than one symbol at a time; a morphophonemic rule.
(Lyons, 1968, 243.) See also MORPHOPHONEMIC RULE.

Phonological redundancy rule.   *G–2.* One of the set of morpheme structure
rules which operate prior to the phonological rules, giving a fuller specification to the phonological distinctive feature matrix of a lexical entry and
defining the notion of phonological admissibility (Chomsky, 1965, 168–
169); a rule in one of two sets of redundancy rules, that is: sequential
constraint rules, which supply otherwise distinctive features that are unspecified for a segment in a particular environment, and blank-filling
rules, which specify nondistinctive features that are independent of surrounding segments (Harms, 1968, 84–85). Also called a **Contingency
statement.** (King, 1969, 21). See also SEQUENTIAL CONSTRAINT RULE,
BLANK-FILLING RULE, MORPHEME STRUCTURE RULE.

Phonological representation.   *G–2.* The abstract underlying representation
of the phonological features of a formative after the application of all
readjustment rules (Chomsky and Halle, 1968, 10–11, 236); the input
to the phonological component (Chomsky, 1966a, 77); the underlying
representation of a segment (Langacker, 1968, 158–159); a marked/
unmarked representation (Postal, 1968a, 167); a morphophonemic representation (Chomsky, 1966a, 79); a systematic phonemic representation
(Postal, 1968a, 163). Phonological representation is much like conventional orthography. (Chomsky, 1966a, 90.) *G–2S.* Some phonological
representations are provided in the transformational component; some are
necessary for proper inflectional and derivational formation; and some
require prior semantic interpretation. (Bach, 1968, 117–118.) Compare
PHONETIC REPRESENTATION.

Phonological rule.   *G–1a.* A rule which operates on T-terminal strings of
formatives, deleting items, rearranging them, introducing new items, etc.
—unlike phrase structure rules, but more like transformational rules. The
first set of rules, the morphophonemic rules, convert strings of morphemes
into strings of phonemes, giving a phonemic representation, while the
remaining rules provide a phonetic description. (Bach, 1964, 126–127.)
G–1b. One of the rules of the phonological component which relate a
phonemic matrix, which is a representation of binary abstract markers,
to a phonetic matrix, which is a transcription of multinary articulatory
markers. The rules of the phonological component modify these matrices

in various ways—supplying values to nonphonemic features, changing values of features—in assigning phonetic interpretations. (Halle, 1959, 333.) *G–2a.* One of the rules in the two subcomponents of the phonological component of a generative grammar, which are the **Morpheme structure (MS) rules** and the **Phonological (P) rules proper**—earlier called **Morphophonemic rules.** (Harms, 1968, 84.) The MS rules operate before the P rules, converting redundant values of features within morphemes to plus or minus values—not deleting or rearranging features—and defining possible and impossible morphemes. (Postal, 1968a, 164.) The phonological rules proper operate in an ordered cycle after the MS rules, applying first to the syntactic string of morphemes—the precycle and cyclic rules—erasing the syntactic brackets in the process, and then to the phonological string—the postcycle rules—to complete the phonological interpretation. (Harms, 1968, 96.) *G–2b.* One of the rules in the two ordered subcomponents of the phonological component of a generative grammar, which are the **Readjustment rules**—earlier called **Morpheme structure** rules—and the **Phonological rules proper.** The readjustment rules apply to a syntactically generated surface structure, expressing phonological properties of the lexical formatives in those syntactic environments and modifying the structure in various ways. The phonological rules proper operate in a transformational cycle, making such modifications as laxing and tensing vowels, simplifying clusters, and assigning primary stress. (Chomsky and Halle, 1968, 236–245.) The phonological process is completed by phonetic rules, which assign detailed phonetic specifications to the string of segments. (King, 1969, 23.)

Phonological rule proper.   See PHONOLOGICAL RULE.

Phonological segment.   *G–2.* A set of phonological feature specifications: the natural categorial segment of a phonetic segment. (Postal, 1968a, 70.) Compare PHONETIC SEGMENT. See also SEGMENT.

Phonological surface structure.   *G–2.* The representation of a sentence after readjustment rules have applied to the syntactic surface structure and before phonological rules convert the string into a phonetic representation. (Chomsky and Halle, 1968, 13.) See also PHONOLOGICAL REPRESENTATION. Compare SURFACE STRUCTURE.

Phonology.   *G–1.* That part of linguistics which is concerned with the relationship between phonemes and sounds (Halle, 1959, 329); one of the two major components of a grammar, the other being the syntax (Lees, 1960b, 150). The 'phonology' of a language is independent of its constituent-structure syntax. (Lees, 1960a, 21.) *G–2.* That part of a generative grammar which interprets the relationship between syntax and sounds (Chomsky, 1965, 89; Chomsky and Halle, 1968, ix); the sound structure, or sound pattern, of a language (Chomsky, 1966a, 8). See also PHONOLOGICAL COMPONENT, PHONOLOGICAL RULE.

Phonology, generative.   See GENERATIVE PHONOLOGY.

Phonology, noncyclical.   See NONCYCLICAL PHONOLOGY.

Phonology, systematic.   See SYSTEMATIC PHONOLOGY.

Phrasal conjunction.   See CONJUNCTION.

Phrase.   *G–1–2.* A syntactic structure that can be traced back to a single node. (Chomsky, 1962, 214.) See also PHRASE-MARKER. Compare PHONOLOGICAL PHRASE.

Phrase, agentive.   See AGENTIVE PHRASE.

Phrase-marker.   *G–1.* The set of strings that occur as lines in the derivation of a sentence (Chomsky, 1956, 149); a set of strings that represent a sentence on the level of phrase structure and are equivalent to a branching diagram (Chomsky, 1957, 87); a description that specifies the set of words in a sentence, their order and grouping, and their syntactic categories (Katz, 1966, 125); one of the elements of the structural description of a terminal string: a labeled bracketing of the categories of the string into phrases representable as a labeled tree (Chomsky, 1961a, 121; Chomsky, 1964, 82); one of a set of P-markers: **Underlying P-markers,** usually binary, provided by the phrase structure grammar, and **Derived P-markers,** resulting from the application of transformations (Postal, 1964a, 87). *G–2.* A **Base phrase-marker,** the underlying phrase structure of a single sentence, or a **Generalized phrase-marker,** the underlying phrase structure of a complex sentence, or a **Derived phrase-marker,** the syntactic surface structure of a sentence (Chomsky, 1965, 142–143); the representation of the linear ordering of constituents and the set of dominance relations among them (Langacker, 1969, 169). See also BASE PHRASE-MARKER, GENERALIZED PHRASE-MARKER, DERIVATION.

Phrase-marker, base. See BASE PHRASE-MARKER.

Phrase-marker, derived. See DERIVED PHRASE-MARKER.

Phrase marker, final derived. See FINAL DERIVED PHRASE MARKER.

Phrase-marker, generalized. See GENERALIZED PHRASE-MARKER.

Phrase-marker, matrix. See MATRIX PHRASE-MARKER.

Phrase-marker, superficial. See SUPERFICIAL PHRASE-MARKER.

Phrase-marker, underlying. See UNDERLYING PHRASE-MARKER.

Phrase, nominal. See NOMINAL PHRASE.

Phrase, noun. See NOUN PHRASE.

Phrase, phonological. See PHONOLOGICAL PHRASE.

Phrase, predicate. See PREDICATE PHRASE.

Phrase, preposition. See PREPOSITIONAL PHRASE.

Phrase, prepositional. See PREPOSITIONAL PHRASE.

Phrase structure. *G–1–2.* The constituent analysis of a derivation—that is, a labeled diagram that can be constructed uniquely from a derivation and which retains all of the essential information about that derivation except the order of application of the rules. (Chomsky, 1957, 26–27.) See also PHRASE-MARKER, PHRASE STRUCTURE GRAMMAR, BRANCHING DIAGRAM, LABELED BRACKETING.

Phrase structure configuration. *G–2.* The profile of the underlying structure—or the base—of a sentence, as given in a branching diagram. Also called **Phrase structure representation.** (Rosenbaum, 1967a, 12–13.) See also PHRASE-MARKER.

Phrase-structure expansion rule. *G–1.* An immediate-constituent rule of bracketing. (Lees, 1964b, xxxiv.) Also called **Expansion rule, Phrase structure rule, Constituent-membership rule, String replacement rule, Phrase structure rewriting rule.**

Phrase structure grammar. *G–1.* A grammar of the type [Σ, F]—that is, a set of initial symbols (Σ) and a set of instruction formulas (F) for rewriting these symbols as a sequence of strings, or derivation (Chomsky, 1957, 29–31); an unordered set of rewriting rules which assign a structural description that can be represented as a tree diagram (Chomsky, 1965, 88); one of the three sets of rules in a transformational grammar: phrase structure rules—the phrase structure grammar or PS grammar—, transformational rules, and morphophonemic rules (Chomsky, 1957, 46).

G–2. In second-generation transformational grammar, the phrase structure grammar is replaced by a base component, containing base rules and a lexicon. (Chomsky, 1965, 88.) In *G–2*, a substitution transformation replaces dummy elements in the last line of a derivation with lexical items from the lexicon, in contrast to *G–1*, where the phrase structure grammar rewrote constituents down to and including lexical items. (Katz and Postal, 1964, 103.) Also called **Constituent-structure grammar, Immediate-constituent grammar.**

Phrase structure representation. See PHRASE STRUCTURE CONFIGURATION.

Phrase structure rewriting rule. *G–1–2.* One of a set of context-free base rules, or expansion rules, which expand S (sentence) into NP, AUX, PDP, or NP, AUX, VP, and these constituents into their internal constituents in the generation of underlying sentence structures. (Rosenbaum, 1967a, 1.) Also called **Phrase structure rule, Phrase-structure expansion rule, Expansion rule, Constituent-membership rule, String-replacement rule.** Compare REWRITING RULE, TRANSFORMATIONAL RULE.

Phrase structure rule. *G–1.* An instruction formula (F) of a phrase structure grammar [Σ, F]: either context-free or context-sensitive, either unordered or partially ordered (Chomsky, 1957, 29, 33), and either optional or obligatory (Chomsky, 1956, 149). Phrase structure rules do not permit deletion, permutation, embedding, or conjunction. (Koutsoudas, 1966, 18–19.) *G–2.* One of the rules of the ordered, context-free set of rewriting rules in the base component which generate base phrase-markers. (Chomsky, 1965, 112.) Phrase structure rules permit conjunction and embedding, and can predict deletion. (Jacobs and Rosenbaum, 1968, vii.) Also called **Rewrite rule, Rule of formation** (Lees, 1960b, 151, 152); **PS rule** (Katz and Postal, 1964, 6); **P-rule** (Koutsoudas, 1966, 18); **String-replacement rule, Expansion rule, One-many rule, Constituent-structure rule, Immediate constituent rule, IC rule** (Bach, 1964, 23, 35); **Branching rule, Rewriting rule** (Chomsky, 1965, 112); **Formation rule** (Jacobs, 1968, 10). Compare REWRITING RULE, TRANSFORMATIONAL RULE.

Phrase, subordinate adverbial. See SUBORDINATE ADVERBIAL PHRASE.

Phrase, 'that'-. See 'THAT'-PHRASE.

Phrase, verb. See VERB PHRASE.

Pitch. See INTONATION.

Pivotal noun. *G–2.* The noun which appears in both the matrix and constituent sentences of a relative-complex sentence and permits their conjoining, as in: "Tom liked the *girl*"; "The *girl* lived next door." The pivotal antecedent noun in the matrix sentence is retained, but it is replaced in the constituent sentence by a relative pronoun: "Tom liked the *girl who* lived next door." (Kuroda, 1968, 268.) See also RELATIVIZATION.

Place adverbial. *G–2.* A locative phrase dominated by the optional ADV category in a derivation, as in:

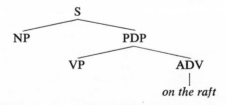

(Rosenbaum, 1967a, 21). See also ADVERBIAL.

Placeholder. *G–2.* The semantically empty morpheme *it*, which is left as a residue when an embedded subject clause is extraposed to the end of the sentence, as when: "That Tom is lazy is obvious" ⇒ "*It* is obvious that Tom is lazy." (Langacker, 1968, 129.) See also EXPLETIVE, IMPERSONAL SUBJECT, PRONOUN 'IT'.

Placement rule, stress. See STRESS PLACEMENT RULE.

Placement transformation, complementizer. See COMPLEMENTIZER PLACEMENT TRANSFORMATION.

Placement transformation, negative. See NEGATIVE PLACEMENT TRANSFORMATION.

Plural. See NUMBER.

P-marker. See PHRASE-MARKER.

Polarization. See SIMPLIFICATION.

Positional constraint. *G–2.* A constraint on the occurrence of a category symbol in a phrase-marker. (Lees, 1964b, xli.) See also STRICT SUBCATEGORIZATION.

Position, neutral. See NEUTRAL POSITION.

Possessive. *G–1.* A nominal transform that is derived from an underlying kernel sentence with *have* by an optional singulary transformation, as when: "Huck has a wart" ⇒ "The wart is Huck's" ⇒ "the wart which is Huck's" ⇒ "Huck's wart." (Koutsoudas, 1966, 320–321.) *G–2.* A noun phrase of the type "Tom's knife," which derives from the underlying structure "the knife of Tom's" by permutation of the noun phrases and deletion of the article and preposition. (Langacker, 1968, 187.) See also GENITIVE, GENITIVE TRANSFORMATION, POSSESSIVE GENITIVE.

Possessive genitive. *G–1.* A genitive construction that is associated with an underlying sentence containing *have*, as in: "Huck *has* a wart" ⇒ "Huck's wart." (Lees, 1960a, 93.) See also POSSESSIVE, GENITIVE, GENITIVE TRANSFORMATION.

Possessive morpheme. *G–2.* The morpheme POSS, which is paired with the morpheme *ing* as one of the complementizers in the predicate complementation system. POSS and *ing* are mutually inclusive, though POSS can be deleted in some instances. (Rosenbaum, 1967a, 24.) See also POSS-ING COMPLEMENTIZER.

Possessive, true. See TRUE POSSESSIVE.

Possible. *G–2.* Occurring as, or in, a grammatical sentence of the language. (Rosenbaum, 1967a, 76.) Compare IMPOSSIBLE.

Possible morpheme. *G–2a.* A sequence of segments, such as *bring*, which passes through the morpheme structure rules of a particular language, as opposed to an 'impossible morpheme,' such as *bning*, which is blocked from passage. (Postal, 1968a, 178–179.) *G–2b.* One of a sequence of marked/unmarked matrices which can be fully specified as plus/minus matrices by the use of universal interpretation rules, as opposed to an 'impossible morpheme,' which requires the use of special interpretation rules. (Postal, 1968a, 178–179.) See also ADMISSIBILITY.

POSS-ing complementizer. *G–2.* The paired morphemes POSS (possessive) and *ing* which together make up one member of the unique set of complementizers distinguishing predicate complementation from other types of complementation. POSS and *ing* are mutually inclusive, in the sense that neither occurs without the other, although POSS can be deleted in some instances, as in: "Huck was worried about Jim('*s*) runn*ing* away." (Rosenbaum, 1967a, 24, 26, 28; Rosenbaum, 1967b, ix.) Also called GERUNDIVE COMPLEMENTIZER.

Post cycle. *G–2*. The series of operations which follow the transformational cycle of a derivation: the morphophonemic rules (M). (Rosenbaum, 1967a, 38, 91.) See also CYCLE, MORPHOPHONEMIC RULE, POSTCYCLE RULE.

Postcycle rule. *G–2a*. A phonological rule that does not belong to the rule cycle but accounts for additional morphophonemic alternations and supplies remaining phonetic detail without the benefit of syntactic information. (Harms, 1968, 100.) *G–2b*. A syntactic rule, or postcyclic rule, that does not belong to the rule cycle but applies after all cyclic rules have applied, such as relative clause reduction: "the boys on the raft" from "the boys *who were* on the raft." (Ross, 1967, 190.) Compare PRECYCLE RULE. See also CYCLE.

Postcyclic rule. See POSTCYCLE RULE.

Postdeterminer. See DETERMINER.

Postnominal-modifier. *G–1*. A modifier of a noun which follows that noun in a noun phrase: Noun+*PNM*, as in: "the street *where you live.*" (Lees, 1960a, 39.) Compare PRENOMINAL ADJECTIVE.

Power, transformational. See TRANSFORMATIONAL POWER.

Prearticle. See DETERMINER.

Precycle rule. *G–2a*. A phonological rule which requires syntactic information for its operation and therefore cannot be part of the cycle, since the cycle requires erasure of the underlying syntactic structure. (Harms, 1968, 100.) *G–2b*. A syntactic rule, or precyclic rule, which applies before the transformational cycle and operates on underlying structures as a whole. (Ross, 1967, 190.) Compare POSTCYCLE RULE. See also CYCLE.

Precyclic rule. See PRECYCLE RULE.

Predeterminer. See DETERMINER.

Predicate. *G–1*. The constituent which follows *be* in a verb phrase: *be* +Predicate. (Chomsky, 1957, 67.) *G–2*. The grammatical relation of a verb phrase directly dominated by an S: [VP, S] 'predicate-of' ("VP is the 'predicate-of' S"; "VP is in the 'predicate-of' relation with S"). (Chomsky, 1965, 71.) *G–2S*. The category P, which is one of the obligatory constituents of S in the deep structure: a one-place predicate (S → P+NP), a two-place predicate (S → P+NP+NP), or a three-place predicate (S → P+NP+NP+NP). P can consist of a verb, an adjective, or a noun. (Langendoen, 1969, 96–97.) Compare SUBJECT, MODALITY, VERB PHRASE.

Predicate, abstract inchoative. See INCHOATIVE.

Predicate adjective. *G–1–2*. The adjective complement of a copulative verb, which is introduced in the phrase structure grammar and is the source, by way of a relative embedding rule, of all attributive adjectives and post-nominal modifiers. (Lees, 1960a, 7, 15; Koutsoudas, 1966, 319; Rosenbaum, 1967a, 39.) See also ADJECTIVE.

Predicate complement. *G–2*. A noun phrase complement or verb phrase complement. Predicate complements are distinguished from other types of complements by a unique set of complementizers, or complementizing morphemes, which appear in initial position in the underlying complement constructions. (Rosenbaum, 1967a, 24.) See also NOUN PHRASE COMPLEMENT, VERB PHRASE COMPLEMENT, COMPLEMENT.

Predicate complementation. *G–2*. Noun phrase complementation and verb phrase complementation, collectively. (Rosenbaum, 1967a, 5, 24.) See also NOUN PHRASE COMPLEMENTATION, VERB PHRASE COMPLEMENTATION, COMPLEMENT SYSTEM. Compare SENTENTIAL COMPLEMENTATION.

Predicate complement system. *G–2*. The rules employed in the description of predicate complementation. (Rosenbaum, 1967a, 8, 82.) See also PREDICATE COMPLEMENTATION, COMPLEMENT SYSTEM.

Predicate inversion, abstract. See ABSTRACT PREDICATE INVERSION.

Predicate, modal. See MODAL PREDICATE.

Predicate nominal. *G–1–2*. A noun phrase which is preceded by a verb of the type *become, look* (like), *act* (like), etc. (Chomsky, 1965, 92.) The number of the subject NP is adjusted to the predicate nominal by transformation. (Lees, 1960a, 5, 14.) Also called **Predicate nominative, Predicate noun.**

Predicate nominative. *G–2*. A noun phrase which follows the transitive verb *be* in the verb phrase of a deep structure, as in: "Tom is *a boy.*" (Jacobs and Rosenbaum, 1968, 113.) Also called **Predicate nominal, Predicate noun.**

Predicate noun. *G–1*. A noun in the predicate which receives its number morpheme by predicate number transformation according to the number of the subject. (Lees, 1960a, 44.) Also called **Predicate nominal, Predicate nominative.** See also NUMBER ADJUSTMENT.

Predicate, one-place. See ONE-PLACE PREDICATE.

Predicate, passive. See PASSIVE PREDICATE.

Predicate phrase. *G–2*. The constituent PDP in the expansion of S as NP, AUX, PDP. The predicate phrase expands into a verb phrase and an optional adverbial phrase:

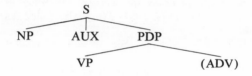

(Rosenbaum, 1967a, 1). Compare PREDICATE.

Predicate, symmetric. See SYMMETRIC PREDICATE.

Predicate, three-place. See THREE-PLACE PREDICATE.

Predicate, two-place. See TWO-PLACE PREDICATE.

Predicate verb-phrase. *G–2*. The constituent of S other than the subject nominal. (Lees, 1964b, xxxiv.) See also PREDICATE, VERB PHRASE, PREDICATE PHRASE.

Predicative sentence. *G–1*. A sentence that contains a copula, followed by a predicate noun or predicate adjective: a copula-type sentence. (Lees, 1960a, 7.) See also PREDICATE ADJECTIVE, PREDICATE NOUN.

Predicative verb. See COPULA-TYPE VERB.

Predict. *G–1–2*. To specify correctly. A rule which specifies a pattern correctly 'predicts' that pattern, and the pattern is said to be 'predictable' from that rule. Irregular patterns, which cannot be specified correctly, are said to be 'unpredictable.' (Koutsoudas, 1966, 85.) The minimal requirement of a particular grammar is that it predict all and only the grammatical sentences of the particular language and assign a correct structural description to each; the minimal requirement of a universal grammar is that it precisely characterize the way in which a particular grammar can 'predict' a given sentence and assign a correct structural description to it. (Bach, 1964, 5–6, 176.) *G–2*. To specify, whether correctly or incorrectly: as for the grammar correctly to specify, or 'predict,' the application of a certain transformation, or for an analysis incorrectly to specify, or predict, the grammaticality of a sentence. (Rosenbaum, 1967a, 39, 89.) Also: **Specify, Enumerate, Generate, Derive, Describe.** See also GENERATE, ENUMERATE.

Predictable. See PREDICT.

Prefix. *G–1–2*. A quasi-productive morpheme which is attached to the left of a stem, either by some internal computation within the lexicon (e.g., *refuse,* to reject) or by transformational process (e.g., *re-fuse,* to fuse again). (Chomsky, 1965, 184–187.) Phonologically, most prefixes are followed by the boundary symbol = (e.g., *re=fuse*) so that they cannot receive primary stress. Little is known about how prefixes should be described—transformationally, in the syntax, or derivationally, in the lexicon. (Chomsky and Halle, 1968, 100, 106.) Compare SUFFIX.

Prenominal adjective. *G–1*. A descriptive adjective that is shifted to pre-nominal position, as in: "The raft is *heavy* ⇒ "The *heavy* raft. . . ." (Lees, 1960a, 97.) Compare POST-NOMINAL MODIFIER.

Prenominal determinative. *G–1*. An article (*a, the*) or demonstrative (*this, that*). (Lees, 1960a, 14.) See also DETERMINER.

Preposing transformation. *G–1*. An optional rule, or preposing rule, which moves certain adverbs and indefinite quantifiers to the left of the subject nominal, as when: "Huck found a hammer *somewhere*" ⇒ "*Somewhere* Huck found a hammer." (Klima, 1964a, 319.) *G–2*. A transformation which moves an adverbial clause to the front of the sentence, as when: "Huck woke up *when he heard the whistle*" ⇒ "*When Huck heard the whistle,* he woke up." (Kuroda, 1968, 276.) Also called **Adverb preposing transformation.**

Preposing transformation, adverb. See ADVERB PREPOSING TRANSFORMATION.

Preposition. *G–1–2*. The first constituent of a prepositional phrase, such as: "*with* Tom" (Chomsky, 1957, 29, 33, 42); the first constituent of the category Prep-P (i.e., *preposition*+NP) (Chomsky, 1965, 94–96, 101–102, 107, 129.) *G–1*. The constituent that is introduced by preposi-tional periphrasis, as in: "The barge hauls coal" ⇒ "a barge *for* coal." (Lees, 1960a, 147.) *G–2*. Prepositions are represented as features of nouns in the deep structure. They may be shifted to the front of the sentence in questions (e.g., "*On* what did the boys ride?"), and they are often deleted from the deep structure by the preposition deletion transformation. (Jacobs and Rosenbaum, 1968, 103, 106, 141.) *G–2S*. One of the possible replace-ments of the K (kasus) category of the case category of a proposition: case → kasus+NP; kasus → preposition. The typical associations of prepo-sitions with the various case categories are: *by* for agentive; *by* or *with* for instrumental; *with* for comitative; *to* for dative; *for* for benefactive; Ø for objective and factitive; and numerous items for locative and temporal. (Fillmore, 1968, 32–33.) See also PREPOSITIONAL PHRASE, PREPOSITION DELETION TRANSFORMATION.

Preposition adjunction. See CONJUNCTION.

Preposition, agentive. See AGENTIVE PREPOSITION.

Prepositional complementation. See PREPOSITIONAL NOUN PHRASE COM-PLEMENTATION.

Prepositional noun phrase complement. *G–2*. A sentence embedded in a prepositional phrase which is a complement in a verb phrase: a complement of a verb (e.g., "Jim counted on *Tom's rescuing him*"); a complement of a noun phrase (e.g., "Tom reminded Huck about *Huck to drop anchor*"); or of an adjective phrase (e.g., "Huck was reluctant towards *Huck to drop the anchor*"). (Rosenbaum, 1967a, 95.) Also called **Oblique noun phrase complement.**

Prepositional noun phrase complementation. *G–2.* The embedding of a sentence in a prepositional phrase which is a complement in a verb phrase: of a verb, of a noun phrase, or of an adjective phrase. Also called **Prepositional complementation.** (Rosenbaum, 1967a, 100, 106.) Also called **Oblique noun phrase complementation.** See also PREPOSITIONAL NOUN PHRASE COMPLEMENT.

Prepositional periphrasis. See PREPOSITION.

Prepositional phrase. *G–1–2.* The PP constituent in a derivation, expanding as PREP, NP: PP   The optional adverbial category,

PREP   NP

dominated by PDP, usually takes the form of a prepositional phrase:

(ADV)   , as does the subordinate phrase, dominated by S:

PREP   NP

SP   . Also called **Preposition phrase.** (Rosenbaum, 1967a,

PREP   NP

17, 19, 83, 102, 105.) See also PREPOSITION.

Preposition deletion. *G–2.* The operation performed by the preposition deletion transformation. (Rosenbaum, 1967a, 83.) See also PREPOSITION DELETION TRANSFORMATION.

Preposition deletion rule. See PREPOSITION DELETION TRANSFORMATION.

Preposition deletion transformation. *G–2.* The partially ordered rule of the predicate complement system which deletes a preposition in case it appears before the pronominal head of a complement marked either for the *that* complementizer or for the *for-to* complementizer, as in: "Huck was surprised (*by*) that Tom was alive"; "Tom decided (*on*) (for) to rescue Jim." Also called **Preposition deletion rule.** (Rosenbaum, 1967a, 7, 21, 83.)

Preposition phrase. See PREPOSITIONAL PHRASE.

Presentence element. *G–2.* An optional element—such as Q (question), Neg (negative), Emph (emphasis), or Imp (imperative)—which is introduced into the derivation by the first phrase structure rule, as in S → (Q) Nom+VP. (Thomas, 1965, 178.) Also called **Scope marker, Formant.**

Present participle. *G–1–2a.* A verb which follows an auxiliary and ends in *ing* (e.g., "is *going*") (Lyons, 1968, 250); the non-tense inflectional form of the verb (e.g., *going*) which indicates progressive aspect (Langendoen, 1969, 118–119, 134). *G–1–2b.* A verbal adjective that is derived from a verb in *ing* and modifies a noun, as in: "a *going* thing." (Lyons, 1968, 250.) *G–2S.* An adjective which occurs with the suffix *ing* as an adjectival predicate in a sentence which selects a dative argument, as in: "The experience was *frightening* to the boys." (Langendoen, 1969, 118–119, 134.) See also PARTICIPLE.

Present tense. *G–1.* The concord morpheme S, in the context NP$_{sing}$——, or Ø, in the context NP$_{pl}$——, which is positioned first in the auxiliary and attached to the right of the following base by auxiliary transformation. (Chomsky, 1957, 39.) *G–2.* The syntactic feature [+present]—syntactic present—of the AUX node in the deep structure. If the AUX is not realized as a copula or perfective form, the tense feature is copied on the verbal by verbal agreement transformation. (Jacobs and Rosenbaum, 1968, 132–133.) *G–2S.* An abstract two-place predicate that occurs in every sentence type: one argument is a time expression, or time adverbial, and the other is a sentence, as in:

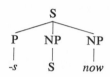

"Huck know*s* better *now*." (Langendoen, 1969, 121–122.) Compare PAST TENSE.

Preterminal string. See STRING.

Preverb. *G–1–2.* One of a class of words, positive or negative, which can occur directly before the main verb (e.g., "Tom *always* works hard") or as part of the auxiliary verb phrase (e.g., "Tom could *seldom* have worked hard"): VP → (Prev) AUX + MV. Negative preverbs such as *seldom, rarely,* and *hardly* cannot generally co-occur with the negative morpheme *not,* which is also a preverb. For example, *"Huck does*n't *hardly* deserve it." (Lees, 1960a, 5–6; Thomas, 1965, 134, 163–164.) See also NEGATIVE PREVERB, NEGATIVE PRE-VERBAL ADVERB.

Pre-verbal adverb, negative. See NEGATIVE PRE-VERBAL ADVERB.

Preverb, negative. See NEGATIVE PREVERB.

Primacy relation. *G–2.* The relation of command—a dominance relation —or of precede—an order relation—which holds between two nodes, for example, A and B: If A commands or precedes B, it has a 'primacy relation' to B, thereby tending to act as a nucleus to the satellite B and being able to pronominalize B. (Langacker, 1969, 167–169.) See also COMMAND.

Primary change. See RULE ADDITION.

Primary linguistic data. *G–2.* The linguistic performance to which the child is exposed, and on the basis of which he constructs a grammar of his language. Primary linguistic data are typically ill-formed, highly restricted, inappropriate, and degraded in quality. (Chomsky and Halle, 1968, 330–331.) See also LANGUAGE ACQUISITION.

Prime. *G–1–2.* One of the atomic elements on a given level of the linguistic theory; a concatenated symbol on a given level. (Bach, 1964, 58, 129.) The 'primes' on the level of phrase structure are category symbols and terminal symbols. The 'primes' on the level of transformations are base phrase-markers and transformations. The 'primes' on the level of phonetic representation are sets of features. A marker is a string of primes or a set of strings of primes. (Chomsky, 1966a, 54.) Also called **Primitive, Atomic element.** See also VOCABULARY.

Primitive. *G–1–2.* Given by the theory. It is said of the initial string S (Bach, 1964, 14) and of the elements out of which rules are built— which are the 'primitive' elements (Chomsky and Halle, 1968, 390). *G–2.* A prime, which is one of the elements out of which rules are built: features, specifications, categories, boundaries, etc. (Chomsky and Halle, 1968, 390.) See also PRIME, ATOMIC ELEMENT, VOCABULARY.

Principle, A-over-A. See A-OVER-A PRINCIPLE.

Principle, cross-over. See CROSS-OVER PRINCIPLE.

Principle, cyclic. See CYCLIC PRINCIPLE.

Principle, erasure. See ERASURE PRINCIPLE.

Procedure, decision. See DECISION PROCEDURE.

Procedure, discovery. See DISCOVERY PROCEDURE.

Procedure, evaluation. See EVALUATION PROCEDURE.

Process, anaphoric. See ANAPHORIC PROCESS.

Process, pseudocleft. See PSEUDOCLEFT PROCESS.

Productive. See PRODUCTIVITY.

Productive class. *G–1–2.* An open class of lexical items with a large and growing membership, such as the class of adjectives of the *clever, wise* type (e.g., "It was *clever/wise* of Huck to escape"), which has several hundred members. (Rosenbaum, 1967a, 106.) See also PRODUCTIVITY.

Productivity. *G–1–2.* The open-endedness which characterizes the categories noun, verb, and adjective—the 'productive' categories—as opposed to the closed nature of the **Nonproductive** categories: article, number, etc. (Chomsky, 1957, 105.) Certain classes of compounds are 'productive' (Lees, 1960a, 143), as are certain prefixes (Chomsky and Halle, 1968, 100, 106). See also PRODUCTIVE CLASS.

Pro-form. *G–1.* An element which replaces a longer and more complex form, such as a pronoun replacing an NP, or the pro-VP *so* replacing all but a subject and auxiliary, as in: "Huck could have been caught, and *so* could Tom (have been caught)." (Chomsky, 1957, 66.) *G–2a.* A form which replaces the universal constituent Pro, which is introduced into a phrase-marker to guarantee unique recoverability of a substitutable major category, as when: "Huck was looking for NP (Indef+Pro)" ⇒ "Huck was looking for *something.*" (Katz and Postal, 1964, 81–83.) *G–2b.* A replacement for a repeated constituent that has been erased by a reduction rule such as pronominalization, as when: "Huck caught the fish, and Tom cleaned *the fish*" ⇒ "Huck caught the fish, and Tom cleaned *them.*" (Langacker, 1968, 123–124.) See also PRONOMINALIZATION.

Progressive aspect. *G–1–2.* Durative aspect, or progressive tense, which is indicated by the selection of the morpheme *ing* in the auxiliary, as in: "Huck was smok*ing* his pipe" (Thomas, 1965, 55)—as opposed to perfect, or perfective, aspect, which selects *en* ("had smok*ed*") (Chomsky, 1965, 64). *G–2.* The feature [+progressive], which conveys the idea of ongoing activity when selected for an English verbal. (Jacobs and Rosenbaum, 1968, 108–109.) *G–2S.* The element *be* (and/or *ing*), which can function as an abstract predicate in a sentence such as "Huck will *be* leaving soon." (Langendoen, 1969, 117, 134.) See also ASPECT.

Progressive morpheme. *G–2.* One of the paired morphemes *be, ing* in the auxiliary, as in: "Huck *was* fall*ing* asleep." (Rosenbaum, 1967a, 27.) See also PROGRESSIVE ASPECT.

Progressive segment transformation. *G–2*. The transformation which introduces, to the left of the verbal, a segment with the features [+copula] [+progressive] when the verbal has the feature [+progressive]. (Jacobs and Rosenbaum, 1968, 109.) See also PROGRESSIVE ASPECT.

Progressive, telescoped. See TELESCOPED PROGRESSIVE.

Project. *G–2*. For a lexical item to impose its features on the constituent which contains it. For example, in the phrase-marker

NP all of

ADJ N

the semantic features of both the adjective and the noun are projected onto the noun phrase. (Langendoen, 1969, 47.) See also PROJECTION RULE.

Projection. See PROJECTION RULE.

Projection rule. G–2a. A rule of one of two types (I, II) in the projection rule subcomponent of the semantic component of a complete linguistic description—that is, outside the grammar. Projection rules produce semantic interpretations of sentences on the basis of their phrase structure, dictionary entries, and transformational history. They select the appropriate senses of the lexical items to provide correct readings for each grammatical structure in the final derived phrase-marker. Projection rules proceed from the bottom of a constituent structure to the top, interpreting the proper reading for each lexical item, amalgamating the readings into an amalgam within a grammatical marker, or bracket, amalgamating these readings within the next higher marker, etc., until the highest marker, or sentence, is associated with a set of readings: its semantic interpretation. (Katz and Fodor, 1963, 493, 505–506.) Type I projection rules operate on the final derived phrase-marker of kernel sentences—which are sentences produced without any optional transformations—providing each such sentence with a semantic interpretation. Type II projection rules provide a separate semantic interpretation for sentences constructed with the use of optional transformations, revealing how a derived sentence is related in meaning to its source sentence(s). (Katz and Fodor, 1963, 514–516; Katz, 1964a, 525–526, 529.) There is a single distinct projection rule for each distinct grammatical relation—subject-predicate, verb-object, etc. (Katz, 1966, 165.) Projection rules are not ordered in respect to each other but apply when their conditions are met. (Katz and Postal, 1964, 64.) *G–2b*. Transformations do not affect meaning. Therefore, projection rules can be said to apply only to underlying phrase-markers. And if generalized transformations are eliminated from the syntactic component, Type II projection rules are no longer needed in the semantic component, since there are no longer any optional transformations. (Katz and Postal, 1964, 23, 66–67.) Projection rules no longer need be considered at all, because of the elimination of transformation-markers and generalized transformations. (Chomsky, 1965, 136.) *G–2S*. Semantic projection rules significantly affect the generative power of a grammar by excluding from the semantic-representation/phonetic-representation pairing any structure on which their functioning is blocked. (McCawley, 1968, 151.) See also SEMANTIC INTERPRETATION, SEMANTIC COMPONENT, SEMANTICS, READING.

Promotion, 'not'. See 'NOT' PROMOTION.

Pronominal. *G–2a*. A derived pronoun, such as the indefinite *somebody*.

(Rosenbaum, 1967a, 116.) *G–2b.* Specifying a pronoun, such as a pronominal feature. (Rosenbaum, 1967a, 13.) See also PRONOMINALIZATION.

Pronominal feature. *G–2.* The feature [+PRO], which, when carried by a noun (i.e., [+N], [+PRO]), specifies the pronoun 'it,' as in: *"It* surprised Huck that Tom was alive." (Rosenbaum, 1967a, 13, 22.) See also PRONOMINALIZATION.

Pronominalization. *G–1.* The transformation which replaces, with a personal pronoun, a noun phrase, in an embedding, that is identical to a noun phrase in the matrix, as when: "Huck gave *Tom* a pipe for *Tom* to smoke" ⇒ "Huck gave Tom a pipe for *him* to smoke." (Lees and Klima, 1963, 149.) *G–2a.* A rule which specifies a noun as [+Pro] if it is identical to another noun in the same sentence (Postal, 1966, 208); the process which replaces a coreferential noun phrase in the deep structure with the corresponding personal pronoun in the surface structure (Reibel and Schane, 1969, 143). *G–2b.* An obligatory cyclic rule which operates after adverb preposing and passive and works in two directions, replacing an NP to the right of an identical NP—forward pronominalization—or replacing an NP to the left of an identical NP—backward pronominalization. (Ross, 1967, 188, 190, 199.) See also FORWARD PRONOMINALIZATION, BACKWARDS PRONOMINALIZATION.

Pronominalization, backwards. See BACKWARDS PRONOMINALIZATION.

Pronominalization, forward. See FORWARD PRONOMINALIZATION.

Pronominalization, reciprocal. See RECIPROCAL PRONOMINALIZATION.

Pro-nominalizing morpheme. *G–1.* A morpheme that is inserted into a sentence in order to keep intact the nominal to be pronominalized, so that the nominal can act as an antecedent for other constituents. (Lees, 1960a, 101.)

Pro-nominal, subject. See SUBJECT PRO-NOMINAL.

Pronoun. *G–1.* An independently chosen noun—that is, a personal pronoun—which can occur in a kernel sentence along with common nouns, proper nouns, etc.—or a pro-noun of the same shape which is introduced transformationally to replace a repeated noun or pronoun. (Lees, 1960a, 100.) Most pronouns in English sentences are introduced late by transformations. (Lees, 1960a, 87.) *G–2a.* A nonanaphoric personal pronoun—all but genitive and objective third person pronouns—which is introduced by phrase structure rules; or an anaphoric or reflexive pronoun which replaces a repeated noun phrase by transformation. (Gleitman, 1965, 98.) *G–2b.* A noun in the deep structure which becomes a definite article in the surface structure. (Jacobs and Rosenbaum, 1968, 93–94.) Pronouns are only syntactic features of definite nouns ([+Pro]) in the deep structure; they are introduced as segments in the intermediate structure to replace [+Pro] nouns and are realized as articles in the surface structure. (Postal, 1966, 203–204.) See also ANAPHORIC PROCESS, REFLEXIVIZATION, PRONOMINALIZATION, PERSONAL PRONOUN.

Pronoun, anaphoric. See ANAPHORIC PRONOUN.

Pronounceable sentence. *G–1.* A sentence to which all rules have applied, including morphophonemic, phonemic, and phonetic rules. (Lees, 1960a, 3.)

Pronoun deletion transformation. *G–2.* The rule which deletes the pronoun 'it' when it occurs immediately before S, as in: "Becky knew (*it*) that she was lost"; "(*It*) that Tom returned surprised Huck." (Rosenbaum, 1967a, 13.) See also PRONOUN 'IT'.

137

Pronoun deletion transformation, indefinite. See INDEFINITE PRONOUN DELETION TRANSFORMATION.

Pronoun, indefinite. See INDEFINITE PRONOUN.

Pronoun, intensive. See INTENSIVE PRONOUN.

Pronoun 'it'. *G–2.* The pronoun which is introduced into pre-complement position in the underlying structure (e.g., *"It* that Tom returned surprised Huck") by the usual lexical insertion rules and is obligatorily deleted, by pronoun deletion transformation, in the absence of extraposition, as in: "*(It)* that Tom returned surprised Huck." (Rosenbaum, 1967a, 22.) See also EXPLETIVE, IMPERSONAL SUBJECT.

Pronoun, personal. See PERSONAL PRONOUN.

Pronoun, reflexive. See REFLEXIVE PRONOUN.

Pronoun, relative. See RELATIVE PRONOUN.

Pronoun replacement. *G–2.* The operation performed by the pronoun replacement transformation. (Rosenbaum, 1967a, 108.) See also PRONOUN REPLACEMENT TRANSFORMATION.

Pronoun replacement transformation. *G–2.* The rule which applies to an extraposed sentence, replacing the initial pronoun 'it' with a noun phrase from the extraposed for-to or POSS-ing complement, as when: "*It* was difficult for Tom to steer *the raft"* ⇒ *"The raft* was difficult for Tom to steer." (Rosenbaum, 1967a, 7, 108.) The pronoun replacement transformation is independent of the extraposition transformation, is ordered before it, and generates a different surface structure. (Rosenbaum, 1967b, ix.) Compare EXTRAPOSITION TRANSFORMATION.

Pronoun transformation. *G–2.* The transformation which adds a pronoun feature to an identical noun phrase and converts it into the correct pronoun form as specified by the other features of the NP: gender, person, number, and case. If no gender is specified, the replacement is *it.* (Jacobs, 1968, 33, 42.) The noun phrases must not be in the same simple sentence: "*Huck* told *Tom* that *Huck* liked *Tom"* ⇒ "Huck told Tom that *he* liked *him."* (Jacobs and Rosenbaum, 1968, 222.) See also PRONOMINALIZATION.

Pronunciation, ideal. See IDEAL PRONUNCIATION.

Proper analysis. *G–1–2.* The structural analysis of a string, which, with its structure index, qualifies it as an appropriate domain for a particular transformation. (Chomsky, 1961a, 131; Chomsky, 1965, 145.) See also ANALYZABLE, STRUCTURAL ANALYSIS, STRUCTURE INDEX.

Proper noun. *G–1.* A noun which does not pattern with a separate determiner or take a separate plural morpheme (Thomas, 1965, 78); a proper name, such as *Hoover Dam* or *Liberty Bell* (Lees, 1960a, 173). *G–2.* A noun which has the feature [−common] in the deep structure (Jacobs and Rosenbaum, 1968, 60); a member of the category of nouns which have the strict subcategorization feature [──] (i.e., no separate determiner and no sentential complement). Proper nouns can also be used as common nouns (i.e., [DET──]), as in: "That isn't *the Hannibal* I used to know"; "And now—*the lovely Becky Thatcher!"* (Chomsky, 1965, 110, 217.) Compare COMMON NOUN.

Proper, phonological rule. See PHONOLOGICAL RULE.

Proper, syntactic feature. See SYNTACTIC FEATURE.

Property, field. See FIELD PROPERTY.

Proposition. *G–2.* A base phrase-marker. (Chomsky, 1965, 225.) *G–2S.*

A tenseless set (P) of relationships among nouns and verbs and embedded sentences in the basic structure of a sentence, as opposed to 'modality', the other constituent of S: S → M+P. The 'proposition' contains the category V (verb) and one or more case categories that subclassify the verb, as in: P → V+A+I+O (rewrite proposition as verb plus the case categories of agentive, instrumental, and objective). (Fillmore, 1966, 366; Fillmore, 1968, 23.) Compare MODALITY. See also CASE GRAMMAR.

Pro-sentence. *G–1.* A short retort type of sentence, reduced from a full sentence, as in: "Tom always gets lost, and *Huck always gets lost*" ⇒ "Tom always gets lost, and *so does Tom.*" (Lees, 1960a, 5.) See also SHORT RETORT.

Prosodic contour. See INTONATION.

Prosodic feature. *G–2a.* One of the two English phonological distinctive features [long] and [stressed], or [accented]. The feature [long] covers quantitative contrasts. The feature [stressed], if positively specified in a phonetic matrix, is realized as one of five relative degrees of accent. (Harms, 1968, 23, 36–37.) *G–2b.* One of the three universal suprasegmental features: pitch or intonation, stress, and length. (Chomsky and Halle, 1968, 15, 300.) See also INTONATION, STRESS, LENGTH.

Proto-sentence. *G–1.* An underlying sentence, or source sentence. (Lees, 1960a, 99.) See also SOURCE SENTENCE.

Pro-verb. *G–1.* The base *do,* which is introduced before an unattached suffix in the auxiliary. (Lees, 1960a, 36.) The pro-verb *do* carries the tense morpheme when no other member of the auxiliary is present. (Lees, 1961, 32.) Also called **Dummy carrier 'do.'** See also 'DO'-SUPPORT.

Pro-VP. See PRO-FORM.

Pruning tree. See TREE PRUNING.

Pseudocleft construction. See CLEFT-SENTENCE.

Pseudoclefted. *G–2.* Transposed to the end of a sentence to which *what* has been preposed and *be* has been postposed. For example, in the sentence "Huck steered the raft," the noun phrase *the raft* can be 'pseudoclefted' as follows: "What Huck steered *the raft* was" ⇒ "What Huck steered was *the raft.*" (Rosenbaum, 1967c, 317.)

Pseudocleft sentence. *G–2.* A sentence which has undergone the pseudocleft sentence transformation. Also: **Pseudo-cleft sentence.** (Rosenbaum, 1967a, 13.) See also PSEUDOCLEFT TRANSFORMATION.

Pseudocleft transformation. *G–2.* The process which converts a sentence with a noun phrase in the predicate (e.g., "Huck caught *fish*") into a sentence, or a pseudocleft construction, beginning with *what* and containing an appropriate form of *be* before the predicate noun phrase (e.g., *"What* Huck caught *was fish"*). The pseudocleft transformation can also apply to noun phrase complements, as when: "Huck hoped *that the fish would bite*" ⇒ *"What* Huck hoped *was that the fish would bite.*" (Rosenbaum, 1967c, 318–319; Rosenbaum, 1967a, 13, 75.) Also called **Pseudocleft process, Cleft transformation, Pseudocleft sentence transformation.** See also CLEFT SENTENCE TRANSFORMATION.

Pseudopassive. *G–1.* A sentence of the form "Tom was looked up to by Huck," which derives from the intransitive kernel structure "Huck looked up to Tom" by the pseudopassive transformation, or pseudopassivization. (Chomsky, 1965, 104–105.) *G–2.* A sentence of the form "Tom was looked up to by Huck," which is the result of regular passivization of the intransitive sentence "Huck looked up to Tom *by*-Passive." (Chomsky, 1965, 104–105.) See also PASSIVE TRANSFORMATION.

Pseudopassive transformation. See PSEUDOPASSIVE.

Pseudopassivization. See PSEUDOPASSIVE.

Psycholinguistics. *G–2.* The investigation of how speakers actually construct or understand sentences (Bach, 1964, 64); the study of linguistic behavior—that is, performance—and the psychological apparatus responsible for it (Langacker, 1968, 6); the study of production (synthesis) and recognition (analysis) (Lyons, 1968, 160); the study of language development in children; the introduction of linguistic theory into psychological problems (Gleitman, 1965, 82). See also LANGUAGE ACQUISITION.

Pure adjective. *G–2.* A word that can occur in the position [DET *very* _____N], from which verbs in *ing* are excluded, as in "a very *interesting* book" (adjective), but not in "a very *reading* book" (verb). (Chomsky, 1965, 151.) See also ADJECTIVE.

Q

Qualifying feature. *G–2.* One of the phonological distinctive features which relate to the lowering or flatting, or the raising or sharping, of acoustic tonality, as measured by a sound spectrograph. The qualifying features 'flat' and 'sharp' indicate the secondary effect, on the graveness or acuteness of a primary articulation, of increasing the volume of the oral cavity by lip rounding or palatalization. (Harms, 1968, 31–33.) Compare ORAL-ARTICULATOR FEATURE. See also CLASSIFICATORY FEATURE.

Quantifier. *G–1.* An article which determines the quantity of the following noun, as in: "*a* boy," "*some* boys" (Klima, 1964a, 279); a modifier which determines the degree of measurement in a following adjective, as in: "*six feet* tall" (Lees, 1961, 308).

Quasi-grammatical sentence. *G–2.* A semi-grammatical sentence, such as one with multiple embeddings, like: "Huck believed that that Tom was safe was true" (i.e., "Huck believed that it was true that Tom was safe"). (Rosenbaum, 1967a, 66.) Also called **Semi-sentence.** See also SEMIGRAM-MATICALNESS. Compare NONSENSE STRING.

Question. *G–1.* An interrogative sentence of the inverted type—a simple or yes-no question—or of the Wh type—a Wh-question or information question—or of the intonational type—an echo question—or of the tag type—a tag question. Yes-no (or yes-or-no) questions are derived by the T_q transformation, Wh questions by the T_w transformation. (Chomsky 1957, 63, 69–72.) Both of them are interrogative transformations. (Lees 1960a, 86.) *G–2a.* An interrogative sentence derived from an underlying declarative sentence structure by means of either a singulary question transformation—a yes-no question, with the morpheme Q in the underlying phrase-marker—or a Wh-question transformation—a Wh-question, with the morpheme Wh in the underlying phrase-marker, later to be attached to the element in the string that is questioned, though that element is not uniquely specified for attachment. The two types of questions have the same underlying phrase-marker except for Q and Wh: yes-no questions do not contain Wh, and Wh-questions do not contain Q. (Katz and Postal, 1964, 79, 86–87, 89, 91.) *G–2b*. Both yes-no questions and Wh questions contain the universal underlying morphemes Q and Wh. The semantic component provides an amalgamation of the reading of Q with the reading of the nucleus—the constituents NP and VP—of the sentence. The scope marker Wh is positioned in the underlying phrase-marker within the noun phrase that is questioned, which is then moved to the front of the sentence. If no particular element is questioned, Wh is deleted, leaving a potential yes-no question; if Q is also deleted, a non-interrogative sentence results. (Katz and Postal, 1964, 79, 86–91, 97–101, 114–115, 130.) See also YES-NO QUESTION, WH-QUESTION. TAG QUESTION, ECHO QUESTION.

Question deletion transformation. *G–2*. The transformation which deletes the Wh-question constituent Wh, when the Wh-question transformation does not apply, as in yes-no questions. (Jacobs and Rosenbaum, 1968, 158.) See also QUESTION, YES-NO QUESTION, WH-QUESTION.

Question, echo. See ECHO QUESTION.

Question, indirect. See INDIRECT QUESTION.

Question marker. *G–2*. The element Q, introduced by the base rules, which conditions the operation of the question transformations. A transformation is obligatory when the question marker is present in the string; it is inapplicable otherwise. (Chomsky, 1966a, 60.) See also QUESTION.

Question, simple. See YES-NO QUESTION.

Question, tag. See TAG QUESTION.

Question, Wh-. See WH-QUESTION.

Question word. See WH-WORD.

Question, yes-no. See YES-NO QUESTION.

Question, yes-or-no. See YES-NO QUESTION.

R

Reading. *G–2*. The complete path representing one distinct sense of a lexical item—viz., a partial reading—or the amalgamation of the partial readings of two or more lexical items in a construction—viz., a derived reading; a semantic interpretation. (Katz and Postal, 1964, 13; Rosenbaum, 1967a, 31.) See also SEMANTIC INTERPRETATION.

Reading, lexical. See LEXICAL READING.

Reading, semantic. See SEMANTIC INTERPRETATION.

Readjustment rule. *G–2*. One of a set of special rules which prepare the syntactic surface structure of a sentence for inputting to the phonological component; one of the types of phonological rules (as opposed to phonological rules proper)—including morpheme structure rules, or lexical redundancy rules—which determine admissible, or possible, and inadmissible, or impossible, classificatory matrices. (Chomsky and Halle, 1968, 369, 382.) See also PHONOLOGICAL RULE, MORPHEME STRUCTURE RULE.

Realization rule, phonological. See PHONOLOGICAL REALIZATION RULE.

Reciprocal conjunction. See CONJUNCTION.

Reciprocal pronominalization. *G–2*. The pronominalization of a plural object noun phrase as *one another* or *each other* if it is a repetition of the plural subject noun phrase of the same sentence, as when: "Huck and Tom helped *Huck and Tom*" ⇒ "Huck and Tom helped *one another/ each other.*" Reciprocal pronominalization is a special form of conjunction. (Lees, 1964b, xlii; Lees and Klima, 1963, 156.) See also PRONOMINALIZA-TION, CONJUNCTION.

Recognition model, speech. See SPEECH RECOGNITION MODEL.

Reconstruction. *G–1*. A postulation, on the basis of a uniform proto lexicon, of the rules that most economically describes the development of each proto-phoneme in each of the daughter languages. The result is a set of proto-phonemes, a set of rules for deriving daughter-phonemes, and a set of daughter-phonemes: an observationally adequate historical phonology. (King, 1969, 176.) *G–2*. A postulation, on the basis of generative descriptions of modern related languages, of the sequences of generative grammars that preceded them, and of the rule additions and losses that relate the grammars in the sequence, insuring that nothing unknown or unlikely in the modern grammars is posited for the earlier structures. (King, 1969, 155–157.) See also HISTORICAL LINGUISTICS, GENERATIVE PHONOLOGY.

Recoverability. *G–2*. The universal constraint on grammars which requires that a deletion transformation cannot apply to a phrase-marker unless, from the output of that transformation and the description of the trans-formational process, the original phrase-marker is correctly predicted: unique recoverability. (Katz and Postal, 1964, 80.) See also RECOVERABLE. Compare ACCESSIBILITY.

Recoverability, unique. See RECOVERABILITY.

Recoverable. *G–1*. Understood as having been a repeated form which was deleted from, or replaced by a pro-form in, the underlying structure of a sentence, as in: "Tom caught more fish than Huck (*caught*)"; "Huck stretched *himself* (i.e. *Huck*) out on the raft." (Thomas, 1965, 88–89.) *G–2*. Traceable to the deep structure, from the surface structure, as a result of the meaning-preserving nature of transformations. For example, the underlying grammatical function of *raft,* in "The *raft* was built by Huck," is recoverable, as direct object, from the surface structure of the passive sentence, where it functions as subject. (Jacobs and Rosenbaum, 1968, 74.) Compare IRRECOVERABLE, ACCESSIBLE.

Recursion. *G–1*. Looping; embedding; self-embedding; nesting; the intro-duction of S into another S by embedding transformation: left recursion (S → S+A), right recursion (S → A+S), nesting (S → A+B; B → S+C). The use of recursive devices—that is, of embedding transformations—simplifies the grammar and permits it to produce infinitely many sen-tences. (Chomsky, 1957, 23–24; Chomsky, 1961a, 123.) Recursion is restricted to the transformational component of the grammar. (Bach, 1964, 39; Katz and Postal, 1964, 12.) *G–2*. The introduction, by the rules of the base component, of the initial symbol S into strings of category symbols—the transformational component being merely interpretive; the recurrence or reintroduction of S in the expansion of NP: S → NP+VP, VP → V+NP, NP → N+S (Chomsky, 1965, 37; Reibel and Schane, 1969, 301; Rosenbaum, 1967a, 9). *Related terms:* A **Recursive rule** is a rule which reapplies indefinitely to its own output. (Katz, 1966, 123.) The **Recursive power** of a grammar, which resides entirely in the syntactic component, is its ability to generate an infinity of sentences. (Chomsky, 1965, 205.) The **Recursive mechanism** is the system of rules which account for the infinite properties of language. (Katz and Postal, 1964, 12.) A **Recursive element** is one from which strings can be derived that contain the same element (e.g., S). (Bach, 1964, 16.) The **Recursive property** of a grammar—its creative aspect—is its provision for embedding sentences within other sentences. (Chomsky, 1968, 27.) See also EMBEDDING.

Reduction. *G–1a.* One of the operations performed by transformations, by which an item in a derived phrase-marker takes the place of several items in the source phrase-marker. (Bach, 1964, 70, 75–76.) *G–1b.* The condition under which one or more sounds are dropped from a morpheme when it combines with another morpheme. (Koutsoudas, 1966, 63.) See also DELETION, TRUNCATION.

Reduction, identical conjunct. See IDENTICAL CONJUNCT REDUCTION.

Reduction, relative. See RELATIVE 'BE' DELETION TRANSFORMATION.

Reduction rule. *G–2.* A syntactic rule, such as pronominalization, which deletes, or erases, a constituent which is identical to another constituent in the same sentence and which replaces it with a pro-form. (Langacker, 1968, 122–123, 182.) See also DELETION, ERASURE, PRONOMINALIZATION.

Reduction rule, vowel. See VOWEL REDUCTION RULE.

Reduction transformation, conjunction. See CONJUNCTION REDUCTION TRANSFORMATION.

Redundancy rule. *G–2.* A rule which acts as a filter on structures which are potential inputs to an interpretive component of the grammar, rejecting, or filtering out, those structures which are not admissible—that is, not properly formed according to the language-particular rules—and accepting those which are admissible, and converting their universal properties to specifications for that particular language (Chomsky, 1965, 168–169; Chomsky and Halle, 1968, 9, 165); a rule of the type $[+A] \rightarrow [\pm B]$, which enumerates the binary values of a hierarchic feature for a particular language, even though those values are not marked in a general specification, where it does not matter whether B is specified $+$ or $-$. (Rosenbaum, 1967a, 25–26.) See also LEXICAL REDUNDANCY RULE, PHONOLOGICAL REDUNDANCY RULE, SYNTACTIC REDUNDANCY RULE.

Redundancy rule, lexical. See LEXICAL REDUNDANCY RULE.

Redundancy rule, phonological. See PHONOLOGICAL REDUNDANCY RULE.

Redundancy rule, syntactic. See SYNTACTIC REDUNDANCY RULE.

Reference. *G–2S.* The semantic specification of nouns as to their referents. (Langendoen, 1969, 48.)

Reference, identical. See IDENTICAL REFERENCE.

Referent. *G–1–2.* The object to which a noun refers. (Lees, 1960a, xx; Langendoen, 1969, 45.) In order for a theory of semantic interpretation to deal with imagination and misconception, the intended referent—that is, the speaker's mental image of the universe—must be distinguished from the actual referent—the real things in the universe. Linguistics should be concerned only with intended referents, not actual referents; but referents of any kind are really nonlinguistic aspects of linguistic description. (McCawley, 1968, 138–139.) See also REFERENTIAL INDEX.

Referential index. *G–2.* One of the integers—subscripts, features, or values—1, 2, 3, etc., which are assigned, by the base component, to the nouns in a sentence, according to their referents, as in: "*Tom Sawyer*$_1$ knew that *Jim*$_2$ had saved *Huck*$_3$." The first noun in the sentence receives the index '1'; the second, '2'—if the referent is different, otherwise also '1'; the third, '3' etc. Two nouns with the same referential index in the same sentence are said to be 'coreferential', as in: "*Tom Sawyer*$_1$ knew that *Tom Sawyer*$_1$ had been saved." Some transformations, such as relativization, pronominalization, and reflexivization, refer to referential indices of the nouns in the string. (Ross, 1967, 188; Langendoen, 1969, 48.) A referential index takes into account the semantic representation of a noun as well as its syntactic representation. (McCawley, 1968, 138–139.) Compare STRUCTURE INDEX.

Reflexive. See REFLEXIVE PRONOUN.

Reflexive conjunction. See CONJUNCTION.

Reflexive object. See REFLEXIVE PRONOUN.

Reflexive pronoun. *G–1.* A personal pronoun in the possessive case, for first and second person, or objective case, for third person, plus *-self* which functions as an object in a sentence whose subject or direct object has the same referent, as in: "Tom Sawyer played *himself* in the skit"; "They left Becky to *herself.*" (Thomas, 1965, 97.) Also called **Reflexive object.** (Lees and Klima, 1963, 154–155.) *G–2.* A pronoun which replaces, by forward pronominalization, an NP with which it is coreferential in the same sentence, as when: "*Tom Sawyer*$_1$ played *Tom Sawyer*$_1$ in the skit" ⇒ *"*Tom* Sawyer played *him* in the skit." The reflexivization transformation here adds the appropriate *-self* form: "Tom Sawyer played *himself* in the skit." (Langendoen, 1969, 81.) Compare INTENSIVE PRONOUN. See also REFLEXIVIZATION.

Reflexive rule. *G–2.* The transformation which attaches the morpheme *-self* to a pronominalized noun phrase, as when: "Tom$_1$ thought him$_1$ to have saved Becky" ⇒ "Tom thought *himself* to have saved Becky." (Rosenbaum, 1967a, 59.) Also called **Reflexivization transformation.** See also REFLEXIVIZATION. Compare REFLEXIVE TRANSFORMATION.

Reflexive transformation. *G–2.* The transformation which adds a pronoun feature and a reflexive feature to a noun phrase object which is identical to the noun phrase subject of the same verb, as when: "*Huck* stretched *Huck* out on the raft" ⇒ "Huck stretched *himself* out on the raft." (Jacobs, 1968, 43.) See also REFLEXIVIZATION. Compare REFLEXIVIZATION TRANSFORMATION, REFLEXIVE RULE.

Reflexive verb. *G–1–2.* A verb whose direct object is either partly or wholly restricted to a reflexive pronoun object, as in: "Tom *behaved* himself, *expressed* himself, *excused* himself, *prided* himself on something." (Lees and Klima, 1963, 154–155; Lees, 1964b, xlii.)

Reflexivization. *G–2.* An erasure operation which uses one noun phrase to delete another noun phrase with the same referential integer, and then introduces the new element *-self,* as when: "*He*$_1$ admired *he*$_1$" ⇒ "He admired *himself*" (Chomsky, 1965, 146); the complex process of pronominalization, definitization, reflexivization, genitivization, and definite article attachment which associates genitve-type definite article features with the features of the noun stem *self.* Reflexivization specifies a noun stem as [+reflexive] and [+pro] if it is identical to another noun stem

in the same simple sentence. (Postal, 1966, 208.) See also REFLEXIVIZA-
TION TRANSFORMATION, REFLEXIVE TRANSFORMATION.

Reflexivization transformation. *G–2*. The transformation which adds a
reflexive feature to the pronoun of a noun phrase which is coreferential
with another noun phrase in the same clause, as when: "Huck stretched
him (i.e., Huck) out on the raft" ⇒ "Huck stretched *himself* out on the
raft." (Langendoen, 1969, 81.) Also called **Reflexive rule.** Compare
REFLEXIVE TRANSFORMATION. See also REFLEXIVIZATION.

Relate. *G–2*. To postulate a common underlying structure for—as to
demonstrate that two sentences with similar surface structures bear a
relation to each other, or are related, by virtue of the fact that they
share the same base. (Rosenbaum, 1967a, 99, 101, 107.)

Related. See RELATE.

Relatedness. *G–2*. The condition which holds between two or more sentences that have a common underlying structure, such as that between
the sentences of a paradigm. (Rosenbaum, 1967a, 34, 106.) Compare
SYNONYMY, IDENTITY. See also PARADIGM, EQUIVALENCE CLASS.

Related sentences. *G–1*. Two or more sentences whose underlying structure
is the same, but whose derived structure is different because of the fact
that one sentence has undergone a transformation which the others have
not, as in: "Huck steered the raft"; "Who steered the raft?"; "The raft
was steered by Huck"; "Wasn't the raft steered by Huck?"; etc. (Koutsoudas, 1966, 37, 57, 254.) Also called **Synonymous sentences.** See also
EQUIVALENCE CLASS, PARADIGM.

Relation. See RELATE.

Relation, category inclusion. See CATEGORY INCLUSION RELATION.

Relation, command. See COMMAND.

Relation, co-occurrence. See SELECTION RESTRICTION.

Relation, dominance. See COMMAND.

Relation, grammatical. See GRAMMATICAL RELATION.

Relation, is-a. See IS-A RELATION.

Relation, primacy. See PRIMACY RELATION.

Relationship, arbitrary. See ARBITRARY RELATIONSHIP.

Relationship, bleeding. See BLEEDING ORDER.

Relationship, feeding. See FEEDING ORDER.

Relative 'be' deletion transformation. *G–2*. The transformation which
deletes the relative pronoun and copula of an embedded relative clause
without affecting the meaning, as when: "The boys *who were on the raft*
were Huck and Tom" ⇒ "The boys *on the raft* were Huck and Tom."
If the relative clause consists of *be*+ADJ, the adjective transformation
must follow the relative 'be' deletion transformation, as when: "The boys
who were lost were Huck and Tom" ⇒ *"The boys *lost* were Huck and
Tom ⇒ "The *lost* boys were Huck and Tom." (Jacobs, 1968, 47.) Also
called **Relative reduction.** (Langacker, 1968, 133.) Compare RELATIVE
PRONOUN DELETION TRANSFORMATION.

Relative clause. *G–1–2*. A sentence that is embedded to the right of a
noun in a nominal phrase: Nom → DET+N+S (Thomas, 1965, 94);
a sentence that is adjoined to an R (restrictive) or an A (appositive)
marked in the NP of another sentence, to the right of the noun: NP →
DET+N+R/A (Smith, 1964, 250–251); a sentence that is embedded
to the right of a noun phrase dominated by another noun phrase: NP →

NP+*S* (a restrictive relative clause); a sentence that is derived from a conjoined sentence which is embedded to the right of an NP in the other conjoined sentence:

(a nonrestrictive relative clause) (Jacobs and Rosenbaum, 1968, 199–211). See also RELATIVIZATION, RESTRICTIVE RELATIVE CLAUSE, NONRESTRICTIVE RELATIVE CLAUSE. *G–2*. A sentence that is embedded within the determiner node of a noun phrase, as in:

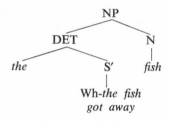

The embedded sentence contains a duplicate, marked 'Wh', of the determiner and noun which surround it: "Wh-*the fish*." This sentence is then inverted with the following noun: "The (Wh-*the fish got away*) *fish*" ⇒ "The *fish* (Wh-*the fish got away*)." Then the repeated phrase is converted into an appropriate relative pronoun: "The fish *that/which* got away. . . ." This example illustrates the two major steps of the relative transformation. (Chomsky, 1965, 128–131, 145.) See also RELATIVE PRONOUN.

Relative clause, appositive. See NONRESTRICTIVE RELATIVE CLAUSE.

Relative clause, nonrestrictive. See NONRESTRICTIVE RELATIVE CLAUSE.

Relative clause, restrictive. See RESTRICTIVE RELATIVE CLAUSE.

Relative clause, sentential. See SENTENTIAL RELATIVE CLAUSE.

Relative clause transformation. *G–2*. The transformation which adds the features [+WH] and [+pronoun] to the identical noun phrase of an embedded relative clause and moves the relative pronoun to the front of the clause. (Jacobs and Rosenbaum, 1968, 199–211.) Compare RELATIVE PRONOUN FORMATION TRANSFORMATION.

Relative-complex sentence. *G–2*. A matrix sentence which contains a relative clause attached to one of its noun phrases. A pivotal noun appears in both the matrix and the constituent sentences. (Kuroda, 1968, 268.) See also PIVOTAL NOUN. Compare RELATIVE CLAUSE.

Relative ordering. *G–2*. The variable order of application of two transformations in respect to each other in a cycle. For example, pronoun deletion, which is partially ordered, may occur before passivization, which is 'strictly ordered,' in one derivation but after it in another, for which reason the transformations are said to be 'relatively ordered' in respect to each other. (Rosenbaum, 1967a, 35.) See also RULE ORDERING, PARTIALLY ORDERED, STRICTLY ORDERED.

Relative pronoun. *G–1*. The form which results from the morphophonemic combination of the morpheme *Wh* and a following personal pronoun, as in: *Wh+he → who; Wh+him → whom; Wh+his → whose; Wh+it → which;* etc. (Chomsky, 1957, 69, 112.) *G–2a.* The morpheme *which* results from the erasure of the following noun phrase, whose features of animateness, case, etc., it has assumed, in an embedded clause because that noun phrase is identical to the preceding noun phrase of the matrix sentence, as in: "The raft (*Wh-the raft* had drifted loose) floated downstream" ⇒ "The raft (*which* had drifted loose) floated downstream." (Chomsky, 1965, 145.) Relative pronouns are either definite (e.g., "the way in *which*") or indefinite (e.g., "the way *that*"). (Katz and Postal, 1964, 133.) *G–2b.* One of the pronouns *who* (*whom, whose*), *which, that, when, where,* or *why.* The latter three—*when, where,* and *why,* which are traditionally relative adverbs—are included as relative pronouns because they are the reflexes of *at which* (*when*), *at/in which* (*where*), and *in/for which* (*why*) and can also undergo optional deletion, as in "Call me the minute (*when*) he arrives"; "This is the place (*where*) he lives"; "That's the reason (*why*) he left." (Langendoen, 1969, 29, 70.) See also RELATIVE CLAUSE, RELATIVE PRONOUN DELETION TRANSFORMATION.

Relative pronoun deletion transformation.   *G–2.* The transformation which deletes a relative pronoun in a restrictive relative clause when the pronoun immediately follows its antecedent and immediately precedes the subject of the relative clause, as when: "The raft *that they built* was not riverworthy" ⇒ "The raft *they built* was not river-worthy." (Jacobs and Rosenbaum, 1968, 211.) Compare RELATIVE 'BE' DELETION TRANSFORMATION, WH-DELETION.

Relative pronoun formation transformation.   *G–2.* The set of rules which move the coreferential noun phrase of the relative clause to the front of that clause and replace it by the appropriate relative pronoun, as when: "The raft (they built *the raft*) was not river-worthy" ⇒ "The raft (*the raft* they built) was not river-worthy" ⇒ "The raft *which* they built was not river-worthy." (Langendoen, 1969, 68–69.) Compare RELATIVE CLAUSE TRANSFORMATION.

Relative reduction.   See RELATIVE 'BE' DELETION TRANSFORMATION.

Relative transformation.   See RELATIVE CLAUSE.

Relativization.   *G–2.* The process by which a sentence is embedded as a modifier in a noun phrase (Reibel and Schane, 1969, 225); sentential embedding of the type "The woman *who punished Tom* was Aunt Polly," which utilizes the Wh morpheme and contrasts with other complementation systems, such as predicate complementation and subordination (Rosenbaum, 1967a, 21). See also RELATIVE CLAUSE TRANSFORMATION, RELATIVE PRONOUN FORMATION TRANSFORMATION.

Release feature.   *G–2.* One of the two phonological distinctive features which apply to the release of closure in stops and affricates: either instantaneous release ([abrupt release]), as with stops, which produces no turbulence; or delayed release ([delayed release]), as with affricates, which produces fricative-like turbulence. (Chomsky and Halle, 1968, 319.)

Reordering.   *G–2.* The historical alternation of the order of a pair of ordered phonological rules: leveling, or bleeding order, in which the promoted rule removes representations to which the lowered rule could apply, and extension reordering, or polarization reordering or feeding order, in which the promoted rule supplies a new set of cases to the lowered rule.

Historically, leveling reordering is minimized, and extension reordering is maximized. (King, 1969, 175.) See also RULE REORDERING, BLEEDING ORDER, FEEDING ORDER.

Reordering, rule. See RULE REORDERING.

Reordering, stylistic. See STYLISTIC REORDERING.

Replacement transformation, 'it'. See 'IT' REPLACEMENT TRANSFORMATION.

Replacement transformation, pronoun. See PRONOUN REPLACEMENT TRANSFORMATION.

Representation. *G–2.* A string of phonological or phonetic symbols which 'represent' a formative or a string of formatives. The **Phonological representation** of an utterance is a string of systematic phonemes; the **Phonetic representation** of an utterance is a string of phonetic segments, or feature matrices. The phonological string is mapped into the phonetic string by the rules of the phonological component. (Postal, 1968a, 53.) See also PHONETIC REPRESENTATION, PHONOLOGICAL REPRESENTATION, LEXICAL REPRESENTATION.

Representation, dual. See CONSTRUCTIONAL HOMONYMITY.

Representation, lexical. See LEXICAL REPRESENTATION.

Representation, phonetic. See PHONETIC REPRESENTATION.

Representation, phonological. See PHONOLOGICAL REPRESENTATION.

Representation, phrase structure. See PHRASE STRUCTURE CONFIGURATION.

Representation, semantic. See SEMANTIC INTERPRETATION.

Residue. *G–2.* The relevant cases not accounted for by a particular rule. (Rosenbaum, 1967a, 14.) See also EXCEPTION.

'Respectively' transformation. *G–2.* The transformation which produces a conjoined noun phrase and a conjoined verb phrase from a pair of conjoined sentences with weakly identical references, and adds *respectively,* as when: "The boys (the boys are old) and (the boys are young)" ⇒ "The boys (the boys and the boys) (are old and young) *respectively*" ⇒ "The boys are old and young *respectively*"—after a collapsing transformation. (McCawley, 1968, 143–145.) See also WEAKLY IDENTICAL.

Restriction, identity. See IDENTITY RESTRICTION.

Restriction, selection. See SELECTION RESTRICTION.

Restriction, selectional. See SELECTION RESTRICTION.

Restrictive relative clause. *G–1.* A relative clause which can follow a noun with an unspecified determiner, such as *any* or *all,* or a noun with a specified determiner, such as *the* or *this,* as in: "*Any* man *who likes fishing* can't be all bad"; "*The* man *who caught the fish* wasn't all bad" (Thomas, 1965, 156–157); a sentence that is adjoined to an R (restrictive) marker at the right of a noun in the noun phrase of another sentence: NP → DET + N + R (Smtih, 1964, 250–251). *G–2a.* A relative clause which belongs to the determiner system, as opposed to a **Nonrestrictive relative clause,** which is a complement of the full NP or of a full sentence, as in:

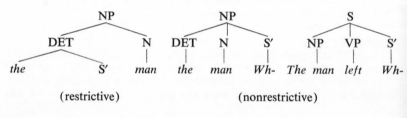

(restrictive)   (nonrestrictive)

(Chomsky, 1965, 128, 217). *G–2b*. A relative clause which derives from an embedding of the type NP → NP+S (e.g., "The raft *that the boys built* was unriverworthy"), as opposed to a nonrestrictive relative clause, which derives from a conjoined sentence: $S_1+S_2 \Rightarrow NP+V+NP-S_2$, (e.g., "The boys built a raft, *and it was unriverworthy*" ⇒ "The boys built a raft, *which was unriverworthy*"). (Jacobs and Rosenbaum, 1968, 259.) Compare NONRESTRICTIVE RELATIVE CLAUSE.

Restructuring. *G–2.* The changes in the underlying representations of sentences that are brought about by the child's internalization of an optimal grammar, which is one based on the original grammars of his parents, plus the innovations which they have made during their lifetime ; the process by which these changes are brought about. (Langacker, 1968, 191–192; King, 1969, 81.) See also LANGUAGE ACQUISITION.

Retort, short. See SHORT RETORT.

Rewrite rule. See REWRITING RULE.

Rewriting rule. *G–1.* An immediate constituent rule of the type X → Y (rewrite X as Y); one of the linearly-ordered constituent structure rules which replace the single, non-null symbol at the left of an arrow with a string of different non-null symbols—one or more—on the right of the arrow, without deleting or rearranging constitutents or rewriting S. (Chomsky, 1961b, 136; Chomsky, 1962, 215.) *G–2.* A rule which generates a base phrase-marker that underlies a sentence (Chomsky, 1965, 72); a rule of the form A → B/X_____Y (rewrite A as B in the context X_____Y); a rule of the categorial subcomponent of the base subcomponent of the syntactic component of a generative grammar (Chomsky, 1965, 66–67); either of two types of base rules: a branching rule, which analyzes a category symbol into a string of terminal or non-terminal symbols, or a subcategorization rule, which introduces syntactic features that form or extend a category symbol. Rewriting rules may rewrite S, but they may not delete or rearrange constituents. (Chomsky, 1965, 112.) Also called **Rewrite rule** (Lees, 1960a, 1), **Instruction formula** (Chomsky, 1957, 29), **Expansion rule, Rule of formation** (Lees, 1960b, 151), **Phrase structure rule, One-many rule, String-replacement rule, Immediate constituent rule, IC rule, PS rule** (Bach, 1964, 35), **Branching rule** (Chomsky, 1965, 112), **Constituent-structure rule, P-rule** (Koutsoudas, 1966, 5), **Constituent-membership rule** (Langendoen, 1969, 20). See also PHRASE STRUCTURE REWRITING RULE, CONTEXT-SENSITIVE RULE, CONTEXT-FREE RULE, PHRASE STRUCTURE RULE, PHRASE-STRUCTURE EXPANSION RULE, EXPANSION RULE, CONSTITUENT-MEMBERSHIP RULE.

Rewriting rule, phrase structure. See PHRASE STRUCTURE REWRITING RULE.

Right-branching construction. *G–2.* A construction which contains one or more embeddings to the right of the dominating phrase in the main sentence, as in: "This is the cat *that caught the rat* THAT STOLE THE CHEESE." (Chomsky, 1965, 13; Chomsky and Halle, 1968, 372.) Compare LEFT-BRANCHING.

Root morpheme. *G–1.* A non-affixal morpheme. (Lees, 1960a, 21.) Compare FREE MORPHEME.

Round. *G–2.* The phonological distinctive feature which is positively specified for sounds that are produced with narrowing of the air passage at the lips—rounded sounds—as opposed to those that are not produced in this manner—nonrounded sounds. All classes of sounds can be rounded, but glides and high back vowels have the most rounding in English. (Chomsky and Halle, 1968, 309.)

Rule. See GRAMMATICAL RULE.

Rule addition. *G–2.* The addition, especially by an adult, of a late phonological rule to his grammar: innovation, a type of primary change, or change in competence. Rule addition is characteristic of adult change in the grammar, but it can also occur in the grammar of the child, especially assimilation. (King, 1969, 116.) See also SOUND CHANGE, PHONOLOGICAL CHANGE, LINGUISTIC CHANGE, SIMPLIFICATION. Compare RULE LOSS.

Rule, ad hoc. See AD HOC RULE.

Rule, alpha-switching. See ALPHA-SWITCHING RULE.

Rule, alternating stress. See STRESS PLACEMENT RULE.

Rule, base. See BASE COMPONENT.

Rule, blank-filling. See BLANK-FILLING RULE.

Rule, bleeding. See BLEEDING RULE.

Rule, boundary insertion. See BOUNDARY.

Rule, branching. See BRANCHING DIAGRAM.

Rule, clause transportation. See CLAUSE TRANSPORTATION RULE.

Rule, constituent-membership. See CONSTITUENT-MEMBERSHIP RULE.

Rule, constituent-structure. See PHRASE STRUCTURE RULE.

Rule, context-free. See CONTEXT-FREE RULE.

Rule, context-sensitive. See CONTEXT-SENSITIVE RULE.

Rule, context-sensitive subcategorization. See CONTEXT-SENSITIVE SUBCATE-GORIZATION RULE.

Rule, contraction. See CONTRACTION.

Rule convention, noniterative. See NONITERATIVE RULE CONVENTION.

Rule, deformation. See DEFORMATION RULE.

Rule, detail. See DETAIL RULE.

Rule, early. See EARLY RULE.

Rule, exception. See EXCEPTION.

Rule, exchange. See ALPHA-SWITCHING RULE.

Rule, expansion. See EXPANSION RULE.

Rule, feeding. See FEEDING RULE.

Rule, formation. See PHRASE STRUCTURE RULE.

Rule, grammatical. See GRAMMATICAL RULE.

Rule, higher-level. See HIGH-LEVEL RULE.

Rule, high-level. See HIGH-LEVEL RULE.

Rule, immediate constituent. See PHRASE STRUCTURE RULE.

Rule, inversion. See INVERSION RULE.

Rule, kernel sentence. See KERNEL SENTENCE RULE.

Rule, late. See LATE RULE.

Rule, lexical. See LEXICAL RULE.

Rule, lexical redundancy. See LEXICAL REDUNDANCY RULE.

Rule loss. *G–2.* The nonacquisition, by the child, of a rule that is present in the grammar of his parents: a type of simplification, or primary change. (King, 1969, 47–50, 64, 77.) See also SIMPLIFICATION. Compare RULE ADDITION.

Rule, lower-level. See LOW-LEVEL RULE.

Rule, low-level. See LOW-LEVEL RULE.

Rule, main stress. See MAIN STRESS RULE.

Rule, major. See MAJOR RULE.

Rule, minor. See MINOR RULE.

Rule, morpheme structure. See MORPHEME STRUCTURE RULE.

Rule, morphographemic. See MORPHOGRAPHEMIC RULE.

Rule, morphophonemic. See MORPHOPHONEMIC RULE.

Rule, morphophonetic. See MORPHOPHONETIC RULE.

Rule, morphophonotactic. See MORPHOPHONOTACTIC RULE.

Rule, nuclear stress. See NUCLEAR STRESS RULE.

Rule of formation. See PHRASE STRUCTURE RULE.

Rule ordering. *G–1.* The strict ordering of the sets of rules of a transformational grammar: phrase structure rules first, transformational rules
second, morphophonemic rules third. Within the sets, the phrase structure
rules, singulary transformations, and morphophonemic rules are 'strictly'
ordered; but generalized transformations are not ordered in respect to
each other. (Chomsky, 1957, 32–33, 44; Koutsoudas, 1966, 38.) 'General'
rules, which apply to an entire class of items, are placed before rules
that divide the class into subclasses, so that the general rule does not have
to name each of the subclasses. (Bach, 1964, 46.) *G–2.* The linear ordering of the rules within the base component, and the sequential ordering
of rules within the phonological component and among the transformations.
(Chomsky, 1965, 134–135.) Generative grammar requires both extrinsic
ordering, imposed by the explicit order of rules, and intrinsic order, a
consequence of rule formulation. (Chomsky, 1965, 223.) Linguistic
generalizations are lost without ordering, because without it the same
facts must be stated over and over, and the predictable facts must be
listed. (Postal, 1968a, 151.) There are ordering relations among transformations; some must apply before others. (Jacobs and Rosenbaum,
1968, 32–33, 235.) Unmarked order is the optimal ordering—and marked
order less optimal—according to the historical direction of rule reordering:
from highly marked to less highly marked. (King, 1969, 88, 194.) In all
known grammars, at least some of the phonological rules are ordered.
(King, 1969, 41.) The discovery of dialects which contain the same
rules, but with different ordering, supports the 'rule ordering' hypothesis.
(Chomsky and Halle, 1968, 343.) See also RELATIVE ORDERING, PARTIALLY
ORDERED, STRICTLY ORDERED.

Rule, permutation. See PERMUTATION.

Rule, phonological. See PHONOLOGICAL RULE.

Rule, phonological realization. See PHONOLOGICAL REALIZATION RULE.

Rule, phonological redundancy. See PHONOLOGICAL REDUNDANCY RULE.

Rule, phrase structure. See PHRASE STRUCTURE RULE.

Rule, phrase-structure expansion. See PHRASE-STRUCTURE EXPANSION RULE.

Rule, phrase structure rewriting. See PHRASE STRUCTURE REWRITING RULE.

Rule, postcycle. See POSTCYCLE RULE.

Rule, postcyclic. See POSTCYCLE RULE.

Rule, precycle. See PRECYCLE RULE.

Rule, precyclic. See PRECYCLE RULE.

Rule, preposition deletion. See PREPOSITION DELETION TRANSFORMATION.

Rule, projection. See PROJECTION RULE.

Rule proper, phonological. See PHONOLOGICAL RULE PROPER.

Rule, readjustment. See READJUSTMENT RULE.

Rule, recursive. See RECURSION.

Rule, reduction. See REDUCTION RULE.

Rule, redundancy. See REDUNDANCY RULE.

Rule, reflexive. See REFLEXIVE RULE.

Rule reordering. *G–2.* The historical change of the order of phonological rules in a particular dialect (Chomsky and Halle, 1968, 343); the result of the borrowing of a rule in a different order in a different dialect (King, 1969, 51–57). The general direction of rule reordering is from highly marked to less highly marked systems. (King, 1969, 88.) See also SOUND CHANGE, PHONOLOGICAL CHANGE, LINGUISTIC CHANGE.

Rule, rewrite. See REWRITING RULE.

Rule, rewriting. See REWRITING RULE.

Rule schema. *G–2.* An abbreviation of a sequence of partly identical rules—viz., schemata—as a single rule by means of enclosing the non-identical parts in braces, through notational convention: $A \to \left\{ \begin{matrix} B \\ C \end{matrix} \right\}$ 're-write A as B'; 'rewrite A as C.' (Chomsky and Halle, 1968, 333; Langendoen, 1969, 31–32.) See also ABBREVIATOR, NOTATIONAL CONVENTION.

Rule, segment structure. See SEGMENT STRUCTURE RULE.

Rule, selectional. See SELECTIONAL RULE.

Rule, sequential constraint. See SEQUENTIAL CONSTRAINT RULE.

Rule, spelling. See MORPHOPHONEMIC RULE.

Rule, stress placement. See STRESS PLACEMENT RULE.

Rule, strict subcategorization. See STRICT SUBCATEGORIZATION RULE.

Rule, string-replacement. See PHRASE STRUCTURE RULE.

Rule, stylistic. See STYLISTIC RULE.

Rule, syntactic redundancy. See SYNTACTIC REDUNDANCY RULE.

Rule, traffic. See TRAFFIC RULE.

Rule, transfer. See TRANSFER RULE.

Rule, transformational. See TRANSFORMATIONAL RULE.

Rule, verb deletion. See VERB DELETION RULE.

Rule, vowel reduction. See VOWEL REDUCTION RULE.

Rule, vowel shift. See VOWEL SHIFT RULE.

S

Scale of grammaticalness. *G–1–2.* The scale along which utterances range from fully grammatical (e.g., "Huck had a good idea") through various degrees of semigrammaticalness (e.g., "Huck had a green idea") to the most ungrammatical expressions still to be yielded by the grammar (e.g., "Huck had an idea green"). (Lees, 1960a, 121–122; Chomsky, 1966a, 36.) See also GRAMMATICALNESS, GRAMMATICALITY, DEGREE OF GRAMMATICAL-NESS.

Schema, rule. See RULE SCHEMA.

Scope marker. *G–2.* A universal marker which specifies the 'scope' of a transformation, such as Wh for questions and Neg for negation: $S \to$ Wh+NP+VP; $S \to$ Neg+NP+VP. (Katz and Postal, 1964, 101, 152.) Also called **Formant, Presentence element.**

Second-generation transformational grammar. *G–2.* A term used by Jacobs (1968, 62) to describe the generative theory found in or based on Chomsky's *Aspects of the Theory of Syntax* (1965), which synthesized the newly refined theories of interpretive semantics (Katz and Fodor, 1963), transformational syntax (Katz and Postal, 1964), and generative phonology (Halle, 1962). *Aspects* 1) redefined transformations as singulary and obligatory, triggered by optional elements in the base rules, such as QUES and NEG; 2) removed optional and generalized transformations; 3) ordered the transformations and applied them before embedding or conjoining; 4) introduced optional rules in the base component to provide for the recursion of S; and 5) integrated syntax with semantics and phonology. Second-generation transformational grammar (*G–2*) presupposes a more abstract notion of underlying constituent structure than *G–1* and makes freer use of syntactic features which are not themselves constituents but are assigned to constituents for the correct operation of transformational and lexical rules. (Lyons, 1968, 268, 387–388.) *G–2* establishes a dichotomy between deep structure, which contains all syntactic information relevant to semantic interpretation, and surface structure, which contains all syntactic information relevant to phonological interpretation. In *G–2,* transformations do not affect the meaning established in the deep structure; they apply cyclically from the most deeply embedded S to the topmost S; and they are often stated in ordinary language rather than in formal notations. Subclassification of lexical categories is provided for by the features of individual lexical items rather than by phrase structure rules, and semantic evidence is used to determine sets of related sentences and to justify the deep structure posited for them. (Reibel and Schane, 1969, viii-ix.) There is also a formulation of underlying representations as complement formatives to be specified later by substitution, a use of pro-formatives for grammatical formatives, and a reduction in the importance of kernel sentence structures. (Lees, 1963, xxvii.) Compare FIRST-GENERATION TRANSFORMATIONAL GRAMMAR, SEMANTIC-BASED TRANSFORMATIONAL GRAMMAR.

Second lexical pass. *G–2.* A second introduction of words or affixes from the lexicon, after all transformations have applied, in order to replace the segments that have been generated by transformations, and to replace certain lexical items that were introduced during the first lexical pass, such as reflexive and relative noun phrases. (Jacobs and Rosenbaum, 1968, 84.) See also LEXICAL PASS. Compare FIRST LEXICAL PASS.

Second passive. *G–1.* An additional passive transform for a sentence containing a *that*-clause, as when: *"Huck* thought *that Tom was sick"* ⇒ *"That Tom was sick* was thought by *Huck"* (regular passive); *"Tom* was thought by *Huck to be sick"* ('second passive'). (Lees, 1960a, 63.) *G–2.* A 'second passive' transformation is unnecessary if the standard passive transformation is followed by the extraposition transformation and the pronoun replacement transformation, as in: "Huck thought (Tom to be sick)"; "It (Tom to be sick) was thought by Huck" (passive); "It was thought by Huck (Tom to be sick)" (extraposed); "Tom was thought by Huck (to be sick)" ('it' replaced). (Rosenbaum, 1967a, 115). Compare PASSIVE.

Second passive transformation. See SECOND PASSIVE.

Segment. *G–1.* A constituent of a string; a morpheme or category symbol;

whatever is concatenated. (Chomsky, 1957, 62.) *G–2a*. A phonological matrix with a single column of feature specifications (Chomsky, 1965, 81); a phonetic segment or its natural categorial segment—viz., a phonological segment (Postal, 1968a, 70); a phoneme or morphophoneme—that is, a set of features with no independent linguistic status (Chomsky, 1966a, 69). *G–2b*. A cluster of syntactic features representing a lexical category, such as the noun segment [+N] [+common] [+concrete] [−animate], which can be replaced by a noun such as *raft*. (Jacobs and Rosenbaum, 1968, 66–68.) See also PHONETIC SEGMENT, PHONOLOGICAL SEGMENT, NATURAL CATEGORIAL SEGMENT.

Segment, affix. See AFFIX SEGMENT.

Segmentalization. *G–2*. The insertion of a segmental element, such as an article, into a phrase-marker on the basis of underlying syntactic feature specifications. (Postal, 1966, 209–210.) Compare SEGMENT TRANSFORMATION.

Segment, lexical. See LEXICAL PASS.

Segment, natural categorial. See NATURAL CATEGORIAL SEGMENT.

Segment, phonetic. See PHONETIC SEGMENT.

Segment, phonological. See PHONOLOGICAL SEGMENT.

Segment structure rule. *G–2*. A rule which subcategorizes a terminal constituent of the deep structure of a sentence before a lexical item is introduced to replace it, as in: N → [[+N] [±singular]]—the category of noun dominates a noun segment with either singular or plural number. Segment structure rules make it unnecessary to specify the number of a lexical item in the lexicon. (Jacobs and Rosenbaum, 1968, 66.) See also SUBCATEGORIZATION.

Segment transformation. *G–2*. The transformation which introduces a segment, such as an article or a noun-suffix, into the deep structure of a sentence, to be replaced by a word or affix in the second lexical pass. (Jacobs and Rosenbaum, 1968, 90.) Compare SEGMENTALIZATION. See also SECOND LEXICAL PASS.

Segment, universal phonetic. See UNIVERSAL PHONETIC SEGMENT.

Selection. See SELECTIONAL RULE.

Selectional feature. *G–2a*. A contextual feature which is associated with a rule that restricts a verb or adjective containing this feature to certain syntactic and semantic contexts—that is, to certain grammatical relations. A selectional feature refers only to heads of related grammatical constructions. Failure to observe a selectional rule results in a deviant string, such as "Hookey played Tom." (Chomsky, 1965, 148, 164–165; Chomsky, 1966a, 73.) *G–2b*. A semantic feature for verbs and adjectives which makes reference to semantic features specified for the noun phrases with which these lexical items occur. The meaning of verbs and adjectives is tied up with their relationship to noun phrases—that is, they impose, or project, their features on the noun phrases which select them. The entire meanings of verbs and adjectives can be expressed in terms of selectional features. (Langendoen, 1969, 44.) See also SELECTIONAL RULE, SELECTION RESTRICTION.

Selectional restriction. See SELECTION RESTRICTION.

Selectional rule. *G–1*. One of the rules that determine which constituents can co-occur in a simple sentence. (Chomsky, 1962, 215.) *G–2*. One of the rules which analyze a complex symbol in respect to the syntactic features of the frames in which it can appear; a rule which expresses a selection restriction or a restriction of co-occurrence for verbs and adjectives in terms of preceding or following nouns, as in: [+V] → complex symbol/ [——DET[+animate]] (Chomsky, 1965, 196–197); a rule which defines a selectional relation between two positions in a sentence, as in: N+V, or V+N. Selectional rules not only assign features of the subject and object to the verb but also assign features of the verb to the subject and object. (Chomsky, 1965, 113–114.) Violation of selectional rules results in such deviant sentences as "Colorless green ideas sleep furiously." (Chomsky, 1965, 115.) Selectional rules insert verbs and adjectives into various positions in generalized phrase-markers on the basis of the inherent features of the adjacent nouns. (Chomsky, 1965, 227.) Nouns must also contain selectional features restricting the selection of their subjects. The dominating noun need not even be in the same simple sentence. (Bach, 1968, 116.) See also SELECTIONAL FEATURE, SELECTION RESTRICTION.

Selection, complementizer. See COMPLEMENTIZER SELECTION.

Selection restriction. *G–2a.* A feature at the end of each reading in the dictionary entry of a lexical item, determining the combinations that that reading can enter into with the readings of other lexical items. That is, two readings will be amalgamated by the projection rules if one reading satisfies the selection restriction of the other. (Katz and Postal, 1964, 15, 21.) Selection restrictions are given within the dictionary entries of verbs in a semantic theory and operate between the verb and the semantic properties of an entire subject noun phrase. (McCawley, 1968, 132.) *G–2b.* A syntactic restraint on a particular verb in relation to its possible selection by a particular noun, as expressed in a selectional rule, or a restriction of co-occurrence. These restrictions are treated in the base component of the grammar and therefore are syntactic selectional restrictions operating between two lexical items, a verb and a noun. (McCawley, 1968, 132.) Each syntactic feature of the preceding and following noun is assigned to the verb as a selectional subclassification of its complex symbol. (Chomsky, 1965, 95, 97.) *G–2S.* Semantic selectional restrictions (as in Katz and Fodor) provide an adequate account of selection, without the use of syntactic selectional features or complex symbols. Any information relevant to the semantic representation of a lexical item can figure in a selectional restriction, and no other type of information except semantic plays a role in selection. The semantic representation of an entire noun phrase, not just the head noun, must be examined to determine whether it meets a given selectional restriction. Selectional restrictions are separate from the base component, which generates deep structures without regard to satisfaction or violation of selectional restrictions. (McCawley, 1968, 134–135.) Also called **Co-occurrence relation.** (Bach, 1964, 114.) See also SELECTIONAL FEATURE, SELECTIONAL RULE.

Self-embedding. *G–1.* The process of embedding, or nesting, a sentence inside, not to the left or right, of another sentence, as in:

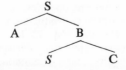

The number of times that a constituent can be self-embedded (up to unintelligibility) determines the degree of a phrase-marker. (Chomsky, 1961a, 123–127.) Self-embedding is a characteristic of context-free grammars. (Bach, 1964, 166.) Self-embedding is a reflexive property of rewrite rules. (Lees, 1960a, 2.) *G–2.* A clause that is completely enclosed within another clause, up to a comprehensibility depth of approximately three in one sentence, as in: "The report that the medicine that Mark Twain took killed him was greatly exaggerated"—two self-embeddings. (Langendoen, 1969, 141–142.) See also NESTING, MULTIPLE EMBEDDING.

Semantic. See SEMANTICS.

Semantic-based transformational grammar. *G–2S.* An ad hoc term employed in this *Glossary* for neotransformational modifications of generative grammar, which assume a semantic basis for syntax: the development in transformational grammar which maintains that the semantic representation of a sentence constitutes its deep structure, thus removing the need for an interpretive component that operates on syntactic deep structures. (Reibel and Schane, 1969, ix.) The syntactic component and the semantic component of second-generation transformational grammar are replaced by a single system of rules which convert semantic representations into surface syntactic representations. Semantic representations can be regarded as trees of linearly ordered constituents labeled with syntactic category symbols. The rules map ordered labeled trees onto ordered labeled trees by the usual syntactic operations plus lexical insertion transformations, which replace portions of trees with lexical items. (McCawley, 1968, 167–168.) In a semantically justified universal syntactic theory the semantic deep structure is an underlying, order-free representation which is mapped onto the surface form by syntactic rules. These rules begin by assigning segmental order to the concepts in the semantic deep structure. Syntactic deep structure is an artificial intermediate level between semantic deep structure and phonological surface structure. The properties of semantic deep structure have to do with the nature of human language rather than the methodology of grammarians. (Fillmore, 1968, 88.) See also SEMANTIC BASIS FOR SYNTAX, SEMANTIC DEEP STRUCTURE, CASE GRAMMAR. Compare FIRST-GENERATION TRANSFORMATIONAL GRAMMAR, SECOND-GENERATION TRANSFORMATIONAL GRAMMAR.

Semantic basis for syntax. *G–2S.* The modification of transformational grammar in which semantic representation constitutes the deep structure without the help of a separate semantic component. (Chomsky, 1965, 78.) See also SEMANTIC-BASED TRANSFORMATIONAL GRAMMAR, SEMANTIC DEEP STRUCTURE, CASE GRAMMAR.

Semantic component. *G–2a.* The component of a complete linguistic description other than the grammar, which consists of a syntax and a phonology. The semantic component provides an explanation of the speaker's ability to determine the meaning of novel sentences in his language. It consists of a dictionary and a set of projection rules. The input to the semantic component is the output of the syntactic component. The semantic component operates on strings of formatives, along with their structural descriptions, producing a semantic interpretation for each string. (Katz and Postal, 1964, 12–13.) *G–2b.* The component of a transformational grammar other than the syntactic component and the phonological component. The semantic component determines the semantic interpretation of sentences—a purely interpretive function. All information necessary for semantic interpretation is provided in the semantic component. (Chomsky, 1965, 16, 75.) The semantic component interprets the meaning of the output of the base component. (Harms, 1968, 4.) The semantic rules refer primarily to the deep structure of the sentence, but possibly also to certain aspects of the surface structure. (Chomsky and Halle, 1968, 6–7.) See also PROJECTION RULE, DICTIONARY, DICTIONARY ENTRY, SEMANTIC INTERPRETATION, SEMANTICS.

Semantic deep structure. *G–2S*. The underlying, order-free representation, in a semantically justified universal syntactic theory, which is mapped into the surface form of a sentence by syntactic rules which begin by assigning segmental order to the concepts. Syntactic deep structure is an artificial intermediate level between semantic deep structure and phonological surface structure. Semantic deep structure is empirically discoverable, and its properties have to do with the nature of human language. (Fillmore, 1968, 88.) See also SEMANTIC-BASED TRANSFORMATIONAL GRAMMAR, SEMANTIC BASIS FOR SYNTAX, CASE GRAMMAR.

Semantic feature. *G–2*. A general feature, or basic element, of meaning, such as 'human', 'male', 'young', etc. (Langendoen, 1969, 34–37); one of the set of universal inherent features which are not mentioned by any syntactic rule (Chomsky, 1965, 142); an innate property of the human mind and human perception, as opposed to a property of the physical world; an inherent feature such as [animate], or a selectional feature, such as [——[+animate]], which is specified for individual lexical items (Langendoen, 1969, 34–37); a semantic marker (Katz, 1964a, 523). Compare SEMANTIC MARKER. See also INHERENT FEATURE, SELECTIONAL FEATURE.

Semantic feature, hierarchic. See HIERARCHIC SEMANTIC FEATURE.

Semantic interpretation. *G–2*. A description of the meaning of a sentence, including a characterization of the meaning of every syntactic structure and every constituent in the sentence (Katz and Postal, 1964, 1, 20); the meaning of a sentence as determined by the underlying syntactic structure (Postal, 1964c, 25); the result of applying dictionary and projection rules to a sentence; the output of the semantic component for a particular sentence (Katz, 1966, 153); a determination of the meaning of a sentence on the basis of the grammatical relations expressed in the abstract deep structure (Chomsky, 1965, 162–163); a semantic representation, which has no phonological aspect (Postal, 1968a, 203); a semantic reading (Harms, 1968, 4; Rosenbaum, 1967a, 74). The underlying syntactic structure of a sentence determines how the semantic information in the dictionary entries of its lexical items must be combined by projection rules. (Katz and Postal, 1964, 1, 20.) Sentences with the same underlying structure—such as the active and passive versions of a sentence—have the same semantic interpretation. (Rosenbaum, 1967a, 70, 89–91.) *G–2S*. The notion of interpretive semantics, as well as the notion of syntactic deep structure, is abandoned in semantic-based transformational grammar. (Langacker, 1968, vi.) The semantic rules and the syntactic rules are merged in *G–2S* into a single system of rules that convert semantic representations into surface structure representations. Semantic representations are trees of linearly ordered constituents labeled with syntactic category symbols. The rules map ordered labeled trees onto ordered labeled trees by the usual syntactic operations, plus lexical insertion transformations. (McCawley, 1968, 167–168.) See also SEMANTIC COMPONENT, SEMANTIC DEEP STRUCTURE, SEMANTICS, SEMANTIC BASIS FOR SYNTAX, SEMANTIC-BASED TRANSFORMATIONAL GRAMMAR.

Semantic marker. *G–2.* A formal element in the dictionary entry of a lexical item, such as 'human' or 'animal' or 'male,' which expresses a systematic semantic relation between that item and the rest of the items in the vocabulary of a language (Katz, 1964a, 523; Katz and Fodor, 1963, 497; Katz and Postal, 1964, 14); a reading; an abstract atomic element representing the conceptual context of a lexical item; a primary descriptive object of a semantic theory, uninterpreted in respect to the nonlinguistic world (Postal, 1964c, 32); a symbol for one of the conceptual elements into which a sense is decomposed by a reading (Katz, 1966, 154–155). Compare SEMANTIC FEATURE.

Semantic reading. See SEMANTIC INTERPRETATION.

Semantic representation. See SEMANTIC INTERPRETATION.

Semantics. *G–1.* The study of meaning. Grammar is best regarded as a study that is independent of semantics, and grammaticalness as independent of meaningfulness. (Chomsky, 1957, 106.) The study of grammatical structure is independent of meaning; no semantic absolutes are known in advance of grammar. (Chomsky, 1961b, 184–185.) *G–2.* Linguistic description minus grammar, in a complete linguistic description. Semantics takes over the responsibility for understanding sentences where grammar leaves off. (Katz and Fodor, 1963, 484.) There is no way to show that semantics plays a part in the design of the syntactic or phonological components or in the function of their rules. (Chomsky, 1968, 49–50.) Semantic considerations do not determine syntactic structures. (Chomsky, 1965, 229.) Semantics can be studied in isolation from phonology, and vice versa, but not in isolation from syntax; syntax, on the other hand, can be studied without a clear notion of semantics. (Chomsky, 1966, 20.) *G–2S.* Many linguists assume an intimate connection between deep syntax and semantics. (Lyons, 1968, 269.) Semanticbased transformational grammar distinguishes between the semantic characterization of a lexical item and the semantic interpretation of a sentence containing that item, which may be affected by transformations with semantic properties. (Fillmore, 1968, 30, 49.) *G–2S* accepts the belief that syntax and semantics are interrelated, each leading its own kind of existence and each having an integral place in grammatical theory. (McCawley, 1968, 125, 161.) See also SEMANTIC BASIS FOR SYNTAX, SEMANTIC-BASED TRANSFORMATIONAL GRAMMAR, SEMANTIC INTERPRETATION, SEMANTIC COMPONENT, CASE GRAMMAR.

Semantics, universal. See UNIVERSAL SEMANTICS.

Semantic theory. *G–2.* A theory of the speaker's ability to interpret the sentences of his language—but not a theory of how settings determine how an utterance is understood (Katz and Fodor, 1963, 486–487); a theory of the fluent speaker's knowledge of the semantic structure of his language, taking the form of a system of recursive rules that enable him to compose the meaning of a sentence from the meanings of its elements (Katz, 1964a, 519–520). A semantic theory has two components: a dictionary of the lexical items of the language along with their meanings, and a finite system of projection rules which produce semantic interpretations. (Katz,

1964a, 519–520; Katz and Fodor, 1963, 493.) The input to a semantic theory is the output of the grammar. (Katz, 1964a, 521.) See also SEMANTIC COMPONENT, SEMANTIC INTERPRETATION, SEMANTICS, DICTIONARY, PROJECTION RULE.

Semi-derivation. *G–2*. The derivation which accounts for the generation of a semi-sentence. A 'phrase structure semi-derivation' begins with the initial symbol SS and proceeds by the application of transfer rules and phrase structure rules. A 'transformational semi-derivation' begins with a phrase structure semi-derivation and proceeds by transfer rules and transformational rules. (Katz, 1964b, 412.) See also SEMI-SENTENCE, TRANSFER RULE.

Semigrammatical. See SEMIGRAMMATICALNESS.

Semigrammaticalness. *G–2*. The result of an incorrect choice of subcategories (e.g., "Colorless green ideas sleep furiously," a semigrammatical sentence) as opposed to ungrammaticalness, or syntactic ill-formedness, which is the result of improper application of syntactic rules. (Lees, 1964b, xxxviii; Chomsky, 1966a, 35.) Also: **Semi-grammaticalness.** (Chomsky and Halle, 1968, 418.) See also GRAMMATICALNESS, GRAMMATICALITY. Compare UNGRAMMATICALNESS, UNGRAMMATICALITY.

Semigrammatical sentence. See SEMIGRAMMATICALNESS.

Semi-sentence. *G–2*. A sentence fragment (Postal, 1964c, 34); a contextually reduced version of a fully grammatical sentence (Katz and Postal, 1964, 90); an utterance that is not well-formed, or is ungrammatical, but can be understood, or is intelligible; a partly-structured, partly-unstructured string which is understood in terms of its well-informed parts; a sentence-like string that can be understood though it is not strictly well-formed either grammatically or semantically; a string that instances a degree of deviation from full grammaticality but is short of nonsense—'word salad' (Katz, 1964b, 400–402). A theory of semi-sentences divides ungrammatical strings into intelligible semi-sentences and unintelligible nonsense strings, and explicates the native speaker's ability to distinguish them and to interpret or paraphrase the former. (Katz, 1964b, 403). Also called **Quasi-grammatical sentence.** See also SEMIGRAMMATICALNESS. Compare NONSENTENCE, NONSENSE STRING.

Semivowel. *G–1*. One of the three glides [w], [j], [h], which are the positional variants of the lax vowels [u], [i], [ə], respectively. Semivowels are specified [−consonantal], [−vocalic]. (Halle, 1959, 327–329, 331.) *G–2*. A glide which corresponds to one of the vowels [u] or [i] (i.e., [w] or [y]), or the glottal [h]. (Harms, 1968, 23, 31.) See also GLIDE, DIPHTHONG.

Sensitive to. *G–2*. Activated, or triggered, by. A transformation is said to be 'sensitive to' a structure, both its constituents and their features, if that structure triggers the application of that transformation. (Rosenbaum, 1967a, 26, 39, 69, 81.) Also: **Defined on/upon/over.** (Rosenbaum, 1967a, 40, 42, 45, 78, 80.) See also NECESSARY CONDITION, STRUCTURAL CONDITION.

Sentence. *G–1*. One of the products of the grammar of a language; one of the infinite set of grammatical sequences which define a particular language; one of the members of the corpus of a language; the initial symbol 'Sentence' of a terminated derivation (Chomsky, 1957, 11, 13, 14, 26–27); a well-formed string; a grammatical utterance (Postal, 1964b,

137). A grammar of English is the only complete definition of 'sentence in English.' (Thomas, 1965, 44.) *G–2.* A surface structure with no violations; a well-formed surface structure (Postal, 1968a, 205); a grammatical string of formatives (Chomsky, 1965, 16); a structured string of words (Jacobs and Rosenbaum, 1968, 10); a string of elements that consists of an output of the syntax and an input to the phonology (Chomsky, 1966a, 54); sentence → noun phrase+predicate (Katz, 1966, 125); sentence → scope marker+nucleus (Katz and Postal, 1964, 104); #-S-# → NP+predicate phrase (Chomsky, 1965, 129); S → NP+AUX+VP (Jacobs and Rosenbaum, 1968, 47). *G–2S.* A predicate with from one to three arguments: S → P+NP (NP) (NP) (Langendoen, 1969, 97, 137); a modality and a proposition: S → M+P (Fillmore, 1968, 83). Compare NONSENTENCE, SEMI-SENTENCE, QUASI-GRAMMATICAL SENTENCE, SENTOID.

Sentence, active. See ACTIVE SENTENCE.

Sentence, adverbial. See ADVERBIAL SENTENCE.

Sentence adverbial. *G–1.* An adverb or adverbial transform which is an attribute of an entire sentence and is thereby permitted to stand first in the sentence, as in: *"Certainly* Huck can swim" (also *generally, in general, in particular, of course, yes, no).* (Thomas, 1965, 162–163.) *G–2.* A constituent of the deep structure of every sentence that is questioned by means of the Wh-interrogative transformation: sentence → Q+*sentence adverbial*+NP+VP. The sentence adverbial constituent dominates Wh and *either* (or) and is deleted when preceded by Q. (Katz and Postal, 1964, 96–97.) Compare ADVERBIAL.

Sentence boundary. *G–2.* The morpheme #, which occurs first and last in an underlying sentence. If the final sentence boundary follows the main verb in a sentence containing an embedded subject complement, the extraposition transformation is obligatory, as when: #That Tom returned happened# ⇒ "It happened that Tom returned." (Rosenbaum, 1967a, 72.) See also BOUNDARY. Compare WORD BOUNDARY.

Sentence, cleft. See CLEFT SENTENCE.

Sentence, cognate. See COGNATE SENTENCE.

Sentence, complement-. See COMPLEMENT-SENTENCE.

Sentence complement. *G–2.* A sentence which is a complement of the impersonal *it* in an underlying noun phrase, as in: "It (*that Tom fell overboard*) amused Huck." (Chomsky, 1965, 100–101.) Also called **Complement sentence.** (Jacobs and Rosenbaum, 1968, 174). Compare SENTENTIAL COMPLEMENT.

Sentence, complex. See COMPLEX SENTENCE.

Sentence conjunction. See CONJUNCTION.

Sentence, constituent. See CONSTITUENT SENTENCE.

Sentence, copula-type. See COPULA-TYPE SENTENCE.

Sentence, derived. See DERIVED SENTENCE.

Sentence, embedded. See EMBEDDED SENTENCE.

Sentence, generic. See GENERIC DETERMINER.

Sentencehood. *G–1.* Status as a grammatical sentence of a particular language, characterized by permitted sequences of word-types. (Lees, 1964a, 139.) A grammar is a theory of sentencehood. (Lees, 1960b, 150.) A recursive language has a decision procedure for sentencehood, for determining whether any given utterance is or is not a sentence. (Postal, 1964a, 83.) See also GRAMMATICALNESS.

Sentencehood, theory of. See SENTENCEHOOD.

Sentence, including. See MAIN SENTENCE.

Sentence, kernel. See KERNEL SENTENCE.

Sentence, main. See MAIN SENTENCE.

Sentence, matrix. See MATRIX SENTENCE.

Sentence, maximal. See MAXIMAL SENTENCE.

Sentence, modal. See MODAL SENTENCE.

Sentence negation. *G–2*. Negation of the entire sentence, as a result of the presence in the derivation of the single independent negative element Neg, whose simple reflex is *not*. The pre-verbal particle Neg can be attributed to a particular element in the sentence and be ultimately fused with that constituent (e.g., *nobody, never, neither*). Sentence negation is thus unary —analyzed by the presence of a single element—and mobile—fusing with other constituents in the sentence—and it can also be described as strong, permitting the *neither* tag, or weak, according to how far down the derivation Neg remains pre-verbal. A sentence that is embedded in a negative sentence must also be negative, by negative agreement, but the reverse does not hold. (Klima, 1964a, 270, 290, 294–295, 311–312, 316.) Compare CONSTITUENT NEGATION. See also NEGATION.

Sentence, negative. See NEGATIVE SENTENCE.

Sentence, noncleft. See NONCLEFT SENTENCE.

Sentence, novel. See NOVEL SENTENCE.

Sentence, passive. See PASSIVE SENTENCE.

Sentence, predicative. See PREDICATIVE SENTENCE.

Sentence, pronounceable. See PRONOUNCEABLE SENTENCE.

Sentence, pseudocleft. See PSEUDOCLEFT SENTENCE.

Sentence, quasi-grammatical. See QUASI-GRAMMATICAL SENTENCE.

Sentence, relative-complex. See RELATIVE-COMPLEX SENTENCE.

Sentence, semigrammatical. See SEMIGRAMMATICALNESS.

Sentence, simple. See SIMPLE SENTENCE.

Sentence, simplex. See SIMPLEX SENTENCE.

Sentence, source. See SOURCE SENTENCE.

Sentences, related See RELATED SENTENCES.

Sentences, synonymous. See SYNONYMOUS SENTENCES.

Sentence trapping. *G–2*. One of a number of semantically empty elements that are introduced into surface structures, often as duplicates of information found elsewhere in the sentence; an embellishment, or trapping, in a sentence, such as *that, to, ing,* the agreement marker, etc. (Langacker, 1968, 125–127.) See also EMPTY MORPHEME.

Sentence type. *G–1*. One of the various classes of sentences, such as active-passive, assertion-question, main clause-subordinate clause, etc. (Lees, 1960a, 2); one of the four basic arrangements in kernel sentence structures, as determined by the nature of the verb: NP+*be*+predicate; NP+intransitive verb+∅; NP+transitive verb+NP; NP+copulative verb +complement (Thomas, 1965, 35–37). *G–2*. One of a range of sets of sentences which are judged to be syntactically related and are consequently assumed either to have identical underlying structures or to have the same universal morpheme, such as Q, Wh, Neg—the sentence-type markers. (Katz and Postal, 1964, 119.) *G–2S*. A group of sentences that share a linguistic property, such as the same number of arguments in the main predicate. (Langendoen, 1969, 155.) Compare KERNEL SENTENCE.

Sentence, ungrammatical. See UNGRAMMATICAL SENTENCE.

Sentence, verbal. See VERBAL SENTENCE.

Sentential complement. *G–2*. A sentence that is the complement of a noun phrase: NP → DET+N+*S'*, as in: "The belief *that Tom was dead . . .*"; "The chance *for him to return . . .*"; "The job *of steering the raft. . . .*" (Chomsky, 1965, 100.) Compare SENTENCE COMPLEMENT.

Sentential complementation. *G–2*. The embedding of a sentence as a complement within another, main, sentence: relativization, subordination, complementation. (Rosenbaum, 1967a, 1, 21.) See also PREDICATE COMPLEMENTATION.

Sentential compound. See CONJUNCTION.

Sentential embedding. See SENTENTIAL COMPLEMENTATION.

Sentential relative clause. *G–2*. A relative clause which is adjoined to an entire sentence, as in: "Huck was a good cook, *which was a lucky thing*"; "Huck was a good cook, *which Tom was the first to admit.*" A sentential relative clause can replace a nonrestrictive relative clause that has been adjoined to an adjective, but not vice versa, as in: "Becky was homely, *which was not her fault*" (replacing *which she was*); *"That the raft leaked, *which she was . . .*" (replacing *which was not their fault*). (Ross, 1969, 357.) See also NONRESTRICTIVE RELATIVE CLAUSE.

Sentoid. *G–2*. A string of formatives with a unique structural description—that is, one which is syntactically unambiguous—as opposed to a 'sentence,' which is a string of formatives regardless of its structural description. (Katz and Postal, 1964, 24.) Compare SENTENCE.

Separable verb. *G–1*. A two-word verb of the type verb+particle, in a construction of the type verb+particle+nominal, the parts of which can be separated by the nominal object, or must be separated if the nominal is a pronominal, as in: "Huck *hauled in* the fish" ⇒ "Huck *hauled* the fish *in*" or "Huck *hauled* it *in*." Most separable verbs are of Germanic origin. (Lees, 1960a, 11.) See also TWO-PART VERB, PARTICLE, PARTICLE MOVEMENT TRANSFORMATION, PARTICLE INVERSION TRANSFORMATION, SEPARATION TRANSFORMATION.

Separation, particle. See PARTICLE.

Separation transformation. *G–1*. The simple transformation which inverts the order of a verb particle and a following noun phrase object, as in: "Huck tied *up the raft*" ⇒ "Huck tied *the raft up*." The separation transformation is obligatory if the NP is a pronoun (e.g., *"Huck tied *up it*" ⇒ "Huck tied *it up*"); otherwise it is optional. (Chomsky, 1957, 75–76, 112.) Also called PARTICLE MOVEMENT TRANSFORMATION, PARTICLE SHIFT, PARTICLE INVERSION TRANSFORMATION.

Sequence, natural categorial. See NATURAL CATEGORIAL SEQUENCE.

Sequential constraint rule. *G–2*. One of the types of phonological redundancy rules, or morpheme structure rules, which supply nondistinctive features for segments on the basis of the limitations placed upon them by their linear segmental environment. For example, the features [continuance] and [voicing] need not be specified for the obstruent that is preceded by an [s] but will be supplied by sequential constraint rules. (Harms, 1968, 84.) See also PHONOLOGICAL REDUNDANCY RULE, MORPHEME STRUCTURAL RULE, BLANK-FILLING RULE.

Set, comprehension. See COMPREHENSION SET.

Sex-antonymy. *G–2*. The relation which holds between a pair of words that have identical dictionary paths except for the semantic markers 'male' and 'female,' as in: *man/woman; aunt/uncle; boy/girl.* (Katz and Fodor, 1963, 496.) See also SEMANTIC MARKER.

Shift, particle. See PARTICLE SHIFT.

Shift rule, vowel. See VOWEL SHIFT RULE.

Short retort. *G–1.* An elliptical transform or tag, as in: *"He did, did he?"* (Lees, 1960a, 40.) Also called PRO-SENTENCE.

Simple question. See YES-NO QUESTION.

Simple sentence. *G–1.* A sentence with no conjoined or embedded elements. (Koutsoudas, 1966, 232.) *G–2.* A sentence that contains only one occurrence of S in its base form. (Kuroda, 1969, 338.) *G–2S.* A deep structure sentence composed of a verb and only one case category. (Fillmore, 1966, 375; Fillmore, 1968, 41.) Also called **Simplex sentence, Simplex, Kernel sentence, Kernel.** Compare COMPLEX SENTENCE.

Simple transformation. See SINGULARY TRANSFORMATION.

Simplex. *G–1.* A kernel sentence, as opposed to a complex sentence or matrix sentence. (Lees, 1960a, 101; Lees, 1964b, xxxix; Lees and Klima, 1963, 148, 150.) Also called **Simple sentence, Kernel, Kernel sentence, Simplex sentence.**

Simplex sentence. *G–1.* A sentence to which only simple transformations have applied. (Lees, 1960a, 42, 101.) Also called **Simple sentence, Kernel, Kernel sentence, Simplex.** Compare COMPLEX SENTENCE.

Simplex transformation. See SINGULARY TRANSFORMATION.

Simplicity. *G–2.* A measure of grammatical generality and economy. Given two descriptions of the same data in the same approximate form, the one without superfluous assumptions or ad hoc apparatus is preferred for its 'simplicity.' (Lees, 1964b, xxxi.) The simpler the grammatical analysis, the better it characterizes human linguistic competence. (Rosenbaum, 1967a, 9, 82.) See also SIMPLICITY METRIC.

Simplicity metric. *G–2.* A measure for the formulation of grammatical rules according to the criteria of descriptive adequacy, generality, and intuitive soundness (King, 1969, 215); a hypothesis about the nature of language which reflects the generality, and consequent economy, of the rules (Harms, 1968, 8); a method for determining the more highly valued grammar—that is, the more general, and consequently more economical, system of rules—from among alternative solutions (Harms, 1968, 13). The addition of a simplicity metric to a linguistic theory permits it to define the possible language underlying a set of data. (Postal, 1968a, 89.) Simplicity is a systematic measure applied to grammars rather than to individual rules. (King, 1969, 193.) Also called **Simplicity measure.** See also SIMPLICITY, ADEQUACY.

Simplification. *G–1.* Leveling of alternations, or extension of the domain of a restricted alternation (polarization)—traditionally attributed to imperfect learning. (King, 1969, 175.) *G–2.* The activation of the universal marking condition; the generalization of grammatical rules; a type of primary change, including rule loss and rule reordering; optimization, which occurs primarily in the grammar of the child. (King, 1969, 74–81.) See also LINGUISTIC CHANGE, PHONOLOGICAL CHANGE, SOUND CHANGE.

Single-base transformation. See SINGULARY TRANSFORMATION.

Singulary transformation. *G–1.* An optional or obligatory transformation which adds or deletes terms (Chomsky, 1961a, 136); a transformation which derives one of a related pair of sentences from the other, such as negatives, passives, and interrogatives from affirmative, active, declarative sentences (Katz and Postal, 1964, 74); a permutation, deletion, or adjunction transformation which is applied before the generalized transformations (Katz and Postal, 1964, 46). The outputs of optional singulary transformations are stylistic variants with the same cognitive meanings as the input sentences. (Katz and Postal, 1964, 112–113, 171.) *G–2.* An obligatory transformation which repositions a question, negative, or imperative morpheme (Katz and Postal, 1964, 74); a transformation which applies cyclically to a generalized phrase-marker: first to constituent sentences, and last to matrix sentences (Chomsky, 1965, 134; Chomsky, 1966a, 62); a transformation which operates on a single phrase-marker at a time (Katz and Postal, 1964, 11–12); an obligatory transformation which applies to a string which contains an appropriate marker: Neg, Q, Pass, etc. Singulary transformations are linearly ordered. They interrelate the semantic interpretations of phrase-markers but cannot introduce meaning-bearing elements. (Chomsky, 1965, 133.) Also called **Single-base transformation** (Lyons, 1968, 265), **Elementary transformation** (Koutsoudas, 1966, 27), **Simple transformation** (Chomsky, 1957, 114), **Unary transformation** (Gleitman, 1965, 90), **Simplex transformation** (Lees, 1965, xlvi.) See also ELEMENTARY TRANSFORMATION.

Sonorant. *G–2.* The phonological distinctive feature which is positively specified for sounds produced with a cavity configuration that permits spontaneous voicing—that is, for vowels, liquids, nasals, and glides—as opposed to **Nonsonorants,** or obstruents, in which spontaneous voicing is impossible; a member of this class. (Chomsky and Halle, 1968, 302.) Compare OBSTRUENT.

'So' transformation. *G–1.* The generalized transformation which replaces everything following the finite verb in a conjoined sentence with the constituent *so,* then inverts *so* and the subject NP, as when: "Huck could swim like a fish, and *Tom could swim like a fish*" ⇒ "Huck could swim like a fish, and *so could Tom.*" (Chomsky, 1957, 65–66, 113; Chomsky, 1962, 228.) See also PRO-FORM.

Sound change. *G–2.* An abrupt change in the grammar, typically by the addition of a rule to the phonological component, although the added rule may function for generations without changing particular lexical representations (Chomsky and Halle, 1968, 249–251); the addition of a rule by an adult, or the reformulation of a grammar by a child (Postal, 1968a, 270); a change in competence, often without effect on performance, which has nothing to do with the change (King, 1969, 108–111). Sounds do not change; grammars do. Sound change would be designated better as phonological change. (King, 1969, 111, 115.) The direction of sound change is not toward phonological symmetry but perhaps toward phonetic symmetry. (Kiparsky, 1968, 184–185.) Sound changes that are not due to language contact are caused by the universal tendency for stylistic change to serve various social functions. (Postal, 1968a, 303.) Also called **Phonological change.** See also LINGUISTIC CHANGE, RULE ADDITION.

Sound structure. See PHONOLOGY.

Source sentence. *G–1–2.* An underlying sentence; one of the expressions from which a sentence is said to be derived by a transformational rule. (Lees, 1960a, 3; Lees, 1964b, xxxvi.) Also called **Constituent sentence.** Compare KERNEL SENTENCE.

Speaker-hearer, ideal. See IDEAL SPEAKER-HEARER.

Speaker, normal. See NORMAL SPEAKER.

Species-specific. See LANGUAGE ACQUISITION.

Species-uniform. See LANGUAGE ACQUISITION.

Specification, feature. See FEATURE SPECIFICATION.

Specification, negative. See NEGATIVE SPECIFICATION.

Specify. See PREDICT.

Speech. *G–1–2.* The actual linguistic behavior which results from the speaker's performance. (Katz, 1966, 116–117.) See also PERFORMANCE.

Speech, part of. See PART OF SPEECH.

Speech production model. *G–2.* A model of the process of producing an utterance—going from message, a set of readings for an S node, through various encodings, to phonetic representation, and eventually to the activation of physiological mechanism. (Katz and Postal, 1964, 169–171.) Compare SPEECH RECOGNITION MODEL.

Speech recognition model. *G–2.* A model of the way in which a speaker uses his linguistic knowledge to understand and disambiguate the sentences he hears. (Katz and Postal, 1964, 167.) Compare SPEECH PRODUCTION MODEL.

Spelling rule. See MORPHOPHONEMIC RULE.

Stage, intermediate. See INTERMEDIATE STAGE.

Stative adjective. See STATIVE VERBAL.

Stative verb. See STATIVE VERBAL.

Stative verbal. *G–2.* A verb or adjective, plus copula, which does not take the progressive aspect, or participate in the imperative or do-so transformations, or appear in the frame "He persuaded NP to _____," as in: *"*know* the difference" (a stative verb); *"be *tall*" (a stative adjective). (Lakoff and Peters, 1966, 115.) Compare NONSTATIVE VERBAL.

Status, derivational. See DERIVATIONAL STATUS.

Stem-forming vowel. *G–2.* One of the vowels /i/ and /u/ which appear in the entries of certain lexical items and remain before certain affixes, but are deleted in final position: "confident-*i*(al)"; "contract-*u*(al)"; "reptil-*i*(ous)"; "tempest-*u*(ous)"; etc. (Chomsky and Halle, 1968, 130.)

Stop. *G–1–2.* A natural class of sounds which are specified [+consonantal], [−vocalic], [−continuant] (interrupted, along with affricates and nasals), [−strident] (mellow, as opposed to fricatives and affricates), and [+abrupt offset] (abrupt release, as opposed to affricates); a member of this class. (Harms, 1968, 33–34.)

Stop, glottal. See GLOTTAL STOP.

Stress. *G–2a.* One of the four or five degrees of accent which can be accounted for by an accent morphophoneme plus boundary markers. Stress rules operate on a string of forms with the vocalic nuclei either stressed or unstressed in numbered brackets, reducing the values in a cycle, from inside out. (Bach, 1964, 136–137). *G–2b.* Accent. The accented-unaccented distinction is so marginal that stress cannot be regarded as a phonological distinctive feature. (Chomsky, 1966a, 89.) The only functional distinction of English stress is the single relative differentiation that distinguishes *black bírd* from *bláckbird*. (Chomsky, 1966a, 88.) Systematic phonemics requires no stress markings in phonological representations. Without grammatical information, only main stress can be positioned correctly. It is simpler to specify the positions of strong stress than of weak stress. (Postal, 1968a, 25–27, 121, 169.) See also PROSODIC FEATURE, STRESS PLACEMENT

RULE, MAIN STRESS RULE, NUCLEAR STRESS RULE, STRESS-SUPERFIX. Compare INTONATION.

Stress adjustment rule. See STRESS PLACEMENT RULE.

Stress-pattern, compounding-. See COMPOUNDING-STRESS-PATTERN.

Stress placement rule. *G–2.* One of the several types of phonological rules which govern the initial placement of primary stress (i.e., the main stress rules), move it to the right (i.e., the nuclear stress rule), move it to the left in non-compounds (i.e., the alternating stress rule), move it to the left in compounds (i.e., the compound rule), and weaken nonprimary stresses within a word (i.e., the stress adjustment rule). (Chomsky and Halle, 1968, 41–84, 92, 115, 119, 156.) See also MAIN STRESS RULE, NUCLEAR STRESS RULE, COMPOUND RULE.

Stress rule, alternating. See STRESS PLACEMENT RULE.

Stress rule, main. See MAIN STRESS RULE.

Stress rule, nuclear. See NUCLEAR STRESS RULE.

Stress-superfix. *G–1.* The stress pattern / +\ for nominal compounds and /\+ / for nominal phrases, as in *bláckbìrd* and *blâck bírd* respectively. (Lees, 1960a, 181.) See also COMPOUNDING-STRESS-PATTERN.

Strictly ordered. *G–2.* Permitted to apply only in a fixed sequence in a transformational cycle. For example, some of the transformations necessary to the predicate complementation system are strictly ordered—1. Complementizer placement, 2. Identity erasure, 3. Passive, 4. Extraposition, etc. Others are partially ordered in respect to each other—pronoun replacement before obligatory complementizer deletion but after preposition deletion. (Rosenbaum, 1967a, 5, 47, 51–52.) Compare PARTIALLY ORDERED. See also RULE ORDERING, CYCLE.

Strict subcategorization. *G–2.* The marking of the lexical entry of a verb to describe its permitted occurrence in specific syntactic environments, for instance, as transitive [NP____NP] or intransitive [NP____]. Also called **Strict subclassification.** (Rosenbaum, 1967a, 15, 81, 88, 120.) See also STRICT SUBCATEGORIZATION RULE, STRICT SUBCATEGORIZATION FEATURE.

Strict subcategorization feature. *G–2.* A contextual feature that specifies categorial frames in which an item may appear (Chomsky, 1966a, 72); a contextual feature which is associated with a particular rule that limits the contexts in which a positively specified lexical entry can occur, such as the strict subcategorization features transitive, intransitive, pre-adjectival, etc. for verbs (Chomsky, 1965, 148–149); a syntactic feature which subcategorizes verbs in regard to the presence or absence of other categories but does not refer to the feature specifications of these other constituents (Langendoen, 1969, 43). Failure to observe a strict subcategorizational rule can result in a deviant string such as *"Tom found happy." (*Find* is [+____N] but not [+____ADJ].) (Chomsky, 1965, 148–149.) Also called **Strict subcategorization marker, Strict subclassificational feature.** (Rosenbaum, 1967a, 81.) See also STRICT SUBCATEGORIZATION, STRICT SUBCATEGORIZATION RULE, STRICT SUBCATEGORIZATION MARKER.

Strict subcategorization marker. *G–2.* A feature specification in the lexical entry of a verb which describes the verb's permitted occurrence in specific syntactic environments. For instance, the verb *to tend* (have a propensity to) is marked [+____S] in the lexicon: "The raft tended *to leak.*" Also called **Strict subclassificational feature.** (Rosenbaum, 1967a, 15, 81, 88.) See also STRICT SUBCATEGORIZATION FEATURE.

Strict subcategorization rule. *G–2.* A rule which analyzes a complex symbol in terms of its syntactic context, as in: V → complex symbol/ _____ {NP, ADJ, PredNom} (rewrite the category symbol V as a complex symbol in the categorial context of a following noun phrase or adjective or predicate nominal—each of these contexts is a 'frame'). Strict subcategorization rules are restricted to strictly 'local' transformations—internal, for example, to the VP. Verbs are strictly subcategorized into transitives, intransitives, pre-adjectival, etc. (Chomsky, 1965, 95–96, 105.) See also STRICT SUBCATEGORIZATION FEATURE, STRICT SUBCATEGORIZATION MARKER.

Strict subclassificational feature. See STRICT SUBCATEGORIZATION MARKER.

Strident. *G–1–2.* A phonological distinctive feature that is positively specified for consonant sounds whose production generates considerable friction or turbulence or noisiness (Halle, 1959, 327); a feature of obstruent continuants and affricates, as opposed to stops, liquids, nasals, and glides, which are **Nonstrident** (Chomsky and Halle, 1968, 327–329); one of the manner features of consonants, applying to alveolar fricatives and affricates, as opposed to stops and nonfricatives, which are **Mellow** (Harms, 1968, 34).

String. *G–1–2.* A concatenation of one or more vocabulary symbols (Chomsky, 1956, 142; Koutsoudas, 1966, 5–6); a sequence of alphabetic symbols of a language; a line of derivation: an initial string or sentence, a preterminal string or non-terminal string (Koutsoudas, 1966, 15), or a terminal string, viz., the last line of a terminated derivation, containing lexical items (Chomsky, 1957, 29–30; Chomsky, 1965, 84); the configuration of the constituency of a structure at a particular stage of its derivation, given either as a linear succession of the constituents or as a labeled bracketing of their structure (Rosenbaum, 1967a, 33, 35–37). See also BASIC STRING, INITIAL STRING, TERMINAL STRING, C-TERMINAL STRING, T-TERMINAL STRING.

String, base. See C-TERMINAL STRING.

String, basic. See BASIC STRING.

String, C-terminal. See C-TERMINAL STRING.

String, initial. See INITIAL STRING.

String, intermediate. See INTERMEDIATE STRUCTURE.

String, kernel. See KERNEL SENTENCE.

String, nonsense. See NONSENSE STRING.

String, null. See NULL STRING.

String, preterminal. See STRING.

String-replacement rule. See PHRASE STRUCTURE RULE.

String, terminal. See TERMINAL STRING.

String, T-terminal. See T-TERMINAL STRING.

Strong cluster. *G–2.* A string of phonological segments which consist either of a simple vocalic nucleus—a short vowel or schwa—followed by two or more consonants, or of a complex vocalic nucleus—a long vowel or diphthong—followed by zero or more consonants, as in: EvAd (*evade*, SS—strong, strong). (Chomsky and Halle, 1968, 29.) Compare WEAK CLUSTER.

Strong generative capacity. *G–1–2.* The capacity of a grammar to assign a correct structural description to any string that it generates (Bach, 1964, 168); the capacity of a grammar to generate a correct set of structural descriptions, as well as to weakly generate a set of sentences. A theory is descriptively adequate if the system of structural description for all languages is included in its strong generative capacity. (Chomsky, 1965, 60–61.) Compare WEAK GENERATIVE CAPACITY.

Strongly adequate. See ADEQUACY.

Strongly identical. *G–2a.* Identical both terminally—viz., weakly identical —and in respect to higher-order constituents. This is a condition necessary for certain deletion and substitution transformations, for example the substitution of the relative noun for the head noun: "The *raft* Wh-a *raft* appeared" ⇒ "The *raft which* appeared. . . ." (Katz and Postal, 1964, 150.) *G–2b.* Identical both in meaning—viz., weakly identical— and in reference. This is a condition necessary for the application of the identical conjunct reduction transformation, as when: "That boy (Tom) slept and that boy (Huck) steered" ⇒ "That boy and that boy slept and steered, respectively" (not "Those boys slept and steered"). (Jacobs and Rosenbaum, 1968, 258.) Compare WEAKLY IDENTICAL.

Strong verb. See IRREGULAR VERB.

Structural ambiguity. *G–2.* The condition which holds when a phonetic representation has two or more deep structure origins. (Postal, 1968a, 15.) See also AMBIGUITY.

Structural analysis. *G–1.* The description of the phrase structure to which a structural change applies, such as the structural analysis of the 'Do'-Transformation—$\# + $affix—and the structural change—$X_1 + X_2 \Rightarrow X_1 + do + X_2$ (Chomsky, 1957, 113); the condition which defines the class of phrasemarkers to which a transformational rule applies; the analysis of the terminal string of a phrase-marker into successive parts (Chomsky, 1966a, 51). See also STRUCTURAL DESCRIPTION. Compare STRUCTURAL CHANGE.

Structural change. *G–1.* The generalization of the operation which a particular transformation performs, such as the change which the particle separation transformation effects on the structural analysis X—V—Prt— Pro: X_1—X_2—X_3—$X_4 \Rightarrow X_1$—X_2—X_4—X_3 ("They called *up him*" ⇒ "They called *him up*") (Chomsky, 1957, 112); the right-hand side of a transformational rule, which describes the form of the derived phrasemarker after the application of the rule; a transform (Koutsoudas, 1966, 24). Compare STRUCTURAL ANALYSIS.

Structural condition. *G–2.* One of the necessary properties which a string must possess in order for a particular transformation to apply. (Rosenbaum, 1967a, 72.) See also NECESSARY ENVIRONMENT.

Structural description. *G–1.* A structural analysis or structure index (Bach, 1964, 61); the left-hand side of a transformational rule, which specifies the domain of the rule, as opposed to the right-hand side of the rule, which specifies the structural change or transform (Koutsoudas, 1966, 24–25); a specification of the constituents and structural relations of a phonetically possible utterance: a phrase-marker (Chomsky, 1964, 51, 53). *G–2.* The full syntactic description and phonological and semantic representations that are assigned to a sentence by the grammar (Chomsky and Halle, 1968, 7); a formulation of the structural conditions necessary for the application of a transformation, describing only the necessary environment, including feature specifications, with irrelevant environments symbolized by the variables X, Y, and Z. The structural description is accompanied by a sequence of structural indices—only one index number for each constituent, in order—and is followed by an analysis of the

structural change, represented by the reordered indices and by Ø for the loss of a constituent. For example, the structural description for the auxiliary transformation is: X + affix + base + Y; and the structural change
$$\underset{1}{\quad}\quad\underset{2}{\quad}\quad\underset{3}{\quad}\quad\underset{4}{\quad}$$
is: 1, Ø, 3 + 2, 4 (i.e., X + base − affix + Y). (Rosenbaum, 1967a, 26, 35, 41, 51, 92.) See also STRUCTURAL ANALYSIS. Compare STRUCTURAL CHANGE.

Structural index. *G–2.* One of the sequence of numerical markers (1, 2, 3, 4, etc.) of the linear order of constituents—one structural index for each constituent, in order—in a structural description and a structural change. Also called **Structure index.** (Rosenbaum, 1967a, 5–7, 92.) See also STRUCTURE INDEX, STRUCTURAL DESCRIPTION, STRUCTURAL ANALYSIS.

Structural linguistics. *G–1–2a.* Linguistics generally (Klima, 1964b, 228); synchronic linguistics generally (King, 1969, 3). *G–1–2b.* Modern linguistics, which is the field of linguistics, roughly within the period 1930–1960, which was based primarily on the discovery of the phoneme. (Postal, 1968a, ix.) From the point of view of the transformationalists, structural linguistics: 1) assumed that grammar must be defined in terms of the notions phoneme and morpheme; 2) limited grammatical description to organization of primary linguistic data; 3) assumed that discovery of a grammar resulted from segmentation and classification of items; 4) was based on the assumption that deep and surface structures were the same (Chomsky, 1965, 202–203, 205, 209); 5) defined language as a set of behavioral patterns common to a speech community; 6) was preoccupied with observable data—actual speech, physical phonetics, tape recordings, sound spectrograms—and the induction of general laws from these events; 7) was a prescientific task of providing materials upon which a science of language could operate; 8) was preoccupied with efficiency and putative discovery procedures; 9) provided taxonomic classification without evaluation; 10) provided an arrangement of the data without claims about the nature of the data; 11) rejected introspection and intuition of the analyst; 12) held the belief that the mind is inaccessible to scientific investigation (Rosenbaum, 1965, 467–472); 13) was primarily concerned with language as a system of phonological units, the modification of these units, the relations among them, their patterns; 14) assumed that systematic procedures of segmentation and classification could isolate and identify all significant elements of a language; 15) assumed that a grammar of a language consists of a catalog of elements, along with their relations and distributions (Chomsky, 1966b, 6); 16) claimed that knowledge of language amounts to a stored set of overlearned patterns modified only by analogy; 17) consisted of taxonomic analysis of surface structure signals into syntagmatic and paradigmatic patterns; 18) was an antipsychological, antimentalistic behavioral science (Chomsky, 1968, 4, 10, 16–17, 58–59); 19) had little interest in specifying the notions 'grammar' and 'rule of grammar' (Postal, 1964b, 141); 20) essentially amounted to discovery of efficient transcription systems (Lees, 1964a, 137, 138); 21) consisted of an intensive study of artifacts (Chomsky, 1964, 60). Also called: **Modern linguistics, Modern structuralism, Modern structural linguistics, Modern descriptive linguistics, Descriptive linguistics, Structural-descriptive linguistics, American descriptive linguistics, Bloomfieldian linguistics, Post-Bloomfieldian linguistics, Neo-Bloomfieldian linguistics, Classificatory linguistics, Taxonomic linguistics, Mechanistic linguistics, Behavioristic**

linguistics, Anthropological linguistics. Compare TRADITIONAL GRAMMAR, GENERATIVE GRAMMAR, TRANSFORMATIONAL GRAMMAR.

Structure. See CONSTRUCTION.

Structure, common underlying. See COMMON UNDERLYING STRUCTURE.

Structure, conceptual. See CONCEPTUAL STRUCTURE.

Structure, deep. See DEEP STRUCTURE.

Structure, deep-level. See DEEP STRUCTURE.

Structure-dependent. *G–2.* Dependent on the particular organization of a string of words for application—said of a grammatical transformation. (Chomsky, 1968, 51–52.) See also SENSITIVE TO, DEFINED ON/UPON/OVER.

Structure, derived. See DERIVED STRUCTURE.

Structure index. *G–2.* A numerical index which defines the domain of a particular transformation. For example, the structure index for the particle separation transformation is: NP—V—Prt—Pro (a terminal string falls
1   2   3   4
under the domain of the particle separation transformation if its first part is a noun phrase, its second part a verb, its third part a particle, and its fourth part a pronoun—e.g., "Tom helped *out him*"). (Katz and Postal, 1964, 9.) Also called **Structural index.** Compare REFERENTIAL INDEX.

Structure, intermediate. See INTERMEDIATE STRUCTURE.

Structure, phrase. See PHRASE STRUCTURE.

Structure, sound. See PHONOLOGY.

Structure, superficial. See SUPERFICIAL STRUCTURE.

Structure, surface. See SURFACE STRUCTURE.

Structure, surface-level. See SURFACE STRUCTURE.

Structure, syntactic. See SYNTACTIC STRUCTURE.

Structure, underlying. See UNDERLYING STRUCTURE.

Stylistic inversion. *G–2.* The inversion of two major constituents of a sentence for stylistic reasons, perhaps determined by performance rules, as in: "That place I never want to visit again" (from "I never want to visit that place again"). Stylistic inversion seems to be universal, though tolerated more extensively by richly inflected languages. It is superficial and cannot be handled by grammatical transformations. Stylistic inversion is a type of stylistic reordering. (Chomsky, 1965, 126–127, 222–223). See also STYLISTIC REORDERING.

Stylistic reordering. *G–2.* The reordering of major constituents of a sentence, short of ambiguity, for stylistic reasons. In English, stylistic reordering amounts to stylistic inversion. (Chomsky, 1965, 126–127, 222–223.) See also STYLISTIC INVERSION.

Stylistic rule. *G–1.* An optional rule of the grammar, following all of the obligatory rules for normal forms, which generates stylistic variants such as ellipses and contractions. (Lees, 1960a, 33, 41.) See also STYLISTIC VARIANT.

Stylistic transformation. See INVERSION.

Stylistic variant. *G–1.* A contraction or ellipsis which is the result of an optional stylistic rule at the end of the grammar. (Lees, 1960a, 33.) See also STYLISTIC RULE.

Subcategorization. *G–2.* The analysis of a syntactic category of lexical formatives into subcategories which are cross-classificational rather than strictly hierarchical. Subcategorization can be eliminated from the system of rewrite rules and assigned to the lexicon, but without semantic determination. Context-free subcategorization rules introduce inherent features of lexical items. Thus, *boy* is a count noun, a common noun, etc. (Chomsky, 1965, 75, 79, 120.) Subcategorization constraints are different from positional constraints and domination constraints. (Lees, 1964b, xli). *G–2S.* Semantic information is relevant to subcategorization. The dictionary entry of a lexical item must specify all of the information needed to characterize that item, including its meaning. (McCawley, 1968, 136.) See also STRICT SUBCATEGORIZATION FEATURE, STRICT SUBCATEGORIZATION RULE, CONTEXT-SENSITIVE SUBCATEGORIZATION RULE.

Subcategorization feature, strict.   See STRICT SUBCATEGORIZATION FEATURE.

Subcategorization marker, strict.   See STRICT SUBCATEGORIZATION MARKER.

Subcategorization rule, context-sensitive.   See CONTEXT-SENSITIVE SUBCATEGORIZATION RULE.

Subcategorization rule, strict.   See STRICT SUBCATEGORIZATION RULE.

Subcategorization, strict.   See STRICT SUBCATEGORIZATION.

Subclassificational feature, strict.   See STRICT SUBCATEGORIZATION MARKER.

Subcomponent, transformational.   See TRANSFORMATIONAL SUBCOMPONENT.

Subconstituent.   *G–2.* A constituent of a constituent of a sentence—that is, a constituent that is not an immediate constituent of S, such as *the raft,* in "Huck steered *the raft,*" which is a constituent of VP and a subconstituent of S. (Langacker, 1968, 98.) Also called **Substituent.** (Katz and Postal, 1964, 49.) Compare SUB-TREE, SUBSTRING.

Subject.   *G–1–2.* The grammatical relation, or function, of NP directly dominated by S: [NP, S], subject of; the relation between the NP of a sentence of the type NP+PredP and the whole sentence (Chomsky, 1965, 70–71); a noun phrase immediately dominated by S in the deep structure (Jacobs, 1968, 26). The subject of a deep structure is a **Deep subject,** and the subject of a surface structure a **Surface subject.** (Jacobs and Rosenbaum, 1968, 72, 74–75.) The surface structure subject is not necessarily the deep structure subject. For example, in "Tom was rescued by Huck," *Tom* is the grammatical (surface structure) subject; but *Huck* is the logical (deep structure) subject ("Huck rescued Tom"). (Chomsky, 1965, 70–71.) *G–2S.* The propositional actant that is placed to the left of the auxiliary by transformation—a surface structure phenomenon only. If there is only only one actant, it becomes the subject. (Fillmore, 1966, 368; Fillmore, 1968, 33.) Compare DIRECT OBJECT.

Subject complement.   *G–2.* A sentence embedded as the complement of a noun in the noun phrase subject of an underlying structure, such as "(It) *that Tom returned* surprised Huck," which is an instance of subject noun phrase complementation, or subject complementation. (Rosenbaum, 1967a, 5, 71.) Compare OBJECT COMPLEMENT.

Subject complementation.   *G–2.* The type of complementation in which a sentence is embedded in a subject NP: NP → DET+N+*S* (e.g., "the fact *that Tom returned*"). A noun phrase complement is a subject complement if the entire NP in which it is embedded can be shifted to the end of the sentence under passivization, as when: "*The fact that Tom returned* surprised Huck" ⇒ "Huck was surprised by *the fact that Tom returned.*" (Rosenbaum, 1967c, 320.) Subject complementation is an instance of noun phrase complementation. Also called **Subject noun phrase complementation.** (Rosenbaum, 1967a, 5, 71, 79.) Compare OBJECT COMPLEMENTATION.

Subject, deep. See DEEP SUBJECT.

Subject, derived. See DERIVED SUBJECT.

Subject, impersonal. See IMPERSONAL SUBJECT.

Subject, implicit. See IMPLICIT SUBJECT.

Subjectivalization. *G–2S.* The transformation which selects one of the arguments (NP's) of a sentence as the subject of the sentence and moves it to the left of the predicate: $P+NP \Rightarrow NP+P$; $P+NP_1+NP_2 \Rightarrow NP_1+P+NP_2$ or NP_2+P+NP_1. Also called **Subjectivization, Topicalization.** (Langendoen, 1969, 98.) See also TOPICALIZATION.

Subjectivalization transformation. See SUBJECTIVALIZATION.

Subjectivization. See SUBJECTIVALIZATION.

Subject nominal. *G–1.* A noun phrase subject. (Lees, 1964b, xxxiv.)

Subject noun phrase complementation. See SUBJECT COMPLEMENTATION.

Subject noun phrase, underlying. See UNDERLYING SUBJECT NOUN PHRASE.

Subject-object inversion transformation. *G–2.* The transformation, in the verb phrase complement system, which inverts the subject and object of a main sentence containing a sense verb, placing the underlying object noun phrase in first position and moving the underlying subject noun phrase, plus *to,* to final position following a verb phrase complement, as in: "*The food* tasted good *to Tom*" from "*Tom* tasted *the food* (for the food to be) good." (Rosenbaum, 1967a, 6, 98–99.)

Subject pro-nominal. *G–1.* The pronoun *it,* as in "*It* was tough to lose," from the structure "To lose was tough." (Lees, 1960a, 32.) Also called **Impersonal subject, Expletive, Pronoun 'it.'** See also EXTRAPOSITION.

Subject, superficial. See SUPERFICIAL SUBJECT.

Subject, underlying. See UNDERLYING SUBJECT.

Subordinate adverbial phrase. *G–2.* The constituent SP in the expansion of S as NP, PDP, SP. This constituent can expand into Prep, NP; and the NP can expand as DET, N, S—that is, it can contain a noun phrase complement, as in:

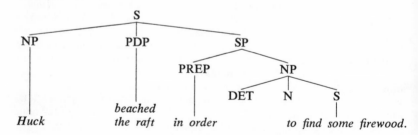

(Rosenbaum, 1967a, 17, 23.) Compare SUBORDINATE CLAUSE. See also ADVERBIAL CLAUSE.

Subordinate clause. *G–1–2.* A clause which is subordinate to the sentence or to one of its constituents: an adverbial clause, a nominal complement, an appositive complement, an embedded question, or a relative clause. (Lees, 1960a, 2; Ross, 1967, 192.) Compare MAIN CLAUSE, SUBORDINATE ADVERBIAL PHRASE.

Substantive universal. *G–2.* One of the primitive items of the fixed universal vocabulary of a linguistic theory: distinctive features, syntactic categories, semantic concepts. (Katz and Postal, 1964, 160; Chomsky,

1965, 29; Chomsky and Halle, 1968, 4.) See also ATOMIC ELEMENT, PRIME, VOCABULARY. Compare FORMAL UNIVERSAL.

Substantivization transformation. *G–2.* The transformation which, when triggered by an abstract complementizer, converts an adjective or verb, in an embedded complement of *it,* into the substantive head of the noun phrase, as when: "It (that Tom will be a pilot was *possible*) didn't impress Huck" ⇒ "The *possibility* that Tom would be a pilot didn't impress Huck"; "It (Huck *knew* that Tom will be a pilot) didn't impress Huck" ⇒ "The *knowledge* that Tom would be a pilot didn't impress Huck." (Ross, 1967, 196–197.) See also NOMINALIZATION.

Substituent. See SUBCONSTITUENT.

Substitution test. *G–2.* The test which can be used to determine the similarity of type of two or more constituents of a sentence. The test replaces one of the constituents with the other, and if a grammatical string results, the constituents are of the same type. (Jacobs and Rosenbaum, 1968, 13.)

Substitution transformation. *G–1.* A transformation which performs the operation of substituting one constituent for another, as when: A+B+C ⇒ A+D+C; a replacement transformation. (Koutsoudas, 1966, 33.) *G–2.* The transformation which substitutes a lexical item—that is, the features of that item—for an occurrence of the dummy element △ in a phrase-marker. (Chomsky, 1966a, 73.) See also OPERATION, DUMMY ELEMENT.

Substring. *G–1–2.* A string which is a constituent of another string. (Lyons, 1968, 259.) Also: **Sub-string.** (Lees, 1960a, 2.) Also called **Sub-tree.** Compare SUBCONSTITUENT.

Sub-tree. *G–1.* A branching which is part of another branching, such as the branching NP → Art+Adj+N in the sentence S → NP+VP. (Lees, 1960b, 151.) *G–2.* The tree of an embedded sentence. (Lees, 1964b, xxxix.) Also called **Substring.** Compare SUBCONSTITUENT.

Suffix. *G–1–2.* A lexical item that is not a word but can be attached to the end of a word; a derivational or inflectional ending, as in: "fool-*ish*"; "final-*ize*"; "act-*ion*"; "fool-*s*"; "fool-*ing*"; "fool-*ed*"; "fool-*'s*"; etc. (Langendoen, 1969, 129.) Compare PREFIX. See also INFLECTION, DERIVATIONAL SUFFIX.

Suffix, attributivizing. See ATTRIBUTIVIZING SUFFIX.

Suffix, derivational. See DERIVATIONAL SUFFIX.

Superficial phrase-marker. *G–2.* The labeled bracketing of the actual string of morphemes and words which are directly related to the phonetic manifestation, or pronunciation, of a sentence. The superficial phrase-marker is derived by transformations from its abstract underlying, or deep, structure. (Postal, 1964c, 22–23, 28, 30.) Also called **Surface level structure, Surface structure.** Compare UNDERLYING PHRASE STRUCTURE, DEEP STRUCTURE.

Superficial structure. *G–2.* The superficial phrase-marker of a sentence. (Rosenbaum, 1964c, 27, 31.) Also called **Surface structure, Superficial phrase-marker.**

Superficial subject. *G–2.* The subject of a superficial sentence structure, as opposed to an 'underlying subject,' which is the subject of an underlying phrase-marker. The superficial subject noun may have a different grammatical function in the underlying structure, as in: "Huck worked with *Tom"* (object of preposition in underlying structure); "Huck and *Tom* worked together" (subject conjunct in superficial sentence). (Lakoff and Peters, 1966, 124–125.) Also called **Derived subject.** Compare UNDER-LYING SUBJECT, DEEP SUBJECT.

Superfix, stress-. See STRESS-SUPERFIX.

Suppletion. *G–2.* The condition which holds in a derivation when the phonetic shape of a formative is totally unpredictable from its phonological representation, or when one realization is totally unlike another realization, as in: /go/ + /ed/ → [went]. The copula *be* illustrates more suppletion than any other English formative: *be, am, are, i*(s), *was, were.* (Postal, 1968a, 162.)

Support, 'do'-. See 'DO'-SUPPORT.

Suprasegmental. *G–2.* Prosodic—that is, pertaining to length, stress, and tone. So called because these features are marked above the segmental symbols in a phonemic transcription. (Langacker, 1968, 151.) See also PROSODIC FEATURE, STRESS, LENGTH, INTONATION.

Surface level. *G–2.* The level of representation of a sentence which corresponds to its overt, physical form, as opposed to the abstract, underlying, deep level. For example, an imperative sentence lacks a 'surface-level' subject but has a 'deep-level' subject. (Langendoen, 1969, 14.) Compare DEEP LEVEL.

Surface-level structure. See SURFACE STRUCTURE.

Surface structure. *G–2a.* The superficial form of a sentence, in which grammatical relations are not associated with unique configurations of constituents—superficial structure (Postal, 1964c, 28); the outer aspect of language (Chomsky, 1966c, 35); a labeled bracketing which segments a derived sentence into its successive constituents, categorizes them, and further segments these constituents (Chomsky, 1966a, 16–17, 37); a categorization of a sentence into morphemes, words, and phrases—a surface syntactic structure (Postal, 1968a, x, 114–115). Surface structures do not indicate grammatical relations with any semantic significance. (Chomsky, 1966a, 16–17.) The presence of an element in the surface structure does not necessarily mean that it was present in the deep structure, and the presence of an element in the deep structure does not necessarily mean that it will be present in the surface structure. (Postal, 1966, 203.) *G–2b.* The superficial organization of units into categories and phrases which is directly associated with the physical signal and determines the phonetic interpretation (Chomsky, 1966c, 33; Chomsky, 1968, 25); the actual organization of the physical signal into phrases, words, particles, inflections, etc. (Chomsky, 1966b, 4–5); the output of the syntactic component and the input to the phonological component (Chomsky and Halle, 1968, 9, 163); that aspect of the syntactic description which determines its phonetic form (Chomsky, 1966a, 16–17). The grammar contains readjustment rules for converting the syntactic surface structure into a form appropriate for the phonological component—that is, into a phonological representation. (Chomsky and Halle, 1968, 9, 163.) Also called **Surface-level structure** (Langendoen, 1969, 24), **Superficial structure** (Postal, 1964c, 27). Compare DEEP STRUCTURE, UNDER-LYING STRUCTURE.

Surface structure, phonological. See PHONOLOGICAL SURFACE STRUCTURE.

Syllable. *G–2.* The universal pattern CVC, which is unmarked throughout.

(Postal, 1968a, 138, 181.) The syllable is not a basic unit of the grammar, though it is relevant to the operation of certain phonological rules. (Harms, 1968, 116). Syllables are characterized as possible, admissible, permissible, and as impossible, inadmissible, on the basis of the phonological redundancy rules of the language—viz., the morpheme structure rules. (Postal, 1968a, 138, 181.) See also ADMISSIBILITY, PHONOLOGICAL ADMISSIBILITY.

Symbol. *G–1–2*. One of the three types of abstract grammatical elements: vocabulary symbols, which represent grammatical classes (N, V, etc.); operators, which symbolize operations performed by the grammatical rules (+, #, →); and abbreviators, which conflate existing rules ({}, [], ()). Only the vocabulary symbols are counted as structural elements of the string. (Koutsoudas, 1966, 6.) See also OPERATOR, ABBREVIATOR, VOCABULARY.

Symbol, complex. See COMPLEX SYMBOL.

Symbol, cover. See COVER SYMBOL.

Symbol, dummy. See DUMMY SYMBOL.

Symbol, nonterminal. See NONTERMINAL SYMBOL.

Symbol, vocabulary. See VOCABULARY.

Symmetric predicate. *G–2S*. A verb or adjective or noun which functions as the predicate of two arguments which can be interchanged or conjoined as subject without significant change of meaning, as in: "The riverboat *collided* with the raft" ⇒ "The raft *collided* with the riverboat" ⇒ "The riverboat and the raft *collided*"; "Honey is *similar* to molasses" ⇒ "Molasses is *similar* to honey" ⇒ "Honey and molasses are *similar*"; "Aunt Polly is a *relative* of Tom" ⇒ "Tom is a *relative* of Aunt Polly" ⇒ "Aunt Polly and Tom are *relatives*." (Langendoen, 1969, 94–95.) See also IRREFLEXIVE.

Synonymous. *G–2*. Having the same semantic interpretation, as an automatic consequence of a common underlying structure—said of two related sentences with contrasting surface structures, such as the active and passive versions of the same deep structure; related. (Rosenbaum, 1967a, 60, 74, 78, 90, 104.) Compare IDENTICAL. See also RELATED SENTENCES, SYNONYMOUS SENTENCES.

Synonymous sentences. *G–2S*. Two or more sentences which have different surface structures but the same underlying conceptual structure, such as: "Tom skipped school"—Tom played hooky from school"; "Huck started up the fire"—"Huck started the fire up." (Langacker, 1968, 117–118.) Also called **Related sentences.**

Synonymy. *G–2*. Sameness of semantic interpretation of two sentences, as an automatic consequence of their common underlying structure. Also called **Truth value synonymy.** (Rosenbaum, 1967a, 60–61, 78, 89–90, 103–105.) Compare RELATEDNESS, IDENTITY.

Synonymy, truth value. See SYNONYMY.

Syntactic. See SYNTACTIC STRUCTURE.

Syntactic ambiguity. See AMBIGUITY.

Syntactic base. See BASE.

Syntactic change. *G–2*. A change in the transformational component of a grammar through time by addition, loss, and reordering of rules—along the same lines as phonological change. The base component rules show little change through time, however. (King, 1969, 143.) See also LINGUISTIC CHANGE. Compare SOUND CHANGE, PHONOLOGICAL CHANGE.

175

Syntactic component. *G–1.* The syntax, one of the two major components of a grammar—phonology being the other component—consisting of two kinds of rules, besides a lexicon. The rules are those which enumerate kernel sentences (viz., phrase structure rules) and those which generate derived sentences (viz., transformational rules). The syntax enumerates an infinite set of strings of grammatical symbols, each with its correct structural description. (Lees, 1960b, 150–151; Chomsky, 1966a, 51.) *G–2a.* One of the two components—the other being a phonological component—of a grammar, which in turn is one of two components, along with a semantic component, of a linguistic description. The syntactic component contains a constituent structure component, a lexicon, and a transformational component. The syntactic component is the generative source in a linguistic description. It enumerates the set of formal structures underlying sentences and assigns to each a structural description and a transformation marker. (Katz and Postal, 1964, 1, 6.) *G–2b.* The component of a linguistic theory, or grammar, which generates strings of formatives and their structural descriptions, providing for each sentence a semantically interpretable deep structure and a phonetically interpretable surface structure, along with a statement of the relation between these two structures. (Chomsky, 1964, 52–54.) The syntax consists of a base component, containing a categorial component and a lexicon, and a set of transformational rules. (Chomsky, 1965, 120, 128.) See also SYNTAX.

Syntactic deep structure. See DEEP STRUCTURE.

Syntactic description. *G–1.* The specification, for a string of formatives, of a set of underlying phrase-markers, a derived phrase-marker, and a transformation-marker. (Chomsky, 1964, 84.) *G–2a.* The specification, for a sentence, of its set of words, their order, their grouping, and their syntactic categories; a phrase-marker; a branching diagram. (Katz, 1966, 124.) *G–2b.* An abstract object—an SD—which uniquely determines the semantic interpretation of the sentence that it is associated with. (Chomsky, 1966a, 13.) *G–2c.* An account of the intuitions of grammaticality of a fluent speaker; a 'black box,' which inputs linguistic objects and outputs structural descriptions and descisions on grammaticality. (Langendoen, 1969, 17.) Compare STRUCTURAL DESCRIPTION. See also SYNTACTIC COMPONENT.

Syntactic feature. *G–2a.* One of the syntactic properties of the complex symbol of a lexical category which are specified for each lexical formative that is a member of that category, as in: N → [+N, ±common]: *boy* → [+N, +common]; *Huck* → [+N, −common]. Syntactic features can be represented in a binary branching diagram or as a set of rewritings, as shown here. (Chomsky, 1965, 83.) *G–2b.* One of the two types of properties of lexical formatives: those which are relevant to the syntactic rules—syntactic features proper—and those which are relevant only to the phonological rules—morphological features, or properties of entire morphemes, which divide up the vocabulary according to historical source. (Postal, 1968a, 120–123.) Compare MORPHOLOGICAL FEATURE, SEMANTIC FEATURE.

Syntactic feature proper. See SYNTACTIC FEATURE.

Syntactic redundancy rule. *G–2.* A rule in the grammar of a particular language which states a general property of lexical entries, thereby eliminating redundant specifications from the lexicon. (Chomsky, 1965, 168–169.) See also LEXICAL REDUNDANCY RULE.

Syntactic structure. *G–1.* A sentence structure; a sentence; sentence structure. In the broad sense, the study of syntactic structure is grammar, as opposed to semantics. In the narrow sense, the study of syntactic structure is syntax, as opposed to morphology and phonemics. (Chomsky, 1957, 5.) *G–2.* The by-product of a generative grammar. In the broad sense, a syntactic structure is the product of both the syntax and the interpretive components—that is, the semantics and the phonology. In the narrow sense, it is the product of the subcomponents of the syntax —the base component and the transformational component. (Postal, 1968a, 279, 281.) See also SYNTAX, SYNTACTIC COMPONENT, PHRASE STRUCTURE, DEEP STRUCTURE, SURFACE STRUCTURE.

Syntactic tense. *G–2.* The present or past time feature of an auxiliary segment in the deep structure of a sentence. The syntactic tense is copied onto the verbal segment unless the auxiliary contains a modal, *have,* or *be.* (Jacobs and Rosenbaum, 1968, 121–125.) See also TENSE.

Syntactic theory. *G–2.* The theory which defines the notions 'deep structure' and 'surface structure' and states precisely how the syntactic rules generate a syntactic description. (Chomsky, 1966a, 55.) See also LINGUISTIC THEORY.

Syntax. *G–1.* The study of the principles and processes of sentence construction in particular languages—that is, the grammar. (Chomsky, 1957, 11.) *G–2a.* The component of a transformational grammar which derives abstract underlying phrase-markers by phrase structure rules and final derived phrase-markers by transformational rules. (Postal, 1964c, 25–26.) *G–2b.* A base system which generates deep structures and a system of transformations which map deep structures into surface structures. The 'syntax' of an expression is its deep structure. (Chomsky, 1966c, 42, 47.) *G–2S.* The system of rules which convert abstract semantic representations into surface syntactic representations. (McCawley, 1968, 167.) The 'semantics' of an expression is its deep structure. (Fillmore, 1968, 88.) See also SYNTACTIC COMPONENT, SYNTACTIC DESCRIPTION.

Syntax, abstract. See ABSTRACT SYNTAX.

Syntax, semantic basis for. See SEMANTIC BASIS FOR SYNTAX.

Synthesis, analysis by. See ANALYSIS BY SYNTHESIS.

Synthetic grammar. *G–1.* A grammar which takes the point of view of the speaker. (Chomsky, 1962, 240.) See also ANALYSIS BY SYNTHESIS.

Systematic. See SYSTEMATIC GRAMMAR.

Systematic archiphoneme. See ARCHIPHONEME.

Systematic grammar. *G–2.* A grammar which distinguishes between underlying and superficial levels of structure in the syntactic and phonological components and accounts for their relationship by rules of the transformational type. (Postal, 1968a, 215–216.)

Systematic phoneme. *G–2.* One of the set of segments, containing only distinctively specified features, which underlies the phonetic segments of morphemes before any redundancy rules have applied (Harms, 1968, 2); one of the underlying segments used to spell morphemes; one of the segments which contain the minimum number of distinctive feature-specifications to account for the phonetic form of morphemes; a phoneme, written in slashes, such as /p/ (Harms, 1968, 1, 2); a bundle of distinctive features (Postal, 1968a, 110); one of the segments of the input to the phonological component, earlier called **Morphophoneme** (Postal, 1968a, xi-xii, 14). The number of features in various lexical instances of the same phoneme may differ according to their environments, as in: /pin/ (aspirated) vs. /spin/ (aspiration not specified). (Harms, 1968, 2.) See also SYSTEMATIC PHONEMICS.

Systematic phonemics. *G–2.* The level of representation of a string in terms of segments and junctures, with the derived constituent structure still marked—it is 'systematic,' that is, the choice of elements at this level is determined by both the syntactic and the phonological components (Chomsky, 1964, 87); the binary phonemic level of distinctive features at which nondistinctive features have not yet been specified by redundancy rules (Harms, 1968, 17–18); the deep phonological structure representation which underlies a phonetic surface form (King, 1969, 126); an approach to phonology which recognizes only one significant level above the phonetic level: the systematic phonemic level, which is a labeled bracketing—approximately a morphophonemic representation (Postal, 1968a, xi-xii); the theory which assumes that the input to the phonological component consists exactly of the output of the syntactic rules (Postal, 1968a, xii); the theory that a sentence has two types of phonological structure, viz., a systematic phonemic representation—which is a labeled bracketing of a string of systematic phonemes and boundaries: the output of the syntactic component—and a universal phonetic representation—which are instructions for speech production: the output of the phonological component—plus a set of rules which convert the former into the latter through various intermediate representations; the theory which reconstructs the natural relation between phonological and phonetic structures embodied in the naturalness condition (Postal, 1968a, 34, 56, 58). The theory of systematic phonemics demands that a dictionary entry consist of some kind of morphophonemic representation of unpredictable aspects of pronunciation of that morpheme. (Postal, 1968a, 162–163.) Compare SYSTEMATIC PHONETICS. See also SYSTEMATIC PHONOLOGY.

Systematic phonetics. *G–2.* The level of representation of the output of the phonological component, in terms of phones and phonetic junctures (Chomsky, 1964, 87); the level of the phonetic output of the phonological component, as opposed to the systematic phonemic level of representation of morphemes, which constitutes the input to this component. On the systematic phonetic level, utterances are represented as sequences of fully specified feature matrices, or phones, and syllable boundaries. (Harms, 1968, 14). The systematic phonetic representation does not consist of actual perceptual cues but of abstract matrices of specifications for universal phonetic features of phonetic segments. (Postal, 1968a, 58–59.) Compare SYSTEMATIC PHONEMICS. See also SYSTEMATIC PHONOLOGY.

Systematic phonology. *G–2.* The component of a systematic grammar which provides a systematic phonemic and phonetic representation for each sentence that is generated, along with many intermediate representations according to the number of ordered rules which apply. (Postal, 1968a, 215–216.) See also SYSTEMATIC PHONEMICS, SYSTEMATIC PHONETICS, SYSTEMATIC PHONEME.

System, complement. See COMPLEMENT SYSTEM.

System, feature. See FEATURE SYSTEM.

System, marker. See MARKER SYSTEM.

System, motivated. See MOTIVATED SYSTEM.

System, object complement. See OBJECT COMPLEMENT SYSTEM.

System, predicate complement. See PREDICATE COMPLEMENT SYSTEM.

T

Tag question. *G–2.* A sentence which derives from the postposing of the initial interrogative marker of an underlying simple (yes-no) question and the inclusion of that marker in a duplicate 'tag' sentence which is negative if the main sentence is affirmative, and affirmative if the main sentence is negative, as in: "Wh-Tom fell overboard" ⇒ "Tom fell overboard, Wh-Aux-Neg-Pro" ("Tom fell overboard, *didn't he?*"); "Wh-Tom didn't fall overboard" ⇒ "Tom didn't fall overboard, Wh-Aux-Pro" ("Tom didn't fall overboard, *did he?*"). (Klima, 1964a, 319.) See also QUESTION.

Taxonomic linguistics. See STRUCTURAL LINGUISTICS.

Telescoped progressive. *G–2.* The progressive morpheme *ing*—as opposed to the complementizing morpheme *ing*—when deleted from the verb to which it was affixed. For example, *ing* is a telescoped progressive in "Huck felt the raft move" (from "Huck felt the raft mov*ing*"). (Rosenbaum, 1967a, 28, 118.) See also PROGRESSIVE ASPECT.

Tense. *G–1.* The obligatory element C in the auxiliary, which can be developed as one of the morphemes: -S in the context NP_{sing}___, Ø in the context NP_{pl}___, or Past in any context (Chomsky, 1957, 39); the obligatory morpheme {tn}, which can be rewritten as either {Pres} (simple present) or {Pas} (simple past) (Thomas, 1965, 128–131). *G–2.* One of the syntactic features of the AUX node of S in the deep structure: [+present] (syntactic present) or [−present] (syntactic past). If the AUX is not realized as a copula or perfect form, the tense feature is copied on the verbal by verbal agreement transformation. (Jacobs and Rosenbaum, 1968, 132–133.) *G–2S.* An abstract two-place predicate which occurs in every sentence type. One argument is a time expression, or time adverbial, and the other is a sentence, as in:

Considering the tense constituent to be a predicate accounts for the relationship between verb tense and time adverbs. (Langendoen, 1969, 121–122.) See also PRESENT TENSE, PAST TENSE. *G–1–2.* The phonological distinctive feature which is positively specified for sounds, both consonants and vowels, that are articulated with deliberate prolonged muscular effort above the glottis, as opposed to **Nontense** or **Lax** sounds, which are articulated more rapidly and with less muscular effort. 'Tense' vowels are markedly longer than nontense vowels and deviate more from the neutral position. (Chomsky and Halle, 1968, 324–325.) See also LENGTH.

Tense affix. *G–1.* The finite verb affix 'present' or 'past.' Also called the **Verbal affix.** (Lees, 1960a, 19.) See also TENSE.

Tense, past. See PAST TENSE.

Tense, present. See PRESENT TENSE.

Tense, syntactic. See SYNTACTIC TENSE.

Terminal string. *G–1.* The string of morphemes which make up the last line of a terminated derivation (Chomsky, 1957, 30, 46); a string of terminal, irreplaceable symbols produced by the phrase structure rules (Halle, 1959, R&S, 49–52). *G–2.* The last line of the last of the sequential derivations generated by the rewriting rules of the base, consisting of a string of lexical and grammatical formatives. (Chomsky, 1965, 67–68.) Also called **Kernel string, C-terminal string, Basic string, Basis.** Compare T-TERMINAL STRING. See also STRING.

Test, cleft sentence. See CLEFT SENTENCE TEST.

Test, pair. See PAIR TEST.

Test, passive. See PASSIVE TEST.

Test, substitution. See SUBSTITUTION TEST.

Test, time-place. See TIME-PLACE TEST.

T-grammar. See TRANSFORMATIONAL GRAMMAR.

T-grammarian. *G–2.* A transformational grammarian. (Lees, 1964b, xxxiii.) See also GRAMMARIAN.

'That'-clause. *G–1.* A nominalization of the type "that Tom was alive," as in the sentence *"That Tom was alive* was a miracle" or "Huck knew *that Tom was alive"* or "Aunt Polly was glad *that Tom was alive."* (Lees, 1960a, 58.) Also called **'That' phrase.** See also NOMINALIZATION.

'That' complementizer. *G–2.* The complementizing morpheme *that,* which occurs alone as a complementizer of sentences embedded in noun phrases, as in: "Huck knew (it) *that* Tom was lost," which is an example of object complementation. (Rosenbaum, 1967a, 24, 26–27; Rosenbaum, 1967b, ix.) See also 'THAT'-CLAUSE, 'THAT' PHRASE.

'That'-deletion transformation. *G–2.* The transformation which deletes the clause-introducer *that* from an extraposed 'that'-clause, as when: "It *that Tom had escaped* seemed impossible" ⇒ "It seemed impossible *that Tom had escaped"* ⇒ "It seemed impossible *Tom had escaped."* (Langendoen, 1969, 63–64.) Also called **Optional complementizer deletion transformation.** (Rosenbaum, 1967a, 38–39). Compare 'THAT' INSERTION.

'That' insertion. *G–2S.* The rule which optionally inserts *that* before a sentence which is embedded in an object noun phrase, as shown in: "Huck realized *Tom was in trouble"* ⇒ "Huck realized *that Tom was in trouble."* *That* is a 'sentence trapping,' representing nothing in the conceptual structure. (Langacker, 1968, 126.) Compare 'THAT'-DELETION TRANSFORMATION.

'That' phrase. *G–2.* A noun phrase complement with a *that* complementizer, as in: "Huck thought *that Tom was dead."* (Rosenbaum, 1967a, 12.) Also called **'That'-clause.**

Theory, formal. See FORMAL THEORY.

Theory, grammatical. See GRAMMATICAL THEORY.

Theory, linguistic. See LINGUISTIC THEORY.

Theory of sentencehood. See SENTENCEHOOD.

Theory, semantic. See SEMANTIC THEORY.

Theory, syntactic. See SYNTACTIC THEORY.

Theory, universal phonetic. See UNIVERSAL PHONETIC THEORY.

'There,' introductory. See INTRODUCTORY 'THERE.'

Three-grammatical. *G–1.* The degree of grammaticalness of a semi-sentence, which contains an ill-formed word, or phrase, category relation and is theoretically, but not always actually, incomprehensible to a fluent speaker, as in: "Catches fish Huck?" (Katz, 1964b, 406.) Compare ONE-GRAMMATICAL, TWO-GRAMMATICAL.

Three-place predicate. *G–2S.* A predicate—that is, an adjective or verb or noun—which has three arguments, or noun phrases, one of which must contain an embedded sentence: S → P+NP+NP+NP(-S), *"used by-Huck with-rope to-bind-by-Huck-the-logs"* (i.e., "Huck used rope to bind the logs"). (Langendoen, 1969, 97, 106.) Compare ONE-PLACE PREDICATE, TWO-PLACE PREDICATE.

Time adverbial. *G–2.* A temporal phrase dominated by the optional ADV category in a derivation, as in:

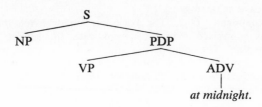

(Rosenbaum, 1967a, 21.) See also ADVERBIAL.

Time-place deletion transformation. *G–2.* The transformation which operates on the noun phrases *at the time when* and *at the place where,* deleting all but *when* and *where,* as when: "Tom arrived *at the time when* the family was grieving" ⇒ "Tom arrived *when* the family was grieving"; "Huck left the raft *at the place where* he found it" ⇒ "Huck left the raft *where* he found it." (Jacobs and Rosenbaum, 1968, 208–209.) See also TIME ADVERBIAL, PLACE ADVERBIAL.

Time-place test. *G–2.* The test for determining whether a clause is an adverbial clause. The test is: if a string can be shifted to the front of the sentence by adverb preposing transformation, it is an adverbial clause, as is the case in: "Tom slept *while Huck stood watch*" ⇒ *"While Huck stood watch,* Tom slept." (Jacobs and Rosenbaum, 1968, 209–210.) See also ADVERB PREPOSING TRANSFORMATION.

T-marker. See TRANSFORMATION MARKER.

To-be deletion transformation. *G–2.* The transformation which deletes *to be* from the infinitive complement of certain verbs, such as *seem,* as when: "Huck seemed *to be* tired" ⇒ "Huck seemed tired." (Langendoen, 1969, 62.)

'To' deletion transformation. *G–2.* The transformation which optionally or obligatorily deletes the *to* complementizing morpheme in certain instances of transitive verb phrase complementation, as in: "Tom helped Huck *(to)* build the raft"; "Huck let Tom *(to)* do the cooking." (Rosenbaum, 1967a, 97.) Compare 'TO' INSERTION.

'To' insertion. *G–2.* The rule which replaces the tense morpheme of a subordinate clause with *to,* which is a semantically empty morpheme, or sentence trapping, as when: "Huck wanted (Tom *Tense* steer)" ⇒ "Huck wanted Tom *to* steer." Not every verb permits 'to' insertion. (Langacker, 1968, 126–127.) Compare 'TO' DELETION TRANSFORMATION.

Topicalization. *G–2.* The use of topic-comment, rather than subject-predicate, constructions by the child, as in: *"The doggy—he likes me."* Here a noun phrase topic is followed by a predication as comment. The child who is acquiring language first produces sentences without subjects (S →

VP), then produces topic-comment constructions (S → NP+S′), then produces adult-type sentences (S → NP+VP). (Gruber, 1967, 447.) *G–2S.* The selection of a surface subject, or topic, for a sentence from among particular case categories. This is the process for bringing into focus, as topic, one particular constituent of a sentence. **Subjectivalization,** another term for 'topicalization,' consists of primary topicalization—establishment of position and number concord—and secondary topicalization—stress assignment, cleft sentence construction, late word-order changes. (Fillmore, 1968, 52, 57.) Also called **Subjectivization.** See also TOPIC AND COMMENT, CASE GRAMMAR.

Topic and comment. *G–2.* The basic grammatical relation of surface structure, as contrasted with subject-predicate, the fundamental relation of deep structure. The topic-of the sentence is the leftmost noun phrase immediately dominated by S; the comment-of the sentence is the rest of the surface structure string. (Chomsky, 1965, 221.) Also called **Topic-comment.** (Gruber, 1967, 447.) See also TOPICALIZATION, SUBJECTIVALIZATION.

Topic-comment. See TOPIC AND COMMENT.

Traditional grammar. Not a technical term of transformational grammar, but frequently used, often with favorable connotation, to refer to: 1) inexplicit generative grammar, containing vague rules, gaps, and a reliance on the intuition of the reader (Chomsky, 1964, 78); 2) a descriptive methodology which assumed an abstract logical structure for sentences and sought to discover the grammatical constituents of these sentences on the basis of intuitive judgments about the logical constituents (subject, verb, etc.): a matter of observation and description rather than explanation and justification—an art rather than a formal system (Rosenbaum, 1967a, 109, 110, 113). The major goal of all traditional grammars was to tell the reader how to construct sentences correctly according to a set of explicit recipes. (Lees, 1960b, 148.) Traditional grammars relied on the intelligence and linguistic intuitions of the reader to provide the structural descriptions of items not in the collection. (Chomsky, 1961b, 176.) Though the goals of traditional grammar where high, to account for competence, traditional grammars were handicapped by not being explicit and by employing vague semantic notions. (Lees, 1964a, 137–138.) Traditional grammars did not actually formulate the rules of the grammar, but rather appealed to the intelligence of the reader to determine the grammar on the basis of hints and examples. (Chomsky, 1966a, 11.) The insights of traditional grammar were not too far from the current views—viz., speech and writing are intimately related, language can be equated with logic, any language can be forced into the Latin mold, etc. (Langacker, 1968, 8–9.) Compare STRUCTURAL LINGUISTICS, GENERATIVE GRAMMAR, TRANSFORMATIONAL GRAMMAR.

Traffic rule. *G–1.* One of the rules that order the procedures in a derivation: a traffic direction; a control unit in a grammar which directs the order of application of rules, permitting both single recursions and loops. (Lees, 1960a, 1, 55, 112.) *G–2.* One of the systematized rules which restrict the number and kind of violations by transfer rules, in order to prevent semi-sentences from becoming so ill-formed that they are totally unintelligible. (Katz, 1964b, 414.) Compare TRANSFER RULE. See also EPI-RULE, SEMI-SENTENCE.

Transcription, phonetic. See PHONETIC TRANSCRIPTION.

Transfer rule. *G–2.* One of the system of rules which transfer the meanings of a comprehension set of sentences to the semi-derivation of a semi-sentence, telling how the corresponding grammatical rule—the phrase structure rule or transformation—can be violated without generating a nonsense string. There is at least one 'transfer rule' for each rule of the grammar. (Katz, 1964b, 412.) Compare TRAFFIC RULE. See also COM-PREHENSION SET, SEMI-SENTENCE, SEMI-DERIVATION.

Transform. *G–1–2a.* To convert a sentence with a given constituent structure into a sentence with a derived constituent structure (Chomsky, 1956, 149); for a sentence to change its structure—for example, for an action verb to 'transform' into an action nominal using *of* (Lees, 1960a, 8). See also CONVERT, MAP. *G–1–2b.* A derived constituent structure, as opposed to a kernel—basic or simple—sentence structure; the structure which results from the application of a transformation. (Chomsky, 1956, 149, 150.) *Related terms:* A **Transformation** is a rule which transforms underlying structures into derived structures, or transforms. (Chomsky, 1956, 149.) A grammar which utilizes transformations is called a **Transformational grammar** (Lees, 1963, xxviii) or a **Transformation grammar** (Lees, 1964a, 150). A grammar which supplies structural descriptions to its grammatical outputs is a **Generative-transformational grammar** (Langendoen, 1969, 24) or a **Transformational generative grammar** (Chomsky, 1966a, 7). A linguist who investigates transformational grammar is sometimes called a **Transformational grammarian,** or **T-Grammarian** (Lees, 1964b, xxxiii), or a **Transformationalist** (Thomas, 1965, 4, 163). See also TRANSFORMATION, TRANSFORMATIONAL GRAMMAR.

Transformation. *G–1.* An optional or obligatory rule which effects a simple or generalized structural change on a structural description, potentially also changing the meaning. (Chomsky, 1957, 44.) *G–2.* An obligatory rule which effects a single structural change in a phrase-marker, other than embedding and conjunction, without changing its meaning. (Chomsky, 1965, 142–143.) Transformational rules of the phonological component are 'local' transformations. (Chomsky, 1965, 89.) *G–2S.* A rule, or set of rules, which converts a semantic deep structure into a syntactic surface structure, potentially also changing the meaning. (Fillmore, 1968, 48–49.) See also TRANSFORMATIONAL RULE, GRAMMATICAL TRANSFORMATION, LOCAL TRANSFORMATION. Compare PHRASE STRUCTURE RULE, REWRITING RULE.

Transformation, accusative. See ACCUSATIVE TRANSFORMATION.

Transformation, adjective. See ADJECTIVE TRANSFORMATION.

Transformation, adverb preposing. See ADVERB PREPOSING TRANSFORMA-TION.

Transformation, affirmation. See AFFIRMATION TRANSFORMATION.

Transformation, affix. See AUXILIARY TRANSFORMATION.

Transformation, agreement. See AGREEMENT TRANSFORMATION.

Transformational ambiguity. *G–1.* Ambiguity which arises from two distinct transformational origins for a sentence: structural ambiguity; constructional homonymity on the transformational level, as in "Flying planes can be dangerous." It is possible that all cases of constructional homonymity occur on the transformational level rather than on the phrase structure level. (Chomsky, 1957, 87.) See also AMBIGUITY, CONSTRUCTIONAL HOMONYMITY.

Transformational apparatus. See TRANSFORMATIONAL MACHINERY.

Transformational cycle. *G–2a.* The cyclic application of phonological rules in determining the phonetic form of a syntactic string of phonemes according to the composition specified by the derived phrase-marker (Chomsky, 1964, 54); the general principle which governs the application of the rules of the phonological component to a labeled bracketing of the surface structure of a sentence. The rules first apply, in order, to strings containing no brackets, then erase the bracketing of those strings, then apply in order to the larger strings containing no brackets, etc., until the entire string has been given a phonological interpretation. (Chomsky and Halle, 1968, 15.) *G–2b.* The cyclic application of phrase structure rules, which return to the first rule in the sequence whenever a new occurrence of S is encountered, and then run through the entire sequence of rules again; the cyclic application of transformations, which apply first to the most deeply embedded S structure, then reapply to the next most deeply embedded S structure, etc., until the transformations apply to the initial S (Katz, 1966, 146–147); the application of transformational rules to underlying structures as a whole (precyclic rules), or within the cycle (cyclic rules), or after the cycle (postcyclic rules) (Ross, 1967, 190). See also CYCLE, ITERATIVE CYCLE, PHONOLOGICAL RULE.

Transformational generative grammar. *G–1–2.* An explicit, formalized, generative grammar—a transformational grammar—as opposed to a traditional grammar, which is generative but neither formal nor explicit (i.e., is not transformational). (Chomsky, 1966a, 7—the only occurrence in the corpus.) See also TRANSFORMATIONAL GRAMMAR, GENERATIVE GRAMMAR, GENERATIVE-TRANSFORMATIONAL GRAMMAR.

Transformational grammar. *G–1a.* A set of rules that can be adjoined to the phrase structure grammar; a grammar of transformations. (Chomsky, 1956, 149; Lees, 1963, xxviii.) *G–1b.* A generative grammar which contains a grammar of transformational rules (Lees, 1963, xxviii); a grammar consisting of a finite sequence of context-restricted rewrite rules and a finite set of transformations (Chomsky, 1961a, 136); a T-grammar: a grammar that describes how the sentences of a language are put together (Lees, 1964b, xxix). *G–2a.* A theory of sentencehood: a transformation grammar (Lees, 1964a, 150); a general, language-independent theory (TG) which characterizes linguistic universals such as the form of grammatical rules in all languages (Postal, 1964a, 98). *G–2b.* A characterization of linguistic competence, consisting of a set of ordered rules which recursively specify the sentences of the language; a system which reveals the regularities underlying a given natural language. (Rosenbaum, 1965, 474, 477.) See also GENERATIVE GRAMMAR, GENERATIVE-TRANSFORMATIONAL GRAMMAR, TRANSFORMATIONAL GENERATIVE GRAMMAR. Compare TRADITIONAL GRAMMAR, STRUCTURAL LINGUISTICS.

Transformational grammar, first-generation. See FIRST-GENERATION TRANSFORMATIONAL GRAMMAR.

Transformational grammar, generative-. See GENERATIVE-TRANSFORMATIONAL GRAMMAR.

Transformational grammar, nongenerative. See NONGENERATIVE TRANSFORMATIONAL GRAMMAR.

Transformational grammar, second-generation. See SECOND-GENERATION TRANSFORMATIONAL GRAMMAR.

Transformational grammar, semantic-based. See SEMANTIC-BASED TRANSFORMATIONAL GRAMMAR.

Transformational history. *G–1.* A representation on the transformational level (Chomsky, 1957, 91); a description of the order and result of the application of transformations in the derivation of a sentence (Koutsoudas, 1966, 28); a transformation-marker (Chomsky, 1964, 54). Also: **T-history.** (Lees, 1964b, xxxix.) See also TRANSFORMATION-MARKER.

Transformationalist. *G–1.* One of a group of linguists who are primarily concerned with describing a general theory of grammar which will specify the possible form of a grammar, the method for evaluating grammars, and the grammar of any given language. (Thomas, 1965, 4, 163.) Also called **T-grammarian.**

Transformational machinery. *G–2.* The transformations, orderings, cycles, and other derivational apparatus necessary for the generation of sentences in a particular linguistic system. Also called **Transformational apparatus.** (Rosenbaum, 1967a, 61, 88, 93, 101.) See also TRANSFORMATIONAL SUB-COMPONENT.

Transformational morphology. See MORPHOLOGY.

Transformational power. *G–2.* The ability of a transformation to map an underlying structure onto a new derived structure—a power possessed by no other type of rule in the syntax. (Rosenbaum, 1967a, 25.) See also TRANSFORMATION.

Transformational rule. *G–1.* A simple transformation or a generalized transformation (Chomsky, 1957, 114); a rule which effects a structural change in a structural description (Chomsky, 1962, 222); an optional or obligatory rule—a T-rule—which converts an underlying phrase-marker into a derived phrase-marker (Koutsoudas, 1966, 23). Transformational rules always rewrite full sentences, even if the rule affects only a single constituent in the sentence. (Lees, 1960a, 32.) *G–2.* One of a set of rules, usually called 'transformations,' which perform the singulary operations necessary to map deep structures into surface structures, but not to convert one sentence into another or to embed one sentence within another or to conjoin two sentences (Rosenbaum, 1965, 475); a rule of the syntactic component which interprets an object provided by the phrase structure rules, marks it as well-formed or ill-formed, and maps the well-formed underlying structure onto a new, derived structure; a rule with transformational power; a filter (Rosenbaum, 1967a, 1, 25). See also TRANSFORMATION, GRAMMATICAL TRANSFORMATION.

Transformational subcomponent. *G–1.* The component within the syntactic component of a transformational grammar, aside from the constituent structure subcomponent, which consists of a partially ordered set of optional and obligatory operations known as 'grammatical transformations.' (Chomsky, 1964, 54.) *G–2.* The component within the syntactic component of a generative grammar, aside from the base component, which is responsible for generating the surface structure of a sentence from its base, or basis. (Chomsky, 1965, 17.) See also TRANSFORMATIONAL GRAMMAR, SYNTACTIC COMPONENT.

Transformation, article. See ARTICLE TRANSFORMATION.

Transformation, attachment. See ATTACHMENT TRANSFORMATION.

Transformation, auxiliary. See AUXILIARY TRANSFORMATION.

Transformation, auxiliary incorporation. See AUXILIARY INCORPORATION TRANSFORMATION.

Transformation, case. See ACCUSATIVE TRANSFORMATION.

Transformation, causative. See CAUSATIVE TRANSFORMATION.

Transformation, cleft. See CLEFT SENTENCE TRANSFORMATION.

Transformation, cleft sentence. See CLEFT SENTENCE TRANSFORMATION.

Transformation, collapsing. See COLLAPSING TRANSFORMATION.

Transformation, comparative. See COMPARATIVE TRANSFORMATION.

Transformation, complementation. See COMPLEMENT.

Transformation, complementizer deletion. See COMPLEMENTIZER.

Transformation, complementizer placement. See COMPLEMENTIZER PLACE-
MENT TRANSFORMATION.

Transformation, complex. See GENERALIZED TRANSFORMATION.

Transformation, compounding. See COMPOUND.

Transformation, conjunction. See CONJUNCTION.

Transformation, conjunction reduction. See CONJUNCTION REDUCTION
TRANSFORMATION.

Transformation, copula. See COPULA.

Transformation, double-base. See GENERALIZED TRANSFORMATION.

Transformation, elementary. See ELEMENTARY TRANSFORMATION.

Transformation, elliptic. See ELLIPTIC TRANSFORMATION.

Transformation, elliptical. See ELLIPTICAL TRANSFORMATION.

Transformation, emphasis. See AFFIRMATION TRANSFORMATION.

Transformation, erasure. See ERASURE PRINCIPLE.

Transformation, extraposition. See EXTRAPOSITION TRANSFORMATION.

Transformation, filter. See FILTERING.

Transformation, flip-flop. See AUXILIARY TRANSFORMATION.

Transformation, generalized. See GENERALIZED TRANSFORMATION.

Transformation, genitive. See GENITIVE TRANSFORMATION.

Transformation grammar. See TRANSFORMATIONAL GRAMMAR.

Transformation, grammatical. See GRAMMATICAL TRANSFORMATION.

Transformation, identity erasure. See IDENTITY ERASURE TRANSFORMATION.

Transformation, imperative. See IMPERATIVE.

Transformation, indefinite pronoun deletion. See INDEFINITE PRONOUN
DELETION TRANSFORMATION.

Transformation, indirect object inversion. See INDIRECT OBJECT.

Transformation, infinitival clause separation. See INFINITIVAL CLAUSE
SEPARATION TRANSFORMATION.

Transformation, interrogative. See QUESTION.

Transformation, 'it' deletion. See 'IT' DELETION TRANSFORMATION.

Transformation, 'it' replacement. See 'IT' REPLACEMENT TRANSFORMATION.

Transformation, local. See LOCAL TRANSFORMATION.

Transformation, manner adverbial. See MANNER ADVERBIAL.

Transformation-marker. *G–1.* A specification of the elementary operations
to be performed by the transformational rules (Lees, 1960a, 31); the
formal representation of the transformations which have been applied in
the derivation of a string of formatives: a transformational marker or T-
marker (Katz and Postal, 1964, 6); the transformational history of a sentence: the T marker (Bach, 1964, 82); the system of transformations
that apply in the course of a derivation (Chomsky, 1966a, 52–53). Any
transformational derivation can be represented as a T-marker: the full
transformational history of a derived sentence. (Chomsky, 1966a, 54).
G–2. The deep structure of a sentence (Chomsky, 1966a, 55); the transformational history of the derivation of a sentence from its basis; an
informal representation of the transformational structure of an utterance,
which can be represented formally as a set of base phrase-markers and

transformations (Chomsky, 1965, 130–135). With the introduction of S into the right-hand side of the base rules, the notion of 'transformation-marker' disappears. (Chomsky, 1965, 130–135.) See also TRANSFORMATIONAL HISTORY. Compare PHRASE-MARKER.

Transformation, negative. See NEGATIVE.

Transformation, negative adjunction. See NEGATIVE ADJUNCTION TRANSFORMATION.

Transformation, negative placement. See NEGATIVE PLACEMENT TRANSFORMATION.

Transformation, nominalization. See NOMINALIZATION TRANSFORMATION.

Transformation, nominalizing. See NOMINALIZING TRANSFORMATION.

Transformation, nonrestrictive clause. See NONRESTRICTIVE CLAUSE.

Transformation, noun segment deletion. See NOUN SEGMENT DELETION TRANSFORMATION.

Transformation, noun suffix. See NOUN SUFFIX TRANSFORMATION.

Transformation, NPN. See NPN TRANSFORMATION.

Transformation, number. See NUMBER TRANSFORMATION.

Transformation, obligatory. See OBLIGATORY TRANSFORMATION.

Transformation, obligatory complementizer deletion. See OBLIGATORY COMPLEMENTIZER DELETION TRANSFORMATION.

Transformation, optional. See OPTIONAL TRANSFORMATION.

Transformation, optional complementizer deletion. See OPTIONAL COMPLEMENTIZER DELETION TRANSFORMATION.

Transformation, particle inversion. See PARTICLE INVERSION TRANSFORMATION.

Transformation, particle movement. See PARTICLE MOVEMENT TRANSFORMATION.

Transformation, particle segment. See PARTICLE SEGMENT TRANSFORMATION.

Transformation, passive. See PASSIVE TRANSFORMATION.

Transformation, preposing. See PREPOSING TRANSFORMATION.

Transformation, preposition deletion. See PREPOSITION DELETION TRANSFORMATION.

Transformation, progressive segment. See PROGRESSIVE SEGMENT TRANSFORMATION.

Transformation, pronoun. See PRONOUN TRANSFORMATION.

Transformation, pronoun deletion. See PRONOUN DELETION TRANSFORMATION.

Transformation, pronoun replacement. See PRONOUN REPLACEMENT TRANSFORMATION.

Transformation, pseudocleft. See PSEUDOCLEFT TRANSFORMATION.

Transformation, pseudocleft sentence. See PSEUDOCLEFT TRANSFORMATION.

Transformation, pseudopassive. See PSEUDOPASSIVE.

Transformation, question deletion. See QUESTION DELETION TRANSFORMATION.

Transformation, reflexive. See REFLEXIVE TRANSFORMATION.

Transformation, reflexivization. See REFLEXIVIZATION TRANSFORMATION.

Transformation, relative. See RELATIVE CLAUSE.

Transformation, relative 'be' deletion. See RELATIVE 'BE' DELETION TRANSFORMATION.

Transformation, relative pronoun deletion. See RELATIVE PRONOUN DELETION TRANSFORMATION.

Transformation, relative pronoun formation. See RELATIVE PRONOUN FORMATION TRANSFORMATION.

Transformation, 'respectively'. See 'RESPECTIVELY' TRANSFORMATION.

Transformation, second passive. See SECOND PASSIVE.

Transformation, segment. See SEGMENT TRANSFORMATION.

Transformation, separation. See SEPARATION TRANSFORMATION.

Transformations, family of. See FAMILY OF TRANSFORMATIONS.

Transformation, simple. See SINGULARY TRANSFORMATION.

Transformation, simplex. See SINGULARY TRANSFORMATION.

Transformation, single-base. See SINGULARY TRANSFORMATION.

Transformation, singulary. See SINGULARY TRANSFORMATION.

Transformation, 'so'. See 'SO' TRANSFORMATION.

Transformation, stylistic. See INVERSION.

Transformation, subjectivalization. See SUBJECTIVALIZATION.

Transformation, subject-object inversion. See SUBJECT-OBJECT INVERSION TRANSFORMATION.

Transformation, substantivization. See SUBSTANTIVIZATION TRANSFORMATION.

Transformation, substitution. See SUBSTITUTION TRANSFORMATION.

Transformation, 'that'-deletion. See 'THAT'-DELETION TRANSFORMATION.

Transformation, time-place deletion. See TIME-PLACE DELETION TRANSFORMATION.

Transformation, to-be-deletion. See TO-BE-DELETION TRANSFORMATION.

Transformation, 'to' deletion. See 'TO' DELETION TRANSFORMATION.

Transformation, two-case. See TWO-CASE TRANSFORMATION.

Transformation, two-string. See GENERALIZED TRANSFORMATION.

Transformation, verb suffix. See VERB SUFFIX TRANSFORMATION.

Transformation, Wh-question. See QUESTION.

Transitive. See TRANSITIVE VERBAL.

Transitive adjective. *G–2*. A verbal marked [+VB], [−V] which can be followed by a noun phrase or embedded sentence, as in: "Huck was *tired* of running away"; "Tom was *able* to stay awake." (Jacobs and Rosenbaum, 1968, 65.) Compare INTRANSITIVE ADJECTIVE. See also TRANSITIVE VERBAL.

Transitive oblique complement. See TRANSITIVE OBLIQUE COMPLEMENTATION.

Transitive oblique complementation. *G–2*. The embedding of a sentence as a complement of a noun phrase object of a prepositional phrase, which in turn is the complement of a noun phrase direct object:

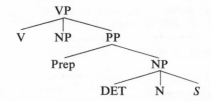

"(Tom) convinced Huck of the fact *that Jim was free.*" A 'transitive oblique complement' cannot become the surface subject of a passive construction, and it cannot be the subject of a pseudocleft construction.

(Rosenbaum, 1967c, 322). Also called **Transitive oblique noun phrase complementation.** (Rosenbaum, 1967a, 4, 87.) See also OBLIQUE NOUN PHRASE COMPLEMENTATION.

Transitive verb. *G–1.* A verb, other than *be,* which is followed by a noun phrase in a string that can undergo the passive transformation (Chomsky, 1957, 42–43); one of the three primary types of verbs (not *be*): transitive (V_t+NP), intransitive (V_i____), and copulative (V_c+Comp) (Thomas, 1965, 33–34). *G–2.* A lexical item which is marked [+V] and [+____NP] in the lexicon and is therefore permitted to accept manner adverbs freely and to participate in the passive transformation (Chomsky, 1965, 107–109); a verb that can appear in the position ____NP in a verb phrase because it is marked [+transitive] (a contextual, or strict subcategorization, feature) (Chomsky, 1966a, 72); a lexical item, possibly *be,* marked [+V], in a transitive verbal, which is one which requires an object noun phrase in the deep structure (Jacobs and Rosenbaum, 1968, 200). *G–2S.* A verb which is a member of a two-place or three-place predicate in the deep semantic structure and can occur with a following noun phrase object in the surface syntactic structure. (Langendoen, 1969, 25–26, 97.) Compare INTRANSITIVE VERB. See also VERB, VERBAL, TRANSITIVE VERBAL.

Transitive verbal. *G–2.* A verbal, [+VB], either a verb or an adjective, which requires a following noun phrase, as in: "Tom *built* a raft"; "Huck *was* a drop-out"; "Jim was *kind* to the boys." (Jacobs and Rosenbaum, 1968, 65, 113.) Compare INTRANSITIVE VERBAL. See also VERBAL, TRANSITIVE VERB, TRANSITIVE ADJECTIVE.

Transitive verb phrase complementation. *G–2.* The embedding of an infinitivalized sentence in a verb phrase as a complement of a noun phrase direct object: VP → V+NP+*S,* as in: "Tom convinced Huck *to release Jim.*" (Rosenbaum, 1967c, 322–323; Roesnbaum, 1967a, 2, 95–97.) Compare INTRANSITIVE VERB PHRASE COMPLEMENTATION.

Transitive, verb-preposition. See VERB-PREPOSITION TRANSITIVE.

Transparency. *G–2.* The property that is assigned, by special rule, to the category NP when that category dominates a proposition that does not have the internal structure of a noun phrase. The property of 'transparency' permits a noun phrase to be extracted from within the 'transparent' noun phrase, even though this is a violation of the A-over-A principle. The larger noun phrase is said to be 'transparent' to the extraction operation, as when: "Tom thought (Huck had tied up *the raft*)" ⇒ "*What* did Tom think (Huck had tied up)?" (Chomsky, 1968, 44–45.) See also A-OVER-A PRINCIPLE.

Transparent. See TRANSPARENCY.

Transportation rule, clause. See CLAUSE TRANSPORTATION RULE.

Trapping, sentence. See SENTENCE TRAPPING.

Tree. *G–1.* A diagrammatic representation of the derivation of a sentence; a parsing, or immediate constituent analysis of a sentence. (Halle, 1959, R&S, 49.) *G–2.* A representation of relationships within a sentence that are intuitively perceived by a native speaker. (Jacobs and Rosenbaum, 1968, 207.) Also called: **Diagram** (Chomsky, 1957, 27), **Branching tree, Branching-diagram** (Lees, 1960b, 150, 151), **Rooted tree, Labeled branching diagram** (Lees, 1964a, 140, 142), **Phrase-marker, Tree-diagram** (Chomsky, 1965, 64, 184), **Labeled tree, Derivational tree, Labeled tree**

diagram (Koutsoudas, 1966, 16), **Constituent structure tree diagram** (Harms, 1968, 3). See also BRANCHING DIAGRAM. Compare LABELED BRACKETING.

Tree, constituent-structure. See TREE.

Tree pruning. *G–2.* Node deletion, which is a metarule, or convention, that deletes or prunes an embedded S node which does not branch or which does not immediately dominate VP and some other constituent (Ross, 1966, 299); a convention which deletes any type of node which, because of a previous transformation, dominates either nothing or a node of the same category, as when:

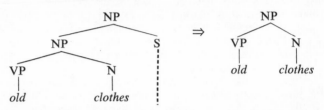

(Jacobs and Rosenbaum, 1968, 205–207). Also called **Node deletion.**

Trigger. *G–2.* To activate a transformation; to cause a transformation to apply. For example, an abstract complementizer 'triggers' the application of a complementation transformation. (Ross, 1967, 197.) See also SENSITIVE TO, DEFINED ON/UPON/OVER.

Trivial. *G–2.* Unrevealing to the theory; insignificant to the analysis; uninteresting to the investigator—obvious, self-evident, superficial (King, 1969, 62); of low-level importance to a system. For example, the assumption that complementizers require a distinctive feature system affects the analysis of predicate complementation only 'trivially,' whether correct or incorrect. (Rosenbaum, 1967a, 27.) Compare INTERESTING.

True consonant. *G–2.* A consonant that is neither a liquid nor a glide (Chomsky, 1965, 168); an obstruent: [+obstruent] or [+consonantal], [−vocalic] (King, 1969, 24). See also CONSONANT, OBSTRUENT.

True diphthong. *G–2.* A vocalic nucleus consisting of a low vowel ([ā] or [ɔ]) followed by a glide ([y] or [w]), such as: [āy], [āw], [ɔy]. (Chomsky and Halle, 1968, 189.) Compare DIPHTHONG.

True possessive. *G–2.* A surface noun phrase of the form *X's Y* or *Y of X* which derives from an underlying sentence of the form *X has Y* by genitive transformation. (Fillmore, 1968, 50.) See also POSSESSIVE, GENITIVE.

Truncation. *G–1.* Optional deletion or reduction. (Klima, 1964a, 268.) See also DELETION, REDUCTION.

Truth value synonymy. See SYNONYMY.

T-terminal string. *G–1.* A transformation-terminal string, which is the string that results from the mapping of one or more phrase-markers of a C-terminal string—a constituent-terminal string—into a derived phrase-marker by the operation of one or more grammatical transformations. (Chomsky, 1964, 54.) Compare C-TERMINAL STRING. See also TERMINAL STRING.

Two-case transformation. *G–2.* A transformation which is sensitive to two different environments in a structural description. For example, the optional complementizer deletion transformation applies either in the case of a POSS-ing complementizer immediately following a verb or adjective, or in the case of a *that* complementizer immediately following a noun phrase following a verb or adjective:

$$X \left\{ \begin{matrix} V \\ ADJ \end{matrix} \right\} \left\{ \begin{matrix} \text{a. } \emptyset \\ \text{b. NP} \end{matrix} \right\} \left\{ \begin{matrix} \text{a. POSS-ing} \\ \text{b. } that \end{matrix} \right\} Y$$

(Rosenbaum, 1967a, 45). See also COLLAPSING TRANSFORMATION.

Two-grammatical. *G–1*. The degree of grammaticalness of a semi-sentence —that is, one which is understandable and has the proper word-category relations but lacks the proper word-subcategory relations, such as: "The raft who enjoyed Tom locates there." (Katz, 1964b, 406.) Compare ONE-GRAMMATICAL, THREE-GRAMMATICAL.

Two-part verb. *G–2*. A transitive verbal which consists of a verb plus a following preposition-like particle that can be moved to the right of the direct object noun phrase by the particle shift rule, or *must* be moved if the object is a pronoun, as in: "Huck *tied down* the canvas" ⇒ "Huck *tied* the canvas *down*." (Langacker, 1968, 118–119.) Also called **Verb-plus-particle construction** (Thomas, 1965, 125–128), **Separable verb** (Lees, 1960a, 11). See also SEPARABLE VERB, SEPARATION TRANSFORMATION, PARTICLE INVERSION TRANSFORMATION, PARTICLE MOVEMENT TRANSFORMATION, PARTICLE. Compare VERB-PREPOSITION TRANSITIVE.

Two-place predicate. *G–2S*. A predicate—that is, an adjective or verb or noun—which has two arguments, or NP's, at least one of which contains an embedded S, as in:

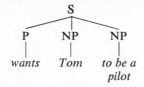

"Tom wants to be a pilot." (Langendoen, 1969, 97.) Compare ONE-PLACE PREDICATE, THREE-PLACE PREDICATE.

Two-string transformation. See GENERALIZED TRANSFORMATION.

Type, sentence. See SENTENCE TYPE.

U

Ultimate constituent. *G–1–2*. A constituent that cannot be rewritten further in a derivation. (Chomsky, 1966a, 17.) See also TERMINAL STRING.

Underlying. See UNDERLYING STRUCTURE.

Underlying object. See UNDERLYING OBJECT NOUN PHRASE.

Underlying object noun phrase. *G–2*. The NP constituent of a VP expanded either as V, *NP* or as V, NP, PP—with PP expanded as Prep,

NP). If the NP of the former case is expanded as DET, N, S, the 'underlying object noun phrase' contains an object noun phrase complement. If the NP of the prepositional phrase in the latter case is expanded as DET, N, S, the underlying object noun phrase contains a 'transitive oblique noun phrase complement,' as in: "Huck doubted (*it*) that Tom would return" and "Huck reminded *Tom* (of) to clean the fish," respectively. (Rosenbaum, 1967a, 4, 33, 87.) Also called **Underlying object.** (Lakoff and Peters, 1966, 124.) See also OBJECT NOUN PHRASE COMPLEMENT, TRANSITIVE OBLIQUE COMPLEMENTATION.

Underlying phrase-marker. *G–2.* The abstract structure, generated by the phrase structure rules and lexical rules, to which transformations will apply to derive the superficial phrase-marker of a sentence. The underlying phrase-marker may contain understood elements—such as *you will* in imperatives—which are lacking in the superficial structure. (Postal, 1964c, 25–27, 29–33, 37.) Also called **Deep structure, Underlying structure.**

Underlying sentence. See SOURCE SENTENCE.

Underlying structure. *G–2.* The sentence structure generated by a set of phrase structure rewriting rules: the base (Rosenbaum, 1967a, 1); the abstract underlying phrase-markers which determine the meaning of a sentence and to which transformations apply to derive a single superficial structure (Postal, 1964c, 22–23, 30–31, 35). Also called **Deep structure.** (Rosenbaum, 1967b, ix.) See also UNDERLYING PHRASE-MARKER. Compare SURFACE STRUCTURE, SUPERFICIAL STRUCTURE, SUPERFICIAL PHRASE-MARKER.

Underlying structure, common. See COMMON UNDERLYING STRUCTURE.

Underlying subject. *G–2.* The subject of the deep structure of a sentence, as opposed to a 'superficial subject,' the subject of the surface structure of a sentence. (Lakoff and Peters, 1966, 124.) Also called **Deep subject.** (Jacobs and Rosenbaum, 1968, 177.) Compare SUPERFICIAL SUBJECT.

Underlying subject noun phrase. *G–2.* The NP in the expansion of S as NP, AUX, PDP. When this NP is expanded as DET, N, S, the underlying subject noun phrase is said to contain a subject noun phrase complement. (Rosenbaum, 1967a, 5, 33, 74.) Also called **Underlying subject, Deep subject.**

Ungrammatical. *G–1–2.* Departing from full grammaticality (Lees, 1960a, 56); violating the rules of English phrase structure (Jacobs and Rosenbaum, 1968, 15); incapable of being assigned a structural description (Langendoen, 1969, 21); incorrectly formed by the grammar; ill-formed; asterisked, as in: *"It was important Tom to do it" (Rosenbaum, 1967a, 14, 37). An ungrammatical sentence requires special treatment for interpretation, such as reference to a particular context. Ungrammatical sentences are not uncommon in use and are not necessarily either unintelligible or bizarre. (Katz, 1966, 133.) Almost all actual utterances are ungrammatical because of repetition, hesitation, interruption, etc. (Fodor and Katz, 1964, 8.) See also UNGRAMMATICALNESS, UNGRAMMATICALITY, GRAMMATICALNESS. Compare GRAMMATICAL.

Ungrammaticality. *G–2.* Ill-formedness of sentences at various stages of generation. A transformational grammar predicts and explains the 'ungrammaticality' of ill-formed sentences and the 'grammaticality' of well-formed sentences. (Rosenbaum, 1967a, 61.) Also called **Ungrammaticalness.** Compare GRAMMATICALITY, GRAMMATICALNESS.

Ungrammaticalness. *G–1–2.* Syntactic ill-formedness, resulting from the wrong derivational history or the wrong transformational history, as opposed to 'semigrammaticalness,' which results from the incorrect choice of subcategories. (Lees, 1964b, xxxviii.) There are several types of ungrammaticalness: **Syntactic ungrammaticalness** (e.g., *"Huck stretched Huck out on the raft"), **Morphological ungrammaticalness** (e.g., *"The boys aggressed against the fish"), and **Semantic ungrammaticalness** (e.g., *"The tail has a fish"). (Kuroda, 1969, 342.) Also called **Ungrammaticality.** Compare GRAMMATICALNESS, SEMIGRAMMATICALNESS.

Unique recoverability. See RECOVERABILITY.

Unit phoneme. *G–2.* A sequence of phones which are interpreted phonologically as a single segment containing secondary features of articulation—such as affrication, aspiration, labialization, etc.—rather than a sequence of segments (e.g., [kʷ] as /k/, which is positively specified for labialization, rather than /kw/). (Harms, 1968, 86.) See also PHONEME.

Universal. See LINGUISTIC UNIVERSAL.

Universal, formal. See FORMAL UNIVERSAL.

Universal grammar. *G–1.* The 'super grammar' which consists of the grammars of all natural languages. (Bach, 1964, 126.) *G–2.* The grammar which determines the universal characteristics of languages, such as grammatical categories, semantic relations, etc. (Katz and Postal, 1964, 159); a theory of the essential properties of language and the nature of the human intellect (Chomsky, 1968, 24); a system of conditions which characterize particular languages and limit the form and organization of their grammars (Chomsky and Halle, 1968, 43); a supplement to particular grammars which describes the underlying regularities that are imposed on all languages (Chomsky, 1965, 6); the principles that govern the conditions which a grammar must meet in order to qualify as a theory of a particular language (Chomsky, 1968, 24). See also LINGUISTIC UNIVERSAL, FORMAL UNIVERSAL, SUBSTANTIVE UNIVERSAL, UNIVERSAL SEMANTICS, UNIVERSAL PHONETIC THEORY. Compare PARTICULAR GRAMMAR.

Universal, language. See LINGUISTIC UNIVERSAL.

Universal, linguistic. See LINGUISTIC UNIVERSAL.

Universal phonetic alphabet. *G–2.* A vocabulary of universal phonetic segments—consonants and vowels—along with a language-independent system for representing them. (Chomsky and Halle, 1968, 28.)

Universal phonetic segment. *G–2.* One of the phonetic elements—a consonant or a vowel—which make up a universal phonetic alphabet. (Chomsky and Halle, 1968, 28.)

Universal phonetic theory. *G–1–2.* The theory which underlies any phonological theory and is implied by a phonological description using articulatory terms. In the phonetic theory of the universal grammar, the phonological rules for all languages are the same. (Bach, 1964, 126.) The theory of universal phonetics is based on Jakobsonian distinctive features. (Chomsky, 1966a, 69.) See also PHONOLOGICAL DISTINCTIVE FEATURE, JAKOBSONIAN DISTINCTIVE FEATURE.

Universal semantics. *G–2.* The undeveloped theory of a language-independent system of semantic representation and the conditions which semantic representations must meet. The prospects for universal semantics seem dim. (Chomsky, 1966a, 13.) See also SEMANTIC BASIS FOR SYNTAX, SEMANTIC DEEP STRUCTURE, SEMANTIC-BASED TRANSFORMATIONAL GRAMMAR.

Universal, substantive. See SUBSTANTIVE UNIVERSAL.

Unpredictable. See PREDICT.

Utterance, novel. See NOVEL UTTERANCE.

V

Vacuous. *G–2*. Empty, without effect. The application of a rule—in a set of rules—is 'vacuous' when its proper environment is not present. (Chomsky and Halle, 1968, 351.) See also VACUOUS APPLICATION. Compare NULL.

Vacuous application. *G–2*. The application of a transformation to a string containing a null environment, possibly resulting in a change in the structure of the string but without change in the constituents or their order. For example, when the extraposition transformation applies to a string containing the null variable Y, it removes the complement sentence from the NP and attaches it to a higher constituent. (Rosenbaum, 1967a, 41–43, 61, 67, 124.) Compare NONAPPLICATION.

Variable. See ALPHA-TYPE VARIABLE, X-TYPE VARIABLE.

Variable, alpha. See ALPHA-TYPE VARIABLE.

Variable, alpha-type. See ALPHA-TYPE VARIABLE.

Variable, greek-letter. See ALPHA-TYPE VARIABLE.

Variable, X-type. See X-TYPE VARIABLE.

Variant, stylistic. See STYLISTIC VARIANT.

Variation, free. See FREE VARIATION.

Verb. *G–1–2*. The obligatory constituent of a verb phrase: VP $\rightarrow$ V+NP (Chomsky, 1957, 111), VP $\rightarrow$ V+{NP, S', Pred} (Chomsky, 1965, 106–107); the obligatory constituent of a main verb: VP $\rightarrow$ AUX+MV, MV $\rightarrow$ V+NP (Bach, 1964, 63); the syntactic category which can be rewritten as a complex symbol in the environment [____NP], [____ADJ], etc. (Chomsky, 1965, 93–94); the [+V] (verb) specification of a verbal: VB $\rightarrow$ [+V] (Jacobs and Rosenbaum, 1968, 57). *G–2S*. The usual replacement for 'predicate': S $\rightarrow$ Pred+NP+NP, Pred $\rightarrow$ V (Langendoen, 1969, 97); the leftmost constituent of a proposition: S $\rightarrow$ modality+proposition, proposition $\rightarrow$ V+case category (Fillmore, 1968, 33). In the lexicon, verbs are classified by frame features according to the propositional environments—the case frames—into which they can be inserted. For example, the frame features for the verb *shut* permit it to be inserted into the case frame [____objective] (e.g., "The door *shut*") or [____objective+agentive] (e.g., "Tom *shut* the door"). (Fillmore, 1968, 26–29.) For subcategorization of the category 'verb', see also: CONTEXT-SENSITIVE SUBCATEGORIZATION RULE, CONTEXTUAL FEATURE, STRICT SUBCATEGORIZATION FEATURE, STRICT SUBCATEGORIZATION RULE, SELECTIONAL FEATURE, SELECTIONAL RESTRICTION, SELECTIONAL RULE, TRANSITIVE VERB, INTRANSITIVE VERB, MIDDLE VERB.

Verb, action. See ACTION VERBAL.

Verb, activity. See ACTIVITY VERB.

Verbal. *G–2*. The single obligatory constituent VB of a verb phrase: VP

→ VB (NP). When the verbal is the only constituent of the verb phrase, it is an **Intransitive verbal**; when it is followed by a noun phrase, it is a **Transitive verbal**. The single category 'verbal' can be either a verb ($[+V]$) or an adjective preceded by *be* ($[-V]$), and these features must be specified for verbals in the lexicon. (Jacobs and Rosenbaum, 1968, 63–65.) Verbs and adjectives are regarded as a single category because of the similarity of their occurrence. That is, members of both classes of items can be transitive (e.g., "That *pleases* me very much"; "That is very *pleasing* to me"), and both can be imperative (e.g., "*Wise* up!"; "Be *wise*!"). (Jacobs, 1968, 21–22.) Also called **Predicate.** (Ross, 1969, 352–353.) See also ACTION VERBAL.

Verbal, action. See ACTION VERBAL.

Verbal affix. See TENSE AFFIX.

Verbal affix, finite. See FINITE VERB.

Verbal auxiliary. *G–1.* One of the verbal elements of the auxiliary. (Lees, 1960a, 4, 6.) See also AUXILIARY.

Verbal, intransitive. See INTRANSITIVE VERBAL.

Verbal marker. *G–2.* An instruction in the lexical entry of a verb or adjective which limits the application of certain transformations to sentences containing that lexical item. (Rosenbaum, 1967a, 72, 104–105.)

Verbal, nonstative. See NONSTATIVE VERBAL.

Verbal sentence. *G–2.* A sentence in which the V constituent is specified as [+verb], rather than as [−verb] (i.e., adjective). (Rosenbaum, 1967a, 101.) See also VERBAL.

Verbal, stative. See STATIVE VERBAL.

Verbal, transitive. See TRANSITIVE VERBAL.

Verb, causative. See CAUSATIVE VERB.

Verb, copula-type. See COPULA-TYPE VERB.

Verb deletion rule. *G–2.* A rule which optionally deletes the last verb in the second conjunct of a conjoined sentence with *too,* provided that that verb is identical to a verb in the first conjunct, as in: "The creek has been rising, and the river has been (*rising*) too." (Langacker, 1968, 121–122.) See also IDENTICAL VERB PHRASE DELETION.

Verb, double-object. See DOUBLE-OBJECT VERB.

Verb, finite. See FINITE VERB.

Verb, intransitive. See INTRANSITIVE VERB.

Verb, irregular. See IRREGULAR VERB.

Verb, main. See MAIN VERB.

Verb, middle. See MIDDLE VERB.

Verb, nonstative. See NONSTATIVE VERBAL.

Verb, parenthetical. See PARENTHETICAL VERB.

Verb particle. *G–2.* A preposition-like word in the surface structure of a sentence which is the reflex of a segment marked [+particle] in the deep structure of the verbal. (Jacobs and Rosenbaum, 1968, 104.) Also called **Particle.**

Verb, performative. See PERFORMATIVE VERB.

Verb phrase. *G–1.* One of the two obligatory constituents of a sentence, the other being a noun phrase: Sentence → $NP+VP$. Verb phrase can be rewritten as $V+NP$ (Chomsky, 1957, 111) or as auxiliary+main verb (i.e., $AUX+MV$) (Bach, 1964, 63). *G–2a.* One of the two obligatory constituents of the nucleus of a sentence, the other being a noun phrase:

S $\rightarrow$ Q+nucleus; nucleus $\rightarrow$ NP+VP. (Katz and Postal, 1964, 34.) *G–2b*. One of the two obligatory constituents of the predicate-phrase, the other being an auxiliary: S $\rightarrow$ NP+PredP; PredP $\rightarrow$ AUX+VP. Verb phrase can be rewritten as copula+predicate or as verb+{NP, S', Pred}. (Chomsky, 1965, 106–107.) *G–2c*. One of the three obligatory constituents of the deep structure of a sentence: S $\rightarrow$ NP+AUX+VP. Verb phrase can be rewritten as verbal+(NP)+{NP, S}. (Jacobs and Rosenbaum, 1968, 57.) *G–2S*. In semantic-based transformational grammar, 'verb phrase' is not a constituent of the abstract deep structure of a sentence. 'Verb,' however, is located either in a predicate, along with tense (Langendoen, 1969, 97), or in a proposition, since tense is a feature of the modality: S $\rightarrow$ modality+proposition; P $\rightarrow$ verb+case category. (Fillmore, 1968, 33.) Compare PREDICATE, PREDICATE PHRASE, MODALITY, PROPOSITION.

Verb phrase complement. *G–2*. A sentence which is embedded in a verb phrase expanded as V, *S*—an **Intransitive verb phrase complement**—or as V, NP, *S*—a **Transitive verb phrase complement**—or as V, PP, *S*—an **Oblique verb phrase complement.** Verb phrase complements utilize only the complementizers *for-to* and *POSS-ing,* the selection of which is dependent on the verb of the main sentence. (Rosenbaum, 1967a, 1–3, 27.) See also VERB PHRASE COMPLEMENTATION.

Verb phrase complementation. *G–2*. The introduction of a sentence into the immediate domination of the verb phrase of another, main, sentence as a 'verb phrase complement': VP $\rightarrow$ V+S. The verb may be transitive (**Transitive verb phrase complementation:** e.g., "They convinced *the audience to nominate Tom*") or intransitive (**Intransitive verb phrase complementation:** e.g., "Huck tended *to withdraw*"). (Rosenbaum, 1967c, 316, 322–323; Rosenbaum, 1967a, 1–3, 115.) Verb phrase complementation is of questionable existence, with few clear cases. (Rosenbaum, 1967b, ix.) See also TRANSITIVE VERB PHRASE COMPLEMENTATION, INTRANSITIVE VERB PHRASE COMPLEMENTATION, OBLIQUE VERB PHRASE COMPLEMENTATION.

Verb phrase complementation, intransitive. See INTRANSITIVE VERB PHRASE COMPLEMENTATION.

Verb phrase complementation, oblique. See OBLIQUE VERB PHRASE COMPLEMENTATION.

Verb phrase complementation, transitive. See TRANSITIVE VERB PHRASE COMPLEMENTATION.

Verb phrase deletion, identical. See IDENTICAL VERB PHRASE DELETION.

Verb-phrase, predicate. See PREDICATE VERB-PHRASE.

Verb, predicative. See COPULA-TYPE VERB.

Verb-preposition transitive. *G–1*. A complex transitive verb consisting of a verb plus a preposition, such as: *step on, look at*. The preposition accompanies the verb under passive transformation, as in: "The picture was *looked at* by both of the boys." (Lees, 1960a, 9.) Compare TWO-PART VERB.

Verb, reflexive. See REFLEXIVE VERB.

Verb, separable. See SEPARABLE VERB.

Verb, stative. See STATIVE VERBAL.

Verb suffix transformation. *G–2*. The rule which converts the [+present], [+3rd person], [+singular] features of a verb or copula into the suffix -*s* (Jacobs, 1968, 33) or the [−present] feature into the suffix -*ed,* past tense

(Jacobs and Rosenbaum, 1968, 133–134). See also AGREEMENT TRANS-
FORMATION.

Verb, transitive. See TRANSITIVE VERB.

Verb, two-part. See TWO-PART VERB.

Vocabulary. *G–1.* One of the sets of symbols employed in the phrase
structure grammar, such as: **Cover symbols**—generalized contexts, such
as X, Y, Z; **Class symbols**—higher-order, nonterminal constituents, such as
NP, VP, etc.; **Morpheme symbols,** such as grammatical markers (*-s, -ed,
ing,* etc.) and lexical morphemes (*green, idea, sleep,* etc.). (Koutsoudas,
1966, 6–7.) *G–2a.* One of the sets of symbols employed in the base
component: **Category symbols** such as S, NP, VP, V, etc., **Grammatical
formatives** such as possessive, plural, etc., and **Lexical formatives** such as
green, idea, sleep, etc. All are called **Vocabulary symbols.** (Chomsky, 1965,
65.) *G–2b.* The primitive conceptual elements which specify universal
relations to the nonlinguistic world; the fixed atomic elements which form
the basis for the two interpretive components: a set of semantic markers
for the semantic component, and a set of phonetic features for the
phonological component. Because these 'vocabularies' are universal, the
child need not learn them or their relations. (Postal, 1964c, 32–33.) See
also ATOMIC ELEMENT, PRIME, SUBSTANTIVE UNIVERSAL.

Vocabulary symbol. See VOCABULARY.

Vocalic. *G–1–2.* The phonological distinctive feature which is positively
specified for sounds that are produced with voicing and an open oral
cavity—that is, having, at the most, constriction but not obstruction. The
'vocalic' sounds are vowels and liquids; all others are **Nonvocalic.** (Halle,
1959, 326; Chomsky and Halle, 1968, 302.) Compare CONSONANTAL.

Voiced. *G–1–2.* The phonological distinctive feature which is positively
specified for sounds that are articulated with vibration of the vocal cords
(i.e., with 'voicing'), as opposed to **Nonvoiced,** or 'voiceless,' sounds, which
lack such vibration. (Halle, 1959, 327). Voicing does not require either
closure or constriction of the glottis; the vocal cords must only be closer
together than for breathing or whispering. (Chomsky and Halle, 1968,
326–327.)

Voiceless. See VOICED.

Voicing. See VOICED.

Vowel. *G–1–2.* A phonological or phonetic segment which is both nonconsonantal and vocalic, or syllabic; one of the four major categories of
segments: true consonant, vowel, glide, liquid. (Halle, 1959, 327; Harms,
1968, 63; Chomsky and Halle, 1968, 408.) Compare CONSONANT, GLIDE,
LIQUID.

Vowel, neutral. See NEUTRAL VOWEL.

Vowel reduction rule. *G–2.* The phonological rule which converts a
weakly stressed, or lax, vowel, which has never received primary stress,
into the neutral vowel 'schwa.' The vowel reduction rule is supplemented
by certain auxiliary reduction rules. (Chomsky and Halle, 1968, 110–113.)
See also NEUTRAL VOWEL.

Vowel shift rule. *G–2.* The phonological rule which has a great-vowel-
shift effect on stressed vowels: $\bar{æ} \to \bar{e} \to \bar{\imath} \to \bar{æ}$ (ā), as in: *grateful* [æy]
→ [ēy]; *serene* [ēy] → [īy]; *derive* [īy] → [āy]. (Chomsky and Halle, 1968,
53, 184.)

Vowel, stem-forming. See STEM-FORMING VOWEL.

Weak cluster. *G–2.* A phonological string which consists of a simple vocalic nucleus followed by no more than one consonant, or none at all, as in: *collide* 'weak'+'strong' [kəlayd]. (Chomsky and Halle, 1968, 29.) Compare STRONG CLUSTER.

Weak generative capacity. *G–2.* The ability of a grammar to enumerate a set of sentences on the level of observational adequacy—which is the capacity of a context-sensitive phrase structure grammar—but not to generate a set of structural descriptions for those sentences. A set of structural descriptions requires strong generative capacity—the characteristic of a transformational grammar. (Chomsky, 1965, 61.) Compare STRONG GENERATIVE CAPACITY.

Weak generative equivalence. *G–2.* The requirement of two equivalent grammars that they generate the same set of strings, though not necessarily the same set of structures. To 'weakly generate' a sentence is to generate its string—that is, to meet the condition of weak generative adequacy, which is not met by context-free grammars. (Chomsky, 1966a, 47–48.) See also WEAK GENERATIVE CAPACITY.

Weakly adequate. See ADEQUACY.

Weakly generate. See WEAK GENERATIVE EQUIVALENCE.

Weakly identical. *G–2.* Having a form identical to that of another constituent, but differing in reference (e.g., *"The King* died and *the King* succeeded"), as opposed to 'strongly identical' constituents, which have both identical form and identical reference (e.g., *"Huck* steered and *Huck* poled"). (Jacobs and Rosenbaum, 1968, 258.) Compare STRONGLY IDENTICAL. See also IDENTICAL REFERENCE.

Well-formed. *G–2.* Correctly derived in respect to one or more of the components of the grammar, as in "Colorless green ideas sleep furiously," which is grammatically and phonologically well-formed, but semantically ill-formed (Lees, 1964b, xxx; Jacobs and Rosenbaum, 1968, 4); interpreted, and marked, by a transformation as being a grammatical sentence of the language, at least at that stage of its derivation; correctly generated; grammatical (Rosenbaum, 1967a, 25). A theory of well-formedness and ill-formedness partially explains acceptability of a sentence. (Lees, 1964b, xxxi.) Also called **Grammatical.** See also GRAMMATICALNESS, ACCEPTABILITY.

Well-formedness. See WELL-FORMED.

Wh-attachment. *G–2.* The introduction of the symbol 'Wh' into the base rules for question formation, the first step in the Wh-question process: Wh+X+pronoun+Y ⇒ Wh-pronoun+X+Y. (King, 1969, 144–145.) Wh-Attachment also applies in relativization, as in "The boat (*Wh*-the boat passed) was a sternwheeler" (Kuroda, 1968, 274), and in pseudo-cleft formation: *"Wh*-pronoun passed was a boat" (Rosenbaum, 1967a, 13). Also called **Wh-placement.** (Chomsky, 1968, 41.) Compare WH-ATTRACTION.

Wh-attraction. *G–2.* The second step in the Wh-question process, which places the Wh-marked noun phrase at the beginning of the sentence, causing inversion of the subject and the auxiliary verb—Wh-inversion

(Chomsky, 1968, 41): Wh-pronoun + subject + AUX + verb ⇒ Wh-pronoun + AUX + subject + verb. (King, 1969, 144–145.) Compare WH-ATTACHMENT.

Wh-component. See WH-MORPHEME.

Wh-deletion. *G–1.* The optional singulary transformation which deletes Wh, and sometimes *be,* from certain restrictive and appositive, or nonrestrictive, relative clauses. When applied to restrictive relatives, Wh-deletion produces postnominal modifiers, some of which are potential prenominal modifiers, as when: "The man (*who is*) in the moon" ⇒ "The man in the moon"; or "The cheese (*which is*) green" ⇒ *"The cheese green" ⇒ "The green cheese." When applied to nonrestrictive relatives, Wh-deletion produces appositives, as when: "The man, (*who is*) my father" ⇒ "The man, my father." (Smith, 1964, 252.) See also RELATIVE PRONOUN DELETION TRANSFORMATION, RELATIVE 'BE' DELETION TRANSFORMATION.

Wh-morpheme. *G–1.* The morpheme *wh* (or Wh or WH), which is attached to nominals and adverbials for questions and relative clauses. Also called the **Wh-component.** (Lees, 1960a, 36, 45.) See also WH-ATTACHMENT.

Wh-morphophonemics. *G–1.* The morphophonemic rules for deriving Wh-words. (Lees, 1960a, 47–48.) See also WH-WORD.

Wh-placement. See WH-ATTACHMENT.

Wh-question. *G–1a.* The interrogative sentence which results from the operation of the Wh-question transformation on a simple question transform. (Chomsky, 1957, 69.) The noun phrase of the simple question sentence is brought to the front of the sentence, where it is attached to the marker *wh.* Simple questions and Wh-questions have the same underlying declarative form. (Kuroda, 1969, 332.) On the basis of word order and intonation, Wh-interrogatives resemble declarative sentences more than they do questions. (Chomsky, 1962, 240.) *G–1b.* To apply the Wh-question transformation. (Lees, 1960a, 108.) *G–2a.* The interrogative sentence which results from the operation of a Wh-question transformation on a simple question phrase-marker, which has a form that is different from a statement. The transformation introduces the marker Wh into sentence-initial position and then attaches it to an indefinite pronoun within the sentence by attachment transformation. (Kuroda, 1969, 332.) *G–2b.* The interrogative sentence which results from the non-deletion of a Wh-marker in an underlying phrase-marker in the determiner constituent, without need for an attachment transformation. The Wh-question and the simple question have different base forms. (Kuroda, 1969, 332; Katz and Postal, 1964, 95.) *G–2c.* Any interrogative sentence, whether of the yes-no or Wh type, in which one of the constituents of a base sentence is questioned. In the case of the simple question, it is a sentence adverbial (*either-or*) which is questioned. (Katz and Postal, 1964, 95.) *G–2d.* An interrogative sentence which results from the operation of a Wh-question transformation on a simple question phrase-marker. The transformation replaces the Q constituent with a noun phrase whose noun has the feature [+WH]: Q + NP [+WH] ⇒ NP [+WH]. (Jacobs and Rosenbaum, 1968, 158.) See also QUESTION.

Wh-question transformation. See QUESTION.

Wh-transform. *G–1.* A Wh-question or relative clause. (Lees, 1960a, 37.)

Wh-transformation.   See QUESTION.

Wh-word.   *G–1.* One of the relative or interrogative pronouns which consist of the Wh-marker plus a personal pronoun (e.g., *wh+he* → /huw/, *wh+him* → /huwm/—Chomsky, 1957, 69) or plus an indefinite pronoun (e.g., *wh+something* → *what, wh+somebody* → *who*—Klima, 1964a, 252) or the determiner *wh* plus a noun (e.g., *wh+man* → *who*—Thomas, 1965, 93). *G–2.* One of the relative or interrogative or nominal or adverbial words which represent an underlying noun phrase containing the Wh-marker plus an indefinite pronoun, as in: *the+one+wh+some+Pro* [*+one*] ⇒ *the one who* ⇒ *who; the+place+at+wh+some+Pro* [*+place*] ⇒ *the place at which place* ⇒ *where.* (Kuroda, 1968, 265–267, 274.) Also called **Question word.** (Ross, 1969, 360.) See also WH-QUESTION.

'With'-transformation.   See CONJUNCTION.

Word.   *G–1.* A lexical item which can replace one of the terminal category symbols—that is, N, V, ADJ, ADV, DET, M, etc.—and be bounded by #'s in the terminal string. The inventory of words in the lexicon is finite at any given time; but there is no longest word, and an infinity of new words is potentially available. There are as many words pronounced [wel] as there are lexical selections of this sequence in syntactic strings. (Postal, 1964a, 56.) *G–2.* A lexical item which can replace a category symbol in the base and be bounded by word boundaries (##——##) in the terminal string; a string of formatives contained in, but not containing, the context ##——##. Because certain noncyclic phonological rules apply only to words, the surface structure of an utterance must be regarded as a sequence of phonological words—which are minimum, independent units of pronunciation (Postal, 1964c, 20)—some of which will contain #'s to set off neutral affixes. Nominalization, relativization, and other transformations and lexical processes account for the origin of many derived words. (Chomsky and Halle, 12–13, 366–370; Langendoen, 1969, 129.)

Word-boundary.   See WORD.

Word, derived.   See DERIVED WORD.

Word order.   *G–1.* The order of constituents in a string. (Lees, 1960a, 112.)

Word, question.   See WH-WORD.

Word, syntactic.   See SYNTACTIC WORD.

X

X-type variable.   *G–2.* A symbol, usually W, X, Y, or Z, in the structural description of a transformational rule, either syntactic or phonological, which represents an arbitrary, unspecified, generalized context, possibly null, and permits the simplification of the statement, as in: XAY → XBY, or A → B/X——Y. Also called **Variable X.** (Rosenbaum, 1967a, 41, 50–51; Harms, 1968, 62.) See also COVER SYMBOL. Compare ALPHA-TYPE VARIABLE.

Y

Yes-no question. *G–1*. A sentence which is a simple-question transform of an underlying declarative sentence. A 'yes-no question' questions the entire sentence rather than a particular element within a noun phrase of that sentence, as a Wh-question does. (Thomas, 1965, 178.) Also called **Yes-or-no question.** (Chomsky, 1957, 63.) *G–2*. An interrogative sentence which results from the deletion of a Wh-marker in an underlying phrase-marker in the determiner constituent. The Wh-question and the yes-no question have different base forms. In the yes-no question, a sentence adverbial (*either-or*) is 'questioned.' (Katz and Postal, 1964, 95.) Also called **Simple,** or **Truth value, question.** (Katz and Postal, 1964, 89.) See also QUESTION, WH-QUESTION.

Yes-or-no question. See YES-NO QUESTION.

Z

Zero. *G–1*. An inflectional morpheme, Ø, meaning 'no phonetic value,' which is affixed to a verb in the present tense for all persons other than third singular, and to the noun for singular number, as in: "The rafts float+Ø"; "The raft+Ø floats." (Chomsky, 1957, 64.) *G–1–2*. Null (Ø), which is a symbol used in a phonological or syntactic rule which deletes a segment, as in: obstruent → Ø/ #——obstruent (if two obstruents occur initially, the first is deleted). (Harms, 1968, 44.) See also NULL.

BIBLIOGRAPHY

The following Bibliography is an alphabetical listing, by authors' names, of the works in the corpus described in the Preface. When there is more than one work by a given author, the works are listed in chronological order according to the date of first publication. That date appears in the left-hand column for all of the works. When there is more than one work by the same author in the same year of first publication, the order is chronological according to the date of 'acceptance,' as in the case of a dissertation, or 'delivery,' as in the case of a paper read at a society meeting. When there is more than one work by the same author in the same year of first publication, and the date of acceptance or delivery is also the same, or is unknown, the order is alphabetical by title. On the basis of these criteria, the works by the same author in the same year of first publication are given 'alpha-indices' at the end of the date—for example, 1964a, 1964b, 1964c, etc.

The page numbers that are cited in the *Glossary* refer to the source in the Bibliography entry which immediately follows the date of first publication, not to a source following that one. For example, the Katz and Fodor article, "The Structure of a Semantic Theory," is labeled '1963' below their names in the Bibliography, since that was the date of first publication—in *Language;* but a citation in the *Glossary* from page 500 of this article refers to the 1964 publication in Fodor and Katz, *The Structure of Language,* since that anthology was the source used for this investigation. It is often the case, therefore, that the page references in a *Glossary* entry are not from the publication whose date appears in the left-hand column in the Bibliography.

A reprinted article published earlier in a source that was not consulted for the *Glossary* is dated at the time of the earlier publication, although the page references are to the consulted reprinting. This practice leads to a certain amount of distortion in the case of Morris Halle's article "On the Bases of Phonology," which was originally published in *Il Nuovo Cimento* in 1959, which was not consulted, but appears in revised form in Fodor and Katz, 1964, which was consulted. To complicate the matter, the un-revised "Introduction" and "Part One" of the original article appear in the consulted Reibel and Schane, 1969, under the title "Questions of Linguistics." Despite the differences in form and reprinting dates, both consulted articles are labeled '1959,' but references in the *Glossary* to the Reibel and Schane portion carry the additional label 'R&S.' Another minor discrepancy arises in the case of Noam Chomsky's article "Some Methodological Remarks on Generative Grammar," which is paged according to Allen, 1964 (consulted), but was originally published in *Word,* 1961 (not consulted). The last portion of this full article is excerpted in Fodor and Katz, 1964 (consulted), under the title "Degrees of Grammaticalness." Occasional references to the latter reprinting carry the label 'F&K' preceding the page number.

ALLEN, Harold B.
1964 (Ed.) *Readings in Applied English Linguistics,* 2nd edition. New York: Appleton-Century-Crofts, 1964.
BACH, Emmon.
1964 *An Introduction to Transformational Grammars.* New York: Holt, Rinehart and Winston, 1964.
1968 "Nouns and noun phrases," pp. 91–122 *in* Bach and Harms (1968). Originally read at the University of Texas Symposium on 'Universals in Linguistic Theory,' April, 1967.
BACH, Emmon, and Robert T. Harms.
1968 (Eds.) *Universals in Linguistic Theory.* New York: Holt, Rinehart and Winston, 1968.
CHOMSKY, Noam.
1956 "Three models for the description of language," pp. 140–152 *in* Smith (1966). Originally published in *Transactions on Information Theory,* IT–2:113–124 (1956).
1957 *Syntactic Structures.* Janua Linguarum, Series Minor 4. The Hague: Mouton, 1957. 7th edition (= 7th printing), 1966. Adapted from Chomsky, "Logical structure of linguistic theory," mimeo, 1955.
1961a "On the notion 'rule of grammar,' " pp. 119–136 *in* Fodor and Katz (1964). Originally published in *Proceedings of the Twelfth Symposium in Applied Mathematics,* 12:6–24 (1961).
1961b "Some methodological remarks on generative grammar," pp. 173–192 *in* Allen (1964). Originally published in *Word,* 17:219–239 (1961). Last portion excerpted as "Degrees of Grammaticalness," pp. 384–389 *in* Fodor and Katz (1964).
1962 "A transformational approach to syntax," pp. 211–245 *in* Fodor and Katz (1964). Originally published in A. A. Hill (Ed.), *Proceedings of the Third Texas Conference on Problems of Linguistic Analysis in English, 1958.* Austin: University of Texas Press, 1962, pp. 124–158.
1964 "Current issues in linguistic theory," pp. 50–118 *in* Fodor and Katz (1964). Originally a report to the session on 'The Logical Basis of Linguistic Theory,' Ninth International Congress of Linguists, Cambridge, Mass., 1962. Published separately as Janua Linguarum, Series Minor 38. The Hague: Mouton, 1965.
1965 *Aspects of the Theory of Syntax.* Cambridge, Mass.: The M.I.T. Press, 1965.
1966a *Topics in the Theory of Generative Grammar.* Janua Linguarum, Series Minor 56. The Hague: Mouton, 1966. 2nd printing, 1969. Originally a series of four lectures delivered at the Linguistic Institute of the Linguistic Society of America, Indiana University, June, 1964.
1966b "The current scene in linguistics: Present directions," pp. 3–12 *in* Reibel and Schane (1969). Originally published in *College English,* 27:587–595 (1966). Originally read at the National Council of Teachers of English meeting at Boston, November, 1965.

1966c   *Cartesian Linguistics: A Chapter in the History of Rationalist Thought*. New York: Harper & Row, 1966.

1968   *Language and Mind*. New York: Harcourt, Brace and World, 1968. An expanded version of three Beckman Lectures given at Berkeley under the title 'Linguistic Contributions to the Study of Mind,' January, 1967.

CHOMSKY, Noam, and Morris Halle.

1968   *The Sound Pattern of English*. New York: Harper & Row, 1968.

CLOSS, Elizabeth.

1965   "Diachronic syntax and generative grammar," pp. 395–408 *in* Reibel and Schane (1969). Originally published in *Language,* 41:402–415 (1965).

FILLMORE, Charles J.

1966   "Toward a modern theory of case," pp. 361–375 *in* Reibel and Schane (1969). Originally published as *Project on Linguistic Analysis Report No. 13*. Columbus, Ohio: The Ohio State University Research Foundation, 1966.

1968   "The case for case," pp. 1–88 *in* Bach and Harms (1968). Originally read at the University of Texas Symposium on 'Universals in Linguistic Theory,' April, 1967.

FODOR, Jerry A., and Jerrold J. Katz.

1964   (Eds.) *The Structure of Language: Readings in the Philosophy of Language*. Englewood Cliffs, N. J.: Prentice-Hall, 1964.

GLEITMAN, Lila R.

1965   "Coordinating conjunctions in English," pp. 80–112 *in* Reibel and Schane (1969). Originally published in *Language,* 41:260–293 (1965).

GRUBER, Jeffrey S.

1967   "Topicalization in child language," pp. 422–447 *in* Reibel and Schane (1969). Originally published in *Foundations of Language,* 3:37–65 (1967).

HALLE, Morris.

1959   "On the bases of phonology," pp. 324–333 *in* Fodor and Katz (1964). Revised from original publication in supplement to *Il Nuovo Cimento,* Serie X, 13:494–503 (1959). The unrevised 'Introduction' and 'Part One' of the original article appear as "Questions of linguistics," pp. 45–52 *in* Reibel and Schane (1969).

1962   "Phonology in generative grammar," pp. 334–352 *in* Fodor and Katz (1964). Originally published in *Word,* 18:54–72 (1962).

HALLE, Morris, and Kenneth N. Stevens.

1964   "Speech recognition: A model and a program for research," pp. 604–612 *in* Fodor and Katz (1964).

HARMS, Robert T.

1968   *Introduction to Phonological Theory*. Englewood Cliffs, N. J.: Prentice-Hall, 1968.

JACOBS, Roderick A.

1968   *On Transformational Grammar: An Introduction for Teachers*. Monograph No. 11. Oneonta, N. Y.: The New York State English Council, 1968.

JACOBS, Roderick A., and Peter S. Rosenbaum.

1968   *English Transformational Grammar*. Waltham, Mass.: Blaisdell, 1968.

KATZ, Jerrold J.

1964a "Analyticity and contradiction in natural language," pp. 519–543 *in* Fodor and Katz (1964).

1964b "Semi-sentences," pp. 400–416 *in* Fodor and Katz (1964).

1966 *The Philosophy of Language.* New York: Harper & Row, 1966.

KATZ, Jerrold J., and Jerry A. Fodor.

1963 "The structure of a semantic theory," pp. 479–518 *in* Fodor and Katz (1964). Originally published in *Language,* 39:170–210 (1963).

KATZ, Jerrold J., and Paul M. Postal.

1964 *An Integrated Theory of Linguistics Descriptions.* Research monograph No. 26. Cambridge, Mass.: The M.I.T. Press, 1964.

KING, Robert D.

1969 *Historical Linguistics and Generative Grammar.* Englewood Cliffs, N. J.: Prentice-Hall, 1969.

KIPARSKY, Paul.

1968 "Linguistic universals and linguistic change," pp. 171–202 *in* Bach and Harms (1968). Originally read at the University of Texas Symposium on 'Universals in Linguistic Theory,' April, 1967.

KLIMA, Edward S.

1964a "Negation in English," pp. 246–323 *in* Fodor and Katz (1964). Originally a series of lectures at the University of Pennsylvania Symposium on 'Transformational Analysis,' November, 1959.

1964b "Relatedness between grammatical systems," pp. 227–246 *in* Reibel and Schane (1969). Originally published in *Language,* 40:1–20 (1964).

KLIMA, Edward S., and Ursula Bellugi-Klima.

1966 "Syntactic regularities in speech of children," pp. 448–466 *in* Reibel and Schane (1969). Revised from original publication in J. Lyons and R. J. Wales (Eds.), *Psycholinguistic Papers.* Edinburgh: Edinburgh University Press, 1966, pp. 183–208.

KOUTSOUDAS, Andreas.

1966 *Writing Transformational Grammars: An Introduction.* New York: McGraw-Hill, 1966.

KURODA, S.-Y.

1968 "English relativization and certain related problems," pp. 264–287 *in* Reibel and Schane (1969). Originally published in *Language,* 44:244–266 (1968).

1969 "Attachment transformations," pp. 331–351 *in* Reibel and Schane (1969). Revised from Ph.D. dissertation, M.I.T., 1965.

LAKOFF, George, and Stanley Peters.

1966 "Phrasal conjunction and symmetric predicates," pp. 113–142 *in* Reibel and Schane (1969). Originally published in *Mathematical Linguistics and Automatic Translation,* Harvard Computation Laboratory, Report No. NSF-17, 1966, pp. VI-1 to VI-49.

LANGACKER, Ronald W.

1968 *Language and Its Structure: Some Fundamental Concepts.* New York: Harcourt, Brace and World, 1968.

1969 "On pronominalization and the chain of command," pp. 160–186 *in* Reibel and Schane (1969).

LANGENDOEN, D. Terence.

1969 *The Study of Syntax: The Generative-Transformational Approach to*

American English. New York: Holt, Rinehart and Winston, 1969.

LEES, Robert B.

1960a *The Grammar of English Nominalizations.* Bloomington, Indiana: Indiana Research Center in Anthropology, Folklore, and Linguistics, Publication Twelve, 1960 (=IJAL, XXVI, No. 3, Part II). Fifth printing. The Hague: Mouton, 1968.

1960b "Some neglected aspects of parsing," pp. 146–155 *in* Allen (1964). Originally published in *Language Learning,* 11:171–180 (1960).

1961 "Grammatical analysis of the English comparative construction," pp. 303–315 *in* Reibel and Schane (1969). Originally published in *Word,* 17:171–185 (1961).

1963 "Preface to second printing," pp. xxvii-xxviii *in* Lees (1960a).

1964a "Transformation grammars and the Fries framework," pp. 137–146 *in* Allen (1964). Originally read at the Midwest Modern Language Association meeting at Lincoln, Nebraska, April, 1962.

1964b "Preface to third printing," pp. xxix-xlv *in* Lees (1960a).

1965 "Preface to fourth printing," p. xlvi *in* Lees (1960a).

LEES, Robert B., and Edward S. Klima.

1963 "Rules for English pronominalization," pp. 145–159 *in* Reibel and Schane (1969). Originally published in *Language,* 39:17–28 (1963).

LYONS, John.

1968 *Introduction to Theoretical Linguistics.* Cambridge: Cambridge University Press, 1968.

McCAWLEY, James D.

1968 "The role of semantics in a grammar," pp. 125–169 *in* Bach and Harms (1968). Originally read at the University of Texas Symposium on 'Universals in Linguistic Theory,' April, 1967.

POSTAL, Paul M.

1964a *Constituent Structure: A Study of Contemporary Models of Syntactic Description.* Bloomington, Indiana: Indiana Research Center in Anthropology, Folklore, and Linguistics, Publication Thirty, 1964 (= IJAL, XXX, No. 1, Part III). The Hague: Mouton, 1964.

1964b "Limitations of phrase structure grammars," pp. 137–151 *in* Fodor and Katz (1964).

1964c "Underlying and superficial linguistic structure," pp. 19–37 *in* Reibel and Schane (1969). Originally published in *Harvard Educational Review,* 34:246–266 (1964).

1966 "On so-called 'pronouns' in English," pp. 201–224 *in* Reibel and Schane (1969). Originally published in F. Dinneen (Ed.), *The 19th Monograph on Languages and Linguistics.* Washington, D. C.: Georgetown University Press, 1966.

1968a *Aspects of Phonological Theory.* New York: Harper & Row, 1968.

1968b "Epilogue," pp. 265–289 *in* Jacobs and Rosenbaum (1968).

REIBEL, David A., and Sanford A. Schane.

1969 (Eds.) *Modern Studies in English: Readings in Transformational Grammar.* Englewood Cliffs, N. J.: Prentice-Hall, 1969.

ROSENBAUM, Peter S.

1965 "On the role of linguistics in the teaching of English," pp. 467–481 *in* Reibel and Schane (1969). Originally published in *Harvard Educational Review,* 35:332–348 (1965).

1967a *The Grammar of English Predicate Complement Constructions.* Research monograph No. 47. Cambridge, Mass.: The M.I.T. Press, 1967. Originally a doctoral dissertation at M.I.T. (1965).

1967b "Preface," pp. ix–x *in* Rosenbaum (1967a).

1967c "Phrase structure principles of English complex sentence formation," pp. 316–330 *in* Reibel and Schane (1969). Originally published in *Journal of Linguistics,* 3:103–118 (1967).

ROSS, John Robert.

1966 "A proposed rule of tree-pruning," pp. 288–299 *in* Reibel and Schane (1969). Originally published in *Mathematical Linguistics and Automatic Translation.* Harvard Computation Laboratory, Report No. NSF-17, 1966, pp. IV–1 to IV–18. Originally read at the Linguistic Society of America meeting at Chicago, December, 1965.

1967 "On the cyclic nature of English pronominalization," pp. 187–200 *in* Reibel and Schane (1969). Originally published in *To Honor Roman Jakobson.* The Hague: Mouton, 1967, II, pp. 1669–1682.

1969 "Adjectives as noun phrases," pp. 352–360 *in* Reibel and Schane (1969). Originally read at the Linguistic Society of America meeting at New York, December, 1966.

SMITH, Alfred G.

1966 (Ed.) *Communication and Culture: Readings in the Codes of Human Interaction.* New York: Holt, Rinehart and Winston, 1966.

SMITH, Carlota S.

1964 "Determiners and relative clauses in a generative grammar of English," pp. 247–263 *in* Reibel and Schane (1969). Originally published in *Language,* 40:37–52 (1964).

1969 "Ambiguous sentences with *and,*" pp. 75–79 *in* Reibel and Schane (1969).

THOMAS, Owen.

1965 *Transformational Grammar and the Teacher of English.* New York: Holt, Rinehart and Winston, 1965.